**THE AMERICAS IN THE NEW
INTERNATIONAL DIVISION OF LABOR**

THE AMERICAS IN THE NEW INTERNATIONAL DIVISION OF LABOR

Edited by

Steven E. Sanderson

HM
Holmes & Meier
New York London

First published in the United States of America 1985 by
Holmes & Meier Publishers, Inc.
30 Irving Place
New York, N.Y. 10003

Great Britain:
Holmes & Meier Publishers, Ltd.
Unit 5   Greenwich Industrial Estate
345 Woolwich Road   Charlton, London SE7

Copyright © 1985 by Holmes & Meier Publishers, Inc.
All rights reserved

Book design by Stephanie Barton

Library of Congress Cataloging in Publication Data
Main entry under title:

The Americas in the new international division of labor.

  Bibliography: p.
  Includes index.
  1.Labor and laboring classes—America—Congresses. 2. America—Emigration and immigration—Congresses. 3. Migrant labor—America—Congresses. 4. International division of labor—Congresses. I. Sanderson, Steven E.
HD8045.A44   1985   331'.0973   84-4570
ISBN 0-8419-0971-7
ISBN 0-8419-09672-5 (pbk.)

Manufactured in the United States of America

Contents

Foreword	vii
Helen I. Safa	
Acknowledgments	xiii
Abbreviations	2
A Critical Approach to the Americas in the New International Division of Labor	
Steven E. Sanderson	
Global Proletarianization	26
David Barkin	
The "New" Internationalization of Agriculture in the Americas	46
Steven E. Sanderson	
Some Effects of the Internationalization of Agriculture on the Mexican Agricultural Crisis	69
Ruth Rama	
Political Frameworks for International Migration	95
Robert L. Bach	
Caribbean Cane Cutters in Florida: Implications for the Study of the Internationalization of Labor	125
Charles H. Wood and Terry McCoy	
The Consequences of Dominican Urban Outmigration for National Development: The Case of Santiago	145
Sherri Grasmuck	
Evolving Patterns of Puerto Rican Migration	177
Frank Bonilla and Ricardo Campos	
Contemporary Production and the New International Division of Labor	206
María Patricia Fernández Kelly	
Capital Mobility and Labor Migration	226
Saskia Sassen-Koob	
Segmentation of the Work Process in the International Division of Labor	253
June Nash	
Selected Bibliography	273
About the Contributors	289
Index	291

Foreword

Helen I. Safa

This volume on *The Americas in the New International Division of Labor* brings together several important issues which have heretofore been treated separately in much social science literature: the internationalization of agriculture, the internationalization of industry, the migration of Hispanic and West Indian populations to the U.S., and the impact of these changes on labor in Latin America and the U.S. All of these articles were originally presented at a conference held at the Center for Latin American Studies of the University of Florida in April 1983, which sought to analyze the relationship between these issues and their impact on U.S.-Latin American relations in the period since the 1970s.

The conference arose out of an increasing need at the Center to discover the common elements in several lines of research each of us were pursuing. I had worked for years along with my colleagues María Patricia Fernández Kelly and June Nash on runaway shops and their impact on female labor in Latin America and the U.S. Steve Sanderson made me aware of the similarities between these industrial processes and the internationalization of agriculture, which he had been examining in Mexico. Terry McCoy and Charles Wood were looking at the employment of West Indian migrant labor in the south Florida sugar cane industry and at the impact of their remittances on agricultural development in the islands.

It became clear to us that the new international division of labor represents a new stage in the articulation of the economies of the U.S. and Latin America. We have moved away from simple commodity exchange to the internationalization of production in agriculture and industry, and with it to the internationalization of labor. We buy tomatoes grown in Mexico, blouses sewn in the Dominican Republic, and transistor radios assembled in Barbados. At the same time we continue to receive migrants from the very areas to which these enterprises are moving. How can we explain these phenomena? This is not simply a reversal of earlier patterns of trade and investment, but a new form of integration at the level of production which is having a profound impact on the economies of both the U.S. and Latin America.

As several of the contributors to this volume point out, the Americas have always been joined in an international division of labor. In the early stages, Latin America was primarily a source of raw materials and minerals, which the U.S. exchanged for higher-priced manufactured goods. In order to escape from these terms of unequal exchange, many Latin American countries embarked on an industrialization program geared toward import substitution, in order to help their own manufacturing industries provide for a domestic market. The failure of import substitution industrialization to develop a viable internal market has led many Latin American countries into manufacturing for export, with virtually complete reliance on multinationals for capital, technology, and markets. Agriculture was relegated to second place and cheap food produced by a technologically backward peasantry was used to sustain poorly paid urban wage labor. The result, as Sanderson points out, is that Latin America is increasingly unable to meet its own domestic food needs, and agribusiness is often geared toward export and upper class urban markets.

The consequences of each of these aspects of the new international division of labor have been different in Latin America, particularly in regard to the role of the state and the nature of the labor process. The state in Latin America was strengthened as a result of the policy of import substitution, which required government regulation, subsidies, and tariff protection. This was the beginning of the era of state enterprises, or joint ventures with foreign capital, in response to the lack of domestic risk capital. Continued heavy involvement of the state in the succeeding phase of the internationalization of industry and agriculture has had contradictory effects on the role of the state in Latin America. The state has continued to play a principal role in the internationalization of production, providing tax holidays, industrial plant, infrastructure, and other incentives to foreign capital. As Sanderson notes, this has caused the state to divert scarce resources away from other important domestic needs not only in agriculture and industry but in critical social service such as education, health, and transportation. This has weakened the legitimacy of the state in the eyes of its own citizens, not only peasants and urban workers but entrepreneurs, bureaucrats, and others who find themselves dominated or pushed out by foreign capital. The pressure becomes even more extreme as states attempt to use exports to meet the fiscal crisis aggravated by rapidly escalating foreign debt, itself a product of this process.

The growing pressure on the state plus the need of foreign capital for a cheap and disciplined labor force has also forced the state in Latin America to assume greater control over its labor force. While in earlier stages the state mediated the relationship between employers and workers, now it often sets the guidelines within which these relationships operate, including the right to collective bargaining and strikes, minimum wages, and working conditions. This has tended to erode the paternalistic style of management characteristic of Latin America and to make workers look to the state as both their protector and their enemy. On this basis, it could be predicted that any protest or struggle by workers against the internationalization of agriculture and industry in Latin America is likely to be directed against the state as well as the private sector.

Why should workers revolt? One of the major arguments in favor of the internationalization of agriculture and industry in Latin America is the purported increase in domestic employment generated by these new enterprises. Undoubtedly this increase is real and Fernández Kelly notes that along the Mexican border in a little over a decade almost 200,000 *maquiladora* jobs have been created, most of them held by women. However, it is critical to examine both the kinds of jobs created and the labor recruited for them. While agribusiness continues to displace large segments of the peasantry from smallholder agriculture, they are generally not absorbed by these new productive processes; nor are there jobs for artisans displaced by mass manufacture. Instead, the overwhelming majority of the new recruits are young, single women, particularly in the industrial sector. Most peasants and artisans thus continue to swell the ranks of the informal sector in Latin American cities. This is part of the global proletarianization process to which Barkin refers. It includes workers not only employed in these industries but displaced by them as well. It means an increasing percentage of Latin Americans will have to rely solely on the sale of their labor for survival. At the same time mechanization is reducing the number of jobs available in these enterprises.

The changing nature of the productive process in these new enterprises also has a profound effect on the labor process. This is more evident in export-based industrialization, where the production process has been truly internationalized, across countries as well as plants. The fragmentation of the production process noted in several articles in this volume has led to a deskilling of the labor force and a total loss of identification of the worker with the fruits of his (or more likely her) labor. Often the worker does not even see the final product at the end of the assembly line, since entire plants are often given over to only partial processing or the production of special components. The worker at the same time is forced to carry out the same routine operation day after day, year after year, sewing on buttons or soldering microchips. Only women are thought to have the patience for such tedious work, and even they are let go as they grow older, lose their eyesight, and are burdened with family responsibilities.

These changes in the labor process are not confined to Latin America. The internationalization of production in industry and agriculture has also had a deep impact on the U.S. labor force, particularly with the loss of jobs associated with the movement of production overseas. Public awareness has increased as the loss has affected not only women employed in garment and electronics industries but men in steel and auto plants, the "primary" labor sector. The movement of production overseas can be seen as a response to the high cost of labor in the U.S., particularly in the 1960s with full employment, increasing fringe benefits, strong unions, and the growth of a welfare state. Internationalization has succeeded in reversing many of these gains and greatly weakening the labor movement in the U.S. As in Latin America, the state has been the primary target of labor protest, in an attempt to change the tariffs and trade agreements which allow many of these products to enter the U.S. virtually duty free. Calls for protectionism by U.S. workers only enhance nationalist sentiments and hinder any attempt by labor to organize internationally on a par with capital.

The continuing migration of Hispanic and West Indian workers into an already stagnant labor market has posed another threat to U.S. labor, with corresponding calls to the government to halt the flow through legislation and even force. Sassen-Koob documents the way in which the presence of these migrants has facilitated the restructuring of industry in the U.S., with the movement toward an underground economy based on illegal sweatshops and industrial homework. Here again women become an important part of this vulnerable work force, as Fernández Kelly and Nash demonstrate. Nash shows that gender and race have long played an important role in the segmentation of the work process in the U.S., but segmentation now operates on a global scale. Not only do gender and race pit workers against each other in a particular plant or community, but now migrants are pitted against natives, and workers in one country against those in another. In an effort to recruit a cheap and disciplined labor force, capital manipulates these differences for their own advantage.

Thus, migration of workers into the U.S. and the movement of production abroad must be seen as part of the same economic process. Both represent efforts by capital to weaken labor and lower their production costs. The migrants are often victims of the same proletarianization process referred to earlier, which has been speeded up by the internationalization of agriculture and industry. They are not just displaced or unemployed workers, as the article by Grasmuck on Dominican migrants demonstrates. However, as in the case of the West Indian migrant laborers in south Florida described by Wood and McCoy, they turn to migration and remittances to maintain a life style threatened by changes in the economy, by growing unemployment, and by higher prices. At the same time, this migration reinforces changes in consumer patterns which make continuing migration a necessity.

The growing internationalization of labor and capital make Bonilla and Campos question whether it is possible any longer to distinguish between core and periphery, as in the standard dependency literature. Certainly this would appear to be the case for Puerto Rico, which has now been fully incorporated into the U.S. economy. In many ways, Puerto Rico served as the prototype for the internationalization of production, particularly in industry. The incentives offered by the Puerto Rican government through Operation Bootstrap have been copied throughout the Caribbean and Latin America, and this in turn has led to the flight of industry to areas of cheaper labor. The population has been thoroughly proletarianized, with the total collapse of agriculture, rapid urbanization, and large-scale migration. Nearly two million Puerto Ricans now live in the U.S. Thus, Puerto Rico has served both as a cheap labor reservoir and as a testing ground for the internationalization of production now taking place on a global scale.

It should be clear, then, that the new international division of labor poses a grave threat to labor both in the U.S. and in Latin America. U.S. workers are faced with growing unemployment due to the movement of production both abroad and underground into non-unionized shops often employing immigrant labor. Small farmers cannot compete with imported foodstuffs produced more cheaply abroad. But the workers in Latin America are not benefiting from these changes. They too are suffering from growing unemployment because these new enterprises are unable to absorb the displaced peasants and artisans and instead recruit a new labor force, often young women, into these jobs. At the same time, prices are rising due to the emphasis on export production to the neglect of domestic needs. Many Latin American countries are facing chronic food shortages, as the international division of labor has contributed to the decline in self-sufficiency in food production in Latin America.

The profound structural changes brought on by the new international division of labor have also posed a problem for the state in both Latin America and the U.S. Both are faced with growing protest about unemployment and inflation and increasing demand for social services, partly to cover the needs produced by economic dislocation. Latin American governments have fewer resources to meet these needs, and many of these resources are diverted into providing the infrastructure and incentives necessary to attract foreign capital. The U.S. government has cut down on social services, ostensibly to reduce government expenditure but also to discipline and regain control over labor. Migration aids in this process by providing an alternative source of labor, which as Bach notes, helps account for the government's reluctance to enforce stricter immigration controls. The increasing dependence of Puerto Rico on federal transfer payments to meet the needs of its population frightens government officials, who know they cannot afford to duplicate this form of assistance elsewhere.

Thus far, the political responses to these economic pressures have been totally inadequate. As Bach notes, states have been unable to develop an international framework for dealing with the international division of labor. There is no political equivalent to the multinational corporation. Instead, the state in both Latin America and the U.S. has responded by becoming more rigid and repressive in regard to workers, who are constantly losing purchasing power through the decline in real wages. It may be the inability of workers to buy the goods and services produced by the new international division of labor which ultimately restricts its growth, both in the U.S. and in Latin America.

The present volume is rich in theoretical insight and empirical data but still leaves many questions unanswered. Is the hegemony of the nation-state undermined by the new international division of labor? How will labor in the U.S. and Latin America respond to the threats to its integrity and well-being? Does the incorporation of new workers such as women and migrants weaken the labor movement or will they be incorporated in new forms of class conflict? These are some of the questions we need to address. It suggests that the research agenda for Latin Americanists interested in these questions should no longer be confined to Latin America but should expand to the growing articulation between the economies of both North and South in the hemisphere.

Acknowledgments

This study was made possible through the sponsorship of the Center for Latin American Studies at the University of Florida, Gainesville. The papers contributing to this book originated in the 32nd Annual Conference on Latin America, held in Gainesville in April 1983 as part of the Center for Latin American Studies' continuing commitment to scholarship in the region. Through the annual conference and its many other programs, the Center hopes to promote original inquiry in critical areas of cross-disciplinary research and policy studies. For supporting the original contributors to the conference and the publication of this volume, the Center deserves the thanks of the editor, publisher and contributing authors of *The Americas in the New International Division of Labor*.

In addition, various colleagues and friends contributed greatly to the success of this project, while remaining innocent of its conclusions. Luis Crouch, Carlton Davis, Alain de Janvry, Louis W. Goodman, Rene Lemarchand, Gerardo Navas Davila, Mark Rosenberg, Marianne Schmink, Barbara Schmitter, and Christopher Scott participated in the original conference. Robert L. Farris acted as my assistant during the conference and made it appear as if everything were going smoothly. Ruth Beesch, Margaretta DeMar, Rosemarijn Hofte, Brooke Schwartz, and virtually the entire staff of the Center for Latin American Studies were eventually involved in one or more aspects of the long process from conference to book. To all of them, and especially to Helen I. Safa and Terry McCoy, I extend my thanks.

S.E.S.

Gainesville, Florida
April 1984

THE AMERICAS IN THE NEW INTERNATIONAL DIVISION OF LABOR

Abbreviations

AFDC	Aid for Families with Dependent Children
BWICLO	British West Indian Central Labour Organization
CBI	Caribbean Basin Initiative
DOL	Department of Labor
EPZ	Export processing zone
FFVA	Florida Fruit and Vegetable Association
FOJC	Frozen orange juice concentrate
IK	Internationalization of capital
ILWU	International Longshoremen and Warehousemen's Organization
INS	Immigation and Naturalization Service
NIC	Newly industrialized country
OECD	Organization for Economic Cooperation and Development
SAM	Mexican Food System (Sistema Alimentario Mexicano)
SSI	Supplementary Security Income
TNC	Transnational corporation

A Critical Approach to the Americas in the New International Division of Labor

Steven E. Sanderson

In the world economy of the 1980s, fundamental structural changes are transforming the ways goods are produced, distributed, exchanged, and consumed. "World markets" now exist for many goods and labor processes. Those markets imply not only world prices but "worldwide sourcing" for manufactures, "global strategies" of integrated international enterprises, and the "internationalization" of national economies in new and profound ways.

The Americas represent a living example of such changing productive and social relationships. In the Caribbean, "offshore industries" employ local labor at lower cost than their U.S. and European counterparts. In Mexico, the border industries produce manufactured goods in-bond, circumventing traditional tariff barriers. In the Brazilian Amazon region, agricultural growth coincides with the participation of state, local, and international enterprises to orient the national development model toward the world market. Within the United States itself, free-trade zones have been created to facilitate the worldwide sourcing of regionally produced or consumed goods through commercial ports. And in the global restructuring of industries and trade, jobs are lost and won, populations migrate across borders, and rural dwellers leave the country for the city.

As the rest of the world—and particularly Latin America—continues to challenge U.S. "hegemony" in trade, the "globalization" of the relations of production will figure large on the international political agenda. From the recent economic summitry of Williamsburg and Paris to the more prosaic bilateral trade negotiations of the Western Hemisphere, the specter of a fundamental international realignment of production is ever present in the public discourse of economic recovery. The watchwords of the 1980s—"reindustrialization," "food security," "export substitution," and the like—all attest to the rising influence of the new international division of labor on our daily lives.

The impact of the changing productive structure of the Americas is evident in a broad range of social science literature. New studies on the reindustrialization of the United States implicitly treat these international phenomena through the special lens focusing on employment in the industrial heartland, the composition of agricultural trade with other countries in the hemisphere, and the dynamic comparative advantage traditionally enjoyed by the United States in consumer manufactures, agricultural commodities, and high technology goods (Bluestone and Harrison, 1982; Lawrence and Dyer, 1983; Bowles, Gordon and Weisskopf, 1983).

In the literature of international relations, of course, the "interdependence" of the world has long been recognized (Keohane and Nye, 1977; Hopkins and Puchala, 1980; Cooper, 1980; Caporaso, 1978; 1981). Widely varying political positions fit into the general understanding of the regional and global integration of political associations (Axline, 1977; Bergsten, 1976; Katzenstein, 1975; Krasner, 1982; Rosecrance *et al.*, 1977), the quest for international and transnational economic coalitions among nations (Girvan, 1976; Spero, 1981; Rothstein, 1979), and—in many ways the midwife to all these literatures—the realist perception of mutual security interests among allies (Dougherty and Pfaltzgraff, 1980; Herz, 1981; Feinberg, 1983). At the same time, however, another intellectual focus has been the fundamental inequality of interstate relations, not only in the political realm but in development possibilities and trade relations as well. The much-abused "dependency" arguments, along with more general "development of underdevelopment" theories, have contributed mightily to understanding the inequality of mutual integration between North and South (Cardoso and Faletto, 1979; Sunkel, 1971; Chilcote and Edelstein, 1974).

Despite the widespread, if uneven, treatment of the internationalization of world affairs in recent social science literature, a basic problem still confronts analysts who wish to combine the virtues of nation-centric models and theories of global inequality. The mainstream literature still tends to emphasize *inter*national relations and to incorporate global levels of analysis only insofar as global regimes and transnational actors come into play. Even in the discussions of specific global regimes (Keohane and Nye, 1977; Krasner, 1982), the focus is on institutions and functional analysis rather than the overarching dynamics of change at the level of the global system.

Those who have studied global inequality suffer similar problems of scope and level. The nation-centric "inequality of nations" approach (Tucker, 1977; Rothstein, 1977) fails to account for underlying dynamics of inequality, as opposed to merely offering a neorealist understanding of the inexorable quality of misery in the international system. *Dependentistas*, on the other hand, have vacillated between global system and imperialist domination in their analysis of the permanent structural inequality pervading North-South relations.

Our presentation of the new international division of labor, as we shall see in this introductory essay, seeks a beginning resolution of that difficult merger of interstate system with global process, combining both the regional dynamics of interdependence/dependence with the structural development of inequality in the global system.

To discuss such matters as if they were only phenomena of academic interest misses the more basic point of our orientation toward the Americas in the new international division of labor. What we are witnessing in the international economic system is a more mobile, more flexible capitalist organization of production itself, whereby a different labor force—less organized, more mobile, in many instances cheaper, and certainly not "entitled" to participation in programs under the rubric of social welfare and services—is employed for the sake of industrial rationalization at a global level. The U.S. economy engages Jamaican cane cutters and Central American vegetable pickers in Florida. Undocumented agricultural and service sector workers from Mexico appear in the U.S. Southwest and many other regions of the country to "supplement" or replace local labor. Mexican, Caribbean, and Asian garment workers populate the informal sweatshops of Los Angeles, San Francisco, and New York. The internationalization of the labor force means most obviously the migration of peoples from their homes to foreign sites of employment.

The United States is certainly not unique in its use of foreign labor, although it rarely shares the limelight with other migrant worker economies. For years, Mexican coffee plantations have employed Guatemalan workers. The Dominican cane fields are filled with Haitian migrants. And the Venezuelan countryside draws Colombian workers across the frontier dividing those two countries. Other regional examples abound. More important than the regional itemization of the many cases of actual physical movement in the labor force, however, is a more complex argument about the international integration of labor *processes*, standardizing the world's work at the same time that it is differentiated across national and sectoral boundaries. The internationalization of labor implies far more than the simple movement of labor forces, a process that has characterized the Americas since the colonial epoch. If the internationalization of labor is "new," as the concept of the new international division of labor demands by definition, it is partly new for the capacity of the system to reproduce the most advanced labor processes throughout the world, and thereby to integrate not only commodity markets but workers and consumers themselves.

In many ways, the agricultural sector is the most advanced representative of these new labor processes, partly for its importance to all nations of the hemisphere and partly for its relatively early entry into the dynamic of international integration. But if the place of agricultural internationalization in international integration is secure, its nature is still elusive. In the post-World War II world, the commodity trading arrangements of the "old" international division of labor have endured to some extent. That is, Argentina still exports the staples it developed in the nineteenth century to its old trading partners in Europe, especially Great Britain. Likewise, the Caribbean nations remain inextricably tied to traditional exportables such as sugar, cacao, cotton, and rum. If crop shifts displace traditional exports in favor of new crops, the direction and significance of agricultural commodity trade in large measure endure. Nevertheless, as Rama and Sanderson show in this volume, the sector displays important and subtle changes. First, new commodities have appeared in the international system, changing basic relations of production in the countryside. Input industries have generated technologies so significant to Third World development that Mexico and Brazil have developed exports in patented processes, high technology agricultural infrastructure, and other services unknown in previous epochs.

Second, agroindustry has internationalized its production in the wake of import-substitution industrialization, beginning with commercial contracting in such traditional crops as tobacco. Such integration has spawned a whole new mode of industrial integration through production contracting, technological "packaging" for whole industries, and nonequity forms of international control over agricultural production. It has also meant that the distinction between "national" and "transnational" agribusiness processors has given way to the homogenization of production and technology. No longer is the imperialist model of transnational corporate encroachment viable as an explanation of international integration. The international system is "on beyond imperialism."

These processes of internationalization, whether in the form of direct foreign investment in agribusiness, migrating labor forces, or export processing in manufactures, create systemic pressures on trade policy, investment regulations, immigration policy, and rural development designs. It is widely recognized that the debt crisis in Latin America partly stems from the world recession, in which commodity prices fell, trade partners reduced their imports, and the specter of protectionism once again raised its head. In the trade policy of the OECD (Organization for Economic Cooperation and Development) countries, it is hardly clear that Third World recovery will top the list of political priorities that govern choices of liberalization or protectionism.

In turn, such protectionism is often accompanied by developed capitalist countries taking "Third World" political positions against which they railed for the entire post-World War II period. The United States, captain of the free investment and trade ethic, now battles over a domestic content provision to govern key industries; such language comes historically from the import-substituting countries of the Third World. Likewise, "voluntary" export restraints euphemistically describe attempts by the United States and other countries to enhance their domestic production by trade barriers—again, a political weapon characteristic of the newly industrialized countries (NICs). In a word, the mutual integration of the North and the South has meant also a certain homogenization of nationalist trade and investment strategies—with many allowances for specific national experiences, to be sure.

In immigration, though, the inequalities and political distinctions are clearer. "Receiving" countries simultaneously demand migrant labor for certain purposes (to be described by Wood and McCoy, Grasmuck, Bonilla and Campos, and Bach), as other political forces seek their removal as "job thieves" and "welfare burdens." In stark testimony to the painful political demagogy of "labor force adjustment," migrants attracted in many cases by the demand pull of the developed capitalist economies are attacked as the source of labor force mobility in the global system. As we shall see in the essays presented in this volume, not only are their roles in the labor forces of the Americas complex and changing, but they are governed by convoluted ideologies of xenophobia and nativism. To a great extent, such ideological justifications mask a process imposed by the international system—a logic described in succeeding essays as the new international division of labor.

SPECIFIC DETERMINANTS OF THE NEW INTERNATIONAL DIVISION OF LABOR

If it is easy to witness the new international division of labor through anecdotal evidence, it is much more difficult to conceptualize its specific determinants and motor force. In social science literature, such an effort is confused, not only by the differences of intellectual opinion we are about to treat but by the schizophrenic response to the "level of analysis problem" implicit in treating the new international division of labor. The traditions of comparative politics, immigration studies, international relations, and international economics and comparative economic systems all have emphasized an *inter*national focus. That is, phenomena we will consider as part of the new international division of labor have comprised an important part in studies emanating from essentially national and cross-national foci. Indeed, as Bach's essay in this volume shows, such a focus is hardly misplaced in the current epoch, despite the truly transnational character of market and institutional integration. At the same time, however, a national emphasis fails to consider the critical core of the new international division of labor: the transnational organization of labor processes. Multinational corporations in the 1980s are more properly transnational corporations, given their transition to global organizations (vs. national companies with overseas operations). The terms *transnational associations* and *integrated international enterprises* found in leading journals such as *Business Week* attest to the difficulty in the nation-centric analysis so much a part of North American social science tradition. It is to be expected, of course, that an environment of rapid change will generate such conceptual ambiguity.

Nevertheless, social science literature in the past two decades has in some measure responded to the growing recognition that the international system increasingly mediates national prerogatives of development. Nation-centric models of modernization have lost credibility in favor of more international models emphasizing interdependence, dependence, imperialism, and other theoretical constructs focused more directly on the international system and its impact on national development strategies. Recent formulations of the global integration of national economies increasingly include the concept of the new international division of labor. Nevertheless, the contributions of social scientists in this area have been uneven and certainly have lacked theoretical coherence and definitional precision concerning the interaction between national and international levels of understanding social systems. The transition to the international from the national stage has brought with it the levels problem, now posed as a difficulty in determining the role of international versus transnational regimes and processes.

This general theoretical confusion attests to a more specific lack of conceptual clarity. Not only do traditional approaches deserve new scrutiny, but a new transnational comparative analysis is required to define the vague rubric of the new international division of labor. If that theoretical coherence has still proved elusive to some extent in this volume, the quest for it at least allowed us to make a more systematic critique of current concepts of the new international division of labor and an attempt to close the gap between such high and wide-ranging levels of analysis and the necessary work of grounded research. This introductory essay will attempt to combine the themes found in succeeding contributions to the book and to offer a broader critique of traditional approaches to the new international division of labor itself.

Most analysts agree in general that the new international division of labor has something to do with the structural transformation of the world economy, which has been recognized in varying fashion since the wave of recessions and crises beginning in the early 1970s. Such institutional upheavals as the death of the Bretton Woods System, the "oil shocks" of 1973-74 and 1979 and their accompanying shifts in investment capital, the structural change in the export bill of the United States, and the competitive successes of fully recovered Japanese and German economies all have been thrown together into the seemingly endless web of descriptors that are identified with the new international division of labor. Likewise, in the flurry of discussions about the current international debt crisis—as a part of more serious shortcomings of the international financial system in general—a relatively universal assumption seems to be that economic stabilization agreements will inevitably integrate the economic performances of debtor countries more deeply and more "rationally" into the international economic system, guided by the stern hand of the International Monetary Fund, OECD trade policies, the developed countries' central banks, and in-country agents of fiscal austerity.

After this simple and too general agreement, however, analysts begin to differ quickly. Representatives of the international banking community concede in rather simplistic fashion that the international system is increasingly "penetrated" by competing products from developing countries (Kredietbank, 1978). Such a mild admission is all too modest for institutions playing such a critical role in financing direct foreign investment and trade in the Third World. Nevertheless, in the literature describing the decline of U.S. competitiveness in world manufacturing exports, the successes of East Asian and Latin American rivals seem to be the common denominator. And in the dialog about the recovery of debtor countries such as Brazil, Chile, Argentina, Peru, and Mexico, the problems of OECD protectionism and the uneven export performance of Latin American manufactures generally attest to the role of the "interpenetrated" trade system.

The developing country analog, of course, involves the internationalization of national economies in the region, which itself is described with many variations in literature from the United Nations Food and Agricultural Organization and the Economic Commission for Latin America (Gómes and Pérez, 1979; Assael, 1979; Pinto, 1979). Most of these interpretations focus on trade, especially on "export platforms," and imply that the international division of labor is new principally for its reversal of the traditional division of labor in the international system. That is, the new international division of labor restructures the system so that the previous hewers of wood and drawers of water—the Third World raw materials providers—now export a substantial portion of the developed countries' manufactures and processed goods, as well as labor, and quite often are importers of raw materials from developed countries. The cases of Brazil and Mexico certainly fit into this category. Brazil imports a broad array of inputs for agroindustry and other consumer goods; Mexico imports even to the extent of depending on trade in seedlings to produce agricultural crops to challenge traditional U.S. truck farm goods. In contrast, then, to the model described by classical economists of the nineteenth century to account for trade relations between North and South under free trade imperialism, the developed countries of the late twentieth century are threatened with competition, not only in selected agricultural goods but in a number of sectors of industrial and service activities in which they enjoyed an advantage for generations.

Another interpretation of the new international division of labor emphasizes the internationalization of the world economy as a function of the expansion of capital and its valorization and reproduction at a global level (Barkin and Rozo, 1983; Barkin and Suárez, 1982; Hymer, 1972; Palloix, 1977). Rather than treating the symptoms of change in the trade system, this structural approach led by Palloix and Barkin incorporates much of the logic underlying earlier studies of multinational or transnational capital based on the gains from trade and productive implications of international trade (Helleiner, 1977; Myint, 1954), the product life cycle (Magee, 1977; Vernon, 1966), institutional imperatives for expansion (Moran, 1973), and similar models explaining the internationalization of the world economy through the expansion of production itself. This conception further suggests, however, that the transnational corporation is merely an agent—albeit perhaps the most important one—of a process of international integration that crosses sectors and transcends mere trade relations or the power of a single firm.

This is not to say that the internationalization of production eliminates concepts of nation and national economy, but it does suggest that a proper strategy for understanding the character of the new international division of labor involves the discovery of the specific mechanics of national insertion into the global capitalist economic system. Rather than considering domestic development policy and external payments and trade disequilibria to be phenomena of a closed national system, and far from considering such dynamics to be the simple product of traditional modes of dependency and imperialism, the most sophisticated proponents of this approach to the international division of labor argue that both North and South are affected in contradictory and complex ways by their mutual and lasting integration. That the power inequalities in the international system still favor the OECD countries—and hemispheric domination by the United States is still vivid in Latin American daily life—makes that mutual integration painful and politically volatile for the nations of the underdeveloped world.

Even if we agree on one of the above approaches, however, we are still left with problems of focus and level of analysis. The following description will attempt to itemize a set of categories that pass among a variety of levels, incorporating the conceptual richness taken from various empirical studies in the field with a more general "global systems" analysis based on a critical approach to the new international division of labor.

GLOBAL PROLETARIANIZATION

One of the first points of dispute in assessing the international division of labor revolves around the two-step issue of labor process versus industrial organization as a primary focus of analysis. The first aspect of that two-step progression questions whether the new international division of labor has any integrity as a concept, apart from its place in a more general argument about the proletarianization process at a global level. The second, to be treated momentarily, questions whether to focus our understanding of the internationalization process on industrial organization as it changes in the Americas or on the related but perhaps prior element of labor process transformation.

Global proletarianization itself is a problematic analytical category, partly for the unfortunate connotations conveyed by the term. However, the new international division of labor embodies one element of a more general dynamic under which labor processes are changed in a global capitalist system. Obviously, an internationalization of capital through trade, productive investment, state policy, and labor migration mandates systemwide change in labor processes. The most obvious changes, of course, appear in firms where standardized technologies (often sold in turnkey plants, managerial programs, and export processing manufactures) have supplanted traditional forms to rationalize and homogenize labor processes for the benefit of the global integration and valorization of capital. Concretely, the competitive standardization of labor processes—and through it the enhancement of the firm's profitability—has the effect of transforming the conditions of work on a global level. Such systemic homogenization—with many local variations, to be sure—makes it possible for individual capitals to move physically to any part of the globe for the sake of worldwide sourcing, regional comparative advantage, local market enhancement, and other well-known institutional imperatives of investment expansion.

The obverse of this standardization/transformation thesis, however, stipulates the simultaneous differentiation of the work force as well. Although the universalization of labor processes through investment expansion at the level of production allows certain advantages for global profitability, the differentiation of elements of production further enhances the opportunities of individual capitalists. Thus, homogenization and differentiation operate hand in hand, rather than in opposition.

In addition to the institutional reasons for transnational investment, we must add the competitive virtues of worldwide sourcing and regional differentiation of the labor process. The "world car," after all, is not only the product of homogeneous world labor processes marketed in a package appropriate for a global market; it is also a world car for literally having been made all over the world. In high-volume industries with long production runs, for example, consumer durables, the globalization of production removes the historical necessity of confining production to a single country and expanding markets and profits only through commodity trade. Not only are transnational products now available in "host" countries, but certain well-established labor "providers" act as global or regional transmission points for the worldwide marketing of goods. Thus, Caterpillar, Sony, and Atari are not bound by a single production site, a single tax system, or a single market. Effective tariff protection simply changes the locus of production, the amount of value added in a specific site, and the global calculus of local allocation plans. The differentiation of labor processes in high-volume goods, the deskilling of work in general, and the segmentation of the labor force itself are all compatible with the more general rubric of global proletarianization.

The caveat that the concept of global proletarianization carries is a simple one: global proletarianization does *not* mean that all workers become proletarians. While at first glance that assertion might seem to undercut the concept itself, the research of Rama, Sanderson, Barkin, and Sassen-Koob indicates that global proletarianization often incorporates key elements of the work force in a double-edged nonproletarian or semiproletarian fashion. The increasing importance of the "marginal" peasantry to rural wage labor is a case in point. The home worker in the apparel industry also challenges traditional notions of wage labor, in both remuneration and work site. And the systemic involution of family systems of work for reasons of household survival contribute to the process of global proletarianization without expressing a universal face of wage labor. While such modes of labor integration are critical to more general dynamics of labor process transformation (Who can deny the role of the peasant in generating cheap food for the industrial work force?) they do not demand that we witness proletarian forms of work in all walks of life, either in developed capitalist countries or in the farthest reaches of the Third World.

Implicit in this caveat is a further cut at the concept of the new international division of labor: the primacy of labor process over industrial organization as a focus. That appears as a rather post facto realization of the difficulty imposed on our understanding of the new international division of labor by using the firm as the unit of analysis, from two standpoints. First, as is obvious from the uneven proletarianization of individual workers themselves, using industrial organization as a focus carries the danger of missing some key elements of labor force integration, many of which fall outside the direct organizational mandate of individual firms. In a word, industrial organization as an approach is insufficiently subtle to describe the implied cross-sectoral effects of the internationalization of capital.

Second, an initial premise of the internationalization of capital insists that the national affiliation of individual capitals—even transnational firms—is not the determining factor in the internationalization process itself. Clearly, the organization of individual industries and management styles is implicitly interesting as a mode of approaching the strategic planning of industrial investment, possible modes of local appropriation, and the like. But the most revealing aspects of industrial organization research come in those areas describing the global transformation of labor processes themselves (i.e., vertical coordination, integration). Conversely, the equity position of the transnational firm, its collaboration with local and state capital, and the transaction analysis of inter-and intra-industry change increasingly appear to be important but subsidiary points in the new international division of labor.

In sum, then, a critical approach to the new international division of labor involves some aspect of the process of global proletarianization, although its many manifestations from countryside to city and across borders may momentarily obscure the process from view. Implied in this understanding is the wholesale integration of labor activities on behalf of a system of capital accumulation that takes as its "natural" boundary the world economy itself.

CROSS-SECTORAL INTEGRATION AND COORDINATION

A collateral point makes up a second criterion describing the new international division of labor. If I have shifted attention from other, firm-centered analysis of industrial organization, it has been partly in recognition of the cross-sectoral integration and coordination of capital. In the essays that follow, one of the clear integrative threads involves the horizontal and vertical expansion of labor process linkages. In a simple example, production of basic foodstuffs on the farm in Mexico is controlled to a certain extent by input industries, state enterprises, and agribusiness processors and distributors.

The vertical integration of such "food systems" and "agribusiness chains" is not necessarily formal. Nor is it necessarily restricted to a single sector of activity. Agribusiness diversification in the field has meant the coordination of investment strategies based on global commodity markets, international interest rates, bilateral tariff barriers, and differential rates of return within host countries. In addition to the vertical "deepening" of agribusiness linkages—which are to varying degrees repeated in other sectors of activity, according to the logic and technological demands of the sector—horizontal diversification has also broadened the economic decisions governing the cultivation of crops and the labor processes that accompany them. The "spread" of agribusiness intermediaries into varying crop areas, multiple product lines, and capital diversification has changed the face of agricultural production in the Americas. In manufactures, technological services, and capital goods similar processes obtain.

Before treating the effects of such horizontal and vertical integration of capital under the new international division of labor, two points must be qualified. First, it must be asserted that vertical integration is shorthand for integration and coordination. Second, we must clarify the importance of the distinction between this understanding of the new international division of labor and others that posit a different concept of international expansion and global reorganization.

On the first point, vertical integration does not necessarily mean equity participation in successive links in the productive chain. In fact, to pursue the agribusiness example for a moment, there are important indications that the reverse is true: Beatrice, International Multifoods, and other transnational agribusiness enterprises have divested in critical areas in favor of less risky linkages to producers. The much-vaunted colossal farms of the early 1970s have given way to more subtle forms of agribusiness integration.

The keystone of such linkages is the contract, which has the virtue of secure, high-quality supplies without direct investment exposure. Production contracting in agriculture, which in manufactures may take the form of home work or "putting out" and in labor markets may manifest itself as labor contracts, can assume various forms, with countless variations. Least complicated is the direct contract-for-sale, which does not imply forward guarantees or price commitments but which may stipulate hygiene, pesticide content, size, maturity, and other qualifications for sale. Perhaps most sophisticated is the production contract, through which an agribusiness may arrange in advance for the production of certain varieties of produce under very specific cultivation practices, which may even stipulate brands and frequencies of pesticide application. In the United States such production contracting has taken on a rarefied form in livestock industries, especially in pork and poultry. In the U.S. Southeast, for example, feed mills regularly lease sows for farrow, with the stipulation that the offspring be fed protein supplements provided by the mill and that the feed mill be ceded a percentage of the farrow as well as a service fee. Of course, in livestock, animal reproduction services have long been integrated along such lines.

The point of this discussion is not to raise the organizational variations of vertical integration and coordination. Rather, the point for our discussion of the new international division of labor must center on the potential and actual reorganization of labor processes as a result of the integration and coordination of capital at the international level. As we shall see in several case studies, the vertical integration and coordination of capital across borders adversely affects the nation-state's capacity to govern the processes of capital accumulation, let alone to set an agenda of purposive action in food security, employment, or rural development. More on this phenomenon in a moment.

An equally crucial point in the vertical integration thesis is the implicit critique of those theorists who view the new international division of labor as a simple reversal of the old international division of labor, in which Third World countries now become important manufacturing exporters and industrial processors of agricultural commodities, while the OECD countries—led by the United States—in turn, become exporters of raw materials, foodstuffs, and semi-finished goods. Similarly inadequate is the concept of the new international division of labor that focuses strictly on the allocation of new tasks to individual countries, on the basis of dynamic comparative advantage or multinational investment strategies.

Both of these perspectives fall short of understanding the long-term and *mutual* integration of national economies in the Americas, as part of a global reorganization and expansion of capital, and the universalization of capitalist labor processes throughout the international economic system. Without understanding vertical integration and coordination and their importance for labor process transformation, it is possible to view the new international division of labor as a firm-centered set of allocative decisions. Understanding the implications of vertical integration and coordination, we can see that capital is not reorganized on a bilateral or case-by-case basis. Instead, the institutionalization of capitalist labor processes and social relations of production have assumed an international character. Each nation can, in fact, replicate in some fashion the full range of such relations according to domestic endowments, technological capacities, and the like. But the important and subtle point is that no country must, *in the abstract*, be relegated to a single role, whether as hewer of wood, drawer of water, provider of labor, or assembler of semiconductors. Indeed, according to the flexible conditions provided for investment capital and labor process transformation, each country can potentially find a place in a broad range of capitalist processes, *without being excluded because of national size or country market limitations*. Thus, a country such as Chile is no longer inhibited in its international integration by domestic market size, as long as the conditions for the successful valorization of capital and its unrestrained mobility are present. Likewise, Third World countries can enjoy (or labor under) the most modern steel producing facilities in the world, as long as they give proper attention to the world market and the technological demands of the industry. More importantly, the consumption of such internationalized commodities tends to be standardized at a global level through the universalization of tastes in the marketplace, which itself is the product of the competitive annihilation of inefficient national alternatives.

A SHIFT IN THE SIGNIFICANCE OF TRADE IN THE INTERNATIONAL DIVISION OF LABOR

The two points stipulated so far—the global proletarianization of labor processes and the transnational coordination of capital through vertical integration and coordination—both lead to a reconsideration of the role of trade in the international division of labor. Since its classical formulation during the heyday of British free-trade imperialism, trade theory has argued basically that the motive force for international specialization, price competitiveness, and commodity exchange has its roots in the individual country's opportunity for increasing social well-being through trade. The specifications of that complex and changing theory are treated well elsewhere (Sorenson, 1975; Keesing, 1979; Kindleberger and Lindert, 1978; Myint, 1954; Johnson, 1958) and need not be repeated here. For our purposes, however, it is necessary to itemize some specific assumptions of trade theory in order to show its relevance and limits for our understanding of the new international division of labor.

First, trade theory assumes some form of economic comparative advantage to be gained from trade. Initially, that was considered to be a simple function of differential labor costs in a technologically stable, interstate economic system with little capital and labor mobility (Sorenson, 1975, Ch. 3). Whether in its initial single-factor formulations or in more subtle treatments of factor endowments, trade theory rested on the continuing premise of relative cost advantages from trade.

Two further assumptions of trade theory emerged from that first theoretical premise: the assumption of international specialization, and the presumption of gains from trade. Specialization, of course, emerged not only from the "objective" conditions of factor endowment, relative costs, and commodity trade but also from the complex politics of North-South relations in the epoch of British Empire and U.S. hegemony in the late nineteenth and early twentieth centuries. Quite apart from considering the intrusions of empire on orderly markets, traditional trade theory only haltingly treated currency instability, rapid technological change, and the increasingly free movement of capital.

Regarding the gains from trade, it has been argued throughout the literature on economic development and international trade that "backward" countries benefit from commodity trade with advanced industrial nations (Myint, 1954). Not only do global commodity markets offer opportunities for competitive pricing in raw materials, but an export orientation is still seen as a means by which small economies can industrialize and take advantage of the economies of scale and production run available to larger national economic systems. While small economies have continued to bother trade theorists with their fragility in conditions of international price uncertainty and other elements of the warp and woof of the international economic order, few analysts have questioned the virtues of expanded trade as a generator of much-needed foreign exchange, as an employer, and even as the centerpiece of a resolution of current debt crises in the Americas. From the United States to Chile, expanded trade and deeper integration into the international trade system figure large in the recovery plans of the 1980s.

The understanding of trade in this essay differs substantially from that of classical theory. It is not that dynamic comparative advantage does not exist or that the internal integrity of the two-commodity models of relative cost advantage is in question. Rather, this essay questions the virtue of trade for the development of Third World countries and the nation-centric bias of the trade system itself. Additionally, understanding the new international division of labor requires that a broader logic be imposed on the trade system in order to account for the changes in labor process and capital movement in the post-World War II epoch.

First, as Rama, Barkin, and Sanderson show, comparative advantage is not a neutral patron. Commodity trade means that food security plans disappear in the face of export and import dependence. In times of exchange rate and liquidity crises, national models of development bow before the limits of the international trade system. Likewise, factor endowments are not neutral, nor do they necessarily emanate from "natural" endowments. Labor-abundant economies sometimes come as a product of high population growth and rural dislocation. But these are hardly natural processes that can be equated with superior climate and rich soil. As the Bonilla and Campos, Grasmuck, and Bach studies show, the logic of labor force migration and its political implications are likewise far from natural. The political economy of overpopulation, rural marginalization, emigration, and the like are the specific results of centuries of colonization and dependence and rapid modernization. Trade has played a central role in the development of labor-abundant economies characterized by gross maldistribution of resources and income, low levels of labor organization, and other "efficiencies" of residual economies in the world market. If such evidence is insufficient to question an unqualified embrace of trade as a generator of development, we can look to the cases of rural development and international trade experienced by the leaders of the Latin American development experience: Mexico and Brazil. Both are also leaders in income maldistribution, gross foreign debt, and overurbanization.

On a more theoretical plane, our argument about the new international division of labor differs from others in stipulating that the role of trade in creating the division of labor has diminished in favor of the internationalization of capital at the level of production itself. That is, in contrast to the "interpenetration" thesis, which may be limited to an examination of trade in the international division of labor, and in contrast to the "export platform" concentration of so many theorists of integration through trade, the orientation described above maintains that the internationalization of capital takes place not only through trade but through the integration of production itself. A number of corollaries to this point are important.

First, to understand the new international division of labor, it is necessary to examine more than simple trade processes. For example, as Rama shows, vertical integration and coordination in the agricultural sector help determine the crop mix of the Mexican economy. New crops that displace basic foodstuffs do not necessarily serve the export economy alone, but they do tend to homogenize all markets through the competitive standardization of labor processes at the level of production. Likewise, in the shifting productive structure of the Americas, Fernández and Sassen-Koob show that trade in labor—however important it still is in national immigration policy (Bach), sector-specific programs (Wood and McCoy), and national development problems (Bonilla and Campos)—does not account for the full range of internationalization in labor processes. In fact, those who would seek to make an argument for labor mobility in the late twentieth century would be hard pressed to do so merely on the evidence of physical movements of labor. Nevertheless, the internationalization of labor does exist, in the internationalization of productive processes in the firm, in the standardization of consumer tastes (which again flies in the face of traditional trade theory's stipulation of fixed national tastes and preferences irrespective of the availability of traded goods), and in the segmentation of the labor force (Nash) in a highly competitive environment. Changes in technology and labor markets affect the character of development as much as commodity trade did in the original international division of labor.

In sum, trade theory has not adequately treated the mutual and lasting integration of the world economy on the basis of labor process transformation but rather has concentrated its attention on the important dynamics of interstate trade. As more trade became the rule in the international system, more anomalies simultaneously appeared in trade theory. The presentation of the new international division of labor offered here seeks not to ignore the important dynamics of trade but to situate them in a larger framework of internationalization, which, in one obvious example, is able to distinguish between the changing significance of international trade and intrafirm trade for the future of the Americas. Likewise, the studies to be presented here offer a social understanding of comparative advantage, not removed from trade theory but inserted more profoundly into the developmental dynamics of the countries and societies of the hemisphere.

THE REORIENTATION OF STATE POWER

To return to our earlier treatment of the role of the nation-state in the international system, one of the consequences of the international division of labor has been a transformation of the role of the state itself. Of course, we can see that national states have traditionally borne heavy responsibilities for exchange rate management, trade promotion, and foreign policies. From the Sterling Bloc to the Marshall Plan, individual "key currency" countries have dominated the international financial system at specific points in history (Gardner, 1956; Bergsten, 1975). Likewise, their counterparts in the Third World have had to negotiate increasingly burdensome foreign public debt, to borrow in international capital markets to enhance domestic investment and credit, and to create the political conditions for the onerous "shock treatments" of internationally supervised economic stabilization agreements. In the mid-1980s, as Latin America faces continuing debt service problems, high interest rates, and shortages of new lending, the traditional role of the state grows outward to meet the exigencies of the international economic system.

But such activities on the part of most states in the Americas would hardly be volunteered as expressions of enhanced state power. In fact, the state has come to act increasingly as the authorized agent of international stabilization policies, while faced with a much more restrictive menu of political choices at home (Sanderson, 1983; Whitehead, 1980; Frenkel and O'Donnell, 1979; Skidmore, 1977; Foxley and Whitehead, 1980; Cline and Weintraub, 1981). In this situation—which is not likely to change radically for the rest of the decade—the state experiences an expansion of its apparatus and responsibility vis-à-vis the international financial community and individual capitals exposed in direct or portfolio investment, while the opportunities for exit from the crisis are shaped more narrowly as a recipe for deeper integration into the international economic system. It is with that understanding of the fundamental *problematica* in the Americas today that we can argue that the power of the state has declined, *at least insofar as that power might represent the enacted capacity to enhance national autonomy of decision making or to negotiate the terms of national participation in the international division of labor.* At the same time, however, *dirigiste* responses to debt crises and stabilization demands show that the overall responsibility of the state for economic management has increased, with all of the attendant implications for legitimacy now unfolding in Chile, Argentina, and Brazil.

Concretely, that contradiction of increasing state responsibility for national integration into the global economic system combined with a reduced capacity to influence the nature of that integration expresses itself at the local level in several ways. First, it is clear that the national state cannot militate for commodity negotiations from a position of strength in a time of drastically low world commodity prices and beggar-thy-neighbor trade and investment policies. The recovery of the Latin American countries depends on export expansion, import restraint, "realistic" exchange rate policies (i.e., downward floats in the high-inflation economies of most countries), fiscal austerity at home, and debt refinancing in an unfavorable climate for borrowing. So, irrespective of political coalitions at the national level, most Latin American states must "obey nurse" in the words of the *Economist* (September 4, 1982), and nurse's therapy hardly prescribes economic nationalism, populist-style domestic protection, or other traditional remedies for the structural inequality that defines Latin America's position in the international system. And to the extent that traditional economic nationalism is moribund for the time being (barring defaults from such nationalist tensions in countries such as Argentina), the national state has lost its single historical response to unremitting and unqualified economic integration into the international system.

Needless to say, such a reality leaves most American states increasingly "vulnerable," in the words of interdependence analysts. And such vulnerability—as we shall see in Barkin's and Bach's essays in particular—leads to more complete global proletarianization and a hemispheric vulnerability to the leading power of the region, the United States. Interestingly, the current conjuncture creates a simultaneous countertrend to globalization: in the midst of global integration, North-South hemispheric domination by the United States resurges momentarily. This time the United States is not the hegemonic power, however, but a political forum for the many voices of international capital. And at home, Latin American nationalist oppositions are left with a limited opportunity to constrain the political bases of "internationalist" authoritarian regimes in the region.

At another level, even the United States faces critical difficulties in state policy toward migrant workers, who enter the country with relatively little sensitivity to short-term national political problems but play an important economic role in critical sectors of the economy. As Wood and McCoy show in this volume, under the guise of the narrowly defined H-2 immigration program, the state actually abdicates some of its traditional authority over contract workers in favor of private sector interests desirous of "managing" the labor supply at the international level for the sake of producer needs to valorize capital and reproduce a labor process specific to its sector. Bach's analysis hints at the casuistry involved in politically justifying the comparative discrimination of U.S. immigration policy.

Returning to our earlier point about the "deindustrialization" of the U.S. economy—or the global restructuration of production—we can see also that the entire realm of state intervention in national economic policy is being called into question, from the United States to Chile. The OECD countries—and particularly the United States, in view of its "low stateness" in economic policy—face systemwide critiques of industrial and foreign economic policies, not only within their national political systems but in ministerial meetings of international organizations and in the dialog over the international debt crisis. The ideologies of "free trade" and "fair trade" are a loose reflection of the reorientation of state power toward economic policy making in an internationalized climate clouded by the necessity of mutual structural adjustment.

MUTUAL STRUCTURAL ADJUSTMENT

The last analytical criterion interwoven in the essays that follow in this volume involves the mutual structural adjustment required by all national economies in the 1980s. In fact, such adjustments, which in reality often appear as lost jobs in automobiles, machine tools, and other "smokestack industries" in the United States or as export promotion in agriculture taking the place of basic foodstuffs in the Third World, among other examples, have produced a number of interesting social phenomena to be addressed in succeeding essays. National political systems typically react to mutual structural adjustment with protectionist nostrums and heavy political cant against competitors, who often become enemies of nativist workers and economically threatened firms. Interestingly, the United States has begun to embrace part of the Third World's traditional political resistance to free trade as the keystone of development. On the other hand, the luxury of protectionism is less available to Third World countries in the grip of economic stabilization and foreign debt refinancing schemes.

The trade politics of the United States and other American countries still remain unclear, however. In fact, the claims of Florida tomato producers or automobile and textile workers against a trade system that allows their disappearance as part of the traditional work force confront a national political system in the United States that, as Nash argues, refuses to assume the welfare and employment responsibilities that emanate from the trade system. At the same time, perceiving such mutual structural adjustment at the national level to be a function of trade alone, rather than the integration of production itself, casts a necessarily protectionist shadow on more fundamental issues of "dematurity" or "reindustrialization" or "human capital" investments. Because the United States has been the champion of free trade in the post-World War II epoch and has abjured a national industrial policy, industrial adjustment is perceived as a trade question instead of a consequence of transnational productive integration. The agenda for coming to grips with the political and social consequences of the new international division of labor is thereby shunted into a traditional political language describing the United States as the friendly giant abused by its predatory neighbors.

In the other American countries, however, the political scene is quite different, both for the nature of their economic adjustment to the internationalization of capital and for the traditional "high stateness" of national economic policy making. While the nature of integration moves parallel to the U.S. experience—Mexico and Brazil face an increasingly competitive and protectionist international system that resists their successes in export competition, from wearing apparel to foodstuffs—national latitude in dealing with the competitive homogenization of labor processes is severely constrained by structural weakness in determining international exchange rate policy, transnational investments, interest rates, and other critical variables in response to the new international division of labor. Whether in cases embracing the "low state" neoliberal authoritarianism of Chile or the "high state" mobilization of Brazil, the political capacity, or power, to guide industrial and agricultural internationalization shrinks before the transnational locus of production changes. The imperatives of export promotion, debt refinancing, import constraint, regressive wage policies, competitive devaluation ("realistic exchange rates"), and fiscal austerity dictate that the states of Latin America have less real capacity to negotiate their entry into the new international division of labor. As all of the essays focusing on Latin American cases show, the political alternatives to unqualified international integration are unclear and perhaps beyond the capabilities of the nation-state in the climate of the early 1980s. As Bonilla and Campos and Rama show, we might hypothesize an inverse relationship between state power in this regard and proximity to the United States.

If the political responses to mutual structural adjustment are limited in obvious ways by the character and timing of international integration, however, likely alternatives are in short supply. Virtually all of the literature focusing on reindustrialization or general U.S. industrial policy seems to argue for a recognition of the job displacement (firings and plant closings) that is the grim currency of structural adjustment. But little in the way of short-term responses is offered, despite the short horizon of individual political leaders and the incapacity of all these social systems to guarantee the survival of workers ground up in the process of readjustment. Our essays are necessarily weak in this regard, partly due to the relative weakness of our case countries with respect to any possible exit from international integration in the 1980s.

Implicit in this confession of prescriptive weakness, however, is a critique that emanates from our understanding of the new international division of labor. If, in fact, we posit global proletarianization, vertical integration and coordination, a reorientation of state power, and the necessity for mutual structural adjustment as the initial premises of the new international division of labor, we must also recognize that the nation-centric response of the United States to these processes ignores the developmental consequences of the internationalization of capital for Latin America. At the level of foreign policy making, the greater processes of mutual structural adjustment get translated into debt management, trade liberalization, and regional security. In the literature of reindustrialization, a national emphasis precludes a transnational perspective guiding political responses to world productive integration. And at the level of the work place, the beggar-thy-neighbor trade policies that infected the pre-World War II international system may be resuscitated as possible political programs for national survival in the 1980s.

The critique that we begin in this volume is twofold: an explicit critique of nation-centered understandings of development and change in an interdependent international environment, in favor of an approach pitched at understanding local change from an international level of analysis; and an implicit critique of political leadership that not only is incapable of treating the national symptoms of the new international division of labor with employment and investment policies but is disinclined to understand the matter of international integration from a transnational perspective that might offer more solidly based analysis of this age of internationalization. With these postulates and criticisms in mind, we begin this set of studies with a modest prolegomenon to recasting the methods and levels, not only of scholarly approaches to development but of national and transnational policy formation as well.

REFERENCES

Assael, Hector. 1979. "The Internationalization of the Latin American Economies: Some Reservations." *CEPAL Review* 7 (April), 41-55.

Axline, W. Andrew. 1977. "Underdevelopment, Dependence, and Integration: The Politics of Regionalism in the Third World." *International Organization* 31:1 (Winter), 83-105.

Barkin, David, and Carlos Rozo. 1982. "La producción de alimentos y la internacionalización del capital." *El trimestre económico* 50:3 (September), 1603-1626.

Barkin, David, and Blanca Suárez. 1982. *El fin de autosuficiencia alimentaria*. Mexico: Nueva Imagen.

Bergsten, C. Fred. 1975. *The Dilemmas of the Dollar*. New York: New York University Press.

Bergsten, C. Fred. 1976. "Interdependence and the Reform of International Institutions." *International Organization* 30:2 (Spring), 361-372.

Bhagwati, Jagdish, ed. 1977. *The New International Economic Order: The North-South Debate*. Cambridge: MIT Press.

Bluestone, Barry, and Bennet Harrison. 1982. *The Deindustrialization of America*. New York: Basic Books.

Bowles, Samuel, David M. Gordon, and Thomas E. Weiskopf. 1983. *Beyond the Wasteland: A Democratic Alternative to Economic Decline*. New York: Anchor.

Caporaso, James A. 1978. "Dependence, Dependency and Power in the Global System: A Structural and Behavioral Analysis." *International Organization* 32:1 (Winter), 13-44.

———. 1981. "Industrialization in the Periphery: The Evolving Global Division of Labor." *International Studies Quarterly* 25:3 (September), 347-384.

Cardoso, Fernando Henrique, and Enzo Faletto. 1979. *Dependency and Development in Latin America*. Berkeley: University of California Press.

Chilcote, Ronald H., and Joel C. Edelstein, eds. 1974. *Latin America: The Struggle with Dependency and Beyond*. Cambridge: Shenkman.

Cline, William R., and Sidney Weintraub, eds. 1981. *Economic Stabilization in Developing Countries*. Washington, D.C.: Brookings Institution.

Cooper, Richard. 1980. *The Economics of Interdependence*. New York: Columbia University Press.

Dougherty, James E., and Robert L. Pfaltzgraff, Jr. 1980. *Contemporary Theories of International Relations*. 2nd ed. Philadelphia: Lippincott.

Fagen, Richard R. ed. 1979. *Capitalism and the State in U.S.-Latin American Relations*. Stanford: Stanford University Press.

Feinberg, Richard. 1983. *The Intemperate Zone: The Third World Challenge to U.S. Foreign Policy*. New York: W.W. Norton.

Foxley, Alejandro, and Laurence Whitehead. 1980. "Economic Stabilization in Latin America: Political Dimensions." *World Development* 8:11 (November), 823-832.

Frenkel, Roberto, and Guillermo O'Donnell. 1979. "The 'Stabilization Programs' of the International Monetary Fund and Their Internal Impacts." In *Capitalism and the State in U.S.-Latin American Relations*. ed. Richard R. Fagen, pp. 171-216. Stanford: Stanford University Press.

Galtung, Johan. 1971. "A Structural Theory of Imperialism." *Journal of Peace Research* 2, 81-118.
Gardner, Richard N. 1956. *Sterling-Dollar Diplomacy*. Oxford: Clarendon Press.
Girvan, Norman. 1976. *Corporate Imperialism*. White Plains, N.Y.: M.E. Sharpe.
Gómes, Gerson, and Antonio Pérez. 1979. "The Process of Modernization in Latin American Agriculture." *CEPAL Review* 8 (August), 55-74.
"Hands off the IMF." 1982. *Economist* 284:7253 (September 4), 15-16.
Helleiner, G. K. 1977. "Transnational Enterprises and the New Political Economy of U.S. Trade Policy." *Oxford Economic Papers* 29:1 (March), 102-116.
Herz, John H. 1981. "Political Realism Revisited." Symposium in honor of Hans J. Morgenthau. *International Studies Quarterly* 25:2 (June), 182-197.
Hopkins, Raymond F., and Donald J. Puchala. 1980). *Global Food Interdependence: Challenge to American Foreign Policy*. New York: Columbia University Press.
Hymer, Stephen. 1972). "The Internationalization of Capital." *Journal of Economic Issues* 6:1 (March), 91-111.
Johnson, Harry. 1958. *International Trade and Economic Growth*. London: Allen and Unwin.
Katzenstein, Peter J. 1975. "International Interdependence: Some Longterm and Recent Changes." *International Organization* 29:4 (Autumn), 1021-1034.
Keesing, Donald B. 1979. "Trade Policy in Developing Countries." World Bank Staff Working Paper, no. 353 (August).
Keohane, Robert, and Joseph Nye. 1977. *Power and Interdependence: World Politics in Transition*. Boston: Little, Brown.
Kindleberger, Charles, and Peter Lindert. 1982. *International Economics*. 7th ed. Homewood, Ill.: Irwin.
Krasner, Stephen, ed. 1982. "International Regimes." Special issue of *International Organization* 36:2 (Spring).
Kredietbank. 1978. "The New International Division of Labor." *Weekly Bulletin* 33:37 (October).
Lawrence, Paul R., and Davis Dyer. 1983. *Renewing American Industry*. New York: Free Press.
Magee, Stephen P. 1977. "Information and Multinational Corporation: An Appropriability Theory of Direct Foreign Investment." In *The New International Economic Order: The North-South Debate*. ed. Jagdish Bhagwati, pp. 317-340. Cambridge: MIT Press.
Malloy, James, ed. 1977. *Authoritarianism and Corporatism in Latin America*. Princeton: Princeton University Press.
Moran, Theodore H. 1973. "Foreign Expansion as an 'Institutional Necessity' for U.S. Corporate Capitalism." *World Politics* 25:3 (April), 369-386.
Myint, H. 1954. "The Gains from International Trade and the Backward Countries." *Review of Economic Studies* 22:2. (no. 58), 129-142.
———. 1958. "The Classical Theory of International Trade and the Underdeveloped Countries." *Economic Journal* 68, (June) 317-337.
Palloix, Christian. 1977. *Las firmas multinacionales y el proceso de internacionalización*. Mexico: Siglo XXI.
Pinto, Anibal. 1979. "The Periphery and the Internationalization of the World Economy." *CEPAL Review* 9 (December), 45-67.

Reich, Robert. 1982. *The Next American Frontier*. New York: New York Times Books.
Rosecrance, Richard, *et al*. 1977. "Whither Interdependence?" *International Organization* 31:1 (Winter), 83-105.
Rothstein, Robert L. 1977. *The Weak in the World of the Strong*. New York: Columbia University Press.
——. 1979. *Global Bargaining: UNCTAD and the Quest for a New International Economic Order*. Princeton: Princeton University Press.
Sanderson, Steven E. 1983. "Presidential Succession and Political Rationality in Mexico." *World Politics* 35:3 (April), 315-334.
Skidmore, Thomas. 1977. "The Politics of Economic Stabilization in Postwar Latin America." In *Authoritarianism and Corporatism in Latin America*. ed. James Malloy, pp. 149-190. Princeton: Princeton University Press.
Sorenson, Vernon. 1975. *International Trade Policy: Agriculture and Development*. East Lansing: Michigan State University International Business and Economic Studies.
Spero, Joan Edelman. 1981. *The Politics of International Economic Relations*. 2nd ed. New York: St. Martin's Press.
Sunkel, Osvaldo. 1971. "Capitalismo transnacional y desintegración nacional en América Latina." *Estudios internacionales* 4:16 (January-March), 3-61.
Tucker, Robert W. 1977. *The Inequality of Nations*. New York: Basic Books.
Vernon, Raymond. 1966. "International Investment and International Trade in the Product Cycle." *Quarterly Journal of Economics* 80:2 (May), 190-207.
Whitehead, Laurence. 1980. "Mexico from Bust to Boom: A Political Evaluation of the 1976-1979 Stabilization Programme." *World Development* 8:11 (November), 843-846.

Global Proletarianization

David Barkin

The most significant change in the international economy today is the expansion of the proletariat. With the integration of individual nations into a global system of production and distribution for profit, the wage-labor relationship is extending to encompass new social groups and to transform new and important aspects of human existence into commodities. Capitalists are employing additional workers in new labor markets to increase profits by supplying goods and services previously produced by the household or through cooperative arrangements within social groups: no aspect of life is exempt from this process of commodification. At the same time, the international diffusion of technology and the spread of new standardized systems of production and distribution are amplifying the effect that the generalization of the social relations of capitalist production has on daily life and social organization. Although all societies are subject to the same set of laws of capitalist accumulation, specific resource endowments and conflicts about the rate and character of economic change are causing the differentiation of national social and productive structures.

The internationalization of capital (IK) is a shorthand expression for this complex but normal process of expansion of capitalism as a productive system (see, e.g., Hymer, 1980; Palloix, 1974, 1975, 1979; Barkin and Rozo, 1981; Rozo and Barkin, 1983a). The process has been underway for several centuries, but only recently it has assumed global proportions. Capitalism expands on several planes simultaneously: within a given society, within social groups in society, and within productive sectors, both nationally and internationally. This expansion rarely takes place at a uniform pace and is always profoundly influenced by the specific characteristics of each setting. Its exclusive concern with the production of commodities for exchange (and for profit) and the seemingly contradictory advance in production and material deprivation have broadened social disparities in the Third World, occasioning abrupt transformations of social structures, productive conditions, and political relations.

These changes require new ways of understanding the evolution of the international economy. In its search for new sources of surplus value and higher rates of exploitation to accelerate the pace of accumulation, capital is continually attempting to expand the proletariat and extend commodity production. Industrialization in the Third World, or industrial redeployment, as it is called in Europe, is a product of this process.[1] The competitive struggle among capitals intensifies the rhythm of technical change and leads to the worldwide spread of new production techniques and commodities. Even while capitalists compete to gain markets by copying one another, their need to increase profit rates obliges them to innovate by developing new technologies and by expanding the areas in which commodity production encroaches upon human activity and needs.

The theory which analyzes the internationalization of capital highlights the convergence of disparate trajectories of national capitals, each of which advances the spread of capitalist social relations of production, often in collaboration with transnational capitals. At one and the same time, the IK transforms individual societies, integrating their productive apparatuses into a preexisting global market. The IK is a dramatic process of socioeconomic and political transformation which inevitably creates its own obstacles to future growth. The accumulation of capital itself is plagued by crises of realization, that is, by the difficulty of selling for a profit the ever expanding volume of commodities created by capitalist expansion. Technological advances, which themselves are an essential component of the expansion process, are often blamed for these problems of the production and reproduction of surplus value. National political and social aspirations also alter the global designs of a now overtly transnationalized capitalist class. Social traditionalism, disorganization, and even rebellion impose compromises, changes of pace, and even, extremely, reorganizations of society which threaten the capitalist organization of production itself.

In this chapter, I analyze the distinctive character of the recent expansion of capitalist class relations for the reproduction of the means of production and the goods required for the reproduction of society and its prevailing system of power relations. Capitalist expansion proceeds in accord with universal laws of accumulation, but its results are astonishingly different in each society. The competitive drive to produce profits and continually to accumulate more capital creates dynamic forces which induce technological change and reorganize production and consumption. The theory of the IK explains how capitalist competition and the struggle for higher profits produces the profound transformations of social organization and material production which have been observed in all societies. Each society appears to imitate patterns of its competitors or forerunners, but natural and institutional factors inevitably leave their unique imprint on national development. It is this pattern of diversity within homogeneity to which this essay is addressed.

THE INTERNATIONALIZATION OF CAPITAL

Capitalism is the dominant system of production today. It is characterized by a system of social relations in which a small group of people who control the means of production employs relatively large numbers of people to produce the goods required for their collective reproduction. Their goal is to accumulate capital by producing profits. To achieve their objectives, capitalists attempt to control the state apparatus and the institutions and mechanisms for technological innovation. They also strive to restructure society and individual demands to make production more profitable while expanding the market for particular commodities.

The social relations of capitalist production are characterized by conflict. The constant struggle of the several social classes (within and between groups) to advance their own (contradictory) interests for controlling the social product is an inherent feature of capitalist society. The struggle dominates the evolution of production, conditions technological advance, and induces the appearance of new commodities during the continuing but uneven process of capitalist expansion. In the Third World, the struggle frequently pits workers who are uprooted from non-capitalist forms of production (e.g., artisans and peasants) against local bourgeoisies committed to introducing and accelerating the advance of capitalism. Ironically, although material and technical progress leads to higher productivity and raises the rate of exploitation of labor, it threatens to reduce the rate of profit, occasioning periodic crises of accumulation.[2] These crises always impose heavy burdens on workers. Many are fired, and others suffer decreases in real incomes. Often this leads to a reorganization of production, with more powerful producers destroying weaker ones.

Historically, capitalist expansion has reorganized and extended production to an ever broadening range of commodities because of the imposition of its characteristic social relations. Production for profit encompasses new social groups, new sectors of production, and new regions. The reorganization of traditional economies wrests control of production from self-employed peasants and artisans, and new industrialized products displace homemade products. This is exemplified by the substitution of packaged bread for traditional products or the contracting of such industrial inputs as vegetables to peasants who no longer have control over their own production. In this way noncapitalist production is replaced by modern processes and products which require the enlargement of the wage-labor force as the basis for capital's further expansion and control over society.

The development of capitalist production and accumulation occasions profound transformations. These are not limited to the developing countries, where the qualitative changes involve much more than a simple reproduction of transposed economic structures. Even in the mature economies of the capitalist world the advance of capitalism has left a dramatic imprint. Diets and even life styles change and regions are destroyed when production moves from one area to another, either within the same country or internationally. Capital is continually reshaping the labor force as workers organize to demand a greater share of their product. To counter these efforts, capitalists progressively incorporate outcasts and women as wage laborers. With the increase in the proletariat and the new life styles brought about by changing production and consumption patterns, social interaction and family life are altered. Capital insinuates itself into areas formerly reserved for the household: child care is transformed, and domestic food preparation and other home services are turned into commodities to be purchased. The result is the broadening of the basis for the production of surplus value. Worker and consumer resistance to the new work processes and the commodification of daily life takes many forms and requires capitalists to modify continually their operational strategies to try to maintain profitability.

Capitalism's viability depends on its ability to find new ways to accumulate capital for promoting its further growth. Normally, as capitalists expand their markets for existing commodities, broaden the range of commodities they produce, and revolutionize their techniques, they simplify the work process and employ fewer workers. Competition obliges firms to expand and innovate, as well as to emulate the latest advances of industry leaders. Innovation and redeployment are mechanisms that respond to worker organization and social struggles in the mature economies as capital searches for new sources of surplus value.

The theory of the IK offers a framework within which to analyze this growth process and its internal contradictions. Initially, capital expands internationally in search of new markets and new resources and finally in search of new sources of labor power to employ in the production of saleable commodities.[3] In its international expansion, capital from the mature capitalist economies has joined together with national capitals everywhere. This means building new productive apparatuses for manufacturing goods for world markets as well as for local markets that emerge in the developing countries. The IK is a response to competition and to the specter of declining profit rates. It leads to the standardization of production and requires producers to keep abreast of and to respond to innovations by competitors. At the same time it leads to differentiation of products and techniques as each firm works assiduously to get ahead by introducing new commodities or changing production methods so as to increase its rate of profit.

One of the principal changes in the postwar period which has accelerated the IK is the consolidation of the transnational corporation (TNC) as a key agent in the international spread of technology, new commodities, and new forms for organizing production. It is important to emphasize that it is not the TNC itself that is the cause of the transformations described here. The TNC does, however, play an important role.[4] Relatively recently, the IK has induced structural transformations which are promoting the articulation of national capitalist economies into a coherent but neither unified nor uniform global system. As a result, the TNCs can no longer afford to discriminate against the peripheral or dependent countries for being latecomers. They need new markets and must integrate new workers into their production. They must, therefore, move their operations into the Third World. But the TNCs cannot simply abandon their facilities and markets in the advanced countries. In the new order, the TNC is becoming more imaginative in designing joint ventures with national capitalists or states throughout the world to facilitate its search for new opportunities to accumulate capital by producing surplus value.

Capitalist expansion has wreaked havoc on the inherited division of labor, replacing it with a patchwork pattern of countries producing parts and assembling "world" consumption goods. In some parts of the Third World this production is for export because the local population is too poor to be able to purchase the goods. Elsewhere it is exclusively for a privileged domestic minority as export opportunities are limited because the same industries are being established in each country. But industrialization is not the panacea some theorists had hoped: industrial production requires additional imports of intermediate goods and machinery and inevitably leads to an increase in foreign indebtedness to pay for the goods needed to keep the new plants operative. Thus, even after forging increasingly complex productive structures, many Third World countries find that they must continue to export raw materials and agricultural products to pay for their imports and service their debts. They also find themselves obliged, in spite of uncertain market conditions, to broaden their industrialization programs to produce a greater range of goods, including some machinery and intermediate goods, in a seemingly endless race to reduce foreign dependency and generate additional foreign exchange earnings.

The very complexity of the Third World economies occasions further problems. With new industrial production and growing commercial agriculture displacing traditional products, it is increasingly common to read about the structural inability of many countries to supply their own basic needs (see George, 1977; Lappé and Collins, 1977; Barkin, 1982). Third World capitalist commodity production rarely attempts to satisfy worker and peasant demands because their low incomes cannot create a dynamic market. The contradictions between local production and local needs deepen as insufficient external demand and foreign exchange lead first to further indebtedness and then to resistance by the international banking community to continued external financing for local production. Even those developing countries with dynamic industrial structures and low labor costs, the "success" stories of recent history, find that international competition and production norms force them to import not only capital equipment but also basic foodstuffs. Thus, in spite of deliberate and often successful programs to diversify production, broaden internal markets, and spread capitalist productive relations, most Third World countries find themselves obliged to return to traditional primary exports as a way of trying to reestablish external balance. Even so, Third World external indebtedness is becoming a more serious problem, while profound structural imbalances increasingly polarize society.

These new development programs also exacerbate local employment problems. The productive transformations created by capitalist expansion effectively reorganize whole societies. They create pressures that inject people into the wage-labor force by displacing traditional activities and oblige them to abandon rural communities in search of new productive employment or other ways to subsist. In every country where this has happened, the modern sectors have been incapable of absorbing both the people displaced from traditional activities and the new entrants into the labor force. As a result, open and disguised unemployment, with the resulting economic hardships and social conflicts, have become endemic in every developing country. One response to these structural inadequacies has been a strong popular resistance to the displacement of subsistence or simple-commodity production and to the destruction of traditional economic and social organizations. Peasants and artisans have grouped together in self-defense to build political organizations capable of demanding government assistance for strengthening their productive base and/or obtaining the necessary subsidies to continue as viable social and economic groups. They argue that they can often continue to produce efficiently the basic food and other products needed for national development with resources (people and land) that might otherwise be idle. Obviously, capital fiercely opposes this resistance within the Third World because it could slow down the pace of accumulation. In general, individual initiatives to promote this alternative in capitalist countries have failed, in spite of the lip service accorded to the abstract principle in international forums.[5] Because of this resistance, the phenomenon of global proletarianization referred to in the title of this chapter must be understood as simply a tendency: capital's unreachable goal. It is unreachable because of capital's inability to provide viable alternatives for hundreds of millions who cannot be productively employed or reasonably controlled within the modern sectors of the new economies.

The IK has increased the volume of international trade and the complexity of the global distribution of commodity production. With the industrialization of the Third World the locality of commodity production and productive structures has changed. Many of the advanced countries are faced with crises because new industrial growth and technological innovation can no longer compensate for problems created by "runaway" shops, declining production of traditional goods, and serious regional and social dislocations. On the other hand, in new developing countries the problems are also heightening. In spite of the accelerated industrialization that produces goods for new markets as well as, in some cases, for markets in the "advanced" countries, there is an increasing indebtedness along with a continuing dependence on primary exports and a growing inability to provide productive employment for most of the population.

Technological Change as a Vehicle of Internationalization

The technological reorganization of production has become a central part of the accumulation process.[6] As with other aspects of social organization and material production, scientific activity has become increasingly subject to the logic of capital accumulation. Decisions about priorities, resource availability, and even the directions of new inquiry seem to be strongly influenced by the search for means to effectively control and simplify the work process and to increase labor productivity.

Technology is particularly important to capital because it directly addresses the need to increase profitability. Technological innovations are useful for modifying social relations within the work place. They promote a process of "deskilling" and reorganization of the labor force in consumer goods production. Also they encourage the transformation of capital goods from craft to mass production by taking advantage of advances in computer-aided design and digital control (see, e.g., UNIDO, 1981). Technological advances in organization and control have facilitated the decentralization of production and even the reintroduction of "putting-out" systems. In some places, self-disciplined workers or petty capitalists organize subcontracting systems, which can increase productivity and profitability for the TNCs.

Scientific and technical workers have extended their influence from direct production to encompass the organization and utilization of information. This means that bureaucratic and administrative functions are being rationalized to increase labor productivity and profitability while assisting the managers to have better control of the firm. With the closer interconnection of scientific activity and the production process, technological progress is best analyzed as a response to competitive entrepreneurial decisions rather than as an autonomous product. In its efforts to produce and redistribute surplus value, management must be concerned about the conception, generation, acquisition, assimilation, adaptation, use, and administration of knowledge for the reorganization of production within the firm and restructuring of industry nationally and internationally. Thus, as capitalist production has spread, so have its most advanced systems of organization.

The IK has both intensified and been accelerated by the subordination of technological developments and scientific activity to the norms of profitability. With global decision making and technological advance concentrated in relatively few firms, new productive capital formation almost invariably embodies the latest technological advances.[7] Even when they wish to change factor proportions, capitalists in labor-abundant societies often find themselves unable to do so because of competition in evolving local and international markets. Technological advances have made it increasingly feasible to subdivide the production process, with components produced in widely dispersed plants in accord with macroeconomic evaluations made by the global firm. But as a result, entrepreneurs must adopt standardized international technologies and norms to ensure that components can be correctly and readily integrated into the final products for which they are designed and to counter the constant threat from competitors to displace them. Although some producers may obtain a measure of state protection, the market transmits these competitive pressures to even the most isolated societies in the capitalist world.

Conclusion

The interrnational mobility of resources, the international transfer of technology, and the global spread of the social relations of capitalist production are now integral parts of the social and productive fabric in all parts of the capitalist world (and even influential in the socialist countries). Competition has intensified as oligopolistic firms have become better able to defend their interests and national capitals everywhere are being obliged to become internationalized in order to survive. National attempts to abrogate or modify the international laws of capital accumulation constantly change the pace of global expansion, but time after time these local efforts fail to alter the underlying pattern of expansion with its resulting process of standardization-differentiation.

The IK must be understood, therefore, as a dynamic process of reproduction and growth. Within the less integrated parts of the system (sectors, regions, social groupings), the process of capitalist accumulation leads to modifications of productive structures, social relations, and even commodities. These are the same changes which are occurring in the more mature parts of the global system. The local accumulation processes are guided by the general laws of production and reproduction, although each is unique because local sociopolitical, productive, and technical circumstances leave a distinctive imprint on the universal drive to expand the capitalist market and increase the profit rate. At the same time, the very process of standardization which creates a tendency toward the homogenization of productive and social relationships produces a countertendency toward differentiation within the valorization process: competition incessantly obliges the large oligopolistic firms which now dominate the global economy to innovate, by introducing new products, by developing new ways of increasing labor productivity, and by better controlling the markets for inputs or outputs.

A caveat is in order, however. The IK works to remake society systematically in capital's image. But this very process of productive and social transformation creates countervailing forces. Capitalist expansion is incapable of productively absorbing the available labor pool into the proletariat, and most governments are unable and unwilling to finance the social welfare programs necessary to provide the unemployed and unemployable with a minimally acceptable standard of living. As a result, capitalism's goal of creating a global proletariat becomes increasingly elusive. In the Third World, this leaves a wide range of opportunities available for people to attempt to strengthen their traditional communities and work organization. Furthermore, as societies require more imports than they can pay for, they accumulate foreign debts which often exceed their ability to pay. The austerity programs imposed by the international banking community place unsustainable demands on the working classes and often provoke violent reactions and authoritarian responses. Finally, divergence between social needs and production possibilities appears to be growing throughout the Third World. For all of these reasons, the underlying tendency toward the IK and the creation of a global proletariat must be understood as tendencies, as social phenomena which are provoking their own opposition and which will inevitably create greatly differing results in each country.

THE NEW INTERNATIONAL DIVISION OF LABOR

The IK has propagated the standardized process of accumulation in all capitalist societies. Competition has led capital not simply to search for new markets or raw materials, as in the past, but to incorporate new social groups into a burgeoning productive process (see also Sassen-Koob, 1982; Wolf, 1982; Portes and Walton, 1981). Manufactured consumer goods, individual parts, and intermediate products are now produced throughout the capitalist world. In spite of converging productive structures, national economies are still differentiated by resources, climate, and technology. Institutional factors related to the character of social history and conflict as well as international political alliances and national political structures also play an important role in differentiating national economies, even as the reorganization of production and the international spread of technology create the possibility of homogenizing production.

The traditional description of the international division of labor in terms of geographic differences in commodity production has been used to justify the preservation of the existing set of productive relations between classes and nations: some areas were predestined to become advanced industrialized producers while others were condemned to be primary producers.[8] The theory reflected the prevailing distribution of power, justifying the "optimality" of the situation by arguing that this would lead to lower costs for all participants in a world system characterized by free trade and mobility of capital.

In this setting, the primary producers participated in world trade as dominated partners. In many cases the commodities they exported were not produced within capitalist productive relations, and their international relations were peripheral to, although exploitative of, their relatively closed internal structures. Some production and circulation responded to the demands and logic of a capitalist world, even though the societies themselves were not capitalist. In fact, the whole structure of international economic relations was tangential to the internal coherence and dynamics of capitalist accumulation. International trade was, in fact, the exchange of commodities between countries whose economies were not articulated, where capitalist development and cyclical movements in one region did not uniquely determine what was happening elsewhere. The early theories of world trade, then, correctly reflected the disarticulated nature of international economic relations in past centuries. But they were unable to identify the impact which capitalist expansion in the twentieth century was having on the Third World, an impact which was finally to forge the capitalist world system that now dominates international economic relations.

Early in the century, international capital had already begun to invest in new industrial production in the "Southern" countries. Some fractions of the traditional landed national bourgeoisies adapted to the new opportunities, joining with other groups to form a dynamic capitalist elite. These capitalists quickly discovered the limited possibilities for further accumulation from primary export production. Commodity traders expanded primary production in noncapitalist areas and engaged in fierce competition, which depressed prices on world markets. Furthermore, the profits from this trade were not systematically reinvested to expand the wage-labor force in other capitalist activities.

The new industrialists began to displace the merchants. They reorganized national economies and state policies to facilitate and accelerate their plans for accumulation. The patterns which emerged in each area depended on local conditions: in Latin America import-substitution industrialization was possible because primary exports could be used to pay for needed capital equipment and intermediate goods imports, while export assembly operations proliferated in East Asia, where raw materials were nonexistent (Singapore, Hong Kong) or where production was not organized for international markets (Taiwan, South Korea). Whatever the chosen path, the underlying result was remarkably similar everywhere: (1) the transformation of an important part of the labor force into a proletariat; (2) a population explosion that combined with an upsurge of rural-urban migration to create elephantine cities; (3) a systematic disregard for domestic food production because export production of food and industrial products were required to pay for expanding import needs; and (4) an investment program incapable of creating sufficient jobs for new entrants into the labor force, much less of absorbing the millions displaced from traditional social organizations and economic activities. Capitalist development reorganized society, attempting to separate direct producers from their property and tools.

With the accelerating rate of technological innovation characteristic of the past quarter-century, still other changes were forthcoming. The large enterprises (called conglomerates at the time) that consolidated diversified industrial structures in the 1950s rediscovered foreign investment as an effective way to raise profits. It was not sufficient to create new products and expand markets. Competition forced the giants to displace or absorb existing producers. The corporate imperative to produce more profit and to continue growing sparked an international flow of capital that began as a virtual North American invasion of Europe (see Servan-Schreiber, 1968), which soon expanded to flood the Third World. These new investments substantially transformed the organization of production worldwide.

As they recovered from the devastating effects of World War II, European capitalists, and later Japanese, successfully challenged American leadership of the world economy. All found it beneficial to set up subsidiaries and branch offices abroad, while many also undertook joint ventures with local capitalists. These were able to take advantage of local markets and special incentives offered by developing countries anxious to attract new investments. With the rapid decline in transport and communication costs and the generalization of an international airline network, the geographic dispersion of production became commonplace. Any problems or costs that might be incurred were outweighed by the benefits that were offered in terms of privileged access to raw materials and new markets, as well as a less expensive labor force.

Although many Third World countries continued to export basic raw materials and other primary products, they also began to export industrial products. International firms used domestic inputs and imported components as part of a pattern of "global sourcing" of production and distribution. Industrialization did not only mean production for export, however, since in most of the newly industrialized countries (NICs) the bourgeoisie joined together with part of the proletariat and the middle sectors to forge new markets for consumer durables and processed nondurables. The cross-class demand for domestic tariff protection became a way to struggle for new jobs and local sources of profit.

Agricultural trade also became more complex as some farmer groups demanded and received protection and subsidies (especially in the European Common Market), while others pushed for increased imports from the Third World. The imports could help hold down the cost of living, reducing the value of labor power so as to increase profits. They also could broaden overseas markets by protecting the fragile economies of the exporting nations, which otherwise could not pay for industrial imports or service their increasingly unmanageable foreign debts.

This is the complex situation which has incited a new body of literature: the discussion of the new international division of labor.[9] To those who examine international trade and specialization in terms of specific commodity flows and their locality, it is clear that the composition and volume of international trade has been dramatically altered (Frobel, Heinrichs and Kreye, 1979). To others, the changes are more difficult to characterize, as a substantial part of the international trade in manufactured parts and finished products must be reevaluated because it is really only an exchange of products within a single TNC (Helleiner, 1979; Grubel and Lloyd, 1975). The burgeoning literature on the new international division of labor is part of the widespread effort to understand the changing nature of North-South relations.[10]

The new pattern of international trade has provoked growing protectionism in the industrialized countries, which seriously threatens the viability of the modernization programs in many NICs. Conflicts arise because the new industrial structures are quite similar to modern segments of sectors already firmly entrenched in the advanced countries as a result of the process of standardization-differentiation discussed in the previous section. Industrial redeployment is transferring consumer goods industries to the NICs, displacing more costly operations in the mature economies. Furthermore, new consumer products and markets in the Third World are often simply copies of already established counterparts elsewhere. Thus, Third World development, as it is currently proceeding, does not necessarily offer a new range of products in world trade but rather a more complex siting of the production of existing commodities, with new markets and a vastly expanded international proletariat.

The world economy is now characterized by a geographically broader and vastly expanded scale of capital accumulation rather than by new products. The profound changes in the way in which production is organized, its impact on the labor force, and the consequent restructuring of social and political relations in each country are far more important determinants of the changing nature of international economic relations than are changes in commodity trade.[11] The new international division of labor is not, then, simply a relocation of commodity production; it is a global restructuring of the labor force to include substantial new segments of the population. Their integration will necessarily broaden local markets, change patterns of social interaction, and alter productive structures. This will be the case not only in the Third World but everywhere, as a result of adjustments which also occur in the mature economies.

Perhaps the most notable productive change is the decline in self-sufficiency among the countries of the Third World. The inability of many countries throughout the world to feed themselves is a new phenomenon. Historically, food has been grown locally for regional needs: transportation costs and spoilage were too high for society to depend systematically on regional or national imports to satisfy the daily basic biological needs of its population. This situation prevailed long into the twentieth century. With the spread of new productive relations, the reorganization of the labor force, and the incorporation of agriculture into the circuit of social capital, one country after another has found itself increasingly hard pressed to produce the basic foodstuffs needed for the majority of its population (see Perelman, 1977; Rozo and Barkin, 1983a). It is evident that the transfer of productive resources and labor from basic food production to luxury and nonfood production for local or export markets has systematically created problems of food self-sufficiency throughout the Third World. The market mechanisms which made it profitable to withdraw agricultural resources from basic consumption also created a similar situation in other productive sectors, producing the paradoxical result that many of those countries which have industrialized most rapidly are those very countries least able to supply the basic needs of their population. Even when large segments of the peasantry have not been integrated into the proletariat, state policy systematically discriminates against their basic food production, exacerbating some of the social conflicts which the IK always creates.

These complex changes in national productive relations and structures are the basis for suggesting that *the new international division of labor is* correctly analyzed as *the process of incorporating new groups into a progressively internationalized labor force*. Workers are increasingly subjected to a similar set of productive relationships, even while the patterns of capital accumulation themselves differ greatly from society to society (for reasons discussed previously). As long as our primary concern is with understanding the underlying forces influencing the evolution of capital accumulation in present day society, it is crucial to focus on the mechanisms for the spread of capitalism and the integration of a worldwide capitalist productive system and market.

THE IMPACT OF THE NEW GLOBAL SYSTEM ON DAILY LIFE

The dramatic transformation of international economic relations since World War II is the result of an unprecedented expansion of capitalist production, which systematically revolutionized society by creating a proletariat and multiplying productive forces. The new international distribution of production cannot be explained simply by the restructuring of world trade or by the import demands for raw materials, components, and finished products by the core countries. The expansion of productive investments in the Third World and the worldwide integration of productive processes have profoundly transformed the way goods are produced. The theory of the IK focuses on the advance of capital accumulation and the rhythm of technological change. These lead to the recomposition of production and the subjugation of an ever-widening proportion of the world's population to the conflictive proletarian relationship.

In the new global system capitalist production alters life styles and consumption patterns as societies adjust to the new organization of production.

Old products are displaced by new commodities better suited to the requirements of accumulation. The largest markets are still in the advanced capitalist countries, not because of their large populations but because of their high purchasing power. But even in many of the NICs new consumption demands are growing rapidly as industrialization creates a new proletariat along with a dynamic middle sector. This expansion foments the extension of new consumption patterns to complement the new set of social relations imposed by the generalization of wage labor in production.

The spread of new consumption styles has not been limited to the Third World. Capitalist expansion has placed its imprint on a growing range of household activities which were previously not provided as corporate services. For example, the past few decades have witnessed the growth of meal service as a major area for capitalist investment, not only in the processing of foods for home consumption (which has grown extraordinarily) but also in the reorganization of the preparation and marketing of eating outside the home. Restaurant service has been restructured as capital systematically enters the field, offering standardized fare rapidly and substantially less expensively than traditional restaurants can. These establishments operate not simply to turn a profit that permits individual capitalists to live (as is often the case with the petty bourgeois organization of production) but rather to contribute to a continual multiplication and expansion of productive activities that is the cornerstone of capitalist accumulation. The food processing industry itself has changed as it finds ways to broaden its markets and increase its productivity. Technical change and the effective use of propaganda have made it profitable to break down natural foods and reconstitute them for longer shelf life and faster preparation. These trends have not been restricted to traditional "Western" diets but also have been extended to incorporate new types of foods or styles of cooking from the Third World into the global pattern of capitalist transformation (in a particularly capitalist fashion which often makes the new product only vaguely similar to the original which inspired it). Restaurants offering tacos, Cantonese-style food, and Greek specialties (among others) now diversify the fare available from hamburger, chicken, steak, lobster, and pizza chains started in the United States but now spreading to all potential markets. The internationalization of foods and of restaurant offerings does not require that each establishment or the chain itself be owned by an international capitalist but rather that the concept of food service is now conceived of as a part of a larger process of capital accumulation in which the foods are prepared by waged workers organized to produce a profit with a high rotation of capital. The individual restaurant owned by an isolated entrepreneur working only to produce his or her own livelihood is likely to become a disappearing facet of life in capitalist society.

Food service is a particularly vivid but not isolated example of the way in which the IK is altering daily life in advanced and poor countries alike.

Household services of every type are being modified as local merchants and practitioners find themselves confronting national or transnational organizations trying to displace or absorb them. Examples of the reorganization and commodification of life to fit the needs of valorization abound, as in the case of the retail trade in general or specialty shops, pet and veterinary services, household maintenance and repair, child care, and medical care, all of which have been substantially altered as capitalist organization has expanded to include them.

The IK is not limited to these end products. They are examples of the way in which capitalist expansion has directly altered the organization of daily life. But the changes which we are considering encompass virtually every aspect of human existence in the capitalist world. Although the modifications of life styles are much more profound and perhaps even more unsettling in the Third World, they are perhaps better documented in the advanced countries. As the pace of change has accelerated in the poorer parts of the world, capitalists oftentimes simply transplant established patterns for increasing production, without regard to their potential impact on society or the environment. As a result, the incongruities between material production and social organization are proliferating. In the advanced countries the proletarianization of the labor force has proceeded for centuries. But now capitalists are actively searching for formerly marginal groups and taking advantage of international disparities to recruit immigrants in the advanced countries. This is part of their constant struggle to limit the increase in real wages and to discipline the labor force by threatening its displacement. In other parts of the world the new social relations of capitalist production have had even more dramatic effects. The transformation of workers into wage laborers has incorporated many peasants into industrial and other forms of urban work and reorganized the work day and society itself. The literature on this theme is so large and well known that not even a summary is required here (see Portes and Walton, 1981).

The change in social relations is a result of the expansion of the productive base. New profit opportunities were created by nationalistic demands that domestic markets be increasingly supplied from local production, even when it was controlled by foreigners. The TNCs created and used technology to forge new opportunities for themselves as national economies developed. They reorganized their productive structures to take advantage of tax exemptions, a disciplined and cheap (if poorly skilled) labor force, and financial subsidies offered by authorities in poorer countries and in depressed regions within the richer countries. Consumer goods industries sprang up in response to industrialization plans to supply local markets throughout the developing world. Local capitalists joined with their international counterparts to use domestic savings and international funds to build new plants and recruit new workers in order to take advantage of the attractive financial incentives. On other occasions, the TNCs directly, or through the good offices of local capitalists, organized component production or assembly operations for its worldwide markets.

These changes in commodities and in the locality of production have produced a reorganization of international economic relations. Technical and scientific activity are advancing in response to the demands of capitalist profitability to facilitate the restructuring of production. Assembly operations and the manufacture of components are now an important and growing part of the world economy as technical controls and new equipment permit higher quality for standardized products produced internationally. With the decomposition of production, new industries emerge as commodities are designed to be assembled from components produced in various plants. Global sourcing provides an alternative to, and threatens the viability of, integrated factories where labor conflicts and national political or economic disturbances might upset international corporate planning.

Capitalist expansion is also stimulating the appearance of new internationalized consumption products in the Third World. Although the new commodities are being produced locally for the new proletariat, middle sectors, and elites, they frequently create their own bottlenecks. Domestic production imposes a strict dependency on imports. Now production and employment, not just the consumption standards of the bourgeoisie, depend directly on the availability of imported raw materials, intermediate goods, and equipment. Thus, as foreign exchange becomes scarcer because of the growing burden of debt payments, the increasing difficulty of finding export markets, and the seemingly inevitable need to increase imports of basic consumer goods, the new productive capacity is threatened with idleness. But the new proletariat does not enjoy the benefits of a social welfare system to cushion the effects, as do workers in richer countries.

Finally, the reorganization of national economies occasioned by the IK is producing substantial displacements of traditional production. Peasant production and craft goods turned out in artisan workshops give way to putting-out operations at the service of capitalist enterprises and modern agricultural enterprise. Conflicting demands for official support and a limited revenue base often distort the productive structure further as subsidies are channeled into industrialization and export support programs benefiting a small national capitalist class and responding to the financial pressures of the international financial community. The apparently universal victim of these pressures on the national budget is domestic production of basic food products and other essential goods for mass consumption. Food and other basic products must be imported and distributed at either greatly increased prices or with substantial governmental subsidies—in either case, occasioning inflation with serious consequences for the living standards of the masses. The internationalization of capital, therefore, produces the paradoxical result of increasing society's productive potential while impoverishing its people.

NOTES

* This chapter is part of a research project which the author jointly directs with Carlos Rozo at the Universidad Autónoma Metropolitana (Unidad Xochimilco) on "Technological Adaptation in Agroindustry and the Internationalization of Capital." It is partially financed by the National Science and Technology Council (CONACYT) of Mexico. Gary Howe and Steven Sanderson also provided useful comments on earlier drafts, but final responsibility for this paper rests with the author.

1. A term used frequently in Europe, and especially in publications of the Organization for Economic Cooperation and Development to describe the restructuring of world industry as a result of the expansion of productive capital internationally (Ernst, 1980, 1981). Another term, *delocalization*, is also common, especially in France, to refer to the same process of the global integration of capitalist economies (see, e.g., no. 14 of the new series of *Critiques de l'économie politique* [Jan-Mar. 1981], entitled "Délocalisation du capital et discipline du travail").

2. Discussion of the worldwide crisis of capitalism is increasingly frequent in mainstream as well as radical literature. Two differing but trenchant analyses of the phenomenon can be found in Frank (1980) and Bowles, Gordon and Weisskopf (1983).

3. In this sense, the analysis departs from orthodox Leninist presentations, borrowing from Luxemburg's (1968) insights on the expansion of capitalism to insist on the fundamental importance of the internationalization of productive capital to complete the cycle of social capital internationalized, rather than simply analyze the role of financial and commercial capital in the process.

4. See Barnet and Muller (1974) for a review and popularization of a large literature on the TNC as the principal protagonist or even cause of these transformations.

5. One vivid example of this was the short-lived Mexican government effort to create a peasant-oriented Mexican Food System (SAM) which would strengthen direct producers' capabilities to produce the basic foodstuffs needed for the national diet. The experiment was initiated because growing basic food imports were becoming an embarrassing drain on scarce foreign exchange, while peasant unemployment and vast areas of idle land were creating growing social unrest. In practice, a substantial portion of the sizable volume of official resources assigned to the program went to commercial farmers rather than peasants, and even the gains that were achieved were reversed after less than three years by the subsequent administration's decision to cancel the program and concentrate on commercial agriculture. See Redclift (1981) and Austin and Esteva (1984) for a description and evaluation of this program.

6. This section draws heavily on research done with Carlos Rozo. See Rozo and Barkin, 1983b.

The reorganization of production has been an important tool to facilitate capital's control of work. See, for example, Steven Marglin's (1974) analysis of the transformation of home industries into manufacturing by capital in the eighteenth century. Braverman (1974) also analyzes this process in detail as do many French analysts (e.g., Lipietz, 1982).

7. The literature on technology transfer is replete with laments about the impact of inappropriate technological choices on the pattern of resource utilization in the Third World: new technologies lead to production processes intensive in the use of machinery and equipment, while they often substitute an abundant use of raw materials for a more

intensive use of labor which might conserve them. The technologies are designed to substitute capital for labor, since this often facilitates the control of the work process and reduces costs in societies where wages are high. One good example of this literature is Ramesh and Weiss (1979).

8. The normative content of neoclassical theory is based on the classical writings of Heckscher (1919) and Ohlin (1935), which offer the factor proportions account of world trade. This school insists that specialization based on factor availability will lead to an optimal global distribution of economic activity, in spite of the patent violations of the assumptions of the underlying model. For a discussion and a sympathetic evaluation of this theory by several of its practioners, see Vernon (1970).

9. At present numerous organizations have programs to study the changing organization of the world economy. For example, the International Labour Office has a special office which examines problems of the new international division of labor, while other institutions examine the phenomenon as part of their studies of the new international economic order.

10. The conference on the "Internationalization of Capital and Industrialization in the Periphery" sponsored by the Centro de Investigación y Docencia Económica in Mexico City in January 1983, is one example of numerous conferences sponsored by national and international groups on the subject of the new international division of labor. The proceedings of the CIDE conference were published in 1984.

11. This approach does not start with the prevailing patterns of commodity trade because they themselves will continue to change rapidly as a result of technological advances, protectionism, alterations in level of economic activity in the richer countries, and relative prices of basic raw materials and productive inputs. Political alliances among the NICs or other Third World countries and agreements with members of the socialist bloc as well as austerity programs imposed by the dominant capitalist powers will also profoundly affect commodity flows. For an interesting description of recent patterns of industrialization in Latin America and an imaginative set of propositions for their modification see Fajnzylber (1983).

REFERENCES

Austin, James, and Gustavo Esteva. 1984. *The Mexican Food System* Boston: Harvard University Graduate School of Business Administration. Forthcoming.

Barkin, David. 1982. "The Impact of Agribusiness on Rural Development." In *Current Pespectives in Social Theory* ed. Scott G. McNall, pp. 1-25. Greenwich, Conn.: JAI Press Inc.

Barkin, David, and Carlos Rozo. 1981. "L'agriculture et l'internationalization du capital." *Revue tiers-monde*, 88 (October-December), 723-745.

Barkin, David, and Blanca Suárez. 1982. *El fin de la autosuficiencia alimentaria*. Mexico: Centro de Ecodesarrollo and Nueva Imagen.

Barnet, Richard, and Ronald Muller. 1974. *Global Reach: The Power of the Multinational Corporation*. New York: Simon & Schuster.

Bowles, Samuel, David Gordon, and Thomas Weisskopf. 1983. *Beyond the Wasteland: A Democratic Alternative to Economic Decline*. New York: Anchor.

Braverman, Harry. 1974. *Labor and Monopoly Capital*. New York: Monthly Review Press.
Ellis, H. S., and L. A. Metzler. eds. 1950. *Readings in the Theory of International Trade*. Philadelphia: Blakiston.
Ernst, Dieter. ed. 1980. *The New International Division of Labour, Technology and Underdevelopment: Consequences for the Third World*. Frankfurt: Campus/Verlag.
———. 1981. "Industrial Redeployment and International Transfer of Technology: Trends and Policy Issues." Special issue of *Viertel Jahres Berichte* 83 (March).
Frank, Andre Gunder. 1980. *Crisis in the World Economy*. New York: Holmes and Meier.
Frobel, Folker, Jurgen Heinrichs and Otto Kreye. 1979. *The New International Division of Labor*. New York: Cambridge University Press.
George, Susan. 1977. *How the Other Half Dies: The Real Reasons for World Hunger*. Montclair, N.J.: Allanheld, Osmun.
Giersch, H., ed. 1979. *On the Economics of Intra-Industry Trade*. Tubingen, German Federal Republic: JCB Mohr.
Grubel, Herbert, and Peter Lloyd. 1975. *Intra-Industry Trade*. London: MacMillan.
Heckscher, Eli. 1919. "The Effects of Foreign Trade on the Distribution of Income." In *Readings in the Theory of International Trade*. ed. H. S. Ellis and L. A. Metzler, pp. 272-300. Philadelphia: Blakiston, (1949).
Helleiner, Gerald K. 1979. "Transnational Corporations and Trade Structure: The Role of Intra-firm Trade." In *On the Economics of Intra-Industry Trade*. ed. H. Giersch, pp. 159-181. Tubingen, German Federal Republic: JCB Mohr.
Hymer, Stephen. 1980. *The Multinational Corporation*. Cambridge: Cambridge University Press.
Lappé, Frances Moore, and Joseph Collins. 1977. *Food First: Beyond the Myth of Scarcity*. Boston: Houghton Mifflin.
Lipietz, Alain. 1982. "Marx or Rostow?" *New Left Review*, 132 (March), 48-58.
Luxemburg, Rosa. 1968. *The Accumulation of Capital*. New York: Monthly Review Press.
Marglin, Steve. 1974. "What Do Bosses Do? The Origin and Function of Hierarchy in Capitalist Production." *Review of Radical Political Economics* 6:3 (Summer), 60-112.
Ohlin, B. 1935. *Interregional Trade and International Trade*. Cambridge: Harvard University Press.
Palloix, Christian. 1974. *Les Firmes multinationales et le procès d'internationalization*. Paris: Maspero.
———. 1975. *L'Internationalization du capital*. Paris: Maspero.
———. 1979. *Proces de Production et Crise du Capitalisme*. Paris: Maspero.
Perelman, Michael. 1977. *Farming for Profit in a Hungry World: Capital and Crisis in Agriculture*. Montclair, N.J.: Allanheld, Osmun.
Portes, Alejandro, and John Walton. 1981. *Labor, Class and the International System*. New York: Academic Press.
Ramesh, J., and Charles Weiss. 1979. *Mobilizing Technology for World Development*. New York: Praeger and Overseas Development Corporation.
Redclift, Michael. 1981. "Development Policymaking in Mexico: The Sistema Alimen-

tario Mexicano." Working Papers in U.S.-Mexican Studies, no. 24. La Jolla: University of California at San Diego.

Rozo, Carlos, and David Barkin. 1983a. "La producción de alimentos en el proceso de internacionalización del capital." *El trimestre económico* 50:3 (July-September), 1603-1626.

———. 1983b. "La tecnología y la acumulación." Mimeo.

Sassen-Koob, Saskia. 1982. "Recomposition and Peripheralization at the Core." *Contemporary Marxism* 5 (Summer), 88-100.

Servan-Schreiber, Jean-Jacques. 1968. *The American Challenge*. New York: Atheneum.

United Nations Industrial Development Organization. 1981. *Restructuring World Industry in a Period of Crisis—The Role of Innovation: An Analysis of Recent Developments in the Semiconductor Industry*. Vienna: UNIDO.

Vernon, Raymond. 1970. *The Technology Factor in International Trade*. New York: Columbia University Press for the National Bureau of Economic Research.

Wolf, Eric. 1982. *Europe and the People Without History*. Berkeley: University of California Press.

The "New" Internationalization of Agriculture in the Americas

Steven Sanderson

Latin American agriculture in the 1980s is being internationalized in ways unknown in previous epochs. The production, distribution, exchange, and consumption of agricultural products has been transformed by the "globalization" of agricultural labor processes and by improvements in refrigerated shipping, communications, industrial organization, and technology. The tastes and values of "center" country consumers and agribusinesses have been internalized by Third World populations. The tastes of center country consumers and producers, in turn, have been affected by the transformation of Third World agricultural commodity production. The relations of production governing rural cropping and manufacture have become standardized in keeping with their transnational models. And the shape of agriculture in the Americas is, to some great extent, dictated at the international level, in sales, procurement, technological inputs, cropping, and processing agricultural raw materials.

Given the long history of Latin American primary commodity exports, such a thesis is hardly surprising. From the first colonial export enclaves in Brazil, New Spain, and the Viceroyalty of Peru, the growth of agriculture in Latin America has been understood as an export-dependent phenomenon related to the grand architecture of relationships with the "center" countries of world commerce. To propose that agriculture in Latin America functioned as a growth pole, or generated an "engine of growth" for import-substitution industrialization, or, alternatively, halted or delayed industrialization in smaller economies is hardly an improvement of the broad literature on plantation economies, agricultural modernization, and staple crops. To assert that the relations of production in export-dependent agriculture determine to some extent the generalized benefits of agriculture for the economy at large does not improve significantly on traditional analysis of the region's economic history.

The principal argument of this essay, however, is that the character of internationalization in the agricultural sector throughout the Americas has changed since World War II to reflect a new mode of regional integration in the world economy. Specifically, I will argue that the *new* internationalization of agriculture in the Americas takes place at the level of production itself and is not a simple product of commodity circulation through trade. Second, I will show that the forces of such internationalized productive capital encourage the mutual integration of North and South America, rather than a simpler model of agribusiness imperialism or center-periphery relations. Third, I will try to distinguish between those countries or sectors that are involved in this mutual integration process through the mechanisms of trade, as opposed to those integrated at the level of agribusiness production. Finally, I will address some of the political problems and theoretical concerns implicit in such an approach to agricultural growth in the Americas.

Before proceeding, it must be conceded that this essay does not pretend to offer a uniform or complete picture of agricultural internationalization in the Americas. The methodological obstacles to such a task are well known, as is the tremendous diversity of agricultural systems in the region. Beyond such general obstacles, however, lies the fact that the direct field research on which many inferences herein are based took place in Mexico, which has a "special" quality to its agricultural system. In subsequent primary research, however, and in the academic literature from other countries, I have found many of these processes validated throughout the principal agricultural countries of the region. The purpose of generalizing here is not to defend the uniformity of the Latin American experience but to suggest some common themes that unify the dynamics of agricultural modernization and integration at the international level.

In order to examine such propositions, we must first establish some of the key elements of the internationalization of American agriculture, which in turn is a reflection of hemispheric tendencies in general. First, internationalization in the Americas no longer means foreign domination in the same sense as it applied during the epoch of colonial rule or the heyday of agricultural export enclaves in the late nineteenth century. Internationalization in American agriculture does not observe the canons of the old "international division of labor," in which Great Britain and the United States presided over the bulk of world trade in agricultural commodities produced in the Americas and the economies of Latin America imported virtually all of their manufactured products and much of their capital and technology from center countries (Furtado, 1976, part 2). Currently, many American countries display high levels of intraregional trade outside the United States (e.g. Argentina, Brazil, and the Andean countries) (IDB, 1982; Business International, 1981). The new internationalization of American agriculture implies a domination by trade relations and by the transnational integration of agricultural production itself, not in the context of empire, but through the medium of the internationalization of productive capital.

THE STRUCTURE OF AGRICULTURAL INTERNATIONALIZATION IN THE AMERICAS

When we speak of the agricultural internationalization of the Americas, we must specify that not all countries are equally relevant, either in a productive or trade dimension. Seven countries in Latin America dominate the production and trade profile of the region. As table 1 shows, the GDP of Brazil, Mexico, Argentina, Venezuela, Colombia, Peru, and Chile account for nearly 90 percent of the regional total. Likewise, these same countries account for four-fifths of regional exports and 88 percent of gross debt. As we would expect from the thesis that the new international division of labor is not simply a function of trade dependence, none of these countries has an extremely high reliance on the external sector of its economy, relative to the rest of the region. Brazil and Mexico show the lowest level of reliance on their external sectors of any economies in Latin America (IDB, 1982, p. 24). Among these countries, only Mexico shows great vulnerability to the United States, due to its extraordinary reliance on bilateral trade as a proportion of its total foreign commerce. The other countries have rather more diversified markets, less trade reliance on the United States, and relatively high levels of intraregional trade (IDB, 1982, pp. 30-31). As we shall see, however, such bilateral reliance is only one indicator of transnational integration into the new international division of labor.

One of the vehicles of the internationalization of agriculture is trade, significant for its revelation of the dynamics of capital accumulation in exportables. Recognizing this, we can narrow the list of major participants in agricultural internationalization even further by considering the scale of activities in agricultural exports and agribusiness activities in the region. Chile has modest involvement in agricultural exports; its principal claim to prominence in the trading nations cited above comes from mineral exports and the import consequences of the "free market" philosophy of the military dictatorship since 1973. Before the fall of Allende, Chile had a modest reliance on the external sector as a proportion of total economic activity and little agricultural trade to recommend it as a leader in the region.[1] Likewise, Venezuela is a modest provider of agricultural commodities to the international system; its prominence in table 1 comes principally from its import reliance since the oil boom and its growing exports of petroleum and petroleum products.

The clear leaders among the seven nations in table 1 are Brazil and Mexico, followed by Argentina, Colombia, and Peru. Brazil and Mexico are both major producers of coffee, soya, and citrus, as well as hides and leather goods, sugar, and meat. Argentina, of course, is well known as a major world contributor of wheat and beef and produces coarse grains, maize, sugar, and a growing volume of soybeans for the international market. Colombia is a growing producer of beef and a major exporter of coffee and has contributed to

TABLE 1
Relative Share of the Countries of the Region in Productive Activity and the External Sector, 1980
(percent of regional total)

Country	GDP	Exports of Goods and Services	Gross Public and Private External Debt
Brazil	36.8	19.2	27.5
Mexico	24.0	20.4	24.1
Argentina	9.8	9.2	11.6
Venezuela	6.8	18.4	12.9
Colombia	4.4	4.6	3.5
Peru	3.9	3.9	4.0
Chile	3.2	5.1	4.8
Total	88.9	80.8	88.4
Remaining countries	11.1	19.2	11.6
Regional total	100.0	100.0	100.0

Source: IDB, 1982, table 2.1.

regional exports of sugar, bananas, and cotton as well in recent years. Peru provides a broad range of agricultural crops to the international system as well, although its prominence as an exporter of a single crop is less. Nevertheless, Peru has participated significantly in sugar, fishmeal, and cotton exports, among other crops and primary goods.

This is not to say, of course, that other regions and nations do not participate in this same integrative web. The Caribbean islands have become new targets of trade promotion and agroindustry investment in the 1980s, and the volume of trade between the Caribbean and the United States alone equalled $1.2 billion in 1981 (USDA, 1983). Although I will make occasional reference to such experiences, my attention will remain with the leading nations of the region, for the sake of exploring the full range of the internationalization experience in the most deeply "articulated" agricultural economies.

If we refine our analysis one step further, by concentrating on transnational corporate presence in the leading agricultural export economies of the region, we find that TNCs in the food and beverage processing sectors are prominent in the leading economies listed in table 1. While Colombia in 1976 had one TNC meat packing and processing firm present in the country, Argentina nad four, Brazil six, and Mexico five (UNCTC, 1981, p. 21). Although the dairy industry is more diversified, the concentration in large markets is similar. And in animal feed, transnationals concentrated 23 of their 35 worldwide large market affiliates in the underdeveloped world in Argentina, Brazil, Mexico, Colombia, and Venezuela. In addition, of course, the major economies of the region have their own agroindustrial complexes created under import-substitution strategies after World War II. In the cases of Colombia, Mexico, and Brazil—and part of the long tradition of Argentine export growth—agroindustrial exports have become major influences in the national economy. From refined soya oil in Brazil to soluble coffee in Colombia, canned pineapple in Mexico, and meat extract in Argentina, these countries have integrated the agroindustrial growth model into their external sector as well as their processing for domestic consumers.

Following this summary characterization of trade and agribusiness involvement in Latin America, the rest of this chapter will sacrifice a country-by-country analysis of the Americas in the internationalization of agriculture for the sake of highlighting some of the more dynamic forces of such a process. For the purposes of exposition, I will concentrate on Argentina, Brazil, Colombia, and Mexico, with occasional recourse to examples from other Latin American countries. Because of its complexity and difference from Latin American systems, U.S. agriculture will be treated only briefly, though an extended version of this argument would clearly insist on the *mutual* integration of all American systems of agriculture, and not simply those of Latin America. It must be recognized, of course, that such a concentration qualifies the following general propositions:

First, the internationalization of American agriculture reveals itself in greater volumes of trade in agricultural commodities that are "disarticulated" from domestic producers and lower-class consumers.

Second, the increasing intervention of transnational agribusiness vertically integrates or coordinates the "internationalized" sector of agricultural activities along standardized lines of production most familiar to center country environments. The integration and coordination of agribusiness activities depends not on transnational participation in equity but on the "transnationalization" of productive processes in domestic firms in competition with international agribusinesses.

Third, the internationalization of agricultural production and trade results in a structure of production at the national level that does not coincide with certain producer priorities or the national food interests of the Americas.

Fourth, the effects on national food systems—whether in the countries of Latin America or in the United States—involve the increasing integration of agriculture into the international economy. Such integration often challenges traditional trade relationships, steering capacities at the national level, and control over agricultural investment.

The Disarticulation of Agriculture through Trade

Latin American agriculture has always operated under a clear trade imperative. From the agricultural export enclaves of the independence period, of course, come the notions of "classical dependency" (Evans, 1979) based on the old international division of labor. But even in the rise of import-substitution industrialization, agricultural exports maintained importance in national economic growth plans throughout Latin America, even as they were being decapitalized and shifted away from domestic foodstuff production. During the "easy phase" of import-substitution industrialization—which benefitted from the foreign exchange boom accompanying the Allied war effort—agriculture was the "engine" or "handmaiden" of growth for industrialization (Sanderson, 1981a, ch. 6; Reynolds, 1970). It provided the key foreign exchange required to import industrial inputs for the transforming economies of Brazil, Argentina, Colombia, and Mexico. Agricultural modernization became the prime value of the leaders of the rural sector, both for its domestic potential in feeding the burgeoning urban industrial working class and for its capacity to stimulate the external sector's role in import substitution.

During this period, however, the internal terms of trade operated to the disadvantage of agriculture, as did the priorities of the banking system and the strategies of national entrepreneurs. Capital fled agriculture for industry; state finance favored industrialization; and individuals sought higher and safer returns outside the primary sector. As the industrialization drive proceeded, agriculture declined in importance as a generator of foreign exchange, although in 1981 the Latin American region still counted on agriculture for 80 percent of external sector activity (IDB, 1982, table 10). Likewise, the rural sector employed fewer people, as nonfarm employment skyrocketed (Gómes and Pérez, 1979). But rural life was still important in several respects. It became, first, an adjunct to industrialization, in more than one sense. Agriculture provided the material wherewithal for cheap food policies governed by the state and its marketing boards; the countryside was an important locus for certain "industries of transformation" critical to import substitution; and agricultural exports still played a key role as a traditional element in the export bill of most Latin American countries.

Increasingly, the conditions of agricultural growth and modernization in the 1960s and 1970s created the circumstances of the disarticulated model commented upon by Amin (1975) and de Janvry (1981), among others. First, the productive apparatus of the modernized agricultural sector became separated from the living conditions of the rural poor. Second, the cropping patterns of agriculture shifted away from basic foodstuffs to inputs for agribusiness and new export crops, in addition to the expansion of old export lines; the relationship diminished between productivity increases and wage gains; and more subtly, the domestic wage earner became marginal to the production of agricultural foodstuffs, as wage good production (and indirectly, consumption) took second place to export generation and agribusiness value-added. In these respects, the peasant became doubly disarticulated: once from the circumstances of production, as he became forced into a subsidiary role in the countryside; and again from the products of the Latin American *campo* as they became attuned to the dining tables of the city and the markets beyond the border, whether in the form of frozen strawberries from the Bajio, instant coffee from Colombia, or pullets from Rio Grande do Sul.

To the extent that ideas of comparative advantage dominated the transformation of modernized Latin American agriculture, trade liberalization also became a favored vehicle for increasing export receipts from agriculture, purchasing foodstuffs on world markets rather than subsidizing their production at home, and stimulating the production of cash crops. In the case of economic stabilization experiences in the 1960s and 1970s, such a dynamic is clear—Brazil after 1964, Argentina in 1966-1969, and again in 1976, Mexico in its regime of *desarrollo estabilizador* from 1958 to 1970. It also became true as the agricultural systems of Latin America became more self-sufficient in certain basic foodstuffs and sought relief from their problems of overcapacity (Argentina and Mexico, especially, but also the U.S.) in the international market. Increasingly, however, the trade impetus to agriculture has left the economies of the region actually more dependent on imports of basic foodstuffs from the developed capitalist economies, obliged to hold down the rural wage to stimulate competitiveness in export crops, and impelled to stimulate exports in a new wave of balance of trade and payments deficits which threaten the national economy in general.

The Rise of Agribusiness in the Americas

A complementary aspect of agricultural modernization has been the rise of agribusiness activity in the Americas. Defined as a vertically organized food system from farm to market (Austin, 1974; Goldberg, 1974; Burbach and Flynn, 1980), agribusiness—and especially agroindustry—has come to deepen the disarticulation of export crop production from the producer, to command cropping and technology decisions at the level of the firm, and to shift the yield of the *campo* from basic foods to elaborated manufactures. Interestingly, the agroindustrial component of agribusiness has prospered in conditions opposite to those of trade-impelled agricultural modernization. As has been noted elsewhere (Evans, 1979, p. 74), the protectionism of import-substitution experiences in effect invited transnational corporations to invest in Latin America to avoid tariff barriers and take advantage of incentives to "infant industries" and industries of transformation. Of course, some of the infants were a century old—especially textiles, soap, industrial fibers—and presented favorable climates for agroindustrial investment from transnationals. In any event, throughout the period since World War II, agribusiness investment in the Americas has grown; but more than mere growth, it has displayed integration and coordination as its hallmark.

The two tendencies of integration and coordination—actually phenomena accompanying the transnationalization of accumulation itself—are of a piece. Vertical integration signifies the formal linkage of one aspect of a productive process to another, from farm to market, as it were. Vertical coordination is slightly more subtle, emphasizing contracts and long-term productive associations without formal control or ownership of all phases of the productive process itself (Mighell and Jones, 1963; Morrissy, 1974; Farris and Couvillion, 1975). Both phenomena however, carry the same effect for the rural producer: the diminution of control over rural resources and decisions. The production contract—or the commercial or forward contract—engage the rural producer on specific terms, often with a "technological package," financial assistance, extension, and other support services. While such packaging of agricultural inputs and services seems progressive from the perspective of cost efficiency and productivity, contracting tends to "denationalize" production by shifting the locus of producer control away from the farm toward the agroindustrial enterprise. In turn, that enterprise, be it foreign or domestic, is likely to employ technologies of production emanating from transnational corporations at the international level.

Beyond the question of control, however, to the issue of peasant survival, there arise two dynamics in the "traditional" sector of agriculture. Either the peasant is forced by the intrusion of the marketplace to shift away from subsistence production—or basic foodstuff production for the market—to inputs for agroindustry, or he is made more marginal to the agricultural economy at large, while peasant networks for survival are undercut by modernization. Peasant production often falls victim to forced overproduction in the sector and is manipulated for the sake of price controls by agroindustry. In the celebrated case of barley for malt in Mexico, the agroindustry Impulsora Agricola acts as a broker (and scion) of the brewery industry to engage in contract production of barley in federal irrigation districts. The result is an absence of a "true market" for barley and the control of barley production in the major regions of central Mexico based partly on price and supply expectations and producer militance (Barkin and Suárez, 1982). In such a case, overproduction becomes a rational strategy for the agroindustry as a hedge against price increases, while the same phenomenon destroys on-farm profits, shifts control of production to the agroindustry, and undermines the price mechanism.[2]

In the case of basic foodstuff production, the peasant becomes integrated into agribusiness growth in a number of ways. To the extent agribusiness involves basic food production—as in the case of wheat and maize seed production and sales—the peasant tends to rely less on criollo seed and self-sufficiency as a producer strategy than on improved seed and commercial sales, often impelled by state incentives. At the same time, the growth of unrelated agroindustries, such as the balanced feed industry, challenge the production of basic foodstuffs by substituting sorghum and other cash crops for maize, beans, cassava, and other foodstuffs (Sanderson, 1982). Urban markets and their agribusiness suppliers also affect small-scale production by encouraging the substitution of oilseeds for wheat, or luxury comestibles for basic foodstuffs in general.

MODES OF INTERNATIONAL INTEGRATION IN LATIN AMERICAN AGRICULTURE

As a result of these dynamics of trade, agribusiness growth, and state strategies of agricultural modernization, we find in Latin America three modes of agricultural internationalization, which at first glance correspond to familiar "classical" rural formations but in fact differ substantially in form and implication. Perhaps the least surprising form, given our understanding of Latin American agricultural growth, is the new agricultural export enclave. The second form involves a deeper integration at the level of production: the internationally linked agroindustry. Finally, the most subtle variation is the agribusiness satellite. In a formal sense, at the international level, these three forms are indistinguishable facets of the same phenomenon: the international integration of agriculture in the hemisphere, according to criteria for growth and profitability created outside national boundaries. But in concrete appearance, the forms are different and deserve separate attention here.

The New Agricultural Export Enclave

The traditional notion of Latin American agricultural growth has emphasized one of two trends: the export pole led by a staple crop (Argentine wheat, Guatemalan bananas, Brazilian sugar, then coffee) (Watkins, 1963; Fogarty, 1982); or the relatively isolated hacienda, only marginally linked to commerce and little affected by international forces (e.g. Mexican cattle before 1850, Cuban sugar before the 1830s) (Chevalier, 1963). Naturally, for our purposes here the former is more interesting to compare with current agricultural export enclaves. The new export enclaves differ from traditional circumstance in several respects, as revealed by case studies in the field (Rama and Vigorito, 1979; Mares, 1981; Sanderson, 1981b; Muller, 1979). First, agricultural exports are to a much greater extent governed by internationally standardized technological requirements. All citrus exported fresh from Mexico passes through U.S. Department of Agriculture certified inspection and packing stations (USDA, 1981). All beef packed in Latin America for shipment to the United States must meet USDA standards for hygiene and slaughter (P.L. 90-201). And, for reasons of market appearance and appeal, products emanating from the Americas in general must replicate the fastidious requirements of consumer markets abroad to be successful in competitive industries such as those that characterize international traffic in agricultural commodities. To a great extent such demands are only possible in the current epoch of revolutionary transformations in shipping, disease control, and communication.

Second, agricultural export enclaves are much more likely to be productively integrated via contracts and long-term productive relationships across borders than characterized most auction markets or primary commodity trade arrangements of the old order (Spanish mercantilist restrictions and later nineteenth century British domination notwithstanding). In the case of Mexican winter vegetables—one of the most famous cases of export enclave integration in recent years—producer technology, financing and sales all transcend mere episodic market interaction and involve contract relationships, transnational brokerage, and consignment sales to prearranged markets. The fluctuations of commodity markets dictate with great sensitivity the annual planting priorities of Mexican producers and the marketing prerogatives of their U.S. distributors.[3] The same is true in live cattle exports from the Mexican north, which respond to the broker's and feedlots' expectations of market performance but revolve around production contracts and forward contracts for custom feeding across borders (Sanderson, 1982). Likewise, in Brazilian and Colombian coffee production, state trading arrangements and an international convention dictate the international marketing strategies of producer countries in accordance with a relatively refined understanding of the market and other variables of production.[4] This articulation of agricultural exports with the international market stands in stark contrast to the weak interventions of the Brazilian valorization schemes of the first half of the twentieth century, which intervened principally to manage the marketing of existing stocks rather than to attune production to market conditions per se.

Third, agricultural export enclaves have a more direct impact on domestic markets than in classic cases, with perhaps Argentine beef as the outstanding exception. While most agricultural export enclaves of the *ancien régime* seemed to operate relatively apart from domestic market considerations, the current incarnation of the export enterprise directly relates to provisioning requirements for populations increasingly "sophisticated" (at least in a value-added sense) in their food demands. Exports of Mexican cattle challenge shortfalls in domestic supplies. Winter vegetables threaten basic foodstuff production in irrigation districts. Pineapple exports undermine the popular consumption of fresh fruit at a low price. And sugar exports (in Brazil, at least) must be attentive to increasing domestic demands. To the extent that the export enclave is more sensitive to domestic political and consumer considerations than previously, the growth prospects and nature of state intervention in agroexport activities becomes more problematic, as we shall see.

Finally, the agricultural export enclave must survive in a much more politically sophisticated atmosphere. The old model of agroexport activities came from a historical circumstance in which the Latin American state had little bureaucratic weight and less power. The current state has, since then, weathered the rise of import substitution, presided over the creation of massive social service and social capital investment structures, and acted as midwife to agricultural capital formation in post-Depression Latin America. No longer does the export entrepreneur encounter the client state perhaps more fondly remembered by United Fruit or Standard Brands. Now, if one can still concede that the virtue of many Latin American states is too easily breached, the politics of state management from the exporters' perspective have become much more complicated and interactive with domestic considerations.

The Internationalized Agroindustry

Perhaps the most interesting mode of agricultural internationalization comes in the myriad forms of agroindustrial growth in the Americas. Once again, agroindustries are hardly new to Latin America. From the "Aurora Yucateca" (Cline, 1947) of the nineteenth century, or the rise of bottling, beer, and soft drink industries at the turn of the twentieth century, or even the redoubtable sugar *ingenio* of emerging agricultural capitalism in the Caribbean, Brazil, and Mexico, agroindustries have played an important part in the generation of value-added in the countryside, the articulation of production with the market, and the rise of state intervention and foreign direct investment in the primary sector. The progressive integration of such industries at the international level, however, has led to a qualitative change in their composition in the postwar era.

First, as in the case of the agricultural export enclave, agroindustries are more likely to be integrated into an international standard of technology, labor process creation, and valorization. Concretely that integration has had a twofold effect at the level of production: first, the agroindustrial goods are implicitly more acceptable to international markets; and second, the technology of production, determined to a great extent outside the national boundaries of the Latin American "host" nation, are naturally not necessarily the most appropriate for national agricultural production. The more painful corollaries to these statements involve the generation of agricultural product lines and goods inappropriate for domestic consumption or unnecessarily expensive from the viewpoint of domestic requirements. Likewise, another corollary involves the strain on productive resources imposed by internationalized technologies. In the first case, as may be seen in the export promotion of frozen orange juice concentrate or confinement-fed purebred beef cut to international standards (although with slight variations, we could include frozen strawberries from the Mexican Bajio, cut flowers from Colombia, canned pineapple from Veracruz, granulated sugar throughout the region, or refined safflower oil in Mexico), the productive apparatus of Latin American agroindustries tends to be geared to global markets and technologies, at the expense of domestic consumers.

Latin America has been cited as a locus of increasing domestic animal protein consumption (Winrock International, 1981). Data from leading countries in the region show that per capita consumption of beef has not consistently increased with herd growth (a relationship which itself even understates the separation between the "modern" beef industry and the average consumer) (see table 2). In the case of poultry industry growth, the leading hosts for the

TABLE 2
Per Capita Beef and Veal Consumption, Latin America
(Kilograms)

Country	1961	1970	1980
Argentina	83.2	82.4	88.9
Brazil	18.4	18.6	16.9
Colombia	19.2	19.5	22.7
Costa Rica	11.4	12.1	16.7
Dominican Republic	7.0	6.5	7.0
El Salvador	8.0	5.9	7.3
Guatemala	8.3	7.6	11.1
Honduras	7.2	4.9	5.9
Mexico	9.1	10.6	14.6
Nicaragua	12.9	15.4	11.8
Panama	19.3	22.4	26.0
Uruguay	79.0	77.8	75.2

Source: U.S. Department of Agriculture, *Livestock and Meat Situation*, various issues.

chicken boom—Mexico and Brazil—both validate our observations here. In Mexico, virtually no one in lower-income strata eats poultry, eggs, or any other animal protein on a regular basis (SPP, 1979). In Brazil, rapid growth in modern poultry production has also been accompanied by a declining proportion of production domestically consumed.[5] In the first case, Mexican poultry has failed to address the food needs of the nutritionally deprived, all the while it is touted as a cheap source of popular protein. In Brazil, poultry production has joined the legions of export platform industries, provisioning European markets while denying the domestic consumer improvements in diet. In both cases, of course, the demands for sorghum, soya meal, and other balanced feedstuffs essential to confinement feeding of poultry strain agricultural resources further.

In the case of orange juice concentrate, Brazil has a relatively privileged position in the international market as the world's second largest producer of citrus and frozen orange juice concentrate (FOJC).[6] While the foreign exchange consequences (U.S. $609 million in 1981) of such activities are clearly important to the current Brazilian preoccupation with using agriculture as a means of solving foreign trade deficits, once again Brazil finds itself producing an agricultural manufacture for an international market quite removed from the needs of much of its domestic population and dependent on futures markets dictated by the caprice of weather, Florida land values, Mexican citrus canker, and similar uncertainties. In the case of Mexico, a recent entrant in the FOJC sweepstakes, the costs of production are clearer than in Brazil. Mexico is still much more dependent on imported technologies for processing citrus, still unable to produce all the varieties necessary for a palatable "international grade" FOJC, and still without leverage as a producer of concentrate, compared with the United States and Brazil. At the same time, the consumer profile of Mexico shows little domestic demand among average consumers, for reasons of both income and prices as well as lack of refrigeration.[7]

In all these cases, the agroindustrial growth of the economy has also meant the diversion of scarce public resources to the advantage of externally oriented enterprises, or to enterprises targeted toward a small upper stratum of the domestic consumer market. I will treat this by-product of agroindustrial growth more carefully in a subsequent section, but suffice it to say here that there is a disarticulation of public credit and incentives from domestic food needs, as a "natural" concomitant of comparative advantage and agroindustrial growth. Only in a halting fashion did Mexico attempt to counter that diversion through the now defunct Sistema Alimentario Mexicano.[8] In Brazil, Argentina, and Colombia, one of the primary functions of the state is to arbitrate the successful capitalization of export agriculture, both in the form of primary goods and in agroindustrial processing. Central to the "new wave" of export substitution engaged in by most Latin American states—by which they attempt to integrate their manufactures into the international system through trade liberalization and production incentives programs—is the idea of adding value to agroindustrial exports. Those strategies span the full range of national economic strategies from economic stabilization with its great emphasis on exchange rate and credit incentives for export to the industrialization drive of Mexico in the late 1970s, which sought to expand agroindustrial exports to stave off the petrolization of the external sector of the economy. Naturally, as most of Latin America tries to recover from the international debt crisis through export competitiveness with the rest of the Third World in the 1980s, such export orientation in agriculture and agroindustries will likely accelerate wherever possible.

The Agroindustrial Satellite

As suggested in the brief description of the poultry industry, the rise of agroindustry and export enclaves involves the "satellization" of the agricultural economy at large. Such vertical and horizontal linkages into input and support activities also distinguish the modern internationalization of agriculture from the classic case. The most illustrative examples of the agroindustrial satellite may be found in the balanced feed and sugar industries, although similar cases in barley, maize, manioc, and other crops could be cited. In the case of modern sugar production, the mode of producer dependence differs little at the local level from the old *ingenio* of the Caribbean, Mexico, or Brazil. The cane producer is typically a client of a refinery to which he is beholden not only for the critical processing of his cane but for production financing, water rights, transport, and the like. However, we could hypothesize here that the greater the industrial growth of the national economy of sugar-producing nations in the region, the greater the change in the commercial relations of sugar production. That is, in Brazil, Colombia, and Mexico, as well as Argentina, sugar production is less important as an export crop (as opposed to new exports) and more important as an agroindustrial input and a domestic commodity in refined form.[9] Although the satellite producers have stayed the same, their integration into the international economy has changed.

In the case of the livestock feed industry, the dynamic is different, fundamentally for the lack of a transnationalized balanced feedstuff industry in the classical mode of export enclaves. The rise of feed mills and their producers has come with the rise of modern beef, poultry, and pork industries, emphasizing confinement feeding over range and *traspatio* modes and demanding improved protein for the sake of faster growth rates, better marbling characteristics, lower death rates of livestock, and the like. Immanent in such a rise of sorghum, soya meal, and maize production (as well as some carotene production for cosmetic purposes in the egg industry) is the satellization of traditional peasant producers and some small farmers into the livestock-feedgrain complex, especially in the form of contract production for feed mills and oilseed processors. They become satellites to a highly mechanized and integrated poultry industry, as well as to the feed mills dedicated to other livestock feeding. In Mexico, for example, of the 23 largest poultry companies (all producing over 500,000 birds per cycle), 5 are integrated from hatchery to processor (Agribusiness Associates, 1981, p. 53). The small rural producer of hens for local use has all but disappeared in the Mexican poultry industry, representing only about 8 percent of national production. Fully 69 percent of sorghum cultivation in Mexico goes to the poultry industry for chicken feed (CANACINTRA, 1978, pp. 4,7). Trends in the hog industry and in beef and dairy cattle seem to be moving in similar directions, although data are indadequate to speculate now. Of course, the consumer composition of animal protein—overwhelmingly income-determined—returns us to the question of who is raising what for whom in the integrated satellization of feedgrains and livestock. In this regard, the essence of satellite production for integrated agroindustries is the deepening disarticulation of the producer from national and local needs, the upward income bias of the agroindustry-led food system, and the diminution of local control over production decisions in the countryside.

THE POLITICAL CONSEQUENCES OF INTERNATIONAL AGRICULTURAL INTEGRATION

Clearly, the processes and modes of international integration described above are not politically neutral, particularly in view of the Latin American state's longstanding involvement in agriculture, the importance of the rural sector to the national economies of the region, and the external trade and payments crises currently endemic throughout the Americas. Unfortunately for attempts to generalize about the political attitudes or policy frameworks guiding Latin American agricultural development strategies, the analyst is undone at first look by the great diversity of state apparatuses in Latin America and their widely varying perspectives on the role of state intervention, the significance of the rural sector for national development, and their capacity to attend to rural imbalances and growth prospects.

In the cases of our principal countries of interest—Mexico, Brazil, Colombia, Argentina, and Peru—we find that in the 1970s the latter two have more or less continuously fought external imbalances and financial crisis to the point that political coherence has been threatened by myriad factors, including fiscal crisis and rapid turnover in state managers. Likewise, the political composition of the state differs radically between Mexico and Brazil; even with certain common state policies toward agricultural incentives and frontier development, the two countries can hardly be considered together on most dimensions of rural policy. Other points of difference among all these countries are obvious obstacles to a successful generalization about state policy toward agriculture and the political configuration of the rural sector in Latin America.

Nevertheless, because the political dimension of agricultural internationalization is increasingly important, certain first principles can be considered among all the countries we are analyzing here. The first set of these analytical identifiers involves a shifting logic in state policies toward agriculture, which accompanies the rise of manufacturing through import-substitution industrialization, the growth of a wage-labor force in urban locations, and increasing state interest in integrated rural development strategies linked to agroindustrial growth.

Traditionally, Latin America has been thought of as a region dependent on agriculture as the "engine of growth" for national economies. With the rise of import-substitution industrialization in the 1940s and 1950s, however, the importance of agriculture to national economic well-being changed, although it remained critical to national employment and generated a continued high proportion of exports. The new role of agriculture in the national economies of

Argentina, Colombia, Mexico, and Brazil represented less the engine of growth for the economy in general than the "adjunct of industrialization" under import substitution. In addition to a new subsidiary status for agriculture as a sector of activity in national production, the rural sector was expected to provide "cheap food" to the urban population, both as a concession to the changing consumer profile of industrializing nations and as a hedge against wage increases in manufacturing and services (de Janvry, 1982).

A corollary effect of the poorly managed but important cheap food policies of industrialization drives involved the increase in wage share of national income (or at least the sectoral shift of wage earners into higher income categories and nonfarm occupations). Such changes in wage earners meant greater effective demand for basic foodstuffs and higher-priced food items enhanced (in price, at least) by processing. Because of the high income elasticities of many agricultural products, the increasingly urban work force toiling in a regime of wage labor exerted a major influence on rural society by demanding more meat, more oilseeds, more fresh fruits and vegetables, and more agribusiness inputs for processing into canned goods, beverages, and other consumer items of the "modern" dining table.

The obverse of this dynamic, however, was the monetization of traditional food systems, the proletarianization of the peasantry, and the capitalization of the countryside. For the population in the countryside, the opportunity—however limited—of sustaining life on the basis of subsistence folkways and community support is threatened by the commercialization of agriculture at an international level.

The changing role for agriculture under the industrialization drives of the postwar era meant three fundamental changes in the impetus for agricultural production: the transformation of the agricultural system from the "independent variable" of the growth experience to the "dependent variable" of industrialization; the deepening integration of agriculture with agribusiness activities domestically; and the increasing vulnerability of the food system to changes in demand from the urban consumer and the transnational corporation. The rise in urban demand for animal protein generated a growing beef herd, a transnational poultry complex, and a hog industry in transition toward confinement feeding and vertical coordination. In the countryside, that productive response to urban demand meant shifts in cropping and land use patterns, often with devastating consequences for rural lives and ecologies. Frequently, these shifts industrialized agriculture itself at the expense of rural jobs and ignored rural nutrition and peasant survival. Thus, the very dynamic drawing the peasantry into cash exchange and the wage-labor market was unable to generate enough rural employment to enable them to consume the products of their work.

In keeping with the character of Latin American industrialization, agricultural processes have tended to become industrialized according to the same logic. In the first blush of import substitution, agribusiness enjoyed effective protection from import competition through the tariff structure, incentives to growth through production stimuli and low tax rates, and official state support through programs of export promotion and rural job creation. The parallel growth of agroindustry in this process, however satisfying it may be to the internationalization process in general, has fed on the increasing penetration of both the transnational and the state enterprise. From livestock feed to pesticides to jellies and jams, agribusiness activities have borne the brand of Del Monte, Ciba-Geigy, Hoechst, Anderson-Clayton, Ralston-Purina, Bayer, Dekalb, and scores of other international agribusiness luminaries from the moment of import substitution's conception.

The political consequences of the industrialization of agriculture in general and the reliance on rural production for cheap food include a deepening relationship with the forces militating toward a greater internationalization of Latin American agriculture. In the first place, Latin American economies in the 1970s became greater importers of basic foodstuffs than ever before. Mexico, of course, is the classic case, in which one of the most modern agricultural systems in the Third World increasingly finds itself unable to feed its population basic foods. But Brazil, Venezuela, and Colombia also have fallen into import-dependent positions for basic foods, at least partly due to the industrial shift in agricultural growth and the inattention of state policy toward supports for the producer of basic foodstuffs (see table 3). Such import

TABLE 3
Total Imports of Wheat, Sorghum, and Maize from the United States Selected Latin American Countries
(million metric tons)

Country	1970	1975	1980	1981	1982
Brazil	0.849	0.549	3.659	4.382	2.796
Colombia	0.244	0.318	0.911	0.457	0.656
Mexico	0.406	2.794	7.035	7.630	1.664
Peru	0.148	0.783	0.992	1.212	1.503
Venezuela	0.663	0.851	1.574	2.044	1.827

Source: U.S. Department of Agriculture, *Foreign Agricultural Trade Statistical Report*, various years.

dependence in the basic foods and agroindustrial raw materials areas puts great strain on economies suffering trade and payments imbalances since 1974.

Second, agroindustries have become increasingly important to the growth and trade plans of the region's economies. Since the beginning of import substitution, one of the goals of Latin American economic growth plans has been to reshape exports in favor of manufactures, once domestic demand has been satisfied and infant industries have matured. "Export substitution" became even more important in the 1970s, partly because of the "oil shock" of 1973-1974 and the efforts of regional economies to diversify exports in an epoch of wildly fluctuating primary commodity prices. And in the cases of our country examples, as well as in Chile, Costa Rica, and other nations of Latin America, manufactured exports began to play an increasingly important role in the trade bill (see table 4). Although Mexico suffered somewhat from an

TABLE 4
Growth Rates of Manufacturing Exports
Selected Latin American Countries

Country	Manufacturing as % of Total Trade 1978	Mean Annual Growth Rate			
		1971-1974	1975	1976-1978	1979
Argentina	58.2	7.6	-31.0	23.1	n.a.
Brazil	64.7	23.7	3.6	8.0	12.9
Colombia	25.2	26.5	-4.0	-1.8	7.6
Mexico	38.0	14.4	-30.7	7.0	n.a.
Peru	67.4*	-5.0	-17.1	-3.7	n.a.

Sources: For manufacturing as percent of total trade, United Nations, *Yearbook of International Trade Statistics, 1980*, vol. 1, *Trade by Country*. For mean annual growth rate, IBD, 1982, table 5.2.
* This figure is for 1977.

overvalued exchange rate and Brazil wavered after 1974's oil shock crippled the growth "miracle," all of the countries under consideration increased their total exports of manufactures as a proportion of traded goods. Not surprisingly, given the arguments set forth earlier, foodstuff manufactures led the way, pulling the external sectors of Latin America—and their local rural suppliers—deeper into the internationalization experience.

Unsurprisingly, given the mutual nature of the internationalization of American agriculture, some of these agroindustrial processes and agribusiness activities threaten jobs in developed capitalist countries. To the extent that such threats are politically unacceptable to consumer countries, tariff barriers and nontariff restrictions to trade become part of the North-South agenda in Latin American foreign relations with the developed capitalist countries. Although agriculture remains the single area of tariff protection inviolate before the advances of the GATT, Europe and the United States will hardly soften restrictions limiting the external vulnerability of Latin American agriculture and related industries. Recent evidence of such protectionism has surfaced in the case of Mexican tomatoes and of Latin American beef and sugar throughout the region. More interestingly, in areas not typically as sensitive to tariff pressures (e.g. fibers, wearing apparel, leather goods manufactures), weakened industries in center countries have lobbied with some success against imports from Latin America, *which have often been stimulated by U.S. trade and direct foreign investment policy itself* (Fishlow, 1978; Evans, 1978). Such political conflicts have not only increased the general levels of tension among the nations of the Americas but also have raised questions from the "old" nationalist agenda, including those which doubt the gains from trade altogether.

The industrialization of agricultural processes and its relation to imports of basic foods and raw materials inputs have led to external vulnerability to producers of such goods in other countries. Although it is unclear that such vulnerability is greater in current circumstances than in classical dependency, many of the arguments in defense of import- and export-substitution industrialization are undercut by the continuing weak position of Latin American countries, in regard not only to their rich consumer markets but also to their dependence on imports of primary inputs and raw materials. Perhaps the single most significant change from earlier epochs involves the heavy state participation in creating the agroindustrial complex and export platforms for agricultural goods, which from a fiscal viewpoint has come at the expense of stimulating alternative forms of agricultural growth and modernization more in line with the nutritional and employment needs of the domestic population. It has also left the state exposed in another sense: under such conditions, the public investment limits of the national economy become direct limits on capital formation in the agricultural sector.

With heavy state involvement in agricultural growth and agroindustrial development also comes external reliance on developed world producers of grains for imports of basic foods. The diversion of scarce resources away from basic foods in favor of the industrialization and export orientation of agriculture gives new ammunition to the "food power" advocates in developed countries. Although such power is complex and problematic (Rothschild, 1976; Gelb and Lake, 1974-75; Weber, 1978; Nau, 1978; Paarlberg, 1978), certainly the import content of basic foods supplies becomes more directly dependent on the expansion of state spending (exacerbated by demographic characteristics in many of the countries considered) and the vicissitudes of international commodity prices and concessional lending. And from that vulnerability to world grain markets and rich country producers (with the obvious exceptions of Argentina and Uruguay) many Latin American countries have begun a new discourse of dependency versus autonomy, now using the language of "food power" and "food security" in basic food systems.

At the heart of these external relationships, however, are more important domestic development problems for Latin American states. The growth of the agroindustrial complex has threatened peasant survival and undercut the production of basic foodstuffs in a rural social setting that is self-sustaining. Imbedded in this growth dynamic is the evaporation of remunerative rural employment, the mass migration of the peasantry to the cities or to the borders, the decline in peasant nutrition (especially among the elderly and preschool children), regional shortages in the labor force stimulating migration (from Colombia to Venezuela, from Haiti to the Dominican Republic, from Oaxaca, Mexico, to the Pacific Northwest or the Imperial Valley of California), and other permanent destabilizers of rural development. The state that faces such current integration into the new international division of labor is a particularly weak one, despite its heavy involvement. It is a state typically ravaged by fiscal crisis, externally dependent and short of foreign exchange, and late in its attempts to "steer" the nature of agricultural growth at a national level. While the state may know the limits of private sector agroindustrial investment, it can do little to ameliorate its effects, short of intervening to control economic property itself (which is politically impossible in most nonrevolutionary circumstances). The state is left with the weak strategy of creating "parallel structures" to capital, to ensure that more value-added reaches the producer. How such a modest self-concept could yield a positive structural reform of the rural sector challenges the imagination. But that is the subject of another essay.

Notes

1. In 1970, the external sector in Chile represented 39 percent of GDP; in 1980, 80 percent. This is not to say that copper exports were not a fundamental determinant of state policy before 1970 in Chile, of course. IDB, 1982, table 2.

2. Similar complaints are heard in U.S. hogs and poultry which are further integrated and removed from on-farm management of decision-making. For an example of the growing integration of the hog industry, see Jackson and Malphrus, 1973, pp. 20-22.

3. The evidence for this may be found in SARH, 1979, as well as various studies of the winter vegetable industry in Sinaloa and the United States. In addition to the studies cited in the references, see Zepp and Simmons, 1979; Schmitz, Firch and Hillman, 1981; and "Strano Farms," 1980.

4. Latin American coffee producers attempt to stabilize coffee prices through participation in a price stabilization fund under the aegis of the "Bogota Group," in operation since 1978. For a convenient summary, see Parker, 1980, pp. 7-10.

5. U.S. estimates state that domestic consumption of Brazilian poultry declined from about 90 percent in 1979 to about 75 percent in 1981. Exports at the same time increased as a percentage of production from 8 percent to 20 percent. USDA, 1981, p. 11.

6. Brazilian production of FOJC totalled 533,000 tons in 1981. USDA, 1981, p. 23.

7. In fact, USDA estimates show Mexican per capita consumption to have stagnated throughout the 1970s, despite increasing consumption. See USDA, 1981, table 9.

8. The Sistema Alimentario Mexicano was a multi-agency food security program instituted under the Lopez Portillo administration in Mexico during 1980. It failed to survive the presidential succession, although some of its functions appear to have been assumed by other ministries.

9. Brazil is the most spectacular case, being the world's largest producer of sugar and cane. Although Brazil is a large exporter, per capita consumption continues high, and domestic priorities seem to preempt an overwhelming concern with export promotion.

REFERENCES

Agribusiness Associates. 1981. *The Poultry Breeding Industry and Mexican Development*. Wellesley Hills, Mass.: Agribusiness Associates.

Amin, Samir. 1975. *Accumulation on a World Scale*. New York: Monthly Review Press.

Austin, James E. 1974. *Agribusiness in Latin America*. New York: Praeger.

Barkin, David, and Blanca Suárez. 1982. *El fin de la autosuficiencia alimentaria*. Mexico: Centro de Ecodesarrollo y Nueva Imagen

Burbach, Roger, and Patricia Flynn. 1980. *Agribusiness in the Americas*. New York: Monthly Review Press.

Business International. 1981. *Trading in Latin America: The Impact of Changing Policies*. New York: Business International.

Chevalier, François. 1963. *Land and Society in Colonial Mexico: The Great Hacienda*, trans. Alvin Eustis, ed. Lesley B. Simpson. Berkeley: University of California Press.

Cline, Howard. 1947. "The 'Aurora Yucateca' and the Spirit of Enterprise in Yucatan, 1821-1847." *Hispanic American Historical Review* 27:1 (February), 30-60.

de Janvry, Alain. 1981. *The Agrarian Question and Reformism in Latin America*. Baltimore: Johns Hopkins University Press.

Evans, Peter. 1978. "Shoes, OPIC, and the Unquestioning Persuasion." In *Capitalism and the State in U.S.-Latin American Relations*. ed. Richard R. Fagen, pp. 302-336. Stanford: Stanford University Press.

———. 1979. *Dependent Development: The Alliance of Multinational, State and Local Capital in Brazil*. Princeton: Princeton University Press.

Fagen, Richard R., ed. 1978. *Capitalism and the State in U.S.-Latin American Relations*. Stanford: Stanford University Press.

Farris, D. E., and W.C. Couvillion. 1975. *Vertical Coordination of Beef in the South: Nature of Different Systems*. Southern Cooperative Series Bulletin, no. 192. College Station: Texas A&M University.

Fishlow, Albert. 1978. "Flying Down to Rio." *Foreign Affairs* (Winter), 387-405.

Fogarty, John. 1982. "Staple Theory and the Development Experiences of

Argentina, Australia, and Canada." Paper delivered to the International Congress of Americanists. Manchester, England.
Furtado, Celso. 1976. *Economic Development of Latin America*. 2nd ed. Cambridge: Cambridge University Press.
Gelb, Leslie, and Anthony Lake. 1974-5. "Washington Dateline: Less Food, More Politics." *Foreign Policy* 17 (Winter), 176-189.
Goldberg, Ray. 1974. *Agribusiness Management for Developing Countries—Latin America*. Cambridge, Mass.: Ballinger Press.
Gómes, Gerson, and Antonio Pérez. 1979. "The Process of Modernization in Latin American Agriculture." *CEPAL Review* 8 (August), 55-74.
Hopkins, Raymond, and Donald Puchala. eds. 1978. *The Global Political Economy of Food*. Madison: University of Wisconsin Press.
Inter-American Development Bank. 1982. *Economic and Social Progress in Latin America: The External Sector*. Washington, D.C.: IDB.
Jackson, Hillard, and Lewis D. Malphrus. 1973. *The South's Hog-Pork Industry and Vertical Coordination*. Southern Cooperative Series Bulletin no. 179 (September), 20-22.
Mares, David. 1981. "The Evolution of U.S.-Mexican Agricultural Relations: The Changing Roles of the Mexican State and Mexican Agricultural Producers." Working Papers in U.S.-Mexican Studies, no. 16. La Jolla: University of California at San Diego.
Mexico. Camara Nacional de la Industria de Transformación (CANACINTRA). 1978. *La industria alimenticia animal en México (en cifras)*. Mexico: CANACINTRA.
México. Secretaría de Agricultura y Recursos Hidráulicos. Various Years. *Programa siembra-exportación de tomate*. México: SARH.
México. Secretaría de Programación y Presupuesto. 1979. *La población de México, su ocupación, y sus niveles de bienestar*. México: SPP.
Mighell, Ronald, and Lawrence Jones. 1963. *Vertical Coordination in Agriculture*. Washington, D.C.: USDA.
Morrissy, J. David. 1974. *Agricultural Modernization Through Production Contracting: The Role of the Fruit and Vegetable Processor in Mexico and Central America*. New York: Praeger.
Muller, Geraldo. 1979). "Agroindustria e multinacionais: Acerca da recente expansão da soja no Brasil." Unpublished manuscript.
Nau, Henry. 1978. "The Diplomacy of World Food." In *The Global Political Economy of Food*. ed. Raymond Hopkins and Donald Puchala, pp. 201-235. Madison: University of Wisconsin Press.
Paarlberg, Robert L. 1978. "Food, Oil, and Coercive Resource Power." *International Security* 3:2 (Fall), 3-19.
Parker, Joel R. 1980. "Basin Exporters Move to Stabilize Coffee Prices." *Caribbean Basin Economic Survey* (May-July), 7-10.
Rama, Ruth, and Raul Vigorito. 1979. *El complejo de frutas y legumbres en México*. México: Nueva Imagen.
Rothschild, Emma. 1976. "Food Politics." *Foreign Affairs* 54:2 (January), 285-307.
Sanderson, Steven E. 1981. *Agrarian Populism and the Mexican State: The*

Struggle for Land in Sonora. Berkeley: University of California Press.
———. 1981. "Florida Tomatoes, U.S.-Mexican Relations, and the International Division of Labor." *Inter-American Economic Affairs* 31:3 (Winter), 23-52.
———. 1982. "The Emergence of the 'World Steer': Internationalization and Foreign Domination in Latin American Cattle Industry." Paper presented to the International Congress of Americanists. Manchester, England.
———. forthcoming. *The Transformation of Mexican Agriculture: International Dimensions of Rural Change.* Princeton: Princeton University Press.
Schmitz, Andrew, Robert S. Firch and Jimmye S. Hillman. 1981. "Agricultural Export Dumping: The Case of Mexican Winter Vegetables in the U.S. Market." *American Journal of Agricultural Economics* 63:4 (November), 645-654.
"Strano Farms." 1980. Harvard Business School Case Study (July).
United Nations Center on Transnational Corporations. 1981. *Transnational Corporations in Food and Beverage Processing.* New York: UNCTC.
U. S. Congress. 1967. Public Law 90-201 (81 Stat. 584). "The Wholesome Meat Act." Section 10. Amendment to the Federal Meat Inspection Act of 1964 (52 Stat. 1235).
United States Department of Agriculture. 1981. *Citrus in Mexico.* Washington, D.C.: USDA.
———. 1982. "Brazil: Agricultural Situation, 1981." Agricultural Attache Report. American Embassy, Brasilia (March 5).
———. 1983. *Foreign Agricultural Trade of the United States.* Washington, D.C.: USDA.
Watkins, Melville H. 1963. "A Staple Theory of Economic Growth." *Canadian Journal of Economics and Political Science* 29:2 (May), 150-158.
Weber, William T. 1978. "The Complexities of Agripower." *Agricultural History* 52:4 (October), 526-537.
Winrock International. 1981. *The World Livestock Product, Feedstuff, and Food Grain System.* Morrilton, Ark.: Winrock International.
World Bank. 1982a. *Brazil: A Review of Agricultural Policies.* Washington, D.C.: World Bank.
———. 1982b. "Mexico: Recent Developments in Food and Agricultural Policy". Washington, D.C.: World Bank.
Zepp, G. A., and R. L. Simmons. 1979. "Producing Fresh Winter Vegetables in Florida and Mexico: Costs and Competition." USDA-ESCS Report. Washington, D. C.: USDA.

Some Effects of the Internationalization of Agriculture on the Mexican Agricultural Crisis

Ruth Rama

The internationalization of Mexican agriculture includes processes of modernizing food production and other agricultural products, including innovations in agricultural technology, organizational and economic improvements on rural smallholdings, and new mechanisms of integrating agricultural units with the marketing and processing aspects of primary agricultural materials, which began to be diffused in the country at the start of the 1960s. In its recent development, agriculture is also more and more articulated in the agribusiness food chain (Arroyo, 1979, p. 45). It is necessary to analyze changes that occurred in the same period in the methods of processing, distributing, and consuming foods. As we shall see later, processes of modernization in the form of processing, distributing at the retail level, and food consumption can occur without the modernization of primary production itself.

This process of modernization is driven by national and transnational capitals, and its success would have been limited without the price support policies, transfers to and from agriculture, and supply policies in basic goods undertaken by the state. Still, although it is not the only protagonist, foreign direct investment also plays a role of the first magnitude through the leadership it exercises over agroindustrial enterprises with its innovations in technology, publicity, systems of raw materials supplies, and consumer distribution.

On the other hand, that process has gone hand in hand with the greater insertion of agriculture and—in general—of the Mexican food system with the international economy, through the growth of foreign agricultural commerce, the arrival of a number of subsidiaries of transnational enterprises in agroindustry, and the international homogenization of wage goods that results from the changing traditional Mexican diet (or at least that of city residents) in favor of more "Western" models. These reasons justify our discussion of an "internationalization" of Mexican agriculture.

The internationalization of the Mexican food system consists of a "historical bringing up to date" whereby the country undergoes a technological and organizational revolution that has already taken place in the food systems of the developed capitalist countries, in particular the United States. This concept, which we take from Latin American anthropology,[1] refers to an accelerated movement through which technological revolutions generated in more advanced geographic areas are disseminated to other communities, in counterpoise to the sequential evolution of technologies that has taken place principally in the developed countries.

Obviously, the adoption of a concept from another discipline may involve a series of methodological problems, which I am not going to treat here. I shall limit myself to some characteristics of the "bringing up to date" that adequately describe the phenomenon to be discussed in this chapter: (1) we are dealing with an imitative modernization in an accelerated time frame; (2) this modernization is dependent; and (3) we refer to a new category, not a simple transfer of technology, but a radical change in the mode of producing, transforming, distributing, and consuming foods, which changes a facet of Mexican society totally.

In this case, "modernization" is unleashed by agroindustrial transnational enterprises; but concomitantly, the changes are adopted as their own by the agricultural and industrial entrepreneurs of the recipient country, as well as by the state that carries these processes forward as a part of the national project (Barkin and Suárez, n.d., p. 235). (In that aspect, obviously, the origin of capital comes to take on a secondary explanatory relevance). For that reason, in this chapter the unit of analysis is the international agroindustrial system rather than the transnationals themselves.

Certain sectors of the Mexican food economy are driven by an external activating agent, consisting of a certain measure of "normal" evolutionary advance in technical processes oriented toward the interior of the country.[2] That is to say, in certain cases (the most successful in terms of the level of modernization achieved) a catalyzing movement from outside flows together with a gradual internal process of advances in productive forces, with the latter being strongly reinforced and impelled by the former. In this view, therefore, the internal process of capital accumulation, along with gradual technical advances in the organization of production, are decisive elements in explaining the internationalization of some of the country's food systems.

In this essay I propose to discuss whether such a process of internationalization contributes to the crisis of basic foods production, the decline in the level of self-sufficiency in grains, and the unfavorable agricultural trade balance in Mexico.

I shall analyze the following problems: (1) the effects of Mexican agricultural exports on the country's capacity to become self-sufficient in basic grains; (2) the effects of transnational enterprises and other modern agroindustries on basic grains production and on the export and import of agricultural products; and (3) the effect of the internationalization of decision making on Mexican agricultural policy vis-à-vis the production of basic grains.

Before moving on, however, it is useful to define the principal characteristics of the Mexican agricultural crisis.

THE CRISIS OF MEXICAN AGRICULTURE

Beginning in the 1950s, Mexico experienced a rapid process of development explicable in large part by the structural change of its productive apparatus, wherein more and more importance was assigned to the manufacturing sector, which became the focus of economic growth (Casar, 1982). The agricultural and livestock sector successfully contributed to this development centered on industry from 1946 to 1966. During that same period, the agricultural and livestock sector was effectively organized to provide cheap foods that could maintain low costs in the industrial work force and generate exportable surpluses that would earn necessary foreign exchange to drive import-substitution industrialization. In that period, the flow between agriculture and the rest of the economy was adverse to agriculture. Resources were transferred from the sector to the urban economy through low and lagging prices relative to manufactured goods. Moreover, financial flows were unfavorable to agriculture in net terms.

Most analysts concur that in this systematic drain of resources the expansion of agricultural and livestock investment was undermined, giving rise to one of the reasons for the agricultural crisis that arrived in the mid-1960s. That argument was even more valid with respect to the peasant sector than the commercial sector; even then, commercial agriculture was partly compensated by government investment in irrigation infrastructure, networks of communications, subsidies, and insurance—a phenomenon which occurred to a much lesser degree in the peasant economy.

While in the period 1944-1946 to 1964-1966 Mexican agricultural production grew at a cumulative annual rate of 7.3 percent and per capita production at a rate of 4 percent, from 1964-1966 to 1976-1978, growth in the sector's production was limited to only 1.8 percent, and per capita production went down to -1.5 percent on an annual average. At the same time, while in the first period area harvested increased from 6.6 million to 14.9 million hectares, in the critical second period the agricultural frontier grew only from 14.9 to 15.1 million hectares (CESPA, 1982, 1:22).

During the last three decades, Mexico has been a persistent net exporter of agricultural products and has counted on a surplus in the commercial balance of the sector, except in 1980. Despite that, one study remarks with some justification that "the decade of the seventies marks a brusque change in the historical tendency of Mexican foreign agricultural commerce" (CESPA, 1982, vol. 1). The agricultural and livestock imports that had grown very slowly from the beginnings of the 1950s accelerated markedly after 1966 and, especially from 1969 forward, in such a way that between 1969 and the beginnings of this decade the cumulative annual rate of growth was 17.5 percent. The value of agricultural and livestock imports to Mexico that were at a level of $89 million (in 1977 dollars) in the three-year period 1950-1952 grew to $1.017 billion in the three-year period 1978-1980. In 1980, imports represented 31 percent of domestic grain consumption, 30 percent of maize, and 25 percent of beans, those products being considered the most important foodstuffs.

The evolution in the volume of agricultural and cattle exports from Mexico shows a stagnation from the mid-1960s forward. That situation is partly compensated by a growing evolution in international agricultural prices, through which Mexico enjoys favorable terms of trade during the entire period (CESPA, 1982, vol. 4).

There is very clear evidence, then, of a critical panorama in production and commercial exchange of agricultural commodities from 1965 on, the most important causes of which begin with the unfavorable relationship between the rural and urban economies and the exhaustion of the "easy" expansion of the agricultural frontier and the improvement in technology which—beginning with very low absolute levels—had achieved spectacular results during the boom phase (CESPA, 1982, 1:41). In addition, the decline in Mexican agriculture is generated in a context of a poor ecological milieu. Far from being the horn of plenty that its geography would suggest to some, rural Mexico suffers from 31 percent of its territory being arid and desertic and from a regime of insufficient or unfavorable rainfall. Also, during the critical period, population grew at an average annual rate of 3.4 percent. The per capita share of land is 0.3 hectares, for a population with very low levels of formal and technical education (CESPA, 1982, vol. 1.)

Without a doubt, we could not fail to note the influence of the new international division of labor as another important cause of the post-1965 crisis. Although the country was not a direct recipient of agricultural surpluses from the United States, channeled through P.L. 480 (which many food analysts characterize as "food dumping"), voluminous world food supplies and the tendency toward lower international cereals prices contributed to maintaining low and fixed guarantee prices for grains in Mexico, lowering their production (Rodriguez G., 1979, p. 98). Until 1965, Mexican agricultural policy had emphasized the necessity of supporting not only agriculture for export but also self-sufficiency for the growing urban market (especially with maize, beans, wheat, and sugar cane); however, the availability of great volumes of cereals at low prices in the North American market increased the opportunity to change food storage policies. Because of these factors, the preferred policy to follow appeared to be to import cheaply rather than to maintain reserves, without worrying excessively about food self-sufficiency in the country. As in the previous period, the main criterion continued to be to provide the industrial work force with cheap food, and these staples were available in the international market—at least until the 1972 world food crisis (CEPAL, 1982, p. 24).

EXPORTS AND INTERNATIONALIZATION

For some authors, a decisive facet of the internationalization of Mexican agriculture is the growth of the link between Mexican agriculture and the world market. The export orientation of Mexican agricultural development constitutes, along with the expansion of forage cultivation for animal consumption, the principal cause of insufficient production of basic foodstuffs during the 1960s and 1970s (Sanderson, 1983).

Various case studies show the important international networks that currently shape some of the agricultural export systems of Mexico. The dynamism of these networks is difficult to understand if we do not take into account the action of economic agents and power groups involved in Mexico and the United States. The modern development in Mexico of the systems of fruits and vegetables of the North Pacific region is explained in great measure by the monetary and technical assistance made available by North American brokers, as well as by deep linkages of Mexican farmers with the networks of distribution and commercialization of the United States, and even political alliances achieved in that country (Mares, 1980; Rama and Vigorito, 1979, p. 150). Production in the strawberry zones of the Bajío depends to a great extent on the financing and technological support of packing enterprises and small North American capitalists who operate in the foreign marketing of that fruit (Feder, 1977, p. 25ff). In the case of beef cattle, the northern zone functions as an integrated agroindustrial complex with the feedlots of Texas and California: the raising of calves, being the riskiest phase of the operation, is done on the Mexican side, and the fattening of the animals is completed in the United States (Reig, 1982, p. 124). In this last case, there is an authentic international division of labor, in that the final product comes from sequential production in "parts," "components," or "inputs" in two countries with very differentiated productive specialization.

Without doubt, the agroexport systems of Mexico are internationalizing themselves. Not only are their products marketed internationally, but their organizational forms, the technology used, the economic agents involved, and the complementarity with the production of the purchasing country imply a greater integration with the world economy. The relationship to this last aspect is now much more intimate, rich, and complex than before, and the strictly commercial character of past integration has clearly been superseded.

At the same time that this is occurring, the overall significance of external demand is decreasing and the importance of internal demand increasing. That is, the internationalization of Mexican agricultural production does not simply mean a massive turn toward the world market, accompanied by a displacement of production for internal consumption.

In the period that occupies our attention, there were changes in the international role of Mexico, which declined as an exporter of foods and began to be an exporter of industrial and energy products,[3] and there were changes in the relative importance of export agriculture vis-à-vis the internal market.

As table 1 shows, in the period of agricultural crisis, the percentage of domestic agricultural consumption increases, currently amounting to 86.4 percent of total agricultural production. The growing evolution of production destined for the internal market and the relative stagnation of exports can be appreciated clearly in figure 1. The exported production that had represented about a fourth of the total in 1950-1952 and in 1964-1966, was reduced to only 13.6 percent in 1976-1978. Also, the acreage dedicated to the cultivation of exports went down by half between the beginning of the 1950s and the end of the past decade (only 506,000 hectares, against 14.6 million dedicated to cultivation for the internal market). The slight increase experienced in physical export volume is attributable to a great increase in productivity per hectare.

TABLE 1
Annual Average Mexican Agricultural Production Exported and Domestically Consumed
(millions 1977 pesos)

Agricultural Production	1950-52		1964-66		1976-78	
Total	38,488	100.0	95,143	100.0	120,316	100.0
Exported	8,965	23.3	22,312	23.5	16,310	13.6
Consumed domestically	29,523	76.7	72,831	76.5	104,006	86.4

Source: Elaborated from official data of the Secretaría de Agricultura y Recursos Hidráulicos, Dirección General de Economía Agrícola.
Note: Goods effectively exported expressed in original product and weighted at the same average rural prices of 1977 used for the calculation of physical volume of agricultural production. Numbers in parentheses indicate percentage participation.

On the other hand, during the period 1930-1932 to 1946-1948, agricultural production for the external market enjoyed a richer, more dynamic growth than did production for the internal market; but during the years of the crisis the fall in production for export was much more serious. In effect, production for export stagnated between 1964-1966 and 1976-1978, while production for internal consumption grew at a cumulative annual rate of 3.0 percent.

FIGURE 1
Evolution of Agricultural Production, According to Destination as Exports or for Internal Consumption, Mexico

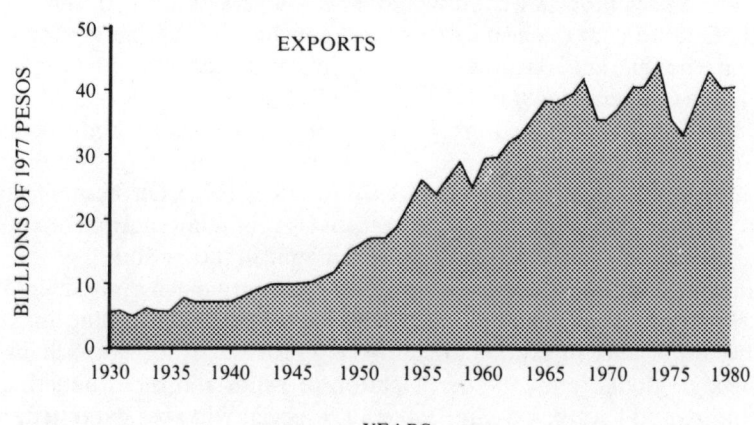

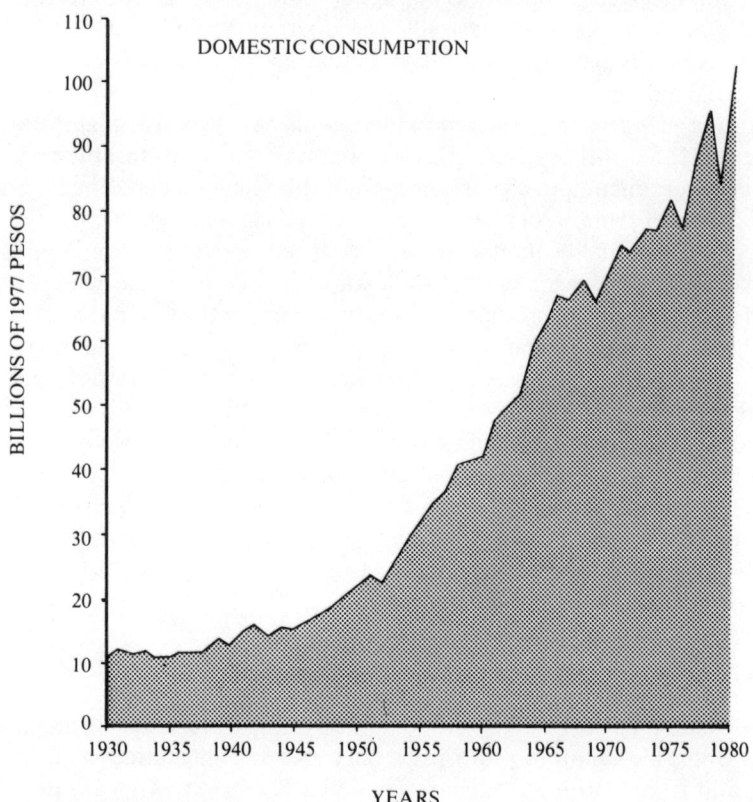

Source: CESPA, 1982.

Regarding Mexican livestock exports, between 1960-1962 and 1978-1980, live bovine exports went down yearly in terms of volume at a rate of -3.2 percent, while beef exports went down at a rate of -2.8 percent (CESPA, 1982, 4:100). One study of the beef cattle system concludes that from 1960 to 1980 "the internal market constitutes the most important structural factor in demand, due to its constant growth" (Reig, 1982, p. 83).

Moreover, the production of beef—which is an export product—grew significantly, although less than the livestock sector as a whole (the sector grew at a 5.6 percent average between 1974-1976 and 1976-1978). On the other hand, livestock production destined almost exclusively for the internal market (pork, meat, poultry, eggs, milk) became more dynamic in this period.

In summary, the various agroexport systems are much more integrated with North American economic agents than in the past. At the same time, the relative importance of export agriculture as a provider of foreign exchange is reduced, in global terms the participation of exports in the production of agriculture and livestock declined overall, especially in area harvested, and production oriented to the world market became less dynamic in its rate of growth than that destined basically for internal consumption. Mexican agriculture is, especially since the mid-1960s, an agriculture clearly oriented to the internal market.

Although in certain specific cases there could have been a displacement of basic crops for export products, it is clear that we cannot attribute the crisis of basic grain production to a generalization of this phenomenon. The internationalization of some agroexport systems—in the sense of a greater participation by international economic agents—does not appear to have implied a massive turn of Mexican agriculture toward the international market that would negatively affect production of basic grains for the internal market.

There are several reasons for this. First, in the period studied, internal demand (stimulated by the process of industrialization, urbanization, and a relative improvement of salary vis-à-vis the price of food) was more dynamic than external demand. Also significant were the policies of provisioning the internal market, as a result of which only surpluses were exported, and the agricultural protectionism of the purchasing countries. Finally, not all Mexican lands are apt for producing export crops; for example, it would be impossible to produce horticultural products in the vast majority of lands currently dedicated to the production of maize.

THE NEW AGRICULTURAL AND LIVESTOCK PRODUCTS

Although of vast proportions, the agricultural crisis of Mexico is not a general crisis. Alongside a majority who are in the process of stagnation, a minority sector that is extraordinarily dynamic and in a clearly expansionary process coexists and prospers.

The Mexican agricultural crisis has its roots in a group of 17 products, including four basic grains (rice, beans, maize, and wheat), that grew at rates inferior to the 3.4 percent demographic increase between 1964-1966 and 1976-1978. That group of products represented 78.6 percent of the physical volume of agricultural production in 1964/66 and 61.2 percent of the same in 1976/78 (CESPA, 1982, 3:32).

As may be seen in table 2, the four basic grains registered rates of growth inferior to 3.4 percent. In particular, maize and beans, which grow overwhelmingly in rainfed regions, show very low, or even negative rates of growth.

Oilseeds show variable behavior. While traditional products such as sesame seed, cottonseed, and copra registered declines in production, the pattern of the new oilseeds (products that appeared in official statistics at the end of the 1950s), such as safflower and soya bean, is notably dynamic and grows during the crisis at a rate of 11.7 and 15.2 percent annual average, respectively.

Sugar cane and other important traditional products for export, such as coffee, cacao, tobacco, henequen, and cotton, show insufficient growth during the crisis.

In summary, basic grains and traditional export products (sesame, cottonseed, copra, sugar cane, coffee, cacao, henequen, and cotton) show a growth rate inferior to the population. In contrast, some crops, including new exports (fruits, legumes, garbanzo), new oilseeds (especially soya, destined principally in paste form for cattle feed), forage crops (barley, sorghum, and alfalfa), and livestock products, all grow at a rate faster than the population.

The rapid growth of various dynamic crops responds to an expansion in cultivated area more than to increases in productivity. This expansion owes its dynamic less to the incorporation of new land than to the displacement of basic grains, a phenomenon especially clear in rain-fed lands. The growth of production in safflower and soya mainly followed the increase in cultivated area, given that yields were comparable from the beginning to those obtained in the United States. In respect to sorghum, growth in production rested also in increases in cultivated area, although there had been some improvement in yields (CESPA, 1982, 3:150).

Conversely, very little increase in basic grains was obtained from higher yields, since the area cultivated in these crops declined by 1.4 million hectares between 1964-1966 and 1976-1978. That reduction in area approximately equals the increase in area harvesting forage and oilseeds, as shown in table 3. Basic grains acreage declined in rain-fed areas, where in particular we can verify crop substitution; in the irrigation districts, forage and oilseeds acreage grew, but so did basic grains (CESPA, 1982: Vol. III, p. 87).

In summary, a series of new crops experienced an extraordinary production boom at the expense of the displacement of traditional crops, especially essential foods and cotton.

We should analyze why and how forage and new oilseeds for the internal

TABLE 2
Groups of Agricultural Products According to Growth in Their Production at Greater or Less than 3.4 Percent per Year, in the Period of the Crisis

Agricultural Products	Less than 3.4%		More than 3.4%	
	1946-48 1964-66	1964-66 1976-78	1964-48 1964-66	1964-66 1976-78
Foods	7.3	0.7	5.4	6.0
Basic grains	7.5	0.9		
Rice	4.8	2.8		
Maize	7.1	0.7		
Wheat	9.2	3.1		
Beans	9.4	-1.0		
Other foods	7.0	0.4	5.4	6.0
Cereals[a]			2.9	6.8
Oilseeds	7.3	-2.8		
Sesame	4.6	-3.0		
Cottonseed	9.9	-4.5		
Copra	10.6	-1.2		
Safflower			—	11.7
Soya			—	15.1
Other[b]	3.5	-0.4		
Sugar cane	7.4	0.6		
Horticultural products, tubers, and dry legumes[c]			5.1	5.4
Fruits[d]			5.2	5.3
Others[e]	6.4	2.1		
Coffee	6.4	2.0		
Cacao	7.5	3.2		
Non Foods	8.2	-3.7	10.2	11.8
Fibers and tobacco	8.2	-3.7		
Cotton				
Henequen	1.9	-3.1		
Tobacco	2.8	0.4		
Forages			10.2	11.8
Grain sorghum			—	13.7
Green alfalfa			5.5	9.0
Total	7.5	-0.1	5.9	7.2

Source: Official data from SARH, DGEA.

[a] Includes oats and barley.

[b] Includes olives, peanuts, and linseed.

[c] Includes garlic, onions, peas, dry chile, green chile, tomatoes, strawberries, melon, watermelon, pineapple, potatoes, camote, garbanzo, and lima bean.

[d] Includes avocado, plums, coconut, peach guava, lemon, mango, apple, orange, nuez encareciada, papaya, pear, banana, tamarind, and grapes.

[e] Includes vanilla.

TABLE 3
Harvested Area in Certain Products and Groups of Products, Mexico
(thousands of hectares)

Product	Annual Average			Difference
	1946-48	*1964-66*	*1976-78*	*1976-78—1964-66*
Basic grains	4,840	10,915	9,598	-1,317
Oilseeds	221	548	995	447
Forages	50	496	1,565	1,069
Cotton	355	772	335	- 437
Subtotal	5,466	12,731	12,493	- 238
Others	1,180	2,185	2,650	465
Total	6,646	14,916	15,143	227

Source: Official data from SARH, DGEA.

market have displaced rice, beans, maize, and wheat, as it is here that we find some of the keys to the internationalization of Mexican agricultural production and commerce.

Modern aviculture emerges in Mexico after World War II as the first commercial farms appear, replacing domestic farms. Using genetically selected birds, these farms turn to importing inputs, such as balanced feed and medicines, in order to produce chickens and eggs for the expanding urban market. In the industrial development of Mexican aviculture, a group of North American transnational enterprises performed a very important role. These companies initiated a change in the productive structure and avicultural technology of the country, involving a new way of utilizing inputs, new avicultural lineage to replace less productive domestic birds, innovative methods of feeding and raising animals, and a system of industrializing the biological cycle in a fashion similar to the assembly line.

Currently, 44 transnational avicultural establishments operate in Mexico, linked to eight networks that maintain the industry's leadership and are integrated vertically into the production of feed, imports of breeding stock, the production of breeders and chicks, the production of chicken and eggs (through contracts with small poultry raisers), and the distribution of the final products for consumption. Transnational enterprises dominate about a third of each one of these diverse markets in the agroindustrial poultry system (Rama and Rello, 1980, pp. 132ff). Later a group of large firms using Mexican capital emerged; they now control the major part of the market for final products and poultry-raising inputs, including genetic materials, which are the nucleus of power of this agroindustrial system.

New aviculture stimulated the rapid growth of the balanced feedstuffs industry, about 69 percent of which is dedicated to poultry production. It channels 18 percent of its sales to its second client, porciculture. (Bovine cattle, especially meat, still employs fundamentally land-extensive and traditional methods, making scarce use of improved feedstuffs).

The animal ration industry is one of the Mexican food industries preferred by foreign capital, which accounts for about 60 percent of total sales. Twenty-nine transnational establishments operate in the country, depending on eight different U.S. companies, among which Ralston Purina and Anderson Clayton stand out.

The balanced feedstuff industry is one of the most dynamic industries from 1960 to 1975, with an annual rate of growth averaging 14.1 percent. It is not surprising, therefore, that it has generated an extraordinary rate of growth in the production of its principal inputs, sorghum and soya.

Mexican sorghum production grew at a rate of 18.1 percent between 1960 and 1978, despite which since 1973 imports represented between 10 and 18 percent of consumption, becoming one of the most important areas of the country's foreign agricultural trade, totaling 18.4 percent of the value of agricultural imports between 1978 and 1980 (see table 4).

TABLE 4
Participation of Principal Agricultural Products in Total Agricultural Imports, Mexico
(millions of current dollars)

Three-Year Period	Barly	Cotton seed	Soya	Sorghum	Wheat	Maize	Cinnamon	Subtotal 7 products	Total Agricultural Imports
1950-52		1.1	0.4		32.3	0.8	0.6	35.2	43.0[a]
Share (%)		2.6	0.9		75.1	1.9	1.4	81.9	100.0
1964-66	3.5	2.8	1.3	1.8	0.4	1.7	2.6	14.1	21.0[b]
Share (%)	16.6	13.3	6.2	8.6	1.9	8.1	12.4	67.1	100.0
1978-80	21.4	10.6	202.2	192.0	150.0	315.7	5.5	897.4	1043.0[a]
Share (%)	2.1	1.0	19.4	18.4	14.4	30.3	0.5	86.0	100.0

Source: Elaborated with official data from the *Anuarios Estadísticos del Comercio Exterior de los Estados Unidos Mexicanos*, Secretaría de Programación y Presupuesto.

[a] If bean imports are included ($3.3 million), the percentage reaches 89.5 percent.

[b] If bean ($0.1 million), rice ($1.3 million), and oilcake (1.3 million) imports are included, the percentage reaches 80 percent.

[c] If bean ($84.0 million), rice ($14.5 million), and oilcake ($26.9 million) imports are included, the percentage reaches 98.1 percent.

The growth in local soya production was also spectacular, but there still exists a growing gap between demand and internal supply, which is filled with voluminous imports (see table 4). As a consequence, Mexican agricultural imports of basic grains for human consumption grew tremendously, but so did forage crops.

The first of various factors contributing to an explanation of the displacement of basic crops by sorghum and the new oilseeds is that the guaranteed prices of sorghum and oilseeds were much more favorable than basic foodstuffs, as a part of the decision to maintain low prices for wage goods. Moreover, in an industrial market hungry for inputs, it is logical that the industries processing balanced feedstuffs and edible oils would be disposed to pay prices higher than the guarantee price. For that reason, the average rural prices of the new oilseeds and sorghum were frequently greater than the government's fixed price, which, of course, was barely a minimum price (Rama and Rello, 1980, p. 75).[4]

Second, the financing that grew most in the past decade went to soya, safflower, and sorghum. In 1978, these three crops received 3.176 billion pesos, while maize and beans received only 2.403 billion (beginning with that year, greater amounts of money were channeled to basic crops)(Gordillo, 1979).

Third, sorghum yields grew relatively more than those of maize. In Mexico, both cereals were cultivated in comparable ecologies. At an equivalent level of technology (rain-fed, mechanized, with high levels of inputs) it was estimated that the net income to cost ratio was 20 percent for corn and 79 percent for sorghum in 1975. This is reason for thinking that the substitution was produced especially in good rain-fed lands and that only those maize producers that were most backward and involved in subsistence consumption had difficulties opting for sorghum (Pereira, 1979).

Finally, another stimulus to the cropping change was the presence of the parastate enterprise CONASUPO (Compañía Nacional de Subsistencias Populares) and of the National Rural Credit Bank (BNCR) as intermediaries between farmers and agroindustrial processors of soya and sorghum. These enterprises, much as in the case of the great poultry farms, count on various supply systems for primary agricultural materials, such as purchases through agents or through contracts with associations of producers and ejidos. Nevertheless, CONASUPO appears to play a role of growing importance (Rama and Rello, 1980, p. 65). For its part, the National Rural Credit Bank has oriented itself systematically toward the most prosperous of the *ejidatarios*, gearing them to the new crops (Rama and Rello, 1980, p. 97).

But in what type of agrarian structures did the substitution of the four basic crops in favor of production destined to internationalized agroindustry occur?

A field study (Rama and Rello, 1980, p. 59) in the zones of crop substitution in the states of Jalisco and Tamaulipas confirms that in those states a backward subsistence agriculture never existed—a result that must be emphasized, given that it is widely assumed in Latin America that agribusiness has had a disintegrating effect on peasant agriculture and that the peasantry becomes functional to such a system due to low pricing of its products (Gómes and Pérez, 1980, p. 29).

In reality, the firms processing sorghum, soya, and safflower purchase their products from large farmers through intermediaries and/or unions of middle-size producers, especially *ejidatarios*, through CONASUPO and the National Rural Credit Bank, which function conjointly.

The same type of agroindustrial suppliers were encountered in fruits and vegetables, where, with the exception of strawberries, it appears that production contracts prevail with large and middle-size farmers. Another similarity can be detected in the case of "brokers" and enterprises marketing fresh fruits and vegetables in the internal and the international markets (Rama and Vigorito, 1979, p. 181). The long organizational tradition of the unions of fruit and vegetable producers for export confirm this finding (Hardy, 1982, p. 9).

Transnational enterprises, and other large producing and marketing firms for fruits and vegetables, and manufacturers of animal rations prefer to locate themselves where they can articulate themselves with middle-size modern rural sectors whose technical abilities and use of inputs are growing at the same time their entrepreneurial independence is declining.

In summary, with respect to some new products (in the sense that they were not previously consumed in the country, or were imported or produced in backward economic structures)—in fruits and vegetables, soya, sorghum, chickens, eggs, part of dairy production (Quintar Salha, 1983, p. 92) and pork—the modernizing expansion of capital covers all of the aspects of the food chain, from primary production to consumption, revolutionizing the sector completely. Transnational enterprises and other modern agroindustries that operate in these agroindustrial systems insinuate themselves into primary production through production contracts or through intermediation along with state marketing and credit enterprises in agriculture. The internationalization of these new agroindustrial systems has implied a displacement of human food crops, but not through a process of the disintegration of the peasant economy, as is frequently assumed.

In fact, the modernizing process took place in commercial agricultural regions of Mexico, where economic agents are strongly predisposed to substitute crops as a response to increased profit margins, adequate marketing channels, official credit, and a dynamic demand from industry. The processes of internationalization operated also through the differentiation of some sectors of peasant agriculture, which by possessing control of relatively propitious factors of production and strong state marketing and credit support were converted into acceptable interlocutors for modern agroindustries, abandoning less profitable human foodstuffs cultivation. This determined a notable increase in the imports of basic crops but also of forage inputs, increasing Mexican agricultural imports from $43 to $1,043 million in three decades (see table 4).

But what would have happened in the absence of crop substitution and with an industrial structure equivalent to that which now exists? It is estimated that even more of an increase of oilseeds imports would be required, as well as imports of fruits and vegetables in which the country is currently self-sufficient; and certain exports would be reduced in absolute terms (CESPA, 1982, 3:163). Given the structure of demand—and especially industrial demand—one may consider the change in crops as an efficient option, to replace less intensive crops with crops that are more intensive (CESPA, 1982, 3:159).

The other hypothetical alternative would have involved the installation of an animal feeds producing industry that would use, instead of sorghum, inputs produced in the tropical zones of the country where grains for human consumption would not be displaced. The use of sugar cane bagasse, cacao, rice and coffee hulls, yucca, and agricultural waste products would have been a more rational alternative from the viewpoint of the country's interest, although from the viewpoint of the companies it would have required a major effort to adapt to available resources. This could contribute to resolving the carbohydrates problem in balanced animal feedstuffs. It is unlikely, nevertheless, that the problem of supplying protein now provided by soya would be resolved. Even in Eastern and Western Europe, the technological problem of finding an oleaginous alternative to soya for cattle feed has not been resolved, for which reason—despite research efforts—North American and Brazilian exports are crucial.

In what magnitude has internationalization directly affected the level of self-sufficiency in cereals? In the case of maize, the impact was notably negative. Maize left out of production in rain-fed zones where there was great crop displacement in 1978 amounted to 90 percent of the tonnage imported that year. In contrast, the amount of wheat that was moved out of production by the same cause was less than 20 percent of the imports of that cereal. One of the differences between the two grains is that there was a relocation of wheat from rain-fed areas to irrigated areas of the north of the country, which compensated in part for its expulsion from rain-fed lands in favor of forage crops (CESPA, 1982, 3:94). In the case of wheat, at least, internationalization had a less direct effect on the crisis of production. Nevertheless, the impact of a guaranteed price policy favorable to that dynamic was important, as well.

NEW CONSUMPTION, TRADITIONAL AGRICULTURE

In contrast to the new food systems just analyzed, in other systems where there was also a process of internationalization, changes have been restricted to the transformation, distribution, and consumption phases of the food chain only, while the productive structure and technology of primary good production, as well as the first industrial processing, remain almost unchanged. These are characteristics of the internationalization process in some traditional Mexican agroindustrial systems, such as beef cattle, tobacco, sweeteners, and cacao (Castillo, 1982; Rama, 1980; Reig, 1982; Teubal, 1982).

These agroindustrial systems are characterized by a great advance of transnational enterprises and in some cases by great connection with the international market. I have already mentioned the vertical integration of an entire subsector of Mexican beef cattle with the feedlot industry of Texas and California. In that system internationalization makes itself evident through the great importance of international financing. In the tobacco system, the impact of transnational enterprises has grown via a process of denationalization and fusion of firms stimulated by the generalized turn of the great cigarette manufacturers toward the developing countries, which have a great mass of potential consumers (youths and women) and have not undertaken antismoking campaigns. The transnational enterprises that are undertaking the second processing of sugar (soft drinks, dessert sweets, and the like) have expanded with unusual rapidity in the Mexican market, as have the processors of cacao derivatives.

In all of these systems there has occurred a noticeable modernization of the product's industrial transformation (above all, in the second phase of transformation controlled by the transnational enterprise) and of the systems of distribution to the consumer: modern refrigeration systems; improvement in the sanitary aspects and in new cuts of meat; innovations in the processing and fermentation of cacao; the use of oleoresins; advances in marketing technologies in chocolate derivatives; new presentations of industrialized cakes and pastries; efficient distributive services in sweets covering the most remote places in the country; and the novel methods of production and merchandizing in the tobacco industry.

Another characteristic common to these systems is that the internal demand for their products has grown unexpectedly in the last twenty years as a consequence of the improvement of the levels of well-being of the middle sectors and urban salaried workers, the demonstration effect at the international level propagated by the publicity apparatus of transnational enterprises, the suitability of the new products for urban life, and the evolution of relative prices in foods. The Mexican diet tends toward a pattern that is more "Western" than in the past, with a growth in the consumption of processed foods and animal proteins and a substitution of wheat for maize in the middle- and high-income social strata, and also among the urban poor.

The linkage between industrial enterprises and the agricultural sector that supplies them with primary goods is constituted by diverse parastate organisms, unions of producers, and public enterprises. These intermediaries are charged with the commercialization of the product and the initial transformation of primary materials (grinding sugar cane, cacao fermentation, etc.). They accomplish the vertical integration of the food chain by supplying credit to the primary producer, supervising production, determining the varieties to plant, and stimulating agricultural investment (at times in a coercive manner), using the power available to them as regional monopsonies and financial resource managers.

But the base is a backward agriculture, and the scarce savings capacity of many small producers puts a brake on the attempt at agricultural modernization undertaken by these institutions (although it is clear that a process of peasant differentiation takes place, from which emerges a group of very significant farmers at the middle level who are capable of using more modern technology). In sugar cane, for example, the forced modernization of agriculture imposed by the sugar refineries concretely affects the technologies and investments absorbed on small parcels. Thus, divisible technological options predominate, such as irrigation, drainage, and fertilization. The limit to productive accumulation lies in investments in agricultural machinery and transport—investments that are very important because of the scarcity of cane cutters and the necessity to transport the cane to the mill rapidly, in order that it not lose its sugar content.

With respect to the cattle system in the northern zone, Reig observes,

> the stability of the productive structure is notable: in the last ten years—in spite of the high density of technological changes and the great changes in internal and external cycles—the type of productive structure remained without great apparent modification, and the cattle and unimproved land remain the focal point of this type of livestock enterprise, with all that that signifies in economic and productive backwardness. (Reig, 1982, p. 147)

With the exception of tobacco enterprises, the processing businesses of other products complain of a scarcity of primary goods. In fact, that problem is identified in case studies as the principal obstacle to the expansion of this group of agroindustrial systems. The lack of harmony between the high rates of growth in these industries and the very low rate of primary materials production was resolved by diverting the bulk of production that was previously exported toward the industrial market. In these systems, which had been oriented toward the external market, the growth focus is now the internal market.

Everything seems to indicate that not even the scarcity of primary materials would incline modern industry to attempt a transformation of the conditions of agricultural and livestock production in these systems. The example of sugar is very illustrative: the solution has been to import that product basically to satisfy growing industrial consumption. In other cases new technologies conserve primary materials (tobacco) or use substitutes (cacao).

In the case of meat, whose internal consumption grew at an average annual rate of 7 percent from 1960 to 1980, while cattle production managed a rate of barely 3 percent, the response involves a broad expansion of the productive base. The strategy of U.S. importers of boned meat, rather than simply to stimulate Mexican production, has been to diversify sources of supply. A clear illustration is the boom in purchases from Central America (Slutzky, 1982, p. 191).

Some reasons why the internationalization process does not include the primary sector appear to include the following: (1) in some cases, as in sugar cane, there have not been technical advances except in the new technology to obtain sugar from maize; (2) discouraging agricultural prices and structures; (3) low comparative advantage in Mexico in the production of some goods, discouraging the transnationals from exporting from that country; and (4) the type of technology utilized by enterprises and subsidies contribute to the fact that these modern agroindustries have few backward linkages with agricultural and livestock production, especially with such low costs for primary goods.

As we can see in table 5, there is a notorious imbalance between the high rates of industrial production and the stagnation in the growth of agricultural and livestock production and in exports from these old systems.

Because industry does not impinge directly on the conditions of primary materials production—in contrast to the transnational enterprises operating in such systems as fruit and vegetables and dairy products—the incongruity between backward agriculture and growing industrial demand has been resolved by the sector's diversion of a grand part of the surpluses that used to be exported toward the internal market, especially the agroindustrial market. This has contributed to a deterioration in the agricultural trade balance, measured in volume. If the agricultural trade balance in value has been positive in the majority of the years of the period under study, it is because of the favorable impact of export prices, which compensated for the decline of export volume (CESPA, 1982, 4:70).

THE INTERNATIONALIZATION OF THE DECISION-MAKING REALM

Mexico has traded foods with other countries since time immemorial. The new aspect is that the emergence of the U.S. as an agroexporting power in the 1960s converted the international basic grains market into one of the crucial elements for Mexican agricultural decision-making policy.

The second aspect to take into account is that, as some authors show, agricultural politics objectively had the effect of accelerating the internationalization of Mexican agriculture, sacrificing the production of basic foodstuffs (Barkin and Suárez, 1982, p. 187).

The transition from a policy stimulating growth in basic grain production, whose objective was to satisfy the growing urban markets of the 1950s and early 1960s, to a policy of importation was very rapid. Just before the beginning of the crisis—more precisely, between 1961 and 1965—the supply of basic products grew at 7 percent, while demand grew at 5.6 percent, as a result of decided

TABLE 5
Evolution of the Tobacco, Cacao, Meat, and Sugar Systems in Mexico

Indicator	Tobacco	Cacao	Beef	Sugar
Annual growth of gross agricultural product 1964-66 to to 1976-78 (tons)	0.4	3.2	4.8	0.6
Annual growth of industrial product (1960 prices)				
1st transformation	—	9.1[b]	13.7[n]	6.3[d]
2nd transformation	5.9[e]	9.5[f]	5.5[g]	29.6[h]
Participation of transnationals in gross industrial product in 1975 (%)	3.4[i]	-	-	6.1[j]
	0.0[k]	63.0[b]	15.1[c]	0.0[d]
	96.8[e]	33.2[f]	15.0[g]	0.0[l]
	0.0[j]			86.1[h]
Annual growth of exports 1964-1978 (1977 dollars)	7.3	—	6.3[m]	-14.1
(tons)	7.3	1.5[n]	-2.8[m]	- 8.7
			-32.0[o]	

Sources: CESPA, 1982, vols. 3, 4; Montes de Oca and Escudero, 1981; Castillo, 1982; Censos Industriales, 1960-1975.

[a] Sugar cane.
[b] Cocoa and chocolate.
[c] Cattle slaughtering.
[d] Sugar and residues.
[e] Cigarettes.
[f] Sweets, bonbons, and confections.
[g] Conserving and packing meat.
[h] Concentrates, jarabes, and colorings.
[i] Cigars.
[j] Soft drinks.
[k] Tobacco curing.
[l] Piloncillo and unrefined brown sugar.
[m] Exports of beef.
[n] Cacao exports refer to the period 1970-1978.
[o] Exports of thousands of live cattle.

policies stimulating the most essential agricultural production (CEPAL, 1982, p. 24).

At the moment of the collapse of international grain prices and the emergence of the U.S. as an agroexporting power, Mexican agricultural policy does a complete turnaround. Although Mexico was not a direct recipient of U.S. food aid under the P.L. 480 program, such programs contributed to inducing a change in grain storage policy and to the abandonment of the politics of self-sufficiency in favor of imports.[5] In the period in which the international price of maize was inferior to the internal price, the criterion was to encourage its replacement by more remunerative crops, whose price was increasing in the world market (Esteva and Barkin, 1981, p. 25).

This type of decision was congruent with cheap food policies, which run as a guiding thread through Mexican agricultural politics from the era of importsubstitution industrialization (and even before), since it was thought that one could resort to the external market whenever necessary to cover cereals shortages at a convenient price.

At least from the rhetorical viewpoint, the intention was to promote export specialization in products in which the country had comparative advantage. Nevertheless, as we have seen before, not only would this not result, but the volume of exports actually fell from the mid-1960s. In fact, basic crops were not replaced by export crops that would draw foreign exchange to the country in order to purchase maize, beans, or wheat but instead were replaced by forage crops and oilseeds destined for the agroindustries of the internal market.

Due to the international food crisis of 1972-1973, when world prices for grains were superior to those prevailing in Mexico, Mexican agricultural price policies took yet another turn. From that date forward, guaranteed prices for basic grains began to increase; and in 1980-1982 a program of much broader reach was put into action, the Sistema Alimentario Mexicano, whose objective was self-sufficiency for the country in those basic products and a reversion to policies emphasizing the extraction of surpluses from peasant producers of maize, beans, and wheat.

CONCLUSION

The crisis of basic foods in Mexican agriculture has among its principal causes the limit of "easy" technological advance in agriculture; the "price" that the sector paid to support import-substitution industrialization; and the internationalization of some of the nation's agroindustrial systems. As a consequence, the country lost, in great measure, its self sufficiency in basic foods. In particular, the process of internationalization exercised, directly or indirectly, a negative effect on the agricultural trade balance, because (1) it contributed to the increase of basic grains imports, which stimulated their displacement in internal production, as well as encouraging imports required by the new agroindustries; and (2) in some systems of traditional exports the superimposition of a modern and dynamic food industry on backward agricultural and livestock structures created an imbalance which was resolved by imposing limits on exportable surpluses.

The crisis of agriculture and livestock in Mexico is great, but it is not a general crisis. Together with the basic grains sector (rice, maize, beans, and wheat), which grows at a slower rate than the population, coexists an unusually dynamic and expansive minority sector, producing forages, new oilseeds (safflower and soya), fruits and vegetables, and animal products. One aspect where it could clearly be affirmed that the internationalization process contributed to the crisis is in the loss of 1.4 million hectares in basic foods cultivation that went to sorghum, soya, safflower, forage crops, fruits, and vegetables in commercial rain-fed agricultural zones or in *ejidos* with certain minimal conditions of capital accumulation and credit and technical support from the state.

These new products are inputs for internationalized agroindustrial systems, where all of the phases of the food chain have been modernized, from industrial transformation to wholesale distribution. As bearers and disseminators of new production technology, transnational enterprises created these systems in Mexico, practically from the ground up. Although currently large national companies, and even state enterprises, participate in these networks, these agroindustrial systems are creatures of transnational enterprises.

We can speak of new systems because (1) the products do not appear in agricultural statistics in Mexico before the end of the 1950s, or (2) there was a process of import substitution in agriculture and livestock raising, or (3) the products were previously produced in a domestic or peasant framework of economic organization. The current organization of this production group, among which we include sorghum, safflower, soya, poultry, eggs, fruits, vegetables, and part of pork and dairy production, dates from the end of the 1950s or beginning of the 1960s.

In some of the old export systems (meat, cacao, tobacco, sugar), the internationalization of the industries of transformation and consumption was not accompanied by a transformation of backward agrarian structures that provide those industries with primary goods. In these cases, the observation generally applicable to the new system—that "the food processing industries support the modernization of agriculture through their necessity to assure a stable and growing supply of products of a homogeneous quality" (Sorj, 1980; Teubal, 1982, p. 45)—is not apparent.

Paradoxically, internationalized agriculture is, more than ever in its history, an agriculture turned toward the internal market. Not only did agricultural exports lose their traditional importance as a source of foreign exchange to be replaced overwhelmingly in that function by industries of transformation and extractive industries, but the area dedicated to export crops has been reduced and represents a small proportion of total cultivated area.

But then what is being internationalized? This general term alludes to the imitative and immediate modernization that is experienced in the production of certain foods, which can include some or all phases of the food chain. In the internationalized food systems of Mexico, the technological processes, organizational methods, demand creation, and articulations employed among economic agents and consumers, are those that operate at the international level, that is, in the developed capitalist countries. Moreover, a good part of the production of those systems is obviously generated by transnational enterprises. Second, the supply system has been internationalized since it depends more and more on imports to feed the Mexican population. Third, the world market of grains provides a constant point of reference for agricultural policy—something that occurred to a lesser extent before the mid-1960s—to the point where internal price guarantees depend more on international prices than on internal conditions of supply and demand.

Millions of Mexicans begin to be fed in accordance with the most "Western" styles, replacing traditional diet. Without a doubt, the diets of the middle and upper classes become more varied and rich in products of quality than in the past; but also—although to a lesser extent—low-income city dwellers tend to substitute white bread, noodles, rice, and increasing amounts of animal protein for the traditional diet of maize and beans. This is a slow process that could eventually be reversed during the current crisis. Nevertheless, two groups of foodstuffs tend to be defined: the new wage goods and the peasant foods (maize and beans), although this does not imply that we are talking about mutually exclusive categories (de Janvry, 1981, p. 78).

Also, there tends to be a change regarding who feeds them, which interdicts the traditional function of the peasant economy within the general model of development. The new element is that basic foods for domestic consumption are produced more than ever before by irrigated agriculture, which in Mexico is associated with the commercial modern sector. The new wage goods such as wheat and rice originate overwhelmingly in irrigated agriculture (96 and 75 percent, respectively). Likewise, one-fourth of beans and maize (i.e., peasant foods) are produced under irrigation (CESPA, 1982, 3:40). The arrival of transnational enterprises has ruined peasant poultry raising since the 1960s. The sweets, soft drinks, and industrialized pastries and appetizers integrated in the food baskets of even the poorest urban dwellers of Mexico also come from modern agroindustries (Montes de Oca and Escudero, 1981).

What is the role of peasant agriculture as a provider of food in this internationalized agriculture? It is necessary to distinguish between two sectors: the peasant producer of maize and beans; and the peasant producer articulated with agroindustries.

Subjectively, peasant foods are losing social prestige. Objectively, the urban workers' purchasing power is increasing for those foods involved in the modernization process. Over the long term, although it is a slow process, peasant agricultural production of basic foods appears to be losing its traditional function of being a supplier of cheap food to the industrial work force. This function will then be undertaken more and more by U.S. farmers, domestic capitalist agriculture, and agroindustries. In the absence of a political option in favor of the peasant economy producing basic foodstuffs, this will militate toward converting the peasant producers into a system of indigents producing for indigents, trapped in a closed circuit, relatively less articulated economically than before, within a model of overall development whose motor is industry.[6]

It is very difficult to quantify which part of peasant agriculture is articulated with agroindustries. In any case, it is known that such industries transform about 57 percent of agricultural and livestock production in the country (SEPAFIN, 1978). It is also known that the intermediaries that market primary agricultural materials, administer rural production, and induce investment in the countryside (be they in the form of sugar refineries, unions of producers, official credit banks for agriculture, etc.) are principally linked—and in this aspect all available case studies agree—with middle-size producers with a modest capacity to generate economic surpluses. Because of that link, it is possible that a substantial and growing part of the *campesinado* does not operate independently any longer but within the various agroindustrial systems.

In these cases an induced and slow accumulation of capital occurs, which carries with it a gradual modernization of agroindustrial cropping. This process permits the emergence of peasant sectors with a minimal savings capacity, removed from entrepreneurial decision making on their plots, with that power remaining in the hands of the state, marketing agents, and refineries.

In synthesis, the insufficient production of basic grains and the changes in Mexican foreign commerce from the 1960s to the present (diminution of food self-sufficiency, vertigenous increases in imports, and the lack of dynamism in exports) cannot be interpreted—from my viewpoint—as simple manifestations of a reorganization of Mexican agriculture. The magnitude of the phenomenon and the qualitative importance of the products involved make them relevant to a crisis that also has nutritional, social, and political aspects (which are beyond the objectives here). Although the process of agricultural internationalization has not become general throughout all the food chains of the country, it has added in a significant way to the crisis through different mechanisms (basic crop displacement, agricultural and commercial policy, and in other cases, a weak linkage between enterprise and agriculture), within a relatively rigid framework of the decelerated expansion of the agricultural frontier.

NOTES

1. "We use the concept of technological revolution to indicate that, to certain prodigious transformations in the realm of human actions over nature, or in warfare, correspond qualitative alterations in a society's entire way of being that oblige us to treat them as new categories in the continuum of socio-cultural evolution" (Ribeiro, 1978a, p.47). "By *evolutionary acceleration* we mean those processes of development of societies that autonomously renew their productive system and reform their social institutions in the sense of making a transition from to another model of socio-cultural formation, as communities that exist for themselves. By *actualización histórica* we designate the processes by which those backward communities in history are compulsively involved in more technologically evolved systems, with a resulting loss of their autonomy..." (Ribeiro, 1978a, pp. 55-56). See also, Ribeiro 1978b, pp. 30-33. Evidently, the internationalization of agriculture in the developing countries is only one part of a much vaster movement of "historical bringing up to date" in industrial, war, service, and other technologies.

2. I refer not only to the technology of production but also to management, administration, and marketing.

3. In 1960, agriculture, forestry, cattle, and fishing represented 54.3 percent of the country's exports; extractive industry contributed 22.0 percent, and industries of transformation 23.3 percent. But the structure of Mexican foreign commerce changed after that, producing a loss of the relative value of agricultural exports and a new insertion—first manufacturing, later energy—of the country in the international economy. From 1971 to 1977, industry is first in exports, surpassing agriculture after that period. From 1977 forward, Mexico is converted overwhelmingly into a petroleum-exporting country; currently, about three-fourths of its exports consist of energy and other extractive industry products (data from the Banco de México).

4. The average rural prices of maize and beans, in contrast, did not differ greatly from guaranteed prices in the years 1960-1975. The average rural price of wheat was, in that period, lower than the guarantee price. Rodríguez G., 1979.

5. "We continue to believe that it is preferable to import [maize] since it is indispensable, instead of maintaining an excessive reserve that, from a number of standpoints, would be seriously antieconomical." México, Secretaría de Agricultura y Ganadería and Secretaría de la Presidencia, 1976, p. 27.

6. This does not mean that peasant agriculture tends to disappear since it continues to fulfill a social and political function, although gradually losing its role of feeding the industrial work force at a low cost.

REFERENCES

Arroyo, Gonzalo. 1979. "Firmas transnacionales agroindustriales, reforma agraria, y desarrollo rural." In *El desarrollo agroindustrial y la economía internacional*, pp. 45-68. México: CODAI-SARH.
———. ed. 1982. *El desarrollo agroindustrial y la economía latinoamericana*. Vol. 1. Documentos de Trabajo para el Desarrollo Agroindustrial, no. 5. México: SARH-CODAI.
Barkin, David and Blanca Suárez. 1982. *El fin de autosuficiencia alimentaria*. México: Nueva Imagen.
———. n.d.. *El complejo de granos en México*. México: ILET/Centro de Ecodesarrollo.
Casar, José I.. 1982. "Ciclos económicos en la industria y sustitución de importaciones: 1950-1980." *Economía mexicana* 4.
Castillo, Donald. 1982. *Cacao. El desarrollo agroindustrial y los sistemas alimentarios*. Documentos Técnicos no. 27. México: CODAI-SARH.
CEPAL. 1982. *Caracterización de la política agrícola mexicana en diferentes períodos de los años veinte a los años setenta*. México: CEPAL.
CESPA. 1982. *El desarrollo agropecuario de México. Pasado y perspectivas*. Five volumes. Vol. 1, *El sistema agropecuario en el desarrollo económico de México*. Vol. 3, *La oferta de productos agropecuarios*. Vol. 4, *El comercio exterior de productos agropecuarios*. Vol. 5, *La problemática alimentaria*. México: SARH-CEPAL.
CODAI-SARH. 1979. *El desarrollo agroindustrial y la economía internacional*. México: CODAI-SARH.
de Janvry, Alain. 1981. *The Agrarian Question and Reformism in Latin America*. Baltimore: Johns Hopkins University Press.
Domínguez, Jorge. ed. 1980. *Mexico: International Implications of its Internal Affairs*. Beverly Hills, Calif.: Sage.
Esteva, Gustavo, and David Barkin. 1981 . "El papel del sector público en la comercialización y la fijación de precios de los productos agrícolas básicos en México." México: CEPAL.
Feder, Ernest. 1977. *El imperialismo fresa. Una investigación sobre los mecanismos de la dependencia en la agricultura mexicana*. México: Campesina.
Gómes, Gerson, and Antonio Pérez. 1980. "De la modernización al desarrollo: Elementos y criterios generales para una política de transformación de la agricultura latinoamericana." Santiago: CEPAL.
Gordillo, Gustavo. 1979. "El nucleo estatal en el medio rural. Algunas consideraciones sobre el crédito agrícola en México." *Investigación económica* 147, (January-March).
Hardy, Clarisa, (with others). 1982. *Las organizaciones gremiales de los empresarios agrícolas*. Mexico: CEPAL.
Mares, David. 1980. "Agricultural Trade, Domestic Interests and Transnational Relations." In *Mexico: International Implications of its Internal Affairs*. ed. Jorge Domínguez, pp. Beverly Hills, Calif.: Sage.
México, Secretaría de Agricultura y Ganadería y Secretaría de la Presidencia. 1976. *México a través de los informes presidenciales*. vol. 5. México: SAG.

México, Secretaría de Patrimonio y Fomento Industrial. 1978. *La estructura de la oferta y la demanda en México. Matrices de relaciones intersectoriales, 1975.* Mexico: SEPAFIN.

Montes de Oca, Rosa Elena, and Gerardo Escudero. 1981. "Las empresas transnacionales en la industria alimentaria mexicana." *Comercio Exterior* 31:9 (September).

Pereira, Gonzalo. 1979. "Tendencias actuales de la agricultura campesina de temporal en México." *Investigación económica* 38:147 (January-March).

Quintar Salha, Aida. 1983. "Las empresas transnacionales en la agroindustra de lacteos: El caso de la compañía Nestle en México." Master's thesis, Universidad Nacional Autónoma de México.

Rama, Ruth. 1980. *Transnacionales, estado y acumulación agrícola: La caña de azúcar en México.* México: Universidad Nacional Autónoma de México.

———, and Fernando Rello. 1980. *Estrategias de las agroindustrias transnacionales y política alimentaria en México.* México: Nueva Imagen.

———, and Raúl Vigorito. 1979. *Transnacionales en América Latina: El complejo de frutas y legumbres en México.* México: Nueva Imagen.

Reig, Nicolas. 1982. *El desarrollo agroindustrial y la ganadería en México.* Documentos de trabajo para el desarrollo agroindustrial. Mexico: SARH-CODAI.

Ribeiro, Darcy. 1978a. *O processo civilizatorio. Etapas da evoluçao socio-cultural.* 4th ed. Petropolis, Brazil: Vozes.

———. 1978b. *Os brasileiros: teoria do Brasil,* vol. 1. Petropolis, Brazil: Vozes.

Rodríguez G., Gonzalo. 1979. "El comportamiento de los precios agropecuarios." *Economia mexicana* 1, (April), 89-119.

Sanderson, Steven E. 1983. *Trade Aspects of the Internationalization of Mexican Agriculture: Consequences for the Mexican Food Crisis.* Monographs in U.S.-Mexican Studies, no. 10. La Jolla: University of California at San Diego.

Slutzky, Daniel. 1982. "La agroindustria de la carne en Honduras." In *El desarrollo agroindustrial y la economía latinoamericana,* ed. Gonzalo Arroyo, vol. 1, México: SARH-CODAI.

Sorj, Bernardo. 1980. *Estado e classes sociais na agricultura Brasileira.* Rio de Janeiro: Zahr.

Teubal, Miguel. 1982. *Tabaco. El desarrollo agroindustrial y los sistemas no alimentarios.* Documentos Técnicos, no. 26. México: SARH-CODAI.

Political Frameworks for International Migration

Robert L. Bach

The large-scale surge of world labor onto international circuits of commodity exchange dramatically highlights the current dimensions of the global division of labor. Indeed, except for the geographical subdivisioning of the microprocessing industry, international migration is cited most frequently as evidence of the "tendency" toward a new international division of labor (Frobel, Heinrichs and Kreye, 1977). Migration draws attention to the diverse, worldwide pools of disposable cheap labor that drive the transnational reorganization of capitalist production.

We now have a widely shared understanding of the primary features of the new international division of labor within which to locate migratory flows. Frobel, Heinrichs and Kreye highlight the following conditions as examples of the qualitative shifts in the global structure since the early 1970s: consistently high unemployment rates; cutbacks in production; leaps forward in the rationalization and automation of the production process; stagnant and declining rates of investment; ever-increasing state financial contributions to private business; large-scale increases in the numbers of newly proletarianized and impoverished workers in underdeveloped countries; a significant rise in the interpenetration of national economies; and the formation of world market-oriented manufacturing in semiperipheral and peripheral countries (Frobel, Heinrichs and Kreye, 1978). Underlying these shifts is the transnational reorganization of private enterprise, especially within manufacturing, that results in a rapid proliferation of the number of productive facilities. The preconditions for this worldwide restructuring include the availability of a huge labor pool, the existence of modernized transport and communication technology, and the continuing fragmentation of production tasks. In turn, the effects of this reorganization involve the formation and expansion of a world market for both labor and industrial sites. It is under these conditions that the familiar, characteristic pattern of contemporary capitalist development emerges and is reproduced: the simultaneous flow of low-wage labor from the periphery and semiperiphery to the core, and the emigration of core capital to the migrants' countries of origin.

As familiar and important as this context is for relating labor flows to the circulation of capital and commodities, there is another set of processes of equal significance that is much less understood. These processes, the *political* divisioning of labor,[1] involve the interaction of the axial division of labor and the interstate system (Hopkins and Wallerstein, 1977). *Together* these constitute the world capitalist system, and only in combination can we understand the tendencies toward a new *international* division of labor. For current restructuring of world capitalist accumulation is as much a crisis of the interstate system as it is an economic transformation.

Some analytical difficulties, however, obstruct a full appreciation of the political processes involved in the contribution of international migration to global restructuring. It is not the case, of course, that political forces, or the state, have been completely ignored as part of the reorganization of capital. Frobel, Heinrichs and Kreye, for example, have been quite explicit:

> The social and political conditions that capital meets or is able to impose or to "encourage" are also decisive. It is decisive whether effective union organization, labor struggles, and strikes are tolerated by the state; whether the state imposes restrictions on capital movements, profit realization, and transfer; or whether the free movement of capital is guaranteed by the state. It is also decisive, furthermore, whether, at the locations of potentially available labor force, the state does or does not offer fiscal subsidies, public contributions to private investment, technical infrastructure, and the training of the labor force (1977, p. 83).

State activities may even be accepted as fundamental to capitalist accumulation: "A central precondition for the realization of the surplus-generating possibilities of a geographic location is the formation of a politically and economically suitable labor supply" (Sassen-Koob, 1980, p. 3). Rather, the analytical problems develop in determining how these state activities form and are transformed. Which relationships, for instance, are involved in creating a politically suitable labor force, and how do the political relationships modify the restructuring goals of world-scale capital? To a large degree, the state—and more importantly, the interstate system—either are treated as an historical backdrop that *characterizes* the diversity of labor conditions from which capital can choose or are invoked instrumentally to explain what should be analytically and historically in doubt: the readiness of labor to succumb to specific demands of capital (Bach and Shraml, 1982).

My goal in this chapter is to examine explicitly the formation and transformation of the state and interstate framework through which post-World War II migrations to the United States have developed. To render such a complex task manageable, I have divided the discussion into four sections. Section one serves as a conceptual introduction, raising questions about the use of the phrase "international division of labor" and concentrating on the interaction of political processes and the global reorganization of capital. This discussion highlights the importance of the political emphasis for the study of international migration.

Section two traces the development of "political frameworks" that organize the flows of Mexican and Puerto Rican laborers into the United States. It provides an account of the historical organization of each migration and the more recent changes in their political frameworks. Throughout this section, the analysis emphasizes the interaction of three sets of relationships: underlying pressures of market formation, political management of commodity and labor exchanges, and the complex entanglement of U.S. domestic class relations.[2]

Section three attempts to integrate a discussion of refugee migrations into the same analytical framework proposed for the labor migrations. The attempt is important not only for the migration literature (these two flows have too often been treated as distinctive types) but as well for research on the international division of labor. This section emphasizes the active political contribution of opposition groups in the world economy to the futures of both world capital and labor. Structural transformations—by which I mean both economic and political—that give rise to refugee flows expose dramatically the continuing uncertainty that faces capital in its desires to reorganize on a world scale. Finally, Section four concludes the discussion with a very brief commentary on the current state of immigration reform.

INTERNATIONAL DIVISIONS OF LABOR

Political Divisioning

Examples of the current or "new" international division of labor and its consequences for labor are drawn typically from either the apparel or electronics industry. For different reasons, each industry has reached an advanced stage of both subdividing labor and dispersing geographically. One of the most important aspects of this current division of labor—and the fundamental problem for workers—is the velocity of private capital's geographical movement (Bluestone and Harrison, 1982; Bonilla and Campos, this volume). For instance, a recent report (N.Y. State Department of Labor, 1982) on the "homework" apparel industry indicates that in one short period nearly 10,000 licenses for legal homework issued to apparel manufacturers had been surrendered or canceled because the employers changed locations.

Frequently, of course, capital's geographical relocation has involved crossing state borders, or at least shipping part of the production process across these boundaries. In part, the object has been to overcome restrictive regulations in one state and to take advantage of the absence of controls in another.

"The apex of the distribution system and the manufacturing apparatus," the above report states, "lies outside the state distribution" (N.Y. State Department of Labor, 1982, p. 31). And it concludes, "The existence of state boundaries has no relevance in the manufacturing process (p. 33)."

This familiar description, which could easily be taken from any number of contemporary accounts of the new international division of labor, actually refers specifically to the division of labor in the garment industry in 1903. More importantly, the *states* mentioned are New York and New Jersey, not the nation-states of contemporary profiles. That such a description of the interstate division of labor could serve us as well today as eighty years ago suggests some ambiguity in our understanding of contemporary processes of capitalist accumulation. It raises questions about what is "new" in the current international division of labor. And more importantly for specific interests here, it focuses on the significance of the type of political divisioning of economic processes; whether, for example, interventions by state goverments (New York) are equivalent in conceptual terms to those of nation-state governments (the United States).

There are, of course, several clear proposals as to what constitutes the *new* form of the international division of labor. Frobel, Heinrichs and Kreye (1978) offer the following distinction:

> In Adam Smith's day, the size of the available market for goods determined the division of labor economically possible and necessary in the enterprise. Today, it is the size of the worldwide labor market, with its different skills and wages, that determines the extent of the division of labor between the different production facilities of the enterprise around the globe. (p. 847)

Others have focused on production: "Internationalization of production is the most novel form of the international division of labor. Internationalization of production takes the form of locating manufacturing plants in the periphery. The level of international specialization varies for different industries" (Sassen-Koob, pp. 220-221).

The alleged novel forms in these proposed definitions, however, expose several conceptual and analytical weaknesses. If we begin, for instance, as Frobel, Heinrichs and Kreye do, with an understanding of the capitalist system as being constituted from its inception as a world division of labor and as emerging historically through the rise of modern nation-states, then clearly the processes of capitalist accumulation have been "internationalized" for several hundred years. Nothing especially new, or qualitatively distinct, is derived from observing an "internationalization of production." Certainly the possibility exists, however, that the current novelty lies in the *scale* of internationalization. Yet even a theoretical emphasis on the scale of internationalization creates at least two analytical problems.

First, as the activities that are "internationalized" grow (i.e., world trade, migration, banking, production sites) so also the world economy as a whole *and* intrastate markets (the so-called national economy) expand. *Proportional* shifts in measured international linkages would be the appropriate indication of a new pattern. I doubt seriously, however, that much evidence exists for more than a few commodities (financial markets are probably the best case for proportional shifts), and over long historical periods, that shows interstate activities have increased as a ratio of intrastate exchanges, assuming a constant world scale.

Second, the scale of internationalization depends on the number and nature of state boundaries. World-level processes can and have become rapidly "internationalized" through a multiplication of states (e.g. decolonization) rather than a fundamental economic restructuring. The strength of borders is equally important. For example, are current commodity exchanges between Vietnam and Kampuchea to be considered "international" simply because they cross a virtually fictitious boundary? And more to our interests here, should exchanges between firms in south Texas and northern Mexico be considered international? After all, the goal of the tariff structure and Border Industrialization Program (in fact, free trade zones in general) is to create areas "free" of state influence.

The answer in each situation depends precisely on whether crossing a state boundary makes a difference for processes of capitalist accumulation. But this answer merely returns us to the initial question: What is meant by an *international* division of labor, and what are the political processes that serve both to integrate and to separate global linkages in production, consumption, and exchange? If we look closely at some answers, the meaning and significance of the international division of labor is surprisingly narrow. Once again, my chosen spokespersons for most of this literature, Frobel, Heinrichs, and Kreye (1978), offer a clear response:

> It can be seen that the old or "classical" international division of labor, by which the underdeveloped countries were on the whole incorporated into the capitalist world economy as mere raw materials suppliers, no longer exists. The underdeveloped countries are increasingly chosen as sites for manufacturing industries producing goods that are competitive in the world market. (p. 845)

Such a contrast, however, depends entirely on only one specific type of division of labor, specialization of product within nation states. Functional specialization by states within the world economy is clearly not an unimportant concern, nor are the following remarks meant to reduce its significance. However, change in the location of product specializations does not necessarily require a transformation of the processes and relationships that constitute either the global division of labor or the interstate system (Bach, 1980a).

To pursue this issue one step further, but only briefly: the primary problem is that in most theoretical discussions we are not told what is being divided, by whom, or for what reason. Instead, we are presented with a wide range of detailed examples from which a general tendency is deduced. These examples, however, by no means illustrate similar economic processes. In addition, the emphasis on an international division of labor fails to differentiate economic relationships by the political forces that "separate" them, and to distinguish among relationships contained within the borders, as opposed to those that cross. For in the available examples we can also find a variety of political processes that operate differentially on both production and exchange activities.

The goal must be to identify a full range of types of divisions of labor, the transformations in each, and especially for our thoughts on labor migrations, the consequences of each for differentiating among types of market exchanges. For example, Adam Smith's classical division of labor, involving the contrast between the isolated producer and "modern" industry, refers to at least two very different economic processes (Bucher, 1968). The one implied previously between the new international division of labor and Smith's classical pattern is the image of specialization. This specialization refers to the separation of the whole production process into various departments or new trades, each of which performs an independent economic step, and each change in ownership of the product involves a change for profits. This "divisioning of production" provides a basis for exchange in which potential buyers and sellers, because of the initial independent control of various producers over their product, face each other in a competitive relationship as autonomous entities. The "invisible hand" has the opportunity to rise up through these divisions among producers to reveal itself on the market. To the extent that these separated producers and buyers and sellers are identified with states, then the international division of labor refers to specialization of a country in a particular trade or product. However, to restate the earlier claim now more fully, a change in specialized trades or products does not necessarily alter the relationship among producers or transform the mechanisms of market exchange.

A very different type of division of labor contained in Smith's examples is one frequently found in contemporary empirical studies. It refers to the breaking up of a department of production (which may be the result of a former division of production—the first example) into simple dependent labor elements, a subdivisioning of labor. In this type, the manufactured "product" does not constitute a completed process. The raw materials used are often already well advanced toward completion, and several transformative stages are required subsequently to reach a marketable product. This division results not in a series of new trades or product specialization but in a chain of dependent employments. Successful utilization of these employments requires the existence of a supply of workers held together by one employer. As a result, the product passes through many hands before completion but undergoes no change in ownership. Exchange of various materials between different points in the production process is not subject to the "regulating" mechanisms of competition among separated producers or buyers and sellers but rather may be treated as "internal distributions." Importantly, political divisioning of these relationships would entail much more direct involvement in the activities of labor and capital than in the first case.

These are simply two of the forms of division of labor in which states may become intertwined. Further discussion requires much more space than is available here. The points to be made here are simply the implications of such distinctions among types of division of labor for how we talk about an international labor force, a world market for labor, and, especially, the political divisioning and organization of commodity and labor exchanges. For example, emphasis on the division of production between states treats the political conditions in specific areas as just another characteristic of competing producers. A world market for industrial sites or even a "world market for labor" poses producers and buyers and sellers at odds in a competitive market where bidding occurs in terms of various prices: commodity prices, labor prices (wages), political prices (taxes, subsidies for capital). The characteristics of different locations or political units are all that is of interest.

A focus on subdivisioning of labor shifts the nature of analytical concerns. Establishing the relationships of state activities to different "places" within the division of labor puts political activities at the top of the list of concerns. What "piece" of the production process the state is involved in often determines the nature of the contending groups, the structural basis of public debates, the direct pressures on work place regulations, and the opportunities and constraints on capital. More importantly here, a primary question becomes how the various subdivided tasks and exchanges between them are organized, not only by single entrepreneurs but by a set of relationships between states (the interstate system), or, differentially, within a single state. In this way, for example, we may take seriously the differences (if they exist) among tasks divided between Mexico and the United States as opposed to New York and New Jersey. And from this vantage point we might better contemplate alternative political futures to the current restructuring of the division of labor.

Interstate Organization

If it is legitimate to press for clarification of what is new about the global division of labor, it must be equally appropriate to ask about the novelty of the interstate system. The response is that, while it may not be new in world historical terms, the current organization of the interstate system is vastly different from its pattern of the last 30 or 40 years. Perhaps more so than economic changes, the late 1960s to early 1970s marks a new period of *international* division of labor in which "no political alternative to the economic 'internationalism' of core capital has emerged as a force in world politics so far" (Arrighi, 1982, p. 108).

After World War II, U.S. dominion over the interstate system provided the organizational political framework that fostered the transnational expansion of capital, the spread of Fordism and Taylorism, and the reconstruction of the unity of the world market (Arrighi, 1982, p. 57). The United States accomplished this, working both regionally and domestically, by providing the political, ideological, and when necessary, military force to create and maintain the following relationships: the sustained pacification of relations among capitalist states, especially within the Western Hemisphere; largely completed decolonization by the late 1960s, and enforced elimination or reduction of quantitative restrictions on trade. Immigration policies and practices, as we shall see, were part of these relationships.

By the mid-1960s, U.S. hegemony reigned virtually unchallenged globally and especially within the hemisphere. Cuba represents an obvious challenge in the early 1960s, but even in this case the early reactions of the U.S. state were predicated on its unsurpassed control and support in the region. The crisis of interstate relations begins with the world monetary crisis in 1968, the U.S. defeat in Vietnam, culminating in 1975, and within the United States, the virtual collapse of the New Deal, postwar compromise between capital and organized labor. The latter effectively unleased an unremitting offensive by capital against both organized labor and the social wage of the U.S. working class in general. The international crises precipitated a decline in U.S. regional influence that unlocked supranational, marketlike forces that seemed autonomous of and in domination of state interests and policies (Arrighi, 1982, p. 61). The best example is the degree to which inflation became a generalized condition, forcing states everywhere to discipline their respective working classes and appearing as an autonomous and world dominant force.

The regional state system and the economy increasingly exhibited a chaotic character. Without a clearly enforceable political and institutional framework, relationships among underdeveloped states grew unruly. Core capital, in turn, was left to dominate the regional market. U.S. capital, however, was increasingly challenged by the unrestrained penetration of Japanese, German, and other nonregional capital. Intercapitalist competition intensified, and in classic style, market mechanisms led to seemingly *uncontrollable anarchic relationships* between states and among social relations in general. The unleashing of large-scale migrations and contradictory attempts by states to regulate them are two of the more evident indications of this unruliness.

On the whole in the 1970s, and thus far in the 1980s, the capacity of states to influence developmental processes in general has declined. What remains, however, is not a complete surrender to capital flows or market regulated exchange. There remains a continuous but rough and sputtering of attempts to regain political control. In the last years, especially under the auspices of the Reagan administration, these attempts have been aimed at accomplishing two of the most fundamental characteristics of hegemony: to establish a monopoly over the use of violence, and to gain disciplinary control over wage workers. In both instances, the scope of such attempts has been regional as well as domestic.

U.S. immigration policy and practice has been battered endlessly by these political and economic forces. Most directly, it has been transformed by the collapse of the New Deal political peace between capital and labor and has become part of the generalized attack on the social wage. Despite his usual myopia, David Stockman, director of the Office of Management and Budget, has identified with uncanny clarity both the nature of the current political battle over immigration reform and the underlying structural chaos that has prevented its resolution.

> This was the core of his [Stockman's] complaint against the modern liberalism launched by Franklin Roosevelt's New Deal. He did not quarrel with the need for basic social welfare programs . . . ; he agreed that the government must regulate private enterprise to protect general health and safety. *But liberal politics in the later stages had lost the ability to judge claims, and so yielded to them all,* creating what he describes as "constituency-based choice-making," *which could no longer address larger national interests.* (Greider, 1981)

Following a climactic decade of reform in the 1960s, U.S. immigration policy, which had been successfully reshaped by New Deal liberalism to overcome the most blatant forms of racism, became increasingly unable to control the diverse global flows centered on the United States. With the exhaustion of the push for fundamental change in the immigration law, subsequent debate foundered as the Democratic party lost its ability to evaluate competing claims and so tried to satisfy them all. Through successive legislative battles, select commissions, and changes in administrations, the primary difficulty has been the absence of sufficient political power on any side of the immigration issue to impose its view on the others and to forge an outcome.

The political crisis signaled by this collapse of New Deal liberalism, however, has not been the only influence on immigration policies. For between the mid-1960s and the present, the crisis of hegemony in the region has rendered the United States incapable of effectively imposing changes in immigration policy unilaterally. And immigration policy has become a major part of the framework—woefully inadequately—for handling the consequences of direct challenge to U.S. hegemony. From Cuba and Southeast Asia, the flow of refugees has announced as much the decline of the U.S.-managed political-institutional framework in the world as have the revolutionary changes in each country.

POLITICAL FRAMEWORKS

Structuring Labor Flows

Formation of an institutional framework for international migrations began long before the emergence of the United States as the hegemonic power after 1945. Following a long-term, secular trend initiated in the nineteenth century, the interstate system has increased its degree of control and management of all world economic forces. States' control over the exit and entry of people has reached a particularly high degree, turning away from classically "liberal" policies of free trade toward restrictive laws and practices (Zolberg, 1978, p. 251). The effects of this long-term movement have included not only the mobilization of labor into market relations worldwide but an increasing politicalization of population exchanges for both interstate relations and national struggles.

As a shorter-term segment of this secular movement, the reform of U.S. immigration policies throughout the post-World War II period involved three phases of interstate and domestic class relations. First, there was the drive to construct an immigration policy compatible with the reunification of the world market following the temporary disruptions of two world wars. The goal was to maintain unevenly developed regional labor supplies and to incorporate them progressively into a common, stable framework that would produce a relatively open labor market. Included was the resettlement of vast numbers of displaced persons, which served as the forerunner of the current refugee policy.

A second phase consists of the culmination of postwar economic and political expansionism in the region and the climax to working-class and minority struggles within the United States during the 1960s. It was also in the late 1960s, however, that signs of the beginning crisis appeared, especially among interstate relations.

Third, the 1970s and 1980s play out the specific terms of institutional collapse, political crises, and economic transformation. It is a period of contradictory, highly charged demands on state regulation. Virtual chaos in the debates and battles over immigration policies fully express this confusion, and only in the 1980s are there signs of potential political clarification.

An interstate framework for integrating disparate pockets of regional labor supplies into developing market networks in the United States was already evident in the early decades of this century. In the Southwest, the expansion of railroads into Mexico and their subsequent reorganization after 1905 combined with the rapid development of commercial agriculture to forge U.S.-centered, binational networks of accumulation (Bach, 1978a). Mexican migrant workers were incorporated into sectors of U.S. capital closely tied not only to the national economy but, in many cases, to world commodity markets (e.g. cotton in Texas). Their participation in these networks, however, was selective, in terms of their place both within the technical and social division of labor and within political divisions. As low-wage workers, few Mexicans were able or allowed to make demands on agricultural land as potential owners, and many circulated seasonally across the border. Already, the special character of Mexican labor—its political separation between Mexico and the United States—was recognized and manipulated by U.S.-based growers and manufacturers (Bach, 1978a).

In this early period, vast differences among regional labor markets *within* the United States created problems for a unified approach to the state management of labor flows. The Immigration Act of 1917, for example, while responding to the restrictionist pressures of the Northeast, threatened to impede the expansion of the use of Mexican workers in labor markets of the Southwest. Fearing restrictions on *their* labor supply, Southwest growers sought exemption from the national rules. The secretary of labor subsequently waived the literacy test, the head tax, and the contract labor clause for Mexican workers, retaining only the right to review regulations for future admission of these workers.

World War I provided a much clearer political context through which the state could manage the developing labor exchanges through national laws and institutions. During this period, for example, President Wilson used the Food Administration and the U.S. Employment Service as both employers and contractors for Mexican workers (Reisler, 1976). Following the war, trade union pressure to restrict the flow also resulted in the extension of the Border Patrol, which to this point had been deployed in the Northeast, to the Southwest border.

The interstate character of this labor exchange subjected it to much broader political concerns (Johnson, 1928). Foreign policy interests, administered directly through the State Department, resulted in an institutional position on immigration policy that would last for most of the century. In this early period, the State Department established its primary concern for the effects of immigration restrictions on "Pan-Americanism." The department's position was that tighter, more selective management of the visa system was preferable to inflexible national quotas, which might threaten regional moves to create a cooperative, open hemispheric political framework.

National restrictions and tighter administration of the visa system combined with expanding and intensifying labor market linkages to create the most characteristic feature of the Mexico-U.S. migratory system, the "illegal" status of large portions of its workers. For both capital and labor, the pressures of competition and wage dependence drove each to draw upon informal, unregulated social networks to achieve the necessary market exchanges. Southwest growers quickly realized the advantages of this illegal status and helped create the incentives and direct social linkages that have served to reproduce this "silent flow" for several decades.[4]

Similar but paradoxical patterns of *regional* market formation and integration were also developing in this early period in Puerto Rico. Terms of labor exchange created for Mexican workers through direct binational regulation and subsequent illegal responses were established for Puerto Rican workers through the open granting of citizenship. As in Mexico, capital expansion and labor import ("internationalization" in the post-War period) brought Puerto Rican workers increasingly into contact and dependence on U.S.-based capital. U.S. citizenship, granted in 1917, established de facto their access to U.S. labor markets (Bonilla and Campos, 1981). But unlike the series of regulatory efforts and contradictory pressures created on the Southwest border, the Puerto Rican-U.S. labor market allowed the movement of workers to go virtually unchallenged. In this latter sense, the Puerto Rican flow became depoliticized and unexceptional. While the relative "strength" of the Mexican state forced an *international* dimension onto the incorporation of Mexican workers in the United States, the cumulative consequences of U.S. military occupation, the Forakker Act of 1900, and the Jones Act removed the state from direct involvement in maintaining matches between workers and employers and allowed both capital and labor to move "freely" between the island and the mainland. Still, in both the Mexican and Puerto Rican cases, the state was equally decisive in establishing, albeit in profoundly different ways, the parameters of the market (Bonilla and Campos, 1981).

The early political distinctions have had important consequences for the long-term labor market conditions of Mexican and Puerto Rican workers and communities *inside* the United States.[5] Although both groups were incorporated as a low-wage labor supply and would develop in relation to similar sectors of capital, the divergent political frameworks set very different conditions on each group. Mexican workers have been integrated under highly politicized conditions, where legal status has persistently divided and separated the interests of different sectors of the U.S.-settled community and, on occasion, has been used to weaken the claims of the Chicano working class. "Repatriations" during the Depression and Operation Wetback, for example, helped to reinforce the persecuted minority status of the Chicano population. Puerto Rican workers, on the other hand, precisely because of their citizenship status, have been rendered virtually politically "indistinguishable" from other sectors of the working class in the United States. They have been incorporated over time in a position similar to the black working class in the United States. As a result, Puerto Rican workers have had little access to state recognition and thus have had little leverage to force improvements in their labor market conditions. This difference helps to explain why the Puerto Rican working class in the United States is relatively worse off than other subordinate "Hispanics" sectors of the U.S. working class.

The geographically limited, developing labor markets before 1945 exploded during postwar recovery, unleashing workers from formerly untapped reservoir onto existing routes of exchange. In both Puerto Rico and Mexico, impressive industrialization programs set agricultural workers and redundant urban laborers adrift economically and geographically. A substantial shift occurred in the residential patterns of both former and new immigrants. In the 1950s, the concentration of the Puerto Rican population on the mainland living in New York City decreased. New urban concentrations included Philadelphia, Miami, Chicago-Gary, northeast New Jersey, and Bridgeport, Connecticut (Hernández-Álvarez, 1968). Mexican immigrants joined the concurrent redistribution of Chicanos into the cities of the Southwest, as well as onto wider circuits destined for the Midwest, Chicago, and even the Northeast. The characteristic feature of both flows, however, was the degree of relative concentration within ever wider dispersion. This pattern of community formation, small pockets or "colonies" inside broad geographical distributions, became a peculiar feature of these working-class labor migrations and contributed to their subordinate status in the U.S economy (Portes and Bach, forthcoming).

As strong as the forces of redistribution were, however, labor exchange in the postwar period was still not fully integrated into a "unified" or "world labor market." Instead, the connections between locations in Mexico and Puerto Rico and the United States and between workers and employers were still sufficiently weak to require recruitment efforts and government subsidies. In an admittedly rough manner, the character of progressive integration of both Puerto Rican and Mexican-U.S. labor markets can be traced trough the following aggregate statistics.

At first glance, net migration of Puerto Ricans between the island and the mainland appears subject over the entire postwar period to full market integration. From 1947 to 1973, for instance, the annual net flow corresponds to changes in relative wage rates (Maldonado, 1976). Following the conventional logic suggested by Bukharin, evidence of price discipline—and thus integrated market relations—is given by similar costs of the same commodity at different locations.[6] Distribution of commodities would be sensitive to differential prices ("wage rates") at various locations.

A more careful look, however, shows that price sensitivity is established only relatively late in the postwar period, and fully in accord with the timing of the increased strength of market forces generally. Table 1 presents the results of the regression of annual net migration (numbers of people) from Puerto Rico to the United States on a selected group of economic characteristics of both places (Maldonado, 1976). Figures for the United States include only the four largest concentrations of Puerto Ricans: New York, New Jersey, Connecticut, and Illinois. The independent variables measure relative economic status, including the ratio of the annual unemployment rate in Puerto Rico to the four states, the ratio of average hourly manufacturing wage rates, and the ratio of average monthly welfare payments.

TABLE 1
Regression of Net Migration Between Puerto Rico and the Mainland on Economic and Socioeconomic Characteristics

Variables	1947-1973		1947-1967	
	b (beta)	t-value	b (beta)	t-value
Unemployment	2.183 (.52)	3.50*	2.295 (.80)	6.28*
Income	-15.597 (-.53)	-2.94*	-7.616 (-.30)	-2.06
Welfare	15.050 (.22)	1.39	22.533 (.26)	1.97
Constant	.969		-3.118	
R^2	.57		.81	

Source: Adapted from Maldonado, 1976, table 2, p. 10.
* Significant at .05 level.

The figures show that for the entire 1947-1973 period, the unemployment ratio and relative manufacturing wages are equally important in predicting yearly migration rates: betas equal .52 and -.53, respectively. Differential welfare payments appear to have no effect on this population exchange. The same figures, however, for the 1947-1967 period show that in these earlier years only differences in the unemployment levels correspond to the net distribution of the population. This variable alone explains 81 percent of the variation in net migration, a considerable increase over the 57 percent explained over the longer period.

Distributive mechanisms in the immediate postwar period were even less affected by differential prices. Between 1947 and 1958, yearly net migration corresponded to three factors: the unemployment differences between the island and the U.S., the price of transportation relative to average income, and the size of the Puerto Rican population already settled on the mainland (Fleisher, 1963). When these regression results are placed together, a relatively clear picture of the *development* of the market begins to emerge.

Following the war, transportation costs from the island were relatively cheap as a result of U.S. subsidies to the airline industry, specifically to facilitate the movement of Puerto Rican workers. These fares also aided the forging or maintaining of social networks to the existing Puerto Rican community already in the U.S. But the significance of the unemployment ratios throughout the entire period demonstrates the primary contribution of the restructuring of the Puerto Rican economy in producing the outmigration. Throughout this period, U.S. unemployment ratios remain low and relatively stable. In this context, the positive coefficient for the unemployment variables in table 1 suggests that each weakening in the employment situation on the island corresponds to an increase in net migration. The incorporation of Puerto Rican workers into the United States resulted apparently from a sustained need to find jobs not provided by the island economy. The regulating effects of prices became evident only after 1967, and by then they signaled much more than simply the full integration of market processes.

A comparable analysis of the Mexican flow offers several striking parallels to the Puerto Rican figures. Although there are serious technical problems with the Mexican figures, there is general evidence that throughout the postwar period the Mexican flow has been sensitive to the relative price of labor power at different locations on both sides of the border (Reynolds, 1981). Yet, once again, a closer view shows that wages distributed workers in only a very selective manner, depending on both the types of jobs and, importantly, the migrants' legal (political) status.

Table 2 presents a roughly comparable multivariate analyses of migration rates from Mexico between 1948 and 1975 (Jenkins, 1978). Jenkins concludes from these figures that the Mexican labor flow is generally unresponsive to conventional market parameters. Rather, a more consistent thesis is that Mexican workers are used as a "social control" mechanism, providing a specific type of labor for particular jobs and contributing to an important political purpose in disciplining the working class. Specifically, these statistics raise three points of special interest. First, as with Puerto Rican workers, pressures on availability of jobs comprised the primary distributive mechanisms throughout the postwar period. Second, specific government-sponsored recruitment efforts and labor market protections (minimum wage) significantly influenced the flow. Finally, the political division of the labor supply—legal immigrants, citizens, illegal immigrants, or braceros—created very different types of exchanges in the market.

The obvious point is that the regional "labor market" was not as unified throughout most of the postwar period as many assume. Most importantly, there are clear—if broad—signs that the formation and reproduction of these labor exchanges fundamentally required the active participation of the state. A quick listing of the institutional elements of the Mexican flow is sufficient to underscore the point, including the Bracero Program, commuter status, Border Industrialization Program, selective amnesties and Operation Wetback.

Of course, the political frameworks extend far more deeply into economic relations integrating Mexico and the U.S. And no single program more clearly demonstrates the depth of such as Operation Bootstrap, the postwar program for industrial expansion in Puerto Rico. Its explicit strategy of attracting

TABLE 2
Regression of Migration Rate from Mexico on Selected Economic Characteristics
(standardized partial Rs)

Variables	Predicted Direction for Labor Supplement	Legal Mexican Immigrants	Illegal Mexican Immigrants	Braceros
Employment of farm workers				
Regular	+	-.03	-.01	+.09
Seasonal	+	-.09	-.25	+.32
Agricultural wages	+	-.08	-.16	-.46
Federal minimum wages	+	-.01	+.13	-.25
Unemployment rate				
Aggregate	-	+.18	+.22	+.23
Farm workers	-	+.21	+.37	+.30
Service occupations	-	+.08	+.12	+.10
Nonfarm laborers	-	+.25	+.45	+.51
Capital investments in agriculture	-	+.03	+.23	+.25

Source: Adapted from Jenkins, 1978, table 2, p. 523.

capital to the island and exporting workers highlights more sharply than any detailed analysis of commodity circuits the interconnections between political control and reproduction of labor supplies. Indeed, the program, because it was conceived and developed as a direct tie to the New Deal, Democratic administration in Washington, establishes the most direct connection between the regional institutional framework and the postwar political agenda in the United States.

Transforming Labor Flows

This section reviews the political battles of the 1960s over immigration reform, specifically as part of the crucial connection between New Deal-type social welfare policy and immigration policy and practice. Like the economic forces analyzed above, these broad political connections were initially forged before World War II, then developed and strengthened following 1945. In the earlier period, selective restrictions on immigrants started with private charitable groups and local government as they moved to deport immigrants in order to ameliorate the worst conditions of native-born labor during deep and recurrent recessions. Under the "liberal agenda" of the New Deal, the connection between social welfare and immigration policy was consolidated and fully institutionalized following post-Depression recovery (Bach, 1978a). During periods of increasing unemployment and social disorder, the presence of foreign labor became highly visible. Their presence was linked causally with worsened economic conditions, and the state intervened to restrict the flow—at least selectively and temporarily. In turn, the state expanded general social welfare programs and benefits to the native population.

This strategy developed in direct relationship to the Mexican flow. It was also applied to the Puerto Rican population, but only ambivalently. Puerto Ricans were treated in one sense as foreign laborers because of the velocity of the circular flow between the island and the mainland. Consequently, part of the pressure for immigration restrictions applied to them. Puerto Ricans' citizen status, however, meant they were also directly connected to the expansion of social welfare programs. As a result, during a period of economic crisis, the *combination* of being migrants and a welfare-linked population rendered Puerto Ricans on the mainland a special target for groups seeking someone to blame for their troubles.

The immigration reforms of the early 1960s were linked to the so-called Great Society "social welfare explosions," both through broad political alignments nationally and in direct, practical, legislative debates. Mechanization and labor displacement in rural areas combined with large-scale migration to the cities to provide a political base for opposition to widespread poverty. These conditions in themselves were inadequate, however, to force policy reforms, especially those related to immigration. Instead, the combination of the civil rights movement, which highlighted the blatant racially discriminatory nature of many federal laws, and organized labor's direct assault on the "imported colonialism" of the state-regulated Bracero Program tied the civil rights movement to the migration issue.

At least three administrations had tried to terminate the Bracero Program before its demise in 1963-64. Success at this time was due primarily to a connection with civil rights legislation. In fact, debate on Public Law 78, which authorized the Bracero Program, was instrumental to the passage of the Civil Rights Act of 1964 (Bach, 1978b). As the Civil Rights Act moved through Congress with widespread political support, Southern legislators who opposed its passage were caught in a fundamental legislative conflict. The civil rights opponents argued that any federal involvement enforcing racial integration of public accommodations represented a fundamental change in the historical relationship between federal and state governments. They were undermined, however, by their own earlier support of a public accommodations provision in article 8 of Public Law 78. This article was incorporated in the law *because of the continuous efforts of the Mexican government* to provide protection of its citizens while working abroad. The article allowed the U.S. federal government to intervene directly to prevent the employment of braceros in communities that barred Mexicans from public facilities. The law had been enforced on several occasions in south Texas by the federal Department of Labor. In supporting Public Law 78, therefore, these Southern legislators had voted a clear, legal precedent to the Civil Rights Act.

Similar connections to civil rights legislation fueled the political debates leading up to the Immigration and Nationality Act of 1965. This act represented the fulfillment of a long series of battles to overcome the inherent racism in the national origin quota provisions of existing laws. The return was successful in 1965 primarily because of its connection to the broader attacks on legal discrimination. Attorney General Robert Kennedy indicated as much when he testified before Congress that "the most remarkable thing is that we did not insist on the reforms long ago" (cited in Bach, 1978b). And the *Washington Post* editorialized: "Once the civil rights bill is enacted into law, immigration policy should be high on the congressional agenda. Discrimination on grounds of race and origin is as un-American at the country's gates as it is inside them" (cited in Bach, 1978b).

In 1964 the U.S. ended the Bracero Program as a generalized labor import program and substituted reliance on the more selective, defensible "H-2 system." The 1965 law replaced national origin quotas with family reunion and highly specialized priority system for nationally needed skilled workers. It also pressed for numerical quotas which were presumably less biased, specifically ending restrictions against Asians. Finally, in an often overlooked policy turn in 1966, the United States adopted the 1951 United Nations definition of a refugee as a person fleeing general persecution, which in law at least ended the Walter-McCarran Act definition of a refugee as a person fleeing communism.

The 1960s reforms were enacted primarily in response to these domestic concerns. But they could only have been achieved within a stable regional framework where U.S. interests dominates. The unilateral nature of these reforms is indicated, for example, by the following briefing Secretary of State Dean Rusk gave President Johnson prior to the President's visit with Mexican President López Mateos:

> The Mexican Government is privately seriously disturbed about the termination of this program [the Bracero Program]. The program has been of substantial economic and political benefit [to Mexico]. Congressional opposition is strong and *you should not commit yourself to continue the program.* Assure the Mexican

President that you understand the problem—your own war on poverty—and that you will do what can be done to help. (Emphasis in original) (cited in Bach, 1980b)

The Mexican government was actually given few options: they hoped for AID funding to help with the anticipated employment consequences but were offered a "food-for-work" program to be financed through a private foundation.

Debate on the 1965 amendments to the Immigration and Nationality Act received greater foreign policy attention. As noted previously, there was explicit recognition as early as the 1920s that Western Hemisphere quotas, which were part of the 1965 changes, might threaten "Pan-Americanism." The State Department pressed "to recognize the common bond uniting the Americas by exempting from any quota restrictions those immigrants who were born in independent countries of the Western Hemisphere" (LBJ Papers, 1965). In a White House memo of May 8, 1965, a presidential aide wrote, "According to Secretary Rusk, if we go along [with attempts to impose Western Hemisphere quotas] we will vex and dumbfound our Latin American friends, who will now be sure we are in final retreat from Pan-Americanism" (LBJ Papers, 1965).

The specific international context of these objections is instructive. Abba Schwartz, administrator of the Bureau of Security and Consular Affairs, described the situation for the secretary of state and the attorney general as of May 20, 1965, as follows: "That imposition of an over-all ceiling [on immigration] at this time would confound our problems with our Latin American neighbors, particularly in view of the Dominican situation and forthcoming Inter-American conference" (LBJ Papers, 1965). This same theme was reflected in one of the two options White House staff prepared for President Johnson's selection: "We should determine whether it is in our best interests in Latin America —*at this time*— to forego immediate passage of the Immigration bill. Let us wait until Santo Domingo is behind us and look again" (LBJ Papers, 1965).

Despite these and other concerns, the drive to pass the amendments to the Immigration and Nationality Act won support from the State Department. "Since the end of World War II," Secretary Rusk testified to the House Judiciary Committee, "the United States has been placed in the role of critical leadership in a troubled and constantly changing world. We are concerned to see that our immigration laws reflect our real character and objectives" (LBJ Papers, 1965). The State Department argued that the racial ancestry, or national origins, feature of the existing law was indefensible from a foreign policy point of view, since it represented overt statutory discrimination against more than one-half of the world's population.

The complex nature of the 1960s reforms reflected the tensions inherent in a political issue that rested on the interface of interstate and domestic relations. The liberal agenda to end discrimination at home merged nicely with continuing attempts to open the world to U.S. political and ideological leadership. But conflict lay submerged not far below the surface of regional control, making it necessary to object to Western Hemispheric quotas, to delay action in the context of military intervention in the Dominican Republic, and, after unilateral passage of the laws, to move administratively in other policy areas to cushion the regional consequences. For example, following these reforms, attempts to change the commuter work traffic between Mexico and the United States rose again as a point of contention between the governments. In a memo prepared for Walt Rostow in the White House, foreign policy again was highlighted:

> In our view, precipitous action now to limit in any way the long established practice of admitting Mexican "commuter" workers would seriously disrupt the economic and social life of the border communities, [and] negate President Johnson's policy of increasingly cordial relations with Mexico.... Mexico already feels that recent U.S. actions (termination of the Migrant Labor Agreement, lower cotton prices, limitations on duty-free goods) have seriously damaged its economy. Any new blow could put serious strains on our relations (LBJ Papers, 1965).

CHALLENGE TO EXISTING POLITICAL FRAMEWORKS

Structuring Refugee Flows

In the midst of political battles and administrative maneuvers over legal immigration and labor import programs, the first serious, successful challenge to U.S. hegemony in the region thrust itself into the practice of immigration policy. But rather than a major, immediate crisis for that policy, refugees from the Cuban Revolution were received fully within the same political framework that had guided other immigration matters. The combination of interests in regional stability (domination) and a domestic immigration policy well connected to social welfare policies yielded a series of militaristic actions in the early 1960s and the formation of a novel domestic program for refugee resettlement.

It is important to situate the Cuban Revolution in its obvious but critical context: it was both a challenge to U.S. regional dominion and an attack on the structure of capitalist accumulation protected and promoted by this framework. The social character of the refugees from each phase of the revolution reflected the nature of this challenge to interstate relations as much as it did explicit disaffection from the revolution. Capitalist development and unchallenged political links to the United States had shaped a social division of labor within Cuba (Acosta and Hardoy, 1973) that resembled similar structures in Mexico, in Puerto Rico, and throughout the region. The United States needed to defend these social relationships as much as it did the specific binational political arrangements.

Those who left Cuba in the first years after the revolution have been described many times. They were landowners, landlords, and professionals.

Of the approximately 280,000 who left between 1959 and 1962, 94 percent were white, the majority were middle-aged, and most were well educated. Even from these earliest days, however, the primary social characteristic of the refugees was their class heterogeneity. The reason was that political and institutional connections to the United States had penetrated the full depth of the social division of labor in Havana. Not only were owners dependent on U.S. dominion, but professionals, civil servants, and organized workers—many of whom were employed by U.S. firms—looked northward for ideological direction and consumption expectations.

The U.S. political reaction in the early years was full of the belligerence one would expect from a hegemonic power. Fiasco at the Bay of Pigs included, the early phase of the radical challenge to Cuba-U.S. relations involved a sustained and largely successful (at the time) attempt to isolate Cuba within the region. In 1962, the Cuban Missile Crisis established the strength of the U.S. position. The successful resolution of the sudden and dramatic boatlift from the port of Camarioca in 1965 to south Florida resulted from this clear division of political power. Success from the U.S. point of view meant the ability to forge a political and institutional solution to the chaos. President Johnson in 1965 was able to arrange an orderly departure program, which for the United States saved its immigration policy from a major crisis. Creation of an "aerial bridge," in addition to winning ground on the regional ideological battlefield, ensured institutionally that the United States had control over who emigrated.

Change in the composition of the refugee flow during the years of the aerial bridge (1965-1973) reflected a transition in the focus of revolutionary reforms in Cuba. As the Cuban government moved in 1968 to socialize most of the remaining sectors of the private economy, smaller commercial sectors and civil servants were among the largest groups affected by these moves. As a result, most of the refugees were still well educated, occupationally skilled, and white. This second wave remained a group directly linked to the undermining of a capitalist social division of labor and thus the lingering political relations to the United States. Welcoming these refugees with open arms was reinforcing the defense of the political framework still intact elsewhere in the region.

The ideological and political significance of a Cuban refugee resettlement effort in Miami, in specific programmatic terms, resulted from the same link between immigration and social welfare policies that governed the resettlement of Mexican and Puerto Ricans. It was not simply that Cuban refugees were more important to the United States that other immigrants. Rather, they arrived initially under very different conditions, in the 1960s as general social welfare programs were expanding. The Cuban Refugee Program was a novel effort in comparison to a long string of previous refugee resettlement experiences. It involved for the first time a strong, direct federal-level financial effort that included much more than the relatively minor social benefits offered earlier European refugees. Indeed, in the earliest years, a significant policy problem was that, given Florida's dismal record on social welfare benefits to its own population, the federally levied programs available to the Cubans appeared especially advantageous to foreigners at the expense of citizens. The program also helped to create a new distinction among immigrants. The initial incorporation of Cuban refugees as a temporary, welfare-assisted population prevented institutional links from forming that may have developed an interest in this group as a labor supply.

The greatest challenge to U.S. global hegemony, of course, emerged from military defeat in Vietnam. But the major casualty was political and, with it, the interstate framework for defending capitalist accumulation. Like Cuba—and much of Central America today—the formation of a refugee flow in Vietnam in 1975 looked as if it developed spontaneously at the first sight of enemy soldiers in the capital city. Yet more fundamental was the long-term intertwining of economic development and political structure. In Vietnam, the most vicious political weapon—war—brought about what years of only slow capitalist penetration could not: the large-scale proletarianization of the countryside. In the early 1960s, for instance, South Vietnam was 80-85 percent rural. By the early 1970s, although accurate data are virtually impossible to find and all estimates here are conservative, about 40 percent of the population lived in cities of 20,000 or more. This population concentration made South Vietnam the second most urbanized country in Southeast Asia (after Singapore) and more urbanized than many industrialized countries, including Switzerland, Italy, and Canada.

Undoubtedly, the intensification of the war following the intervention of U.S. combat troops in 1965 explains most of the geographical redistribution. Yet, although the immediate cause was all too evident, the social basis of the transformation was widely ignored, and with it the direct links to the subsequent emigrations. Samuel Huntington, writing in the midst of such changes in 1968, came closer than most:

> In an absent-minded way the United States in Viet Nam may well have stumbled upon the answer to "wars of national liberation." The effective response lies neither in the quest for conventional military victory nor in esoteric doctrines and gimmicks of counter-insurgency warfare. It is instead forced draft urbanization and modernization which rapidly brings the country in question out of the phase in which a rural revolutionary movement can hope to generate sufficient strength to come to power (Huntington, 1968, p. 652).

As to an "answer" to wars of national liberation, Huntington was clearly misguided. But as a statement of the crucial links between capitalist social divisions of labor and political organization, his observations could not have been more insightful. Juxtaposed was a set of processes, capitalist development, modernization, urbanization, and political order that uncovers the common structural basis behind the movement of diverse peoples from disconnected locations in the U.S.-dominated world economy to ultimate resettlement in the

United States. Whether in Puerto Rico, Mexico, Cuba, or Vietnam. It was the political framework through which capitalist penetration of agriculture liberated people from the land, pushed them to the cities, and thrust them beyond national borders that linked their origins to a common destination.

Beyond the intrusion of this general point, which I placed here only to move the discussion along more quickly, the story of the progressive incorporation of Southeast Asians into U.S. political networks needs full elaboration. Suffice it here to describe only a few of the complexities that make the comparisons with the Caribbean experiences more convincing.

The political reactions to the conditions of massive proletarianization and urbanization tell a familiar tale. Over one and a half million new urbanites were created by the influx of refugees from the countryside in Vietnam. Many were held in refugee camps or settled in "suburbs," while their immiseration was denied by U.S. military and political officials. Only subsequent Senate hearings from Congressional opponents of the war revealed the extent of this displacement. Some observers, however, found among the newly urbanized people the benefits often acquired by those joining modern, city life:

> In one Saigon slum, Xom Chua, in early 1965 before the American build-up, the people lived at a depressed level, with 33 percent of the adult males unemployed. Eighteen months later, as a result of military escalation, the total unemployed population of the slum had dropped to 5 percent and average incomes had doubled. In several cases urban refugees from the war refused to return to their villages once security was restored because of the higher level of economic well-being which they could attain in the city. The pull of urban prosperity has been secondary but not insignificant factor in attracting people into the city (Huntington, 1968, p. 649).

By the early 1970s, the war had created effectively the same conditions that characterized Havana in the 1950s and Puerto Rico and Mexico for most of the post-World War II period. And clearly, by 1975 a substantial portion of the Vietnamese population had become equally tied to U.S. economic and political (including military) networks for survival. That many benefited from these connections with comparatively greater economic rewards simply indicated the character and incentives built into some of the linkages. The first wave of refugees out of Saigon in 1975 were, not surprisingly, those with the greatest connections to U.S. personnel or institutions. As in Cuba, these ties brought more than just directly threatened capitalists, extending well into the lower ranks of the urban social structure. The chaos that surrounded the fall of Saigon added even more to the heterogeneity of this refugee group. Still, in the first years of the flow, large shares of the adult population were either former soldiers, civil servants, or their dependents (students) (Bach, 1983).

Similar economic conditions and political connections throughout Kampuchea and Laos widened the source of refugees. In the earliest years, however, even in the midst of substantial human crises, U.S. policy was able to regulate some of the flow through direct application of the immigration law.

Direct linkages to U.S. personnel gave priority to refugees wanting to resettle in the United States.

Although these overseas circumstances resembled those in Cuba in the 1960s, the resettlement program in the United States for Southeast Asian refugees was different. Signs were already evident of the growing attack in the 1970s on social welfare programs. The Southeast Asian resettlement program followed the Cuban Program in that direct federal intervention organized and underwrote the relocation tasks. Unlike the Cuban Program, however, there was much more concern about the potential costs, with serious national debate over whether a "front-end loading" strategy—a welfare-training assistance program—or an immediate employment, long-run, private retraining effort was more beneficial. In addition, although efforts were made in the early 1960s to distribute Cuban refugees out of south Florida, most of that effort was simply directed at temporarily easing pressure on Florida officials.[7] For the Southeast Asians, wide dispersion throughout the United States has been, and continues to be, enforced policy. Finally, in the earliest years, the level of political and ideological support for the Southeast Asians was less than the Cubans, since the former were clearly refugees from a lost U.S. war. Only later, when international conditions changed, did this flow become nearly as important to U.S. foreign policy as the Cuban exodus. For these and other reasons the incorporation of the Southeast Asians into the United States has had a much more diversified, even ambivalent effect on their relationship to social welfare programs and, especially on their status in the labor market.

Transforming Refugee Flows

Both the Cuban and Southeast Asian refugee flows have undergone major realignments in the economic and political forces driving them. Correspondingly, the resettlement programs for each have changed. While there is an important link between the changes in the origin and subsequent policies at place of destination, each program has been influenced by independent changes in the interstate or domestic framework. Changes in the origins of the refugee flow, and the interstate framework to regulate them, have consisted primarily in the playing out of the decline of U.S. hegemony and in the increasing influence of the market over economic and social relationships. Domestic resettlement programs have been overwhelmed, in turn, by the attack on social welfare and the collapse of the liberal agenda. The result appears to be more than general restrictionism. Rather, there is evidence of a progressive *delinking* of the historic relationships between immigration reform and social welfare policies.

The transformations in the Southeast Asian and Cuban flows are sufficiently similar to discuss them together.[8] The similarities between Vietnam and Cuba lie primarily in the sharp increase in each country's economic problems that can be attributed to world market or underlying structural conditions. In the 1970s, both countries suffered several shortages of consumption items, which, coupled with national management mistakes, put extreme pressure on particular sectors of the population. Both governments have criticized their own efforts at rationing, centralized bureaucratic planning, and collectivization. The consequence of these "excesses," in both cases, has been a major split between the organization of forces in the country: on the one hand, social ownership of the means of production and a political regime representative of the working class and peasantry; and on the other hand, unresponsive bureaucratic management.

In Vietnam, the split was manifested in the continuation of the vast differences between the North and the South. The problem of integrating the South into a national economy was, of course, the major task set before the victorious government. Responding to the collapse of the South, however, many Vietnamese in the region hoarded their wealth and especially their gold. Despite repeated efforts and tactical changes, the new government could not gain control over the regional "currency" and thus was unable to influence and reshape the economy. Uncontrolled black markets in the South continued to provide alternative access to goods and services. Apparently, it was so successful that corruption began seeping northward into a population well disciplined by years of wartime austerity. The threat was to a sorely needed level of social discipline and national productivity.

For Cuba, bureaucratic centralization meant that, given increasing pressure from world commodity markets, virtually the only way to increase productivity was through work place discipline administered from the national government. Since work and social life had become so closely intertwined, the national governmnet launched a social campaign against the lack of discipline.

Although Vietnam and Cuba faced very different problems posed by the world economic crisis, both moved toward market-oriented incentives to promote productive efficiency, and as a corrective to excessive bureaucratic control. In both instances, efforts were also made simultaneously to "clean up" the marketplace. This meant gaining control over the black market through direct police measures and by intensifying the ideological pressures on the population to participate in legitimate transactions. In Vietnam, gold hoarding was outlawed, and private, petit owners were harassed (they were the most likely to have gold). In Cuba, those arrested as participants in the black market, as well as those unwilling to cooperate with the intensified social and ideological push, were targeted as social dregs and "scum." Each in their own way created a group of *potential* refugees awaiting the moment and conditions for flight. In each case, however, when the flow came, the refugees resembled economic migrants more than any of those who had left before.

Changes in the interstate framework to cope with these later flows worked in very different ways to create virtually the same outcome: the inability to achieve the political and institutional structure to control and regulate either the post-1978 Vietnamese outflow or the Cuban Mariel boat lift. The crisis of U.S. hegemony was nowhere more clearly revealed than in relations with Cuba in the 1970s. Indeed, the collapse in these relations accounted for the inability of the Carter administration to obtain an orderly departure agreement with Cuba in 1980, especially when compared with the Johnson administration's success in 1965. In 1980, Cuba was in a reasonable position to defy attempts to negotiate and, instead, offered its own terms for a new bilateral framework: return of Guantanamo, normalization of relations, and lifting of the boycott. Unable to accept these terms, and unwilling to impose a solution militarily, the Carter administration allowed U.S. refugee policy to bear the brunt of the subsequent chaos.

Reeling from political and military defeat in Vietnam, Laos, and Cambodia, U.S. strategy in this region stumbled for a few years. Although the ideological battle against Vietnam continued (Chomsky and Herman, 1979), there was little aggressive action attempting to link the refugee flow to restructuring regional relations. This was one reason why the United States was in such a poor position to reap the easy harvest of international opinion when the Khmer Rouge atrocities were finally discovered. Instead, a transformed U.S. response came only in 1979, and then reluctantly, when the celebrated saga of the "boat people" splashed across the international media. By then, the ASEAN countries, who had now reorganized under a novel militarization pact, demanded help from the United States in relieving the burden of the continuing refugee flow. With much fanfare, the Carter administration took the international lead in the summer of 1979, offering to resettle 14,000 Southeast Asians a month in the United States.

Ironically, this regional posture soon came into conflict with the underlying and increasing economic pressures inside Vietnam that fed the refugee outflow. In talking before the Senate in 1981, one observer noted that "many Lao and Vietnamese probably would not meet a strict interpretation of the term refugee as defined in U.S. and international law" (Suhrke, 1981, p. 1). "If a de facto migration process is treated as a refugee movement," she continued, "the integrity of the refugee program based on the 1980 Refugee Act could be undermined. Preferential treatment of Indochinese as compared to other nationals seeking to escape generalized conditions of insecurity or oppression could have a similar effect" (Suhrke, 1981, p. 1).

Domestic resettlement efforts for the later waves of both Cubans and Southeast Asians have had to contend with stiff pressures opposed to the use of social welfare programs to assist their incorporation into the U.S. labor market. Deeply rooted in the language and intent of the Refugee Act of 1980 was the expectation that refugees were to become "self-sufficient" as quickly as possible. Since 1980, the aim of the Reagan administration has been to separate refugee resettlement and government assistance programs. The goal is to return resettlement to the "private sector," where voluntary agencies and church groups will bear the costs and responsibilities for refugees' immediate futures.

Combined with these domestic reforms, the current administration has pushed to clarify the confused dimensions of refugee flows in the Caribbean and Central America. By administrative fiat, Haitians have been declared economic migrants and Salvadorans refused refugee status. Both moves clearly signal to the states in the Caribbean the kind of political and military framework the present U.S. administration would like to reestablish, if it could.

CURRENT REFORMS

The above changes in refugee policies are, of course, only part of a broader attempt to reorganize U.S. immigration practice. And the major piece of legislation currently under debate, the Simpson-Mazzoli bill, is also only the most public expression of those attempts. More fundamental restructuring has already begun, with little public debate and, more importantly, little serious opposition. For example, in 1980, in the middle of an amendment to social welfare legislation, *legal* immigrants were effectively stripped of their access to transfer programs. The new law, which is now widely enforced, requires that the income of legal sponsors of immigrants be used to calculate the eligibility of the newcomer for Social Security Income (SSI) and Aid for Families with Dependent Children (AFDC) for the first three years of residence in the United States.[9] This change seems entirely consistent with the tightened eligibility criteria for all persons. Yet this policy represents an important conceptual innovation in the immigration law. Immigrants now carry with them for three years in the United States a differential claim to social protection from the state, a separate status outside those directly related to political rights (e.g., voting).

Examples of increasing restrictionism are widely available and easily documented. What is not clear, however, is how the various political battles will turn out: whether, for example, immigration restrictions will be sufficient to pacify organized labor now that it is unlikely that there will be complementary expansion of social welfare programs. In addition, there is little evidence that, in spite of the Reagan administration's militaristic gestures, political control of the region is being reestablished. Under ever tightening market pressures, Puerto Rican migration accelerates, and the crisis of the Mexican peso drives thousands across the Southwest border for work. Restrictionism at home is no longer an adequate framework for regulating regional migration; neither is the Caribbean Basin Initiative. As a migration policy, the CBI is little more than an attempt to duplicate the postwar strategy in Puerto Rico. The lessons from the Puerto Rican experience, however, only point to the failure of previous political frameworks:

Puerto Rico's present singularity lies in having run through the full course of options in these exchanges of capital for people as we now know them, most recently within the framework of commonwealth, a political arrangement regarded as totally inadequate in its present from even by its most ardent advocates. (Bonilla and Campos, 1981, pp. 134-135)

NOTES

1. I specifically use the somewhat awkward form "divisioning" to emphasize the active involvement of social groups in the process.

2. Since I have published my thoughts on the domestic issues elsewhere, I will devote my attention here to the interstate relationships. For a complete study, class relations in each of the countries of origin should also be analyzed. However, this presents an unmanageable task for this type of essay.

3. Although many authors have discussed this topic, I frequently refer to Frobel, Heinrichs and Kreye, since they have written most extensively and frequently about the tendency toward a new international division of labor.

4. For much of the postwar period the growers were actually able to maintain the flow through the formally-arranged Bracero Program. Over the long run, however, this is merely a more legally open form of the political framework underlying this flow.

5. Examination of the long-term, labor market conditions inside the United States is a large portion of the total research project from which this paper is extracted. Those conditions will be discussed in detail in subsequent work.

6. Although his own claims are methodologically weak, Bukharin is cited frequently for this contribution. See Bukharin, 1973.

7. Personal interviews with federal administrators of the program.

8. Of course, a primary distinction must be made at the outset: the atrocities of the Pol Pot regime in Kampuchea are totally without comparison in this analysis. Although many Cambodian refugees who have escaped to Thailand or Vietnam were in some way linked to the U.S.-backed Lon Nol regime, the subsequent attacks on the population of Phnom Penh by the Khmer Rouge involved separate incidents, and their development is to be explained as much by the organization and ideology of the revolutionary government as they are by the consequences of the war and national collapse.

Still, the explanation for many of the events that later affected the composition of the refugee flows out of the region undoubtedly lies in the political vacuum left by U.S. defeat. Vietnam's invasion of Kampuchea resurrected a historical battle over boundaries that has roots hundreds of years old. And the Chinese "punishment" of North Vietnam created thousands of refugees among the latter's long-settled ethnic Chinese population. This regional "unruliness" spread the fighting to the borders of Thailand, where the political intricacies determining which superpower supports what guerrilla group are matched only by the depths of human suffering in the refugee camps.

9. SSI is Supplementary Security Income; AFDC is Aid for Families with Dependent Children.

REFERENCES

Acosta, Mariya, and Jorge E. Hardoy. 1973. *Urban Reform in Revolutionary Cuba*. New Haven: Yale University, Antilles Research Program.

Amin, Samir. 1982. *Dynamics of Global Crisis* New York: Monthly Review Press.

Arrighi, Giovanni. 1982. "A Crisis of Hegemony." In *Dynamics of Global Crisis*, pp. 55-108. New York: Monthly Review Press.

Bach, Robert L. 1978a. "Mexican Immigration and the American State." *International Migration Review* 12:4 (Winter), 536-558.

———. 1978b. "Mexican Immigration and U.S. Immigration Reforms in the 1960s." *Kapitalistate* 7, 63-80.

———. 1980a. "On the Holism of the World-Systems Perspective." In *Processes of the World-System*, Political Economy of the World-System Annuals, no. 3. Beverly Hills: Sage.

———. 1980b. *Past and Present Legislative Reform: The Immigration and Nationality Efficiency Act of 1979*. Hearings before the Senate Judiciary Committee on S. 1763. 96th Cong., 1st sess. Washington, D.C.: Government Printing Office.

———. Forthcoming. "The Entry of Refugee Populations in the Labor Force." In *The Labor Market Impacts of Immigration*, Rockefeller Foundation. New York: Rockefeller Foundation.

———, and Lisa A. Schraml. 1982. "Migration, Crisis and Theoretical Conflict." *International Migration Review* 16:2 (Summer), 320-341.

Bluestone, Barry, and Bennet Harrison. 1982. *The Deindustrialization of America*. New York: Basic Books.

Bonilla, Frank, and Ricardo Campos. 1981. "A Wealth of Poor: Puerto Ricans in the New Economic Order." *Daedalus* (Spring), 133-176.

Bucher, Carl. 1968. *Industrial Evolution*. New York: Augustus M. Kelley.

Bukharin, N. 1973. *Imperialism and World Economy*. New York: Monthly Review Press.

Chomsky, Noam, and Edward Herman. 1979. *After the Cataclysm*. vol. 2. Montreal: Black Rose Books.

Fleisher, Belton M. 1963. "Some Aspects of Puerto Rican Migration to the United States." *Review of Economics and Statistics* 45:3 (August), 245-253.

Frobel, Folker, Jurgen Heinrichs and Otto Kreye. 1977. "The Tendency towards a New International Division of Labor." *Review* 1:1 (Summer), 73-88.

———. 1978. "The World Market for Labor and the World Market for Industrial Sites." *Journal of Economic Issues* 12:4 (December), 843-858.

Greider, William. 1981. "The Education of David Stockman." *Atlantic* 248:6 (December), 27-54.

Hernández-Álvarez, J. 1968. "The Movement and Settlement of Puerto Rican Migrants Within the United States, 1950-1960." *International Migration Review* 2:2 (Spring), 40-52.

Hopkins, Terence K., and Immanuel Wallerstein. 1977. "Patterns of Development of the Modern World-System." *Review* 1:2, 111-145.

Huntington, Samuel P. 1968. "The Bases of Accommodation." *Foreign Affairs* 46:4 (July), 642-656.

Jenkins, J. Craig. 1978. "The Demand for Immigrant Workers: Labor Scarcity or Social Control?" *International Migration Review* 12:4 (Winter), 514-535.

Johnson, A. 1928. "How Present Congress Is Dealing with Proposals to Change Immigration." *Congressional Digest* 7 (May), 152-154.

LBJ Papers. Various years. Memoranda from the Presidential Papers of Lyndon Baines Johnson.

Maldonado, Rita M. 1976. "Why Puerto Ricans Migrated to the United States in 1947-73." *Monthly Labor Review* 99:9 (September), 7-18.

McNeill, W. H., and R. S. Adams, ed. 1978. *Human Migration: Patterns and Policies*. Bloomington, Ind.: American Academy of Arts and Sciences.

Mortimer, D. M., and R. Bryce-Laporte, ed. 1981. *Female Immigrants to the United States: Caribbean, Latin American, and African Experiences*. RIIES Occasional Papers, no. 2. Washington, D.C.: Smithsonian Institution.

New York State Department of Labor. 1982. *Employment Standards: Industrial Homeworkers in New York City*. Albany: New York State Department of Labor.

Portes, Alejandro, and Robert L. Bach. Forthcoming. *Latin Journey, Mexican and Cuban Immigrants in the United States*. Berkeley: University of California Press.

Purcell, Susan K., ed. 1981. *Mexico-United States Relations*. New York: Academy of Political Science.

Reisler, Mark. 1976. *By the Sweat of Their Brow: Mexican Immigrant Labor in the United States, 1900-1940*. Westport, Conn.: Greenwood Press.

Reynolds, Clark W. 1981. "The Structure of the Relationship." In *Mexico-United States Relations*, ed. Susan K. Purcell, pp. 125-135. New York: Academy of Political Science.

Rockefeller Foundation. Forthcoming. *The Labor Market Impacts of Immigration*. New York: Rockefeller Foundation.

Sassen-Koob, Saskia. 1980. "The Internationalization of the Labor Force." *Studies in Comparative International Development* 15 (Winter), 3-23.

———. 1981. "Exporting Capital and Importing Labor: The Role of Women." In *Female Immigrants to the United States: Caribbean, Latin American, and African Experiences*. ed. D.M. Mortimer and R. Bryce-Laporte, pp. 203-234. Washington, D.C.: Smithsonian Institution.

Suhrke, Astri. 1981. Statement before the Subcommittee on Immigration, Refugees and International Law, U. S. House of Representatives. Committee on the Judiciary (September 23), mimeo.

Zolberg, Aristide. 1978. "International Migration Policies in a Changing World System." In *Human Migration: Patterns and Policies*, ed. W. H. McNeill and R. S. Adams, pp. 241-286. Bloomington, Ind.: American Academy of Arts and Sciences.

Caribbean Cane Cutters in Florida Implications for the Study of the Internationalization of Labor

Charles H. Wood and Terry McCoy

Every year since 1943, Caribbean workers have been transported to the state of Florida to harvest sugar cane. The offshore labor program, begun during World War II, currently employs between eight and nine thousand men each season. Brought to this country through the H-2 provision of the 1952 Immigration and Nationality Act, it is currently the largest legal foreign labor force in the United States.

This chapter draws on the results of a case study of seasonal labor in the Florida sugar industry (McCoy and Wood, 1982). The first section presents a description of the organization of production on a sugar plantation and reviews the various institutional mechanisms that govern the process by which employers recruit workers from the Caribbean. This overview provides the background for a discussion of three issues relevant to the study of the internationalization of labor. Beginning with a broad historical perspective, the second section traces the events that led to the creation of the system of seasonal labor migration in the 1940s. The analysis centers on the role of the state and the way immigration policy responded to imbalances in the regional labor markets that evolved in the Southeastern and Southwestern part of the United States in the post-Depression period. The third part examines the notion of "cheap" labor and the way various definitions of this concept enter into the debate between critics and defenders of the offshore labor program. A structural perspective on the relative costs of domestic and Caribbean workers suggests that employers prefer a foreign labor force for reasons that transcend the simple wage consideration. The final section explores some of the factors that have contributed to the continued existence of the H-2 labor force in Florida agriculture. Drawing on comparative data from Hawaii, it is argued that the presence of Caribbean workers, by retarding mechanization and by attenuating the need to upgrade working conditions, reproduces the very circumstances that require the recruitment of foreign as opposed to domestic labor. The presentation of each topic seeks to explore the implications of this particular case study for a more general analysis of the internationalization of capital and labor.

SUGAR PRODUCTION AND OFFSHORE LABOR IN FLORIDA

Sugar cane was first planted in a small, isolated area along the southern rim of Lake Okeechobee in the late 1800s. The crop remained relatively unimportant in the state until 1931, when the U.S. Sugar Corporation began to grow and mill sugar on a commercial basis, opening a second mill in 1947. Prior to 1960, 11 of the 13 attempts to produce sugar on a commercial scale failed. Whereas the techniques existed to grow sugar under local conditions, national policy (composed of a complex and interlocking system of quotas, price supports, and other regulations) and international conditions discouraged its production in Florida (Thompson, 1979).

Between 1960 and 1980, the area devoted to sugar rose from around 50,000 to more than 330,000 acres. Increased production was stimulated by the Cuban Revolution. When Cuba lost access to the U.S. market, its quota was partially reassigned to stateside growers, thereby boosting demand for domestically produced sugar. The revolution also led to the transfer to the U.S. of Cuban capital, technology, and skilled workers, a factor that increased Florida's productive capacity. Florida currently accounts for nearly 20 percent of total (cane and beet) domestic production and 10 percent of all sugar consumed in the United States (*Florida Sugar News*, no. 4, 1981). Its 1980-81 record crop of 1,121,400 tons of raw sugar made Florida the leading domestic producer in that year (*Florida Sugar News*, no. 2, 1981).

A distinctive feature of the Florida sugar industry is its reliance on manual labor for harvesting cane. Whereas all other domestically grown sugar cane is harvested by machine, ecological and technical constraints make the use of such methods more expensive in Florida. Prior to 1943, black Americans harvested sugar and other crops in the state. When this labor force moved north into war-related industries, agricultural producers (primarily citrus and vegetable growers) sought foreign replacements from what were then the British West Indies. The offshore labor program first began recruiting workers from the Bahamas. Later, cane cutters were contracted from Jamaica, British Honduras (now Belize), Antigua, St. Kitts, Montserrat, and British Guiana (now Guyana). At present the program is limited to five Commonwealth Caribbean islands: Jamaica (which provides around 80 percent of the labor force), Barbados (the second largest supplier), St. Lucia, St. Vincent, and Dominica.

Under current immigration law employers can recruit temporary foreign workers only after the Department of Labor certifies that there is an insufficient supply of domestic workers. Once this condition is documented the DOL advises the Immigration and Naturalization Service (INS) of a labor shortage. The INS then grants approval for the importation of foreign workers for prespecified tasks for a period of one year or less (eight months in the case of sugar). The DOL also establishes what is known as the "adverse wage rate." This is a guaranteed hourly wage which should not only attract domestic workers but also, failing to do so, should not adversely affect the wages of U.S. workers in related activities (i. e. agricultural workers). The adverse wage rate is dictated by the DOL on the basis of studies done by the Field Reporting Service of the Department of Agriculture to determine the prevailing wages for farm workers. In the case of sugar, it has always been above the federal minimum wage but not high enough to attract sufficient domestic applicants. In 1980-81 the adverse wage rate of $4.09 per hour was about a dollar above the federal minimum ($3.10).

The recruitment of offshore labor is based on an annual contract between representatives of the sugar industry and those of the West Indian governments and workers. For the industry the program is managed by the Florida Fruit and Vegetable Association (FFVA) and the U.S. Sugar Corporation, with the FFVA representing most employers. Representation of West Indian interests is more complicated. The principal organization is the British West Indian Central Labour Organisation (BWICLO). Its governing council, the Regional Labour Board, is composed of the following: the permanent Jamaican secretary for the Ministry of Labour, who serves as chairman; two other Jamaican government officials; the permanent secretary of the Ministry of Labour from Barbados; the labour commissioner of St. Lucia, representing the three remaining small islands; and a representative from one of the two Jamaican labor unions (depending on which party is in power). The BWICLO, with a permanent office in Washington, D.C., maintains liaison officers in the sugar area. Although the Regional Labour Board and industry representatives meet annually to renegotiate the contract, it remains essentially the same from year to year.

The recruiting process varies by island (McCoy and Wood, 1982) and is carried out by industry representatives with the cooperation of the island governments. The selection is generally completed by early summer, several months before the harvest begins. However, an individual who enters into the pool is not guaranteed work in the sugar fields, as this depends on a final call from the employers for a specific number of workers. Although the industry estimates the number of men it will need in advance, the actual size of the labor force is not established until the harvest is about to begin. As a result, some workers may not be contracted at all; others may be hired only after the harvest is well underway. The implications of this recruitment process are explored in a later section.

With the exception of Barbados, the labor force is drawn primarily from rural areas of the Caribbean. Results of a survey carried out in 1981 (McCoy and Wood, 1982) indicate that the workers are primarily small farmers, recruited from a relatively stable population with low rates of intra- and inter-island migration. The principal reason that motivates individuals to seek stateside jobs as cane cutters is the relatively higher wages in Florida than in the Caribbean. A second reason is the opportunity to purchase items that are either unavailable or more expensive on the islands.

Once recruited, workers are taken by charter aircraft to West Palm Beach and then by bus to the sugar area. Each individual is assigned to a specific grower prior to departure. Housing consists of barracks located on or near the sugar estates. Workers interviewed in 1981 reported an average gross biweekly wage of $420. This amounts to about $4,000 per season, from which numerous deductions are made. The average net wage was $245 a fortnight.

Remittances to the place of origin are made in several ways. The contract agreement stipulates that 23 percent of the worker's pay be transferred to a non-interest-bearing bank account on the worker's home island, where all or some (depending on the island) can be later retrieved in local currency. Workers on their own initiative mail substantial amounts of money to family members and friends (totaling about $4.8 million). They also purchase clothes and other items (valued at $4.6 million). Finally, at the end of the season, each individual returns with a certain amount of cash in hand (amounting to $1.9 million total). Extrapolating from the sample to the total population of workers in 1980-81, the work force remitted nearly $19 million (including the U.S. value of goods purchased) to the sending islands. Analyses of spending patterns, together with information on the destination and purpose of mailed remittances, indicate that the wages earned in the United States are used primarily for the maintenance and reproduction of the worker and his household. Although a small percentage of the work force does invest in capital goods, the majority of the purchases and remittances are for consumption purposes.

THE STATE, IMMIGRATION POLICY, AND LABOR SUPPLY

Throughout the independent history of the United States, capital has never been denied access to a preferred labor pool without either its substitution by a more vulnerable labor source or a protracted political struggle (Portes, 1982, p. 11). Still, an excessively instrumentalist interpretation of state action is to be avoided. Rather than assume that this consistency is a mere reflection of the interests of the dominant class, analysis of government policy must contend with the factors that condition the relationship between the needs of private capital and the power of domestic labor, neither of which is to be treated as homogeneous. It is in the context of the changing supply and demand of low-wage labor to different segments of the U.S. economy that various immigration policies, including the H-2 program, have been formulated. The seasonal employment of Caribbean labor in Florida can thus be viewed as one aspect of a broader historical process.

Massive immigration of European workers played a critical role in the early expansion of industrial production in the United States. The influx of foreign labor soon became the target of opposition by the increasingly organized union movement. The major strikes carried out in the late nineteenth and early twentieth centuries attest to the intensification of working-class struggle against leading corporations in the United States (Bach, 1978). Opposition to European labor became increasingly militant, yet it was not sufficiently powerful in the years preceding World War I to stop immigration. After the war, organized labor in the Northern industrial areas was able to limit immigrant flow with the passage of the National Origins Act of 1924. This legislation coincided in time and represented an integral element of the "historic pact" between capital and organized labor (Portes, 1982, p. 3). Growing labor unrest "demonstrated to an increasing number of the leading representatives of monopoly capital the virtue of bargaining with the more conservative trade unions" (Bach, 1978, p. 544). Such bargaining included the regulation of industrial conflicts in exchange for concessions to workers, such as protection from foreign labor.

If Northern industrialists could accept restrictions on immigration, the same was not true in the West, where the demand for labor was rapidly expanding. In 1918 the commissioner general of immigration (drawing on the statutory authority derived from the Immigration Act of 1917) waived the head tax, contract labor laws, and literacy requirement for Mexican workers. While Mexican labor had already been used extensively in the Southwest, the Department Order of 1918 provided the legal foundation and justification for alternatively relaxing and tightening the border according to domestic demand (Manning, 1981, p. 17). With the onset of the Great Depression, for example, Mexican migrant labor became redundant and the border was quickly closed. No new legislation was necessary as the reinstitution of the earlier requirements (head tax, literacy test, contract labor laws, and public charge provisions of the 1917 act) sharply reduced the number of visas issued to Mexican nationals.

In the early 1940s the border was opened once again, this time in response to the shortage of labor brought on by World War II. A government-to-government agreement to import agricultural workers was signed in 1942. This treaty and subsequent amendments and laws (Public Law 45) granted the commissioner of immigration and naturalization the power to admit aliens applying for temporary admission to the United States. In the years 1942 through 1947 the U.S. government imported at public expense over 219,500 workers from Mexico, most of whom were employed in Southwest agriculture (President's Commission on Migrant Labor, 1951, cited in Manning, 1981, p. 34).

Initially, attempts were made to bring Mexican workers to the Eastern seaboard as well. This effort failed because of transportation costs and language difficulties. Moreover, the Mexican supply was insufficient even for the needs of agriculture in the Southwest so another source of farm labor was sought (Kramer, 1966, p. 1). Ease of transportation by ship and the use of English as the official language suggested the British colonial islands of the Atlantic and Caribbean. The first agreement was made in March of 1943, between the U.S. Department of Agriculture and the Bahamian government. The importation of offshore workers from the Bahamas set the pattern for subsequent agreements with Jamaica, Barbados, and British Honduras. Between 1943 and 1947, 116,124 British West Indians worked on farms or in industry in the United States (Kramer, 1966).

After the expiration of the Emergency Farm Program in 1947, Southwestern growers continued to import Mexican nationals through a series of revised executive agreements which supplemented the 1917 immigration law. In the period 1948 to 1951, individuals were contracted through arrangements between workers and employers. It was not until 1951 that Congress enacted Public Law 78, which created the so-called Bracero Program. The bilateral agreement with Mexico was extended by successive amendments until its expiration in 1964. The demise of the Bracero Program was brought about by a number of factors, including the opposition by organized labor and various Hispanic and religious groups. Also important was the mechanization of agriculture in the Southwest, which made bracero labor increasingly obsolete no matter how cheap it was (Bach, 1978; Manning, 1981).

Following the expiration of the Emergency Farm Program in 1947, events in the Southeastern part of the United States took a different turn, a factor that would ultimately be of critical importance to the survival of the offshore labor program. As in the case of growers in the southwest, those in Florida continued to import Caribbean workers without the direct participation of the U.S. government. Authority for maintaining a privately run offshore program fell wholly under the Immigration and Naturalization Act of 1917 and, later, the Immigration and Naturalization Act of 1952 (Public Law 414). Key sections of SP.L. 414 state:

> (1) The admission to the United States of any alien as a non-immigrant shall be for such time and under such conditions as the attorney general may by regulations prescribe....
> 2) The question of importing any alien as a non-immigrant ... shall be determined by the attorney general after consultation with appropriate agencies of the government upon petition from the ... employer.

The significance of these provisions is that they allow the attorney general, with the advice of other agencies, to determine the regulations for the importation of workers. As the situation has evolved, the attorney general has designated the U.S. Department of Labor as the agency to decide whether offshore workers should be admitted. Unlike the Bracero Program (a government-to-government agreement), the offshore labor program in the Southeast became an arrangement among U.S. employers, workers in the Caribbean, and the BWICLO (an organization representing the worker and this government). Rather than being a direct party to the agreement, the U.S. government, through the Department of Labor, only certifies that labor shortages exist that cannot be filled with U.S. workers.

Because the Department of Labor is the agency in control of the certification process, it has substantial power over the offshore program. In the early period, following World War II, the certification of labor needs presented few problems to the employers, a situation that began to change in the late 1950s. Responding to the same pressures that brought an end to the Bracero Program, the Department of Labor made it increasingly difficult to import foreign farm labor. In december 1964, when the Bracero Program ended, Labor Secretary W. Willard Wirtz claimed that North Americans would work in agriculture if proper wages and living conditions were provided and that foreign labor programs could not be tolerated while Americans were unemployed. Stating that the intent of Congress in ending the Bracero Program would not be subverted through the misuse of P.L. 414, he concluded, "The responsibilities of the Secretary of Labor under Public Law 414 will be strictly administered." Wirtz left little doubt as to the aims of the department's initiatives. "The issuance of the new regulations," he argued, "is essential to the orderly administration of Public Law 414, but it does not imply that there will be any large-scale use of foreign workers in the future. To the contrary, it is expected that such use will be greatly reduced and hopefully eliminated" (cited in Kramer, 1966, pp. 3-4).

Among the new regulations adopted were: (1) the maximum period for which foreign labor could be admitted reduced from three years to 120 days; and (2) employers had to make active efforts to recruit domestic workers both within and outside of the state. These policies placed severe restrictions on the offshore labor program. As late as 1965, Caribbean workers were used in citrus, mixed vegetables (including celery, corn, and tomatoes), tropical fruits, strawberries, and watermelons. After 1966 offshore workers in Florida were denied to all except growers of sugar cane. Peter Kramer, a knowledgeable observer of the offshore labor program (whose work we have drawn on here), wrote in 1966 that it would decline and eventually disappear. Citing key officials in a major Florida sugar producing corporation to the effect that the mechanization of cane harvesting was only about five years away, Kramer (1966, p. 5) anticipated the demise of the offshore program by 1970. How can its continued existence in 1983 be explained?

Events at the international level played an important role. On January 1, 1959, Fidel Castro came to power in Cuba. U.S. foreign policy, designed to put economic pressure on the revolutionary government, included a curtailment of Cuba's sugar quota, which was reassigned in part to domestic producers. The expansion of sugar cultivation in Florida, in turn, created new farm labor needs. The situation in Florida came to be regarded as a unique case. Even Secretary Wirtz, following a fact-finding trip to the state, seemed to agree that cane presented a "special problem" (Kramer, 1966, p. 5). At a time when the Bracero Program was under attack, such special status was particularly valuable. Since the legal existence of the offshore arrangement did not rest on P.L. 78, the decision by Congress to allow the law to expire did not terminate the program in the Southeast. Opposition to the Caribbean labor did not materialize for several reasons. The number of West Indian workers involved was relatively small. Moreover, those who were in the United States were certified by the DOL as being necessary to agricultural production. The offshore labor program, although cut back, was thus able to weather a political environment in the 1960s that posed a significant threat to all foreign labor arrangements.

That cane growers continue to rely on Caribbean workers is also associated with the sugar lobby's considerable political power wielded at the local and national level. The industry has been able to survive by obtaining federal concessions in the form of a complex quota and price support system that shields U.S.-produced sugar from the generally lower price on the international market. In the domestic political realm it can further be argued that the state is involved, not only in the routine bureaucratic dimension of recruiting foreign workers, but more importantly in legitimizing the offshore labor program. Through a series of technocratic functions, the Department of Labor assumes the role of validating the claim that a labor shortage exists. The short-term consequences of the certification process may be costly to the industry, as interviewed representatives are quick to point out. At the same time, such action on the part of the state serves to protect the industry from direct attack by organized labor. In helps to avert the possibility of the industry having to involve itself directly in challenges that might arise in the legislature. Stated in its most general form, the state neutralizes labor's challenge to capital by legitimizing a worker recruitment program that is a key element in this sector of agricultural production.

To note the intersection of state action and the needs of private capital is not to say that the two are invariably compatible. Managers of the state apparatus must deal with immediate political crises, the solution of which determines their own continued existence in power. More generally, the state, as a corporate entity concerned with its own preservation, can and will defend the basic attributes of its sovereignty (Portes, 1982, p. 9). Contrary to an instrumentalist view of the state, this can sometimes result in initiatives that run counter to the interests of the sugar industry and to the continued existence of the offshore labor program. An example of such a situation occurred in the

1970s, when the Florida state government was reeling from the impact of the Mariel boat lift and the influx of Haitian refugees. In the face of the need to absorb these highly visible migrant populations, a plausible course of action was to employ them in the sugar fields. This idea led to a flurry of activity suggesting the state's resolve to enlist the sugar industry in dealing with the political crisis.

Little came of the attempt to get significant numbers of Cubans and Haitians employed in the cane fields. The precise history of the threat to the offshore labor program, and how the industry countered it, has yet to be told. For the purposes of this discussion, the incident (and indeed the entire history of the program) serves to illustrate the political vulnerability of the arrangement to a wide spectrum of pressures that come to bear on the state. Continuous efforts by the industry and its representatives, operating at both the local and national level, are thus necessary to perpetuate the Caribbean offshore labor program.

ON THE CONCEPT OF CHEAP LABOR

The presence of West Indian cane cutters in Florida agriculture can hardly be regarded as a transitory phenomenon. Participating in the labor force for well over 30 years, Caribbean workers have become an inherent component of the state's sugar industry. Yet the permanence of the offshore labor program, as noted above, has not gone uncontested. Nearly every year critics raise the same or similar issues. Why does the U.S. government permit the entry of cheap foreign labor when there is domestic unemployment? Posed in this fashion the question is premised on several assumptions and contains within it a clear policy recommendation. The clear implication is that if sugar growers are denied access to foreign labor, American workers will take their place, thereby causing a decline in the rate of stateside unemployment.

Industry representatives reject this argument on several grounds. Because the adverse effect wage that must be offered to Caribbean labor substantially exceeds the minimum wage in the United States, foreign cane cutters cannot, in the eyes of the industry, be considered "cheap." A second issue concerns the feasibility of replacing offshore labor by domestic workers. Employer's records clearly attest to the short-lived work histories of the few North Americans that have been hired. Not only do very few apply for the job, but those who do rarely last more than a few weeks. Since harvesting cane is a task that is rejected by the U.S. labor force, employers maintain they are compelled to seek foreign substitutes. Third, contrary to the views espoused by critics of the offshore labor program, the recruitment of Caribbean workers is ultimately of benefit to the United States' economy. Sugar production provides a tax base that generates revenue for state and local government, and the continued existence of the industry provides jobs for the technical and managerial personnel involved in refining and transport activities. Thus the presence of foreign workers, in this view, has a positive effect on public finance and on domestic employment.

The crux of the dispute between critics and defenders of the offshore labor program turns, in large measure, on two questions: what one means by cheap labor, and whether foreign workers can be substituted by domestic ones. An analysis of these two issues, which are themselves interrelated, requires us to consider a number of factors. We can begin to unravel some of these issues by turning to the relationships presented in figure 1.

The two curves represent the quantity of U.S. (A) and West Indian (B) labor that is supplied at the different wage levels shown on the Y axis. That curve A lies above B reflects the higher wages that must be paid U.S. workers for them to agree to hand-harvest sugar cane under the working conditions that prevail in south Florida. Why is there this discrepancy between the wage levels demanded by the two labor forces? Part of the answer lies in the relative power of the labor movement in the two national contexts and the standards of living that have been achieved in each case (see Castells, 1975). As a result of labor's historic struggle in the United States, a substantial proportion of the labor force enjoys (by most international standards) relatively good conditions of work, broadly defined to include wages, safety regulations, and job security. Also among the hard-won concessions are unemployment compensation, minimum wage laws, as well as welfare and social security benefits. Together these factors establish the minimal standards of work that labor in the U.S. has come to expect.

The relationship between wages and the quantity of labor supplied can be assumed to have the same general shape in the Caribbean, although at a lower level. However, the underdevelopment of Caribbean economies and the weakness of the labor movement in the countries that comprise the region imply low working standards relative to those that obtain in the United States.

With these historically specific standards as a reference point, the supply of labor available for a particular task is determined by the joint evaluation of the characteristics of the job and the wage that is offered. If the combination is unacceptable, workers will withhold their labor from the market. Thus, at a low wage, say W1 (the minimum wage in the U.S.), there may exist an adequate quantity of Caribbean cutters to harvest the sugar crop in south Florida (Q1), yet no U.S. workers would apply for the job.

As the relationships in figure 1 suggest, the required number of workers (Q1) could be recruited from the U.S. if the wage were high enough (W3). Contrary to what sugar industry representatives often stress, cane-cutting jobs do not go begging solely because they are dirty or arduous. If the characteristics of the job per se were the only determinant of the quantity of labor supplied, it is unlikely that certain occupations, such as coal mining, would exist at all in this

FIGURE 1
Wage Levels and the Supply of Foreign and Domestic Labor

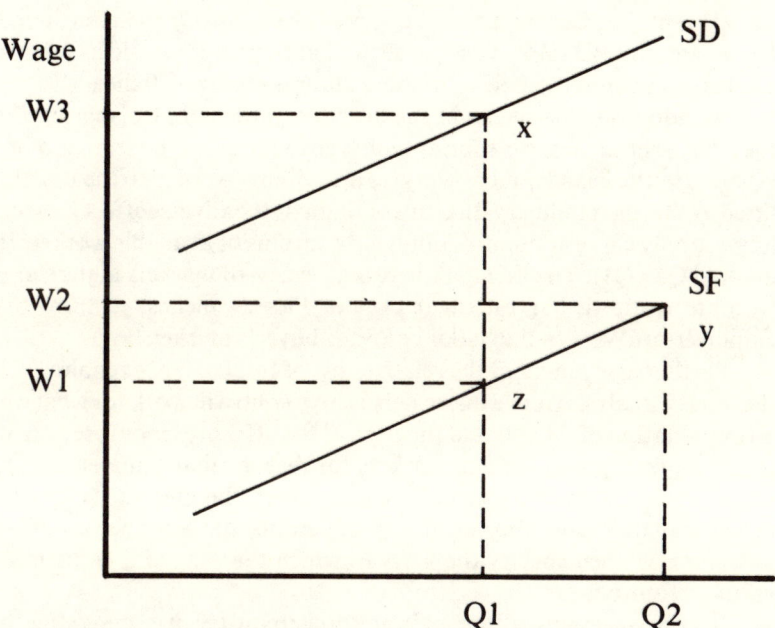

Note: SD is the supply of domestic labor.
SF is the supply of foreign labor.
W1 is the minimum wage in the United States.
W2 is the adverse effect wage rate.
W3 is the wage required to atract domestic workers.

country (Castells, 1975). The key factor, rather, is the level of remuneration offered in return for performing the task. However distasteful the occupation, there is some point at which the wage is high enough to render the job attractive. In the case of hand-harvesting sugar cane this is shown by point x, figure 1.

Having posited the relationship between wages and the quantity of labor supplied, we can now consider whether Caribbean workers can be regarded as a "cheap" labor force. The answer depends entirely on the reference point that is selected. For example, it can be plausibly assumed that the sugar industry, given unhindered access to foreigners, could meet all of its demand for labor by recruiting Caribbean workers and paying them the U.S. minimum wage (point z). Federal regulations, however, set the adverse effect wage (W2) above the minimum wage. From this standpoint the adverse effect wage can be regarded as a *tax* on growers for the use of West Indian workers (by the amount W2 - W1). Therefore, relative to the minimum wage, offshore labor can viewed as "costly."

On the other hand, the adverse effect wage falls short of the level of remuneration required to attract domestic laborers (W3). Using W2 as a reference point, one can conclude that the federal government, by permitting the legal entry of Caribbean workers, provides a *subsidy* to the sugar industry (by the amount W3 - W2). Compared to what employers would have to pay U.S. workers to go into the fields, offshore labor is relatively "cheap."

An additional point can be made with regard to the Caribbean. Because the adverse effect wage is substantially above the average earnings of manual laborers in the islands, more workers are willing to come to the U.S. than are hired by the sugar industry. In terms of figure 1, the adverse effect wage cuts the labor supply curve at point Y, implying a surplus of available workers (by the amount Q2 - Q1). The fact that there is an excess of workers in the Caribbean who are ready to harvest sugar cane in Florida means, in turn, that the employers of West Indian labor enjoy a "buyer's market."

Further assessment of the relative cost of foreign labor requires a shift in the level of analysis from a micro perspective (who will work for what wage) to an examination of the role and function of the offshore labor force as a whole. Sugar growers prefer foreign workers for reasons that transcend the simple wage consideration. To identify the reasons for the preference for offshore rather than domestic labor we must first describe the labor needs of the sugar industry and then specify the ways in which the H-2 work force meets the various requirements.

In large-scale agriculture, as in any other industry, it is imperative that the production process be stabilized and routinized to the greatest extent possible. In the case of sugar cane, the seasonal bulge in labor demand (which can vary in magnitude from one season to the next) implies that a key requirement is the need to ensure a predictable supply of labor. Essential to efficiency is ready access to 8,000-15,000 men who are endowed with the appropriate characteristics. The workers must be skilled in hand-harvesting cane, highly motivated, and willing to accept the wage rate established by the Department of Labor. They must also be on call to begin work the moment they are sent for and accept the living arrangements and working conditions that prevail on the sugar plantations.

The H-2 labor program is tailored to meet such labor needs by regularly supplying a large contingent of seasonal workers from the agricultural sector of less developed countries. In order to identify the various reasons why the Caribbean is an appropriate recruitment site for a work force of the type described above, it is useful to regard the offshore labor program as a longstanding and highly efficient *labor supply system*. A systemic approach stresses the idea that sending and receiving areas, linked by the movement of labor, are functionally interrelated.

Small farmers in the Caribbean comprise the overwhelming majority of the offshore labor force; they sustain themselves much of the year through their own agricultural labor and that of other family members in their country of origin. At the same time, the conditions that prevail in the countryside and the generally low agricultural productivity of small plots compel farmers to supplement their income with off-farm employment. Given the relatively high wages paid in the United States, the chance to harvest sugar cane is a much sought-after option. Whatever slack in the household productive capacity results from the departure of sons and husbands to work in the U.S. is taken up by other members of the domestic unit or kin network, or is filled in by remittances, or some combination of the two (McCoy and Wood, 1982).

Between each harvest season the rural population of the five islands forms a pool of immediately recruitable laborers, many of whom already have extensive on-the-job experience. Once they are approved for employment they wait, sustained by their own resources. They know neither when they will be called on to leave nor how long they will stay in the United States. In some instances, depending on the size of the labor force hired, they may not be employed at all, even though they have successfully gone through the entire recruitment process.

From the standpoint of the industry the important point is that these small farmers in the Caribbean constitute a reservoir of workers awaiting the chance to work in Florida. A labor force with similar characteristics does not exist in the United States. There are, of course, small farmers, sharecroppers, and day laborers in the agricultural sector of the state of Florida. Many wage workers are migrants, both legal and illegal. However, it would logistically difficult to recruit as many 8,000-9,000 domestic cane cutters who must report to work within a period of a few weeks. Equally problematic is the need to count on the availability of a similar number the following year. The social and economic conditions that prevail in the advanced industrial center do not generate and sustain a labor pool of this type.

The characteristics of the work force recruited from the offshore labor reserve are also well suited to the efficient allocation of labor in the process of production. The H-2 program includes only male workers who temporarily live in the United States without wives or family. They are housed in barracks-like quarters, containing up to several hundred men. Breakfast is served in large mess halls staffed by Caribbean cooks. Fleets of buses transport workers to the harvest site in the early hours of the morning. Mobile units serve the noon meal in the fields. In late afternoon the buses return the men to the dormitories, where they eat dinner, rest, wash their own clothes, sharpen tools, and prepare for the next day of work. They normally leave the camps only on payday.

The quality of the living quarters varies by employer. Some places are clean and well kept, housing 10 to 20 men in a series of small, separate buildings. Others are large and crowded places, where the workers frequently complain of substandard food and facilities. From the standpoint of the production process, the important point is that workers without families are housed together in strategically located areas and are organized into subgroups whose activities are coordinated by supervisors and managers through a formal chain of command. Life in the camps and fieldwork is supervised through a system which relies heavily on West Indians as immediate supervisors. At the top of the hierarchy is the camp supervisor. Under his command and in charge of the fieldwork are field bosses, lead men, and ticket writers. The field boss is responsible for the work in his field, while it is the lead man who assigns each cutter his daily task or "row". At the end of the work day, the ticket writer records the day's cut. This housing and organizational arrangement is efficient in terms of the maintenance of the workers and the logistics of transporting labor to the work site.

We must be wary, however, of explaining the presence of immigrant labor solely in terms of the technical demands of production. In a capitalist mode of production the wage level paid by employers is the outcome of the struggle between capital and labor, a process that is conditioned by a wide range of forces that affect the relative strength of the two. A central issue concerns the mechanisms of social control by which capital is able to impose its conditions on the work force. Numerous studies of the economic functions of undocumented aliens in the United States have stressed the importance of nationality and legal status. Because they are vulnerable to deportation, illegal (or undocumented) workers, can be made to work "hard and scared" (Marshall, 1975). The consequence is a docile labor force that is unlikely to bring organized pressure to bear on employers. Relative to the domestic labor force, undocumented workers accept lower wages and work at a faster pace and for longer average work weeks, often under substandard safety conditions with no medical, unemployment, or social security coverage. Jenkins (1978, p. 529) summarizes this well-known line of reasoning as follows: "The threat of deportation plus the desire as a temporary immigrant to make as much money as possible during a short period of time renders illegals ideal targets for superexploitation."

While we do not quarrel with this conclusion, the logic of the argument need not hinge on the question of the legal status of the worker. The crucial issue is maintaining the immigrant labor force under a measure of control (Portes, 1977, p. 36). In the case of undocumented workers this control is exercised indirectly through legal measures: the threat of deportation is not in the hands of the employer but is left to the state.

Caribbean cane cutters represent a variation of the "alien worker" theme. Brought to this country with temporary work permits issued by (or obtained through) the Immigration and Naturalization Service, workers are in the United States legally. The terms of their contract, however, render them equally if not more vulnerable to deportation. Workers who fail to harvest cane at an established rate are sent back to the Caribbean. The decision to terminate the contract and to send the individual home is made directly by the employer (although terminated workers can appeal the decision to the BWICLO liaison officers). Workers with low productivity records, or who do not observe the appropriate standards of labor discipline, are not only sent home but are also blacklisted for future employment by the hiring contractor who collectively represents the entire industry.

The degree of vulnerability of a work force is determined by the control capital exercises over labor, which can be accomplished in numerous ways. The juridical status of being "illegal" undoubtedly enhances the power of employers over undocumented aliens. Yet the same structural advantages can be approximated within a different legal framework. The contract that workers sign to harvest cane in Florida is one example.

As the case of H-2 workers suggests, it is useful to think of the relationship between nationality and the vulnerability of labor in terms of a continuum. If full citizenship is at one end and illegal presence at the other, H-2 status can be seen as some intermediate position that confers certain rights yet denies others. The number of such intermediate statuses may increase in the future as immigration policy evolves in response to the multiple forces that influence its formulation (Manning, 1983). The immigration reform bill now before Congress, for example, establishes a new category of resident aliens who have been in the U.S. illegally since January 1, 1980. Individuals in this category of "temporary resident" would be able to work yet would be denied federal benefits, in spite of the requirement that they pay income and social security taxes. As this example implies, position along the continuum will have different implications (depending on which rights are conferred and which are denied) for the relationship between workers and employers and, hence, the price of labor.

To argue that the H-2 labor force is an efficient system of allocating workers in the production process is to define "efficiency" at the level of the firm. But the concept is also applicable to the macrosocial level. Because migrants occupy the housing facilities described above, their seasonal presence does not require additional expenditures on infrastructure and services by the government or private capital. This would certainly not be the case if an equivalent share of national workers were to live permanently in the area. Government would be compelled to allocate a greater share of its revenue on schools, transportation, and other infrastructure and services to accommodate seasonal workers and their dependents. Wages would have to be sufficiently high (or other employment opportunities available) to sustain the worker and his family between harvests, or public services would have to subsidize the maintenance and reproduction of labor through welfare payments. Employers would be required to contribute to unemployment compensation and social security and to comply with fair labor standards. The seasonal movement of single Caribbean workers thus exempts the host society and employers from a number of expenses that would be encumbered with a comparably large domestic work force.

In view of the cost of transportation to and from the islands, as well as the fact that offshore workers earn about a dollar above the minimum wage in the United States, H-2 workers who harvest Florida sugar cane do not, on the face of it, appear to be "cheap." However, as we have sought to demonstrate here, the cost of labor is a concept whose definition depends largely on the reference point used. Moreover, relative cost of domestic and foreign labor involves a host of factors beyond the hourly wage rate and other direct expenditures borne by the employer.

MECHANIZATION AND THE "NEED" FOR FOREIGN LABOR

The need to recruit Caribbean labor is justified on the grounds that the sugar crop in Florida must be cut by hand. Whereas harvesting procedures in Louisiana and Hawaii are fully automated, mechanical harvesters are rarely used in Florida. The reliance on manual labor is explained by technological deficiencies in the face of ecological constraints. Because Florida sugar is grown on reclaimed swampland, mechanical harvesters do not effectively separate the recumbent cane stalk from the foliage, a factor that increases costs when the crop reaches the mill. Heavy machines also compact the soft muck soil, destroying a portion of the ratoons that produce the following year's crop. Even through machines reduce the wage bill during the harvest itself, from an overall production standpoint manual labor is more efficient.

The unique circumstances that prevail in Florida raise questions as to the relationship between certain sectors of agricultural production and the "need" for foreign labor. The reasoning outlined above posits a clear causal direction: it is the lack of adequate technology that generates the demand for a large contingent of workers. For the reasons noted in the previous section, a labor force on the type required in Florida can be readily found in the Caribbean.

An alternative explanation reverses the direction of causality. In his study of guestworkers in Western Europe, Castells (1975, p. 54) concludes that "immigrant workers do not exist because there are 'arduous and badly paid' jobs to be done, but, rather, arduous and badly paid jobs exist because immigrant workers are present or can be sent for to do them." It is this reasoning that leads Sassen-Koob to conclude that "the availability of immigrant labor reduces the pressure on backward sectors of capital to change techniques of production or to improve conditions of work which are unacceptable to unions and to nationals" (1980, p. 18).

The history of sugar production in Hawaii supports this interpretation. Prior to the Depression, immigrant workers were cheap and plentiful, and the sugar plantations were highly labor intensive. With little incentives for planters to rationalize the production process, technological progress was aimed primarily at increasing crop yields through the use of fertilizers, rodent control, and the development of new varieties of cane. Harvesting activities only began to change as workers became more organized. In 1945 the passage of the Hawaiian Employment Relations Act extended collective bargaining to all agricultural workers on the island. By the end of that year the International Longshoremen and Warehousemen's Union (ILWU) organized workers on 32 of Hawaii's 34 plantations. With unionization in full force, the price of labor rose, causing plantation owners to introduce capital-intensive harvesting techniques. By the end of the 1960s hand labor had been reduced to a minimum as sugar production in Hawaii became the most highly mechanized in the world. The temporal sequence of unionization and mechanization in the Hawaiian sugar industry strongly suggests that the rate of mechanization was retarded by the availability of cheap labor and then accelerated in response to rising labor costs, as has been the case in plantation agriculture around the world (Geschwender and Levine, 1983).

Most Florida growers find manual harvesting to be more profitable. Yet the capacity to cut cane mechanically exists and is currently used on one of the large estates. The plantation that relies on automated procedures is located on somewhat sandy soils, a condition that better permits the used of machinery. Nonetheless, it is significant to note that mechanization was introduced by this company only after a major labor strike. Other growers hold the machines in reserve, to be used in the event of a disruption in labor supply (Reubins, 1978, p. 29). These observations support the contention that the rationalization of production, rather than a management act imposed upon compliant workers, is simply one of the many actions taken by capitalists in the ongoing struggle with labor (Geschwender and Levine, 1983, pp. 353-354).

It is the relative power of capital and labor that also accounts for the general working conditions that prevail in a given industry. Thus, in the case of south Florida, the availability of an easily manipulated labor force not only retards the drive to mechanize the sugar harvest but also attenuates the need to improve the living arrangements on the plantations beyond the minimum standards set by the Department of Labor. Together with the wage level, the housing and working conditions are among the factors that discourage domestic laborers from taking jobs in the industry. It is plausible to conclude, therefore, that the existence of foreign workers in Florida agriculture serves to perpetuate the very conditions that are said to require their presence in the first place.

Conclusion

For those steeped in the abundant contemporary critiques of modernization theory, it may come as a surprise to realize that W. Arthur Lewis's (1954) classic statement on economic development with unlimited supplies of labor anticipated much of the current discussion on the internationalization of capital and labor. With characteristic clarity, Lewis summarizes the tendencies at work at a global level:

> When capital accumulation catches up with the labour supply, wages begin to rise above the subsistence level, and the capitalist surplus is adversely affected. However, if there is still surplus labour in other countries, the capitalist can avoid this in one of two ways, by encouraging immigration or by exporting their capital to countries where there is still abundant labour at a subsistence wage.... [I]n a competitive model the U.S. wage (under conditions of mass immigration) could exceed the Asian wage only by an amount covering migration cost.... This is one of the reasons why, in every country where the wage level is relatively high, the trade unions are bitterly hostile to immigration, except in special categories, and take steps to have it restricted. The result is that real wages are higher than they would be otherwise, while profits, capital resources, and total output are smaller than they would be otherwise.... The export of capital is therefore a much easier way out for the capitalists, since trade unions are quick to restrict immigration, but much slower in bringing the export of capital under control. (Lewis, 1954 pp. 436-437).

Lewis's synthetic statement is a convenient reference point for situating Florida's offshore labor program within the broader context of the tendencies at work at the national and international level. While industry goes abroad for a variety of profit-oriented reasons, capital flight as an "easy way out," to use Lewis's term, is an option available primarily to certain industrial sectors. The prototypical mobile firm is one whose production process is easily and cheaply transported over long distances, as in the case of electronics and textiles (Portes and Walton, 1981, p. 152). Where such mobility is precluded, other means are sought to maintain or increase the rate of profit. Pressuring the state to enact protectionist policies is one route. Another is to reduce the wage bill through mechanization or the recruitment of a cheaper labor force. The sugar industry has pursued both avenues, resorting, on the one hand, to price supports from the federal government and, on the other, to the importation of foreign labor.

It remains to be seen whether Florida sugar (and its reliance on offshore workers) is an economic atavism, or if it portends the course of other sectors of agriculture and industry. Certainly the current policy debate, including proposals to expand the H-2 option by liberalizing the certification procedures, implies that the recourse to foreign workers may indeed become more common (McCoy, 1982). As the case of sugar suggests, the precise factors which lead to such an outcome, or which prevent it, cannot be deduced from analyses carried out exclusively at the world level. The need, rather, is for a greater concern for the concrete subprocesses that occur within the global system. By this is meant greater attention to the labor process (the modes in which workers are controlled and utilized and their reactions to the changing organization of surplus extraction and political domination) within nation-states as they are molded and in turn react to world capitalist expansion. Included in this research agenda are the "shifting character of the working class in response to labor migration and the locational decisions of firms; contradictions within core and periphery class structures provoked by the global strategies of capital; and the forms adopted by the class struggle in response to them" (Portes and Walton, 1981, p. 19). The complexities involved in unraveling these relationships suggest the value of disaggregated analyses of subsectors of industry and case studies of particular firms, if we are to identify the forces that underly the movement of labor and the growing international mobility of capital.

REFERENCES

Bach, Robert L. 1978. "Mexican Immigration and the American State." *International Migration Review* 12: 4 (Winter) 536-558.

Castells, Manuel. 1975. "Immigrant Workers and Class Struggles in Advanced Capitalism: The Western European Experience." *Politics and Society* 5 (Spring), 33-66.

Florida Sugar News. Various dates.

Geschwender, James A., and Rhonda F. Levine. 1983. "Rationalization of Sugar Production in Hawaii, 1946-1960: A Dimension of the Class Struggle." *Social Problems* 30 (Feb.), 352-368.

Jenkins, J. Craig. 1978. "The Demand for Immigrant Workers: Labor Scarcity or Social Control?" *International Migration Review* 12 (Winter), 514-535.

Kramer, Peter. 1966. *The Offshores: A Study of Foreign Farm Labor in Florida*. St. Petersburg, Fla.: Community Action Fund.

Lewis, W. Arthur. 1954. "Economic Development with Unlimited Supplies of Labor." Reprinted in *The Economics of Underdevelopment*, eds. A. N. Agarwala and S. P. Singh, New York: Oxford University Press 1973, pp. 440-449.

Manning, Robert D. 1981. The Interaction of Race, Nationality and Class in the American Labor Market: A Comparative Study of Mexican-American and Afro-American Labor Migration (1842-1981). Master's thesis, Northern Illinois University, Dekalb.

Manning, Robert D. Communication.

Marshall, F. R. 1975. "Economic Factors Influencing the International Migration of Workers." *Mexican-United States Border*. San Antonio, Tex.: Weatherhead Foundation.

McCoy, Terry 1982. "Significance of Comprehensive Immigration Law Reform for the State of Florida: Temporary Workers Provisions." Paper presented to the Fourth Annual Earl Warren Symposium, University of California, San Diego, November 19-20.

———, and Charles H. Wood. 1982. "Caribbean Workers in the Florida Sugar Industry." Gainesville: Occasional Paper, no. 2. Center for Latin American Studies, University of Florida.

O'Connor, James. 1982. *The Fiscal Crisis of the State*. New York: St. Martin's Press.

Piore, Michael. 1975. "Notes for a Theory of Labor Market Stratification." pp. 125-150. In *Labor Market Segmentation*, eds. Richard C. Edwards, Michael Reich and David M. Gordon, Lexington, Mass.: Heath.

Portes, Alejandro. 1977. "Labor Functions of Illegal Aliens." *Society* 14 (September-October), 31-37.

———. 1982. "Of Borders and States: A Skeptical Note on the Legislative Control of Immigration." Paper presented to the Fourth Annual Earl Warren Symposium, University of California at San Diego, November 19-29.

———, and John Walton. 1981. *Labor, Class and the International System.* New York: Academic Press.

Reubins, Edwin P. 1978. "Policy Dimensions of the H-2 Program (Temporary Importation of Foreign Workers). Paper prepared for the National Commission for Manpower Policy, U.S. Department of Labor (Contract no. 99-8-1916-50-54).

Sassen-Koob, Saskia. 1980. "The Internationalization of the Labor Force." *Studies in Comparative International Development* 15: 4 (Winter), 3-23.

Thompson, Holly J. 1979. *An Economic Analysis of the Role of the Sugar Industry in the South Florida Economy.* Master's thesis, University of Florida.

The Consequences of Dominican Urban Outmigration for National Development The Case of Santiago

Sherri Grasmuck

The recent wave of research on the topic of international labor migration has linked the origins of outmigration from the developing to the developed world to the nature of dependency and unequal exchange between these societies. In particular, conditions of relative labor surplus in underdeveloped nations have been associated with the failures of the import-substitution model of development and newer strategies of export reconversion followed by many developing societies to generate adequate employment (Portes, 1978; Alba, 1978; Sassen-Koob, 1978; Vuskovic, 1982). Conditions of relative labor scarcity have typically been linked to the developed societies, although it is also recognized that in some cases the enclave pattern of development (Cardoso and Faletto, 1979) may simultaneously generate conditions of relative labor surplus and relative labor scarcity such that undesirable jobs in one peripheral society come to be filled by workers from another peripheral nation with yet lower average wages (Kritz, 1981; Grasmuck, 1981).

Given the critical problem of underemployment and unemployment in the developing world, it is not surprising that in most discussions of the causes of outmigration from these areas the excess labor force is treated implicitly or explicitly as the most immediate stimulant. Thus statements on the interests of peripheral capitalists concerning outmigration typically portray the local bourgeoisie and the dominant classes of developed societies as mutually benefiting from the labor transfer. The former benefit because migration minimizes the political threat of a large mobilized, unemployed population and the latter because higher profits are obtained via vulnerable low-cost labor willing to work in undesirable jobs with little job security (Castells, 1975; Stoddard, 1976; Alba, 1978). As a result of the increasing interpenetration of the capitalist world, labor migration is seen, therefore, as simultaneously serving the interests of dominant classes in both peripheral and central regions.[1] This conceptualization of the role of migrant labor is certainly in keeping with the policies of most Latin American countries regarding the export of a large percentage of its labor force. These policies have been largely to ignore it, or more aggressively to pressure receiving countries not to restrict it, in exchange for generous concessions to foreign capital in the sending countries. Such policies of laissez-faire emigration of sending countries are based on the assumption that labor exports come predominantly from the labor surplus of the population—namely, the underutilized sectors of labor—and that the net effects of outmigration for the sending society (or its dominant class) is positive.

Not only does labor migration relate to the externally oriented nature of dependent development, but it can be shown to have important correlates in the outmigration of professional workers as well. That is, just as labor exports relate to the importation of industrial technologies inappropriate for the conditions of the Third World, so too the "brain drain" can be seen as a consequence of implanted educational institutions from advanced societies in the underdeveloped context. Thus, Third World societies such as Argentina, South Korea, and Egypt can successfully import technological innovations and train a highly skilled labor force, but the economic and political conditions for absorbing it are often absent (Portes, 1981, p. 39). The costs for underdeveloped societies of a professional group desirous and capable of leaving are tremendous. Scarce resources train students whose dissatisfactions with Third World conditions often increase with their level of training.

A precise determination of the value of labor exports for sending countries cannot be achieved in the abstract because the nature of the labor supply of exporting countries varies. Sassen-Koob has argued that within the labor surplus of underdeveloped societies an "apparent surplus" must be distinguished from a "hard-core surplus" (1978, p. 53). What is usually meant by labor surplus is in fact the hard-core sectors of labor which could not be absorbed even with significantly expanded industrialization. The point is that a share of labor surplus is necessary for significantly expanded industrialization. If labor exports deplete this "apparent labor surplus," the consequences may be detrimental for subsequent development. Thus, although labor exports may be responding to the vagaries of skewed development associated with import-substitution models, if labor exports are coming from the apparent labor surplus, the familiar dependent pattern of development is merely reinforced. In order to examine the role of labor exports effectively, the internal differentiation in the composition of labor exports must be captured.

Relatively few studies exist which attempt an assessment of the impact of Third World emigration on the sending communities themselves. Most of the evidence we have on this question comes form studies which have focused on outmigration from rural sending communities in societies such as Yugoslavia,

Greece, Portugal, Mexico, and the Dominican Republic (Baucic, 1972; Dinerman, 1977; Poinard and Roux, 1977; Reichert, 1981; Weist, 1979; Cornelius, 1978; Pessar, 1982; Grasmuck, 1982). My purpose in this chapter is to assess the impact of urban labor exports on one sending country. Caribbean migration to the United States has been shown to differ from other streams, principally Mexican, in terms of the larger number of Caribbeans who leave from urban rather than rural areas (Urrea, 1982; Gurak, 1981). I will examine the composition of labor exports originating from one urban area of the Domincan Republic and destined for the United States by addressing the following questions: (1) What is the composition of the typical urban migrant household? (2) What share of the migrant population comes from the labor surplus and what share comes from the employed labor force? (3) What share of the formerly employed migrant population may be considered part of an "apparent labor surplus" and what part actually constitutes a "hard-core surplus"? (4) What is the impact of return migration of the urban economy?

The point is not to address the determinants of outmigration associated in much of the literature of this question with the pattern of dependent development but, rather, to examine the likely reciprocal effects of prolonged outmigration on the very conditions which stimulated migration in the first place. The data presented here challenge the generally accepted assumption that labor exports from underdeveloped regions, by drawing from the surplus population, serve to rectify imbalances between low-wage and high-wage regions of the world.

DOMINICAN DEVELOPMENT AND MIGRATION

Dominican industrial development in the post-Trujillo period has paralleled the import-substitution model employed in other parts of Latin America. Early industrial growth was largely financed by foreign capital stimulated originally by easy access to domestic and foreign credit and by liberal tax provisions of a 1966 industrial incentives act. This early industrialization resulted in a growth in the gross domestic product at an annual real rate of 11 percent between 1968 and 1974, one of the highest growth rates in the world (World Bank, 1978, p. 29). After 1974, with the overall worsening of commodity export prices, the national economy seriously declined. The nation's trade deficit tripled between 1972 and 1976, and general economic stagnation set in.

The Dominican economy is marked by an extremely underfinanced, stagnant agrarian sector, which subsidizes cheap food for a relatively low-wage, modern urban sector at the expense of precapitalist and semiproletarianized farmers. The relatively low wages of the modern sector compared to wage labor in the central economies maintains the competitiveness of exports in world markets. This applies to the production of both primary commodities—which in the Dominican Republic are given an additional reduction in production cost by the use of cheap Haitian workers in sugar cane production—and increasingly to manufactured consumer goods (Jalee, 1973; Frobel, Heinrichs and Kreye, 1980; Vuskovic, 1982).

The Dominican Republic well illustrates a sectorally and socially "disarticulated" economy. In a disarticulated economy, industrialization implies external dependency for the acquisition of capital goods and technology; thus, equilibrium in the balance of payments becomes a constraint to industrial expansion. The situation is reinforced by the lack of linkages between agriculture and industrial production (de Janvry, 1981). Unlike developed economies, in socially disarticulated economies there is no objective relation between the overall rate of profit and the level of wages. Indeed, the maintenance of low wages in the peripheral economy assures a competitive position for export goods on the international market.

The shortcomings of the import substitution model of industrialization followed in the Dominican Republic have been especially negative in two areas: employment and income inequality. The stagnation of Dominican agriculture became increasingly acute in the late 1970s and was reflected in a sharp deterioration in the internal relations of exchange between industry and agriculture between 1973 and 1979, to the detriment of the latter (World Bank, 1981, p. 12). The average monthly income of a rural family in 1976-77 was only 55 percent that of the urban household. Unemployment in the rural areas was estimated by the World Bank to be as high as 60 percent in 1976 (World Bank, 1978). The magnitude of rural-urban migration in this context has been explosive, with urban areas expanding at a rate of 5.6 percent per year, compared to 1 percent per year in the rural areas (World Bank, 1981, p. 38). The consequence has been a gradual shift in the focus of unemployment and underemployment from rural to urban areas.

The high growth years did witness the emergence of a new urban middle class in the Dominican Republic. Indeed, state investment during the decade 1966-1976 favored urban middle-class groups, especially in the area of urban residential construction (Catrain, 1980, p. 18). However, the steady growth in GNP per capita from 286 pesos in 1969 to 417 pesos in 1975 (at constant 1962 prices) (World Bank, 1978, p. 129) has not corrected the highly unequal distribution of income. The emergence of a new urban middle class reflected less a redistribution of wealth than a relative loss of total income by the bottom fifth of the population. The bottom fifth of the population earned relatively less in 1973 (1.4 percent of the total) than in 1969 (2.9 percent). The top fifth of the population was able to maintain its share of total income (54.8 percent of total income in 1969 compared with 54.4 percent in 1973). The middle-income groups succeeded in capturing a larger proportion of total income during this period, but this was done at the expense of the poorest sectors of the population and not the most wealthy (27.6 percent in 1969 and 30.2 percent in 1973) (Cabral, 1975, p. 2).

After initially pursuing a path of import substitution, there has been a new emphasis on the establishment of export manufacturing zones. Attuned to the general internationalization of capitalist production, three free trade zones have been established in the Dominican Republic, in La Romana, Santiago de los Caballeros, and San Pedro de Macoris. As of 1969, imports into and exports from these zones are not taxed or restricted in any way. There are 44 firms established in the zones, producing cigars, garments, electronics, and agroindustrial products with a total employment of 6,100 in 1976. The presence of such zones testifies to the low-wage conditions of the Dominican Republic, as firms are primarily attracted by the relatively low average labor costs of 36 cents per hour compared to a range of 25 cents per hour in the Maquila areas of Mexico, and $1.25 to $2.65 per hour in Puerto Rico (World Bank, 1978, p. 58). Whether these free trade zones will contribute to a reduction in unemployment remains to be seen. However, studies of other countries indicate that fewer jobs are created in the export industries than those jobs lost in the area of production for domestic demand (Frobel, Heinrichs and Kreye, 1980, p. 369).

It is from this context of expanded industrial development with sustained high economic growth followed by relative stagnation, and persistently high unemployment, especially visible in urban areas, that the contemporary wave of Dominican outmigration commenced. The yearly average of the number of Dominican immigrants officially admitted to the United States in the decade 1966-1977 was 12,513, for a grand total of 150,155. This is a tenfold increase over any period prior to the assassination of Trujillo in 1961. Further, the number of officially admitted nonimmigrants reached a total of 1,126,000 for the decade.

Early studies of Dominican emigration to the United States assumed that typically migrants originated from rural communities (Gonzalez, 1970; Hendricks, 1974; Garrison and Weiss, 1979). Sometimes this process was described as step-migration, with rural migrants spending some short time in larger urban areas before leaving the country (Kayal, 1978, p. 13), and other times as migration from rural communities directly to the receiving societies (Sassen-Koob, 1978, p. 317). The early studies which suggested a rural-based emigration were typically small community studies whose methodologies did not actually permit generalizations beyond given rural settings. Recent data from ore representative studies reveal that a sizable proportion of the Dominican stream originates from urban areas (Ugalde et al., 1979; Pérez, 1981; Gurak, 1983). One of the more recent studies also suggests a sizeable return migrant population residing in the Dominican Republic (Ugalde, 1979).

The central questions regarding the impact of migration on sending communities are whether or not remittances and savings earned by migrants help to strengthen the local economy in terms of productive investments and the adoption of new technology; whether, in agricultural areas, more egalitarian land tenure relationships or increased agricultural production result; or whether, in urban areas, reductions in the size of the unemployed labor force occur with the consequent reductions in social unrest associated with a languishing urban population. Yet there are relatively few studies of the impact of Dominican migration for the sending communities themselves. The few exceptions have concentrated on the impact of outmigration for rural areas (Pessar, 1982; Grasmuck, 1982; Bray, 1983; Krute, 1983). In view of the sizable component of outmigration emanating from urban areas, the focus of this analysis will be the impact of sustained emigration on one urban zone in the Dominican Republic and the urban impact of return migration.

THE STUDY

The analysis will be based on two different sets of data. The first is a representative survey of the urban area of Santiago de los Caballeros conducted in November 1980. This survey was part of a larger interdisciplinary effort to examine a number of distinct migrant communities in the Cibao regions of the Dominican Republic.[2] The second data set consists of a survey of Dominicans working in New York City conducted in the summer of 1981. The purposes of the two surveys were different, and the sampling techniques differed accordingly.

Santiago de los Caballeros is the second largest city in the Dominican Republic and is, in effect, the capital of the northern region of the country, with a population of approximately 250,000 in 1979 (ONAPLAN, 1981, p. 63). Much of the rapid growth experienced by Santiago during the past two decades resulted from migration from the eastern and western regions, where the majority of the people are sharecroppers or rural day laborers. The tobacco industry has historically been an important sector in Santiago and in the region as a whole, and it remains so today. However, during the high growth of the early 1970s construction was one of the fastest growing industrial sectors (Veras, 1976, p. 35). Santiago is also the base of one of the three free trade zones operating in the Dominican Republic. The limited industrial growth that has occurred has hardly absorbed a fraction of the expanding urban population. A survey conducted by the National Statistics Office in 1979 estimated almost half of the economically active population of Santiago to be openly unemployed or underemployed (ONAPLAN, 1981, p. 129).

The Santiago data was based on a multistage probability sample from a sampling frame provided by the Dominican National Office of Statistics. The sample objective here was twofold: (1) to estimate the proportion of families with members who, at the time of the survey or in the past, had lived abroad for the universe of the urban area of Santiago, and (2) to generate a sufficient number of cases of migrant households in order to compare migrant and nonmigrant households on a variety of dimensions. Known migrant neighborhoods were oversampled in order to maximize the number of migrant households, and these cases were subsequently weighted accordingly. The intent with this data set was to provide representative data of the migrant population.

An interview team consisting of 14 Dominican students largely from the National Catholic University of Santiago received a one-week training session and subsequently conducted the interviews. The survey instrument included information on household size and composition, primary and secondary occupations of all household members, employment history of the household head and spouse; dependence on and use of remittances from abroad, and employment information on all members currently residing outside of the country. The duration of the interviews ranged from 30 minutes to two hours and took place in the homes of the respondents. In 98 percent of the cases the interview was conducted with the head of house or with the spouse of the head of house. The refusal rate was relatively low such that the overall response rate was 91.1 percent, resulting in a working sample of 535 households.

The principal destination of Dominicans bound for the United States is the New York City area. Estimates of the number of documented and undocumented Dominicans living in New York City range from 300,000 to 500,000. The New York survey of our project consists of a "snowball" sample[3] of Dominicans living and working in New York City. The intent was to generate roughly equal numbers of documented and undocumented Dominicans. The original plan was to follow the strategy advocated by Cornelius (1982) by developing a snowball sample of relatives of Dominican contacts we had established by means of our fieldwork in the Dominican Republic. The method proved unworkable given the high costs of locating families in different boroughs of New York and given the acute state of apprehension in which most undocumented Dominicans live. Instead, we selected a group of seven Dominican interviewers who came from different neighborhoods and social circles in New York and generated a chain of interviews originating from the familial and social contacts of the interviewers themselves.

The New York survey consists of 301 interviews with persons born in the Dominican Republic and employed at the time of the survey in New York City. It was permissible for an interviewer to select more than one employed person per household. Of the total sample of 301, 232 interviews represent separate households, with the remaining 22.9 percent of the cases coming from households with more than one case. The interviews typically took place in the residence of the interviewee and generally lasted about one hour. There are many characteristics of the sample which match more representative surveys of Dominicans residing in New York (Gurak, 1981). For example, the sample contains more men than women (58.1 percent to 41.2 percent), has a relatively young median age (32.9 percent), and consists of a large majority whose last residence in the Dominican Republic was urban (79.7 percent). Among other things, the New York survey provides information on the employment history of the migrant, the community of origin in the Dominican Republic, as well as time spent in the community of departure and serves, therefore, as a supplement to the representative survey of the urban area of Santiago.

URBAN MIGRANT HOUSEHOLDS

The Santiago survey reveals that the extent of migration from this urban zone is substantial and that it is also an important place of resettlement for return migrants. Fully 16.7 percent of Santiago households contain at least one member living outside the Dominican Republic (present migrant households), and 11.0 percent of the households contain at least one member who has returned from living in the United States (return migrant households). Combining present with return migrant households we find that 23.0 percent of Santiago residences have been directly touched by migration. Moreover, once a family decides to send one of its members abroad, it often chooses to send a second member as well, with the median number of migrants per migrant household being 1.37.

It is important to underscore the magnitude of this phenomenon and the sheer quantitative impact that migration has had on this urban community. Basing our calculations on the sampling frame unemployed and the total economically active population, we may conservatively calculate the approximate number of adult Santiagüeros living abroad to be 9,941, or 10.0 percent of the urban labor force of Santiago.[4] Likewise, the adult return migrant population is estimated at 6,626, or 7.3 percent of the economically active of Santiago.[5]

These figures actually underestimate the extent to which migration has affected these communities significantly because the surveys by design do not include those families which moved as intact households and thereby left no remaining household members in the community of origin. Indeed, when we employ the term *migrant household* we are effectively describing the true international household, with its members residing on different sides of national borders.

The family members who have left Santiago are predominately male, or 65.9 percent of all migrants. The consequence of this predominately male exodus has been to increase the relative number of female-headed households in the community. Although the number of female households in the community is almost twice as large in migrant households as in nonmigrant households (45.1 percent compared to 22.5 percent, respectively), they, nonetheless do not constitute the majority of the migrant families. The reason for this is the high proportion of cases in which the outside migrant is not the husband or wife of the remaining head but is instead the son or daughter. Table 1 reveals the relationship of the outside migrant to the remaining head of house in Santiago. In 16.6 percent of the migrant households, the first migrant mentioned is the hus-

TABLE 1
Relation of Outside Migrant to Remaining Head of House in Santiago, Dominican Republic
(percent)

Relation	First Migrant Only	All Migrants
Husband	16.6	8.4
Wife	2.4	1.2
Son	32.1	30.5
Daughter	26.2	15.6
Parent or parent-in-law	10.7	15.6
Other	12.0	28.7
Total	100.0	100.0
Weighted Migrant N =	(84)	(167)
Weighted Household N =	(84)	(84)

Source: Santiago Project Data.

band of the remaining female head, in 58.3 percent the migrant is the son or daughter of the head; and in 22.7 percent the outside member is some other relation, most often a sibling or parent of the head of house. Therefore, in our discussion when we refer to the head of a Santiago migrant household, in the majority of the cases we are saying something about the parent who has witnessed the outmigration of his or her child.

An important consideration in urban outmigration is whether or not migrants who have left their country from urban areas had been longtime dwellers in those urban areas or had in fact only recently arrived from the countryside prior to their departure. This point is crucial for an assessment of the extent to which labor exports may be tapping a displaced rural labor force or may be drawing upon the established urban working population. With this in mind, respondents were asked about the last and penultimate places of residence prior to Santiago. Table 2 reveals that present migrant households are no more likely to have recently come from the countryside than are nonmigrant households. The households from which migrants originate have about an equal likelihood of having always resided in the urban area of Santiago as do the nonmigrant households (43.9 percent to 45.0 percent respectively). Among those families who had moved to Santiago from another area, the migrant households were somewhat less likely to have come directly from a rural area (6.1 percent) than were the nonmigrant families who were nonnative Santiagüeros (10.1 percent). Among those who had emigrated from outside Santiago, the migrants were more likely to have come most immediately from smaller urban towns (27.3 percent compared to 21.6 percent, respectively). It

TABLE 2
Place of Last Residence of Head of House Within the Dominican Republic Prior to Residence in Santiago, by Migratory Status
(percent)

Type of Last Residence	Nonmigrant	Present Migrant	Return Migrant	Total
Rural	10.1	6.1	6.4[a]	9.2
Semi-urban (4,900 or less)	21.6	27.3	32.3	23.2
Urban (5,000 or more)	23.3	22.7	19.4	23.0
Native Resident of Santiago	45.0	43.9	41.9	44.6
Total	100.0	100.0	100.0	100.0
Weighted N =	(338)	(66)	(31)[b]	(435)

Source: Santiago Project Data.
[a] Less than 5 cases.
[b] This excludes those case whose prior residence was New York.

may be concluded, therefore, that urban outmigration is not an expression of step-migration, with the real senders being the rural communities and Santiago being only a stopover place. Households which send migrants abroad were just as likely to be native Santiagüeros as the nonmigrant population. Although it is true that a majority of the present migrant households have not always resided in Santiago, this appears to be a reflection of the generally high rate of internal migration characterizing the population as a whole (Ramirez, Tactuk and Breton, 1977) and not a salient feature of the migrant population.

Policy makers from developing societies often point to the positive contributions which remittance payments from abroad make to the balance of payments. Other sources have pointed out that remittances could also have detrimental effects by means of turning significant numbers of agricultural producers into consumers, which could decrease the domestic food supply or contribute to demand-pull inflation (ILO, 1975, p. 65). The difficulty of the issue is compounded by the lack of systematic information regarding the regularity or quantity of remittance payments, especially for areas larger than small villages.

The Santiago survey reveals that one-third (33.8 percent) of the urban families have received at some time in the past some form of aid from relatives living abroad. At the time of the survey, 67.9 percent of the households received no remittances, 12.0 percent received aid but irregularly or only on special occasions, and fully 18.3 percent reported sustained consistent support from outside. Among the regular aid recipients with few exceptions these payments came on a monthly basis.

Table 3 reveals the distribution of the amounts of money being sent on a

TABLE 3
Monthly Remittances Received by Households in Santiago Receiving Regular Payments from Abroad

Amount Received Monthly (D.R.$)	Regular Recipients (%)
Less than $50	23.0
$50-99	21.8
$100-199	26.4
$200-299	5.7
$300 or more	23.0
Weighted N =	(87)
Mean = $ 130.17	

Source: Santiago Project Data.

monthly basis for the households which receive regular payments. Although the majority of families receive payments of less than D.R. $200 a month (71.2 percent), more than one-fifth of them receive more than D.R. $300 a month. The mean amount received per household was D.R. $149.56. These are substantial payments when one considers the fact that the median monthly wage for heads of house in 1979 in Santiago was D.R. $173. Further, extrapolating from the household to that of the city as a whole, we can conservatively estimate that approximately D.R. $16,348,892 is entering Santiago on a regular basis each year.[6] Nor does this figure include the value of appliances, gifts, or savings which migrants bring back during vacations.

One of the most immediate consequences of the increased income for migrant households is the consequent access to modern consumer goods. Indeed, these kinds of remittances combined with the possibility of gifts from relatives living abroad mean dramatically different possibilities for obtaining consumer goods for migrant and nonmigrant families. Table 4 reveals the extent to which migratory status is associated with a lifestyle of "modern consumption." Combining present migrant households with return migrant households and comparing these with nonmigrant families, we see that the former are more likely to have heads which earn $300 pesos or more a month

TABLE 4
Percentage Distribution of Selected Household Consumer Items by Migratory Status by Income in Santiago, 1980
(percent)

	Migratory Status	
Household Consumer Items by Income Levels (D.R. $)	Nonmigrant	All Migrant[a]
Less than $100	15.6	3.2
Electric light	64.9	59.4
Radio	44.9	90.6[b]
$100-300	44.2	48.0
Television	64.8	89.6
Refrigerator	68.9	76.4
Stereo	26.8	42.9
$300 or more	40.1	48.8
Automobile	43.0	56.9
Stereo	57.2	66.4
Color television	5.2	23.4
Weighted N =	(389)	(134)

Source: Santiago Project Data.
[a] Includes present migrant households and return migrant households.
[b] Fewer than 5 cases.

than are nonmigrant households, 48.8 percent compared to 40.1 percent, respectively. Within both of the higher income groups, migrant households are more likely than their nonmigrant counterparts to possess television sets (89.5 to 64.8 percent, respectively), refrigerators (76.1 to 68.9 percent), automobiles (56.9 to 43.0 percent), stereos (66.4 to 57.2 percent), and color televisions sets (23.4 to 5.2 percent). Most of these modern consumer goods which distinguish migrant families are, of course, imported. This inflow of purchasing power for goods in short supply and expensive in the domestic economy can only produce negative effects for the balance of payments. That is, even if dramatic sums of money are entering the city or society as a whole in the form of cash payments, if the consequence is increased demand for imported goods with indirect cost-push pressure, the net contribution to the balance of payments can be assumed to be negative.

There is an important aspect in which the migrant family fares less well than the nonmigrant population, and that lies in the ability of the remaining head to sustain local employment. Table 5 presents employment levels for non-

TABLE 5
Employment by Migratory Status by Sex of Head of House in Santiago
(percent)

Employment Status	Male-Headed			Female-Headed			Total
	Non-migrant	Present Migrant	Return Migrant	Non-migrant	Present Migrant	Return Migrant	
Unemployed	20.3	99.5	29.8	47.0	76.7	78.0	68.2
Employed	79.7	63.4	70.2	53.0	23.3	22.0	31.8
Total	100.0	99.9	100.0	100.0	100.0	100.0	100.0
Weighted N =	(311)	(37)	(39)	(90)	(31)	(16)	(524)

Source: Santiago Project Data.
* Less than 5 cases.

migrant, present migrant, and return migrant households. The return migrants will be treated separately. A much higher percentage of the heads of migrant households are unemployed than are heads of nonmigrant families. Nor is this relatively high unemployment for migrant heads merely a reflection of the greater concentration of female heads among these households. Considering only male heads, 36.5 percent of the migrant households compared to 20.3 percent of the nonmigrant households were unemployed during the week prior to the time of the survey, and among female heads the migrants also reported dramatically higher rates of unemployment than did the nonmigrants, 76.7 percent compared to 47.0 percent. Further, the pattern of relatively high rates of unemployment for migrant heads is reproduced over the five-year period prior to the survey (table 6): only 42.2 percent of the migrant heads reported full employment during the five years, compared to 53.6 percent for the non-migrant heads, whereas 29.1 percent of the migrant heads compared to 19.4 percent of the nonmigrants heads stated that they had been unemployed for two or more of the five years. The fact that many of the heads of migrants households are the parents of the outside migrant may mean that the inability of a parent to secure viable employment was a factor which induced the son or daughter to seek work outside the country or the family to sponsor the trip. Alternatively, the very fact of having a son or daughter working abroad may have tended to produce a dependence on remittance payments rather than local sources of employment.

TABLE 6
Employment Over Five-Year Period by Migratory Status in Santiago
(percent)

Employment Over 5 Years	Nonmigrant	Present Migrant	Return Migrant	Total
Fully employed	53.6	42.2	42.8	51.3
Unemployed for 1 year or less	15.0	7.8	12.1	13.9
Unemployed for 1-2 years	12.0	20.8	15.3	13.3
Unemployed for 2 or more years	19.4	29.1	29.8	21.5
Total	100.0	99.9	100.0	100.0
Weighted N =	(365)	(47)	(53)	(465)

Source: Santiago Project Data.

RELATIVE LABOR SURPLUS AND EMIGRATION

Apart from the issue of what happens to remaining households once a member leaves to find work, it is important to determine the demographic characteristics and class composition of the emigratory population. To the extent to which labor exports come disproportionately from the unemployed population, it can be argued that outmigration results in an increased demand for the remaining labor force, which, if significant enough, will mean a rise in local wage rates. Similarly, if migrants come from the unemployed, their exit becomes a safety-valve for dominant groups against potential social disruption since the physical reminders of economic failures are merely exported. On the contrary, if labor exports draw upon the employed, and within the employed the relatively skilled, then it may be said that the sending society is underwriting the sizable cost of reproducing and training labor for the central and dominant economies. In the discussion which follows information from the survey of Dominicans living in New York will be utilized in order to determine the class background and employment history of the households they leave behind. Since we are interested in analyzing the impact of labor exports of the urban economy, only migrants who reported their last residence in the Dominican Republic to be urban (239) are included here.

The New York data reveal that Dominican labor exports draw from a predominately young, male, educated population. The median age of the New York sampled population is 32.9. Males constitute 58.1 percent of the sample.

The young age of most migrants means that emigration draws disproportionately from the better educated of the home country. As can be seen from table 7, even when we compared the New York migrant population with the

TABLE 7
Educational Levels of New York-Based Migrants from Urban Communities in the Dominican Republic Compared to Santo Domingo Population
(percent)

Years of Completed Education	Urban Migrants	Santo Domingo Population (10 years and older)
0-3	13.0	28.0
4-6	22.4	26.1
7-9	23.9	23.1
10-12	23.5	15.2
13 or more	17.2	7.6
Total	100.0	100.0
	(N = 238)	(N = n.a.)

Sources: For urban migrants, New York Project Data. For Santo Domingo Population, ONAPLAN, 1981, table 27, p. 101.

population of the capital of the Dominican Republic, known for higher than average educational levels compared to the country as a whole, we see a disproportionate concentration of migrants in the higher educational levels. Whereas only 7.6 percent of the population of Santo Domingo has completed 13 or more years of school, this is true of 17.2 percent of the urban migrants living in New York. Moreover, while only 13.0 percent of the sampled Dominican New Yorkers had completed less than three years of school, this was true of 28.0 percent of those living in Santo Domingo. The median number of school years completed by the migrant is 8.2.

With respect to the issue of labor surplus or the extent to which labor exports draw from the working labor force, migrants were asked about the nature of their last employment immediately prior to departure from urban areas in the Dominican Republic. The overwhelming majority, or 69.8 percent, of the migrants reported that they had in fact been working prior to departure (table 8). This means that only 30.2 percent of them were without some kind of employment, and this pattern holds true for males and females alike. It is true, however, that this figure is higher than the unemployment levels of Santo Domingo (19.3 percent) and Santiago (18.5 percent) in 1977, the

TABLE 8
Employment Status of New York-Based Migrants Prior to Departure from Urban Communities in the Dominican Republic
(percent)

Employment Status	Male	Female	Total
Employed	68.8	69.8	69.2
Unemployed	31.3	30.2	30.2
Total	100.0	100.0	100.0
N =	(138)	(96)	(234)

Source: New York Project Data.

two largest urban zones (ONAPLAN, 1981, 6). Thus migrants are more likely to come disproportionately from the unemployed. However, one must keep in mind the fact that most of the migrants are younger that the average age of the economically active in the Dominican Republic. The unemployment levels of younger workers tend to be much higher than that of the population as a whole (ONAPLAN, 1981, 6). Moreover, it is notable that the migrant population sampled in this survey does not come predominantly from an unemployed, displaced labor force.

It is nonetheless possible that migrants with jobs prior to departure were significantly underemployed or occupying insecure and unstable jobs, perhaps in the low-skilled or informal sectors of the economy. In this case their decision to look for foreign employment would not likely cause significant imbalances in the home economy as they would be relatively replaced by the abundant pool of unskilled, unemployed workers concentrated in urban communities. Figures in table 9 compare the occupational attainments of emigrants studied and those of Dominicans living in Santo Domingo. As seen in table 9, migrants do not come disproportionately from the lower strata of the occupational pyramid. On the contrary, they are more heavily represented in three professional and technical jobs than are adult Dominicans in the capital city. Almost one-fifth of the emigrants reported such jobs, compared to only 8.6 percent of the capital city, which is known for a high concentration of professional employment. Most of the other occupational categories are fairly closely matched for the emigrants and the broader Dominican population with the exception of service workers, where the emigrants are substantially underrepresented (12.8 percent compared to 26.3 percent). However, we are not dealing here with a drain of the most highly trained of the professionals. A disaggregated look at the jobs held by migrants *within* the professional and

TABLE 9
Last Occupation of Dominican Urban Emigrants in Home Country and Comparative Figures for the Population of Santo Domingo
(percent)

Occupational Level	Dominican Urban Immigrants	Santo Domingo Population
Professional, technical, and kindred	19.9	8.6
Managers and proprietors	4.5	3.9
Clerical	11.5	9.8
Sales	15.4	14.3
Drivers and kindred	5.7	5.3
Craftsmen and operatives and laborers (except farm)	24.4	28.5
Service workers including private household	12.8	26.3
Other (including agriculture)	5.8	3.3
Total	100.0	100.0
N =	(156)	(2,673)

Sources: For Dominican urban immigrants, New York Project Data. For Santo Domingo Population, ONAPLAN, table 9, p. 17.

technical trades reveals a high concentration within the teaching occupations, especially at the elementary school levels.

It is also important to specify the industrial sector in which migrants were employed in the home economy and to assess the general employment levels of these sectors. This data is presented in table 10 where it is revealed that in general the last jobs held by migrants were in sectors of the economy known for relatively low levels of unemployment, at least as measured in the capital city of Santo Domingo. On the one hand, migrants worked with less frequency in two of the three sectors with the highest rates of unemployment (construction and personal and social service). On the other hand, almost 30 percent of the migrants worked in commerce or in restaurants and hotels, compared with only 20.6 percent of the resident population of Santo Domingo. That such a higher concentration of migrants occurred in this sector is especially significant when the relatively low level of unemployment of this sector (6.5 percent) is taken into account. It is not actually that these persons were particularly

TABLE 10
Last Sector of Employment in Home Country of Dominican Emigrants, Comparative Figures for the Population of Santo Domingo, and Rates of Unemployment by Sector in Santo Domingo
(percent)

Sector	Inmigrant's Last Occupation, 1981	Employment of Santo Domingo Population, 1979	Rates of Unemployment by Sector in Santo Domingo
Manufacturing	20.8	17.1	13.0
Construction	3.1	5.5	32.6
Transport	8.1	5.1	18.2
Commerce, restaurants, and hotels	29.5	20.6	6.5
Personal and social services	28.9	47.3	10.8
Other, including agriculture	9.4	4.4	6.1
Total	100.1	100.0	
N =	(149)	(1051)	(145)

Sources: For immigrants last occupation, New York Project Data. For Santo Domingo population and rates of unemployment, ONAPLAN, table 9, p.17.

* This is the unemployment level of each sector calculated by dividing the number of unemployed in each sector by the total economically active in that sector. Thus the sum of all percentages would not be 100.

threatened by likely redundancy. More probably, migrants employed in such sectors were more likely to have been regularly exposed to foreigners and tourists, who continually exhibit a life style and consumption not attainable by service workers or low-level professionals in the Dominican Republic.

These results contradict the impression that Dominican emigrants, especially illegal ones, are predominantly unskilled, unemployed workers. Nor are these abandoned jobs likely to be the occupations which could easily be filled by other unskilled workers who remain behind in the home community. Yet it is not possible to argue that migrants represent no labor surplus at all, since they were more likely to have been unemployed prior to departure than the total urban population. To the extent that they were unemployed, however, they represent an "apparent surplus" which constitutes a significant societal investment.

RETURN MIGRATION

Another important consideration in an assessment of the impact of emigration on national development is the extent of return migration with its possibilities for new infusions of capital, productive investments, and new skills learned abroad. Returning to our representative sample of Santiago households, we may compare the subsample of households containing return migrants with the rest of the Santiago population in order to typify the experience of those who return and to judge their likely impact on the home economy. As noted above, Santiago is an important site for the resettlement of return migrants, such that 11.0 percent of all households of Santiago have at least one such member.

It has sometimes been argued that international migration exacerbates internal migration, with many rural dwellers using foreign employment to finance a resettlement to an urban area in the sending country. If this were true one would expect a disproportionate number of return migrants reporting former residences in rural areas than the nonmigrant population. The survey data, however, do not confirm this interpretation. The heads of the three household types (nonmigrant, present migrant, and return migrant) have about equal likelihood of having always resided in the urban area of Santiago: 45.0 percent of the nonmigrant households, 43.9 percent of the migrant, and 41.9 percent of the return migrant households (table 2). Among those families who had moved to Santiago from other parts of the Dominican Republic, the present migrant and return migrant families were less likely to have come directly to Santiago from a rural area, 10.6 and 6.4 percent, respectively, than the nonmigrant households (14.5 percent).

Actually a relatively higher proportion of return migrants are native residents of Santiago than table 2 indicates. This is because those cases where the head of a return migrant household reported his or her place of last residence to be outside the country were excluded from the above analysis. However, 65 percent of the return migrants reported that their penultimate residence was the urban area of Santiago. Consistent with this, a slightly higher proportion of the heads of return migrant households were born in the urban area of Santiago, 50.1 percent compared to 44.8 percent for the migrant households, and 43.0 percent for the nonmigrant heads.

Former rural dwellers do not, therefore, form a majority of the returnees. They do, nonetheless, constitute a sizable group. For this reason, perhaps, they have made an indelible impression on the consciousness of many native dwellers of Santiago, who are fond of the stereotype of the rural *campesino* returning from New York with a lot of cash and little capacity for "proper" urban consumption. The Dominican with a rural accent who buys a new house in Santiago in cash may be dominant in popular imagery but, as our survey data indicates, is not in fact the typical case.

The amount of time spent abroad by an adult member away from his or her family and community is important in terms of potential familial and community disruption. It is also true that the longer amount of time spent in the foreign society the less likely the migrant is to return. In this regard the Caribbean migrant stream differs significantly from the Mexican pattern of labor migration to the U.S. In the latter case migrants may easily return to their communities of origin various times a year, and in some cases various times a month (Cornelius, 1976; Portes, 1979; Reichert, 1981). This is true, moreover, for both documented and undocumented workers because of the relative ease with which they may cross the border given a loosely enforced border policy and the relatively low cost of travel home.

In the Dominican case, the cost of the journey from the home community to the protection of the Hispanic community, especially in the New York area, is expensive, and hence Dominican migrants tend to stay for relatively long periods. Table 11 presents the distribution of the duration of stay abroad for

TABLE 11
Time Spent Abroad by Migrants Returning to Santiago
(percent)

Duration of Stay (years)	Return Migrants
1 or less	29.6
1-2	18.5
3-5	21.0
6-10	6.2
10-15	13.6
15-20	11.1
Total	100.0
Weighted N =	(81)

Source: Santiago Project Data.

those Dominicans who have returned to Santiago to live after employment experience overseas. The duration refers to periods of time in which the source of employment was consistently foreign work excluding vacations. Less than one-third of the returnees stayed abroad for less than one year. The median number of years of foreign employment was 3.0. That is, fully one-half of all

Dominicans who leave their country and return home to live have resided outside for more than three years. Some stay for considerable stints; almost one-quarter reported a foreign experience of ten or more years.

The findings of the New York data of higher than average educational attainments for migrants are also confirmed by the Santiago data. Table 12

TABLE 12

Education by Migratory Status for
Heads of Households in Santiago, 1981
(percent)

Years of Education Completed	Nonmigrant	Present Migrant	Return Migrant	Total
0	18.4	24.1	8.9*	18.1
1—3	9.2	14.4	8.3*	9.8
4—6	13.3	13.7	12.3	13.2
7—9	22.0	14.9	13.9	20.0
10—12	28.0	30.6	44.6	30.2
13 or more	9.1	2.3	12.0	8.5
Total	100.0	100.0	100.0	99.8
Weighted N =	(390)	(68)	(57)	(514)

Source: Santiago Project Data.
* Fewer than 5 cases.

reveals the extent to which return migrants are relatively more educated than the general population. They are underrepresented in those groups with no formal education (8.9 percent, compared to 18.4 percent for the nonmigrants) and in all of the lower ranks of educational attainment. Alternatively, almost 45 percent of return migrants report having completed at least one year of high school, compared with only 28 percent for the nonmigrants. Further, slightly more return migrants than heads of nonmigrant households report having completed one or more year of university education. Also notable is the extent to which the heads of present migrant families are overrepresented in the lower educational levels and underrepresented in the higher ranks, particularly university education. This is probably an expression of the fact that many of these family heads are older than the nonmigrant population and hence with fewer years of schooling since we know that many of them are the parents of adult migrants living abroad.

The higher educational levels of return migrant families do not, however, ensure higher labor participation rates. On the contrary, as reflected in the data presented in table 5, return migrant heads are much more likely to be unemployed than are the heads of nonmigrant families. Almost 30 percent of male return migrant heads were out of work, compared to 20.3 percent of the nonmigrant heads. This pattern of relatively higher unemployment rates for returnees is especially marked among female-headed households, with almost four-fifths of the returnees being unemployed, compared to 47 percent of the nonmigrant female heads. Nor is this discrepancy a reflection of the recent return of the migrants. As seen in table 6, the pattern of relatively high rates of unemployment for the returnees compared to the nonmigrant heads is reproduced over the five-year period prior to the survey: only 42.8 percent of the returnees reported full employment during the last five years compared to 53.6 percent of the nonmigrant heads. Whereas 19.4 percent of the nonmigrants had been without work for two or more years, this was true of 29.8 percent of the returnees.

Finally, there is the question of the type of job which the return migrant secures when he or she does find employment. Relevant data are presented in table 13. Despite their relatively high rates of unemployment, return migrants who do work are concentrated in the higher skilled occupations compared to

TABLE 13
Occupation by Migratory Status for Heads of Households in Santiago
(percent)

Occupation	Nonmigrant	Present Migrant	Return Migrant	Total
Professional, technical, managers, proprietors and kindred	14.2	13.7	33.0	16.2
Clerical	3.8	0.4*	8.8	4.1
Sales	19.7	18.4	19.3	19.5
Farmers, farm managers, agricultural and laborers	9.0	0.4*	9.1	8.1
Operatives*	35.0	32.1	25.4	33.5
Service workers, including private household	12.6	28.5	1.4*	13.0
Laborers, except farm	5.7	6.5*	2.9*	5.6
Total	100.0	100.0	99.9	100.0
Weighted N =	(372)	(48)	(53)	(468)

Source: Santiago Project Data.
* Fewer than 5 cases.

the nonmigrant population. Fully one-third of all employed returnees hold professional, technical, or managerial jobs, compared to only 14 percent of the sampled nonmigrant population. Return heads are also more likely to hold clerical jobs (8.8 percent) than are nonmigrant heads (3.8 percent). Similarly, the return migrant heads are significantly underrepresented among the operatives when compared to the nonmigrant heads who occupy such jobs (25.4 and 34.2 percent, respectively). Only 1.4 percent of the return heads hold jobs in personal or domestic service, compared to 12.3 percent of the non-migrant heads.

The dream of many Dominicans when they leave for the U.S. is to work for a temporary period in order to earn enough money to buy a new home in the Dominican Republic and perhaps to start a small business upon returning. There are a variety of firms which have emerged to capitalize upon this aspiration. Indeed the impact of "Dominican-Yorkers" on the residential construction industry in the Dominican Republic has been dramatic. There are presently Dominican construction firms with offices in Manhattan which finance and construct in the Dominican Republic new homes for Dominicans working in New York. The client sees the plans and designs for the house in New York and typically buys it on the island in the summer or during Christmas holidays. There were nine construction firms in Santiago in 1982, building around 400 new constructions each year. One Santiago bank officer and construction firm owner informed me that in 1982 all of the Santiago residential firms were selling principally to Dominican-Yorkers. These are, of course, labor-intensive firms, with the number of employees ranging from 100 to 800. Most of the homes constructed are relatively inexpensive and located in new upper working-class neighborhoods.

The apparent inability of so many Dominicans who have returned to find work, or to find work which is acceptable to them, has important negative implications for the likelihood that they will remain living in the new homes they have built. This same owner of a large construction enterprises told me that many of his clients who buy homes in New York after return to Santiago and start an unsuccessful small business, only to fail and return once more to New York. They continue to rent their homes to low-income Dominicans via lawyers, who collect these rents for a commission. In addition to housing, another service provided by Dominicans from afar takes the form of small loans to island Dominicans via this same set of lawyers, the apparent brokers in the exchange. In the recent years of slow economic growth, the Dominican state has devoted few resources to the construction of low-income housing, with consequent notable housing shortages. Ironically, and without intention, the Dominican-Yorkers are providing this service. They are, in effect, subsidizing the economy in a way the state has failed to do, in the provision of low-cost housing for the urban poor. What was originally a dream house becomes in effect an investment for a small-scale, absentee rentier.

The frustrations of return migrants are graphically illustrated by the data in table 14. All sampled Santiago households were asked if there was anyone in

TABLE 14
Plans for Future Migration Abroad by
Migratory Status for Households in Santiago
(percent)

Do you or other family member have plans to leave in order to live abroad?	Non migrant	Migrant	Return Migrant	Total
Yes	9.5	24.6	36.1	14.5
No	90.5	75.4	63.9	85.5
Total	100.0	100.0	100.0	100.0
	(384)	(69)	(55)	(508)

Source: Santiago Project Data.

the house with plans to leave the Dominican Republic in order to take up residence abroad. More than one-third of all the return households responded that, yes, at least one member had concrete plans to leave, compared to approximately 10 percent of the households with no migration experience. The very fact that fully 14.5 percent of the total sampled population of Santiago answered positively that they had migratory plans reveals the extent to which a stint in a place like New York has been incorporated into the cultural repertoire of strategies which Dominicans realistically consider. The relative predominance of return migrants among these aspirants reveals the failure of the Dominican economy as presently organized to make productive use of the entrepreneurial ambitions, limited capital, and skills of its New York-experienced population.

CONCLUSION

The phenomenon of outmigration from the largest urban zone in the northern region of the Dominican Republic draws predominately upon a labor force of longtime dwellers, if not native inhabitants, of that city. These are not, therefore, displaced rural laborers who have come to the city for a brief period prior to international departure. The number of outside migrants at the time of the survey constituted approximately 11 percent of the active labor force of

Santiago, not even including those cases where families left without leaving household members behind. Santiago is also an important resettlement zone for return migrants, who in 1980 constituted roughly 7 percent of the economically active of Santiago.

The typical Dominican migrant is a relatively young male who has in many cases departed from the household of his parents. The migrant does have a somewhat greater chance of being unemployed than does the population as a whole. One cannot conclude, however, that outmigration represents principally a reduction in the size of a hard-core, unskilled, unemployed population. Rather these migrants represented an "apparent surplus" in the sense that they constitute the type of "human capital" necessary to any meaningful type of expanded industrialization; they are relatively well educated and from relatively skilled occupations, especially at the lower levels of the professional ranks. Moreover, their last jobs were typically in industrial sectors of the economy noted for lower than average levels of unemployment. They therefore represent a rather inelastic supply of labor.

Remittances to the Dominican Republic from migrants living abroad reach approximately one-fifth of the households in Santiago. We estimated that over D.R. $16 million was entering Santiago annually via such payments. Remittances enter the country through the "parallel exchange" market, which varies from an exchange rate of around $1.25-$1.50 D.R./U.S., whereas all other foreign exchanges entering the Dominican Republic must pass through the official exchange marked at the rate of D.R. $1 to U.S. $1. This scale of remittances benefits not only the families receiving them but also a whole array of private exchange dealers. The state, therefore, does not directly capitalize on any of these foreign exchange earnings. The most dramatic expression of the use of remittances is via the purchase or import of consumer goods. Migrant households across all income levels become visible symbols of the relative payoff of wage labor in developed societies. The symbolic importance of these goods only serves to whet the appetite of other aspiring families.

Return migration does not appear to be particularly selective, in the sense that those who return could be distinguished from the overall migrant population. They, like present migrants, are relatively well educated and skilled, with fully one-third of them holding professional or technical jobs. They do, nonetheless, experience relatively high rates of unemployment. Migrants who return to Santiago have spent a median number of three years abroad, and many have stayed more than a decade away. The information presented here regarding the middle-class backgrounds of return migrants confirms earlier findings of Ugalde and his colleagues, based on a national sample of return migrants (Ugalde, Bean and Cardenas, 1979).

In addition to sending remittances, the migrants have played an important role in stimulating the construction of moderate-income housing. The adjustment problems migrants face upon returning, especially the tendency either not to find desirable employment or to start small businesses which fail, have meant that in many cases the return once more to the U.S to become absentee landlords for homes they had originally built for themselves.

The migrants are workers who *because* of their relatively advantageous positions were able to finance a relatively expensive move to the U.S. They seem to be persons motivated by a sense of insecurity, by a desire to improve their wages and type of life, and by a sense that although they themselves had jobs, overall conditions were insecure and would eventually operate against them as well. They aspired to a different kind of consumption pattern, one available to the wage worker in the U.S. and not so to the lower ranks of the middle class in the developing world. One migrant in New York explained to me that when he left Santo Domingo in 1965 he had had a good job as a printer but that all around him he could see smart, talented people without work. Fear of becoming like them coupled with the desire to give a better life to his new wife meant that he made use of his "dreamy" spirit and packed up.

These findings parallel in important ways other research conducted as part of this same project in two agrarian communities in the Dominican Republic known for significant outmigration. There it was found that the impact of outmigration on the community varied according to the infrastructural conditions of the area. In the context of low returns to farming investments, poor soil, and high population growth, migration had contributed to the unproductive use of land because migrant households tended to reduce farming activities. Migrants came from families of medium to large-size landholdings who in becoming dependent on remittances had thereby undetermined the productive base of the community and exacerbated income inequality (Pessar, 1982). Alternatively, in a more soil-rich community with better road transportation and marketing facilities, production had not been hurt by remittance income. In the latter case return migration was more evident and was associated with productive capital investments, notably in egg-producing firms. However, the frustrations of return migrants witnessed in Santiago were also observed in the second agricultural community, where it was discovered two years after the original survey that the bulk of the New York-capitalized egg enterprises had gone bankrupt due to pricing strategies of monopoly firms (Grasmuck, 1981).

These findings underscore the extent to which outmigration expresses not the lack of development but rather the paradoxes of uneven development. The Dominican Republic is one of the most developed Caribbean nations. Yet, in the 1972-1976 period it accounted for 7.9 percent of all America's migrants to the United States (Kritz, 1981, p. 215). This outmigration occurred on the heels of large-scale foreign investment, considerable growth in manufacturing employment, and expansion of higher education. This pattern of high outmigration in the context of high direct foreign investment and manufacturing growth is not unique to the Dominican Republic but has also marked other labor-exporting countries, such as Colombia, Ecuador, Mexico, Hong Kong, Singapore, and South Korea (Sassen-Koob, this volume). Traditional push factors associated with the commercialization of agriculture and displacement of small farmers are not adequate as an explanation for this type of emigration.

It has been suggested that direct foreign investment, especially export-oriented, serves as a triggering mechanism for unleashing regional migration streams. Such investment often mobilizes significant numbers of women and new groups into wage labor and thereby disrupts traditional work structures. Thus the mobilization of women, for example, often contributes to the outmigration of males whose households have been deprived of labor. Further, the high turnover rates of the women in export manufacturing firms often lead to the additional emigration of these "Westernized" women (Sassen-Koob, this volume; Fernández-Kelly, 1981). This type of explanation for large-scale emigration is more adequate to those societies with fairly established export-processing zones, or with well-established patterns of export manufacturing, such as Hong Kong, South Korea, and Mexico. In the Dominican case, early emigration is associated with an emphasis on traditional import substitution, and only later does emigration correlate with the shift to export manufacturing. Dominican labor exports fall somewhere in between the categories of unskilled labor and professional workers. The early emphasis on capital-intensive industrialization meant that the mobilized, unskilled work force could not be adequately absorbed. In addition, a growing percent of the relatively educated, lower-level professional workers have been unable to find secure employment. Yet it is *not* for the most part these workers who migrate.

Labor exports do not draw directly from the large pool of marginalized workers. It is not the unemployed themselves but the relatively skilled and educated whose wages and security are threatened by the existence of a large pool of reserve labor and who choose to migrate. These persons represent significant investments by the developing societies and could be presumed to be fundamental to any future development that was geared to incorporate the broad population into the process of economic development. Most migrants desire to return to the home community. Many have important, albeit limited investments to make in their communities and could presumably be encouraged to do so with limited incentives and state policy initiatives designed to provide credit and pricing breaks for small-scale productive investors. Undoubtedly migration between developed and developing societies represents a grossly unequal exchange, but the most negative consequences associated with outmigration—reductions in agricultural production, exacerbated income inequality, the high failure rates of return migrant firms—could be lessened by some kind of meaningful agrarian reform, by state policies which protect the small investor against monopoly enterprises, and by less repressive labor policies. Until such time, the Domincan state will merely continue to finance the education and training for a labor force which will persist to opt for higher wages in employment at significantly below their skill levels in the U.S.

Outmigration is not only a reflection of a particular pattern of development. In its presently unregulated form its long-term impact serves independently to reinforce the contours of dependent development, notably by stimulating limited growth via remittances and capital investments yet with little redistribution. Policy proposals like the Caribbean Basin Initiative are instruments of U.S. foreign policy ostensibly designed to promote economic development in regions loyal to or controllable by U.S. interests. It is argued that the spread of such labor-intensive firms as have operated in Puerto Rico will provide stimulus to economic development and stability in the area. Yet foreign capital will be attracted to countries like the Dominican Republic only to the extent that low wages are ensured, unions are weak, and taxes are virtually nonexistent. The "private sector strategy" of the CBI may include the creation of a Caribbean Wide Free Trade Zone, which would permit multinational companies to shift their plants out of high-wage areas like Puerto Rico to places like the Dominican Republic.

These kinds of development strategies presuppose the continuation or enforcement of repressive wage policies (Vuskovic, 1982, p. 82). To the extent that employment opportunities are expanded, they provide only for the limited growth of a poorly paid work force. Moreover, research on the impact of export-processing zones on employment indicate that by mobilizing non traditional workers into wage employment these industrialization strategies not only do not reduce the labor surplus but indirectly would create new sources of outmigration (Fernández-Kelly, 1981; Safa, 1981; Sassen-Koob, 1983). As our findings in the Dominican Republic demonstrate, it is the overall depressed wage rates and the inability of the economy to absorb even the skilled labor it trains which provokes migration.

It is important to acknowledge as well the fact that since the relatively better off appear disproportionately to migrate, it could well be the case that in the short run even expanded economic growth with redistribution will provoke further outmigration by enabling more aspiring workers to finance such a move. This is a distinct possibility. It is, nonetheless, uncontestable that the gross disparity of wage income between the receiving and sending countries, which is the basic direct stimulus to outmigration, is the logical extension of the model of development pursued by import substitution and will undoubtedly be exacerbated in the climate of a new international division of labor based on strategies of export conversion and free trade zones.

NOTES

1. The interests of dominant classes in peripheral areas are typically depicted in this literature, broadly defined as dependency, as being served because outmigration reduces the political threat of a large, mobilized, but unemployed, population. Although clearly there are local economic advantages to be had from a large supply of cheap labor, namely, downward pressure on wages in the periphery, the capital-intensive nature of many development models has meant that the absolute size of the unemployed sector often becomes much larger than is necessary for extracting such advantages. It is, in fact, a situation of overkill. Thus the emigration of people (relief of surplus population), especially the young and more ambitious, minimizes the threat that they could otherwise be mobilized politically to resist the very strategies of development adopted by the dominant class (Marshall, 1973, pp.119-128; Castells, 1975; Alba, 1978; Portes, 1981; Sassen-Koob, 1978). It is significant that most of these discussions of the advantages of labor emigration for peripheral capitalists presuppose that labor exports are drawn predominately from the underutilized sectors of labor. This assumption, dominant in most of the literature of international migration, is actually unjustified given the scarcity of reliable data on this question.

2. Dr. Patricia Pessar was the coprincipal investigator of this project. Research was supported by a grant from the National Institute of Child Health and Development (1 RO1 HD14198-01). The author is also grateful to the Oficina Nacional Estadística of the Dominican Republic for important institutional support in various stages of the project, especially to Dr. Julio Cross-Beras, Lic. Méjico Ángel Suárez and Victor Arvelo within that office, to the Center for Research of the National Catholic University of Mother and Teacher (UCMM), and to Lic. Noris Eusebio, who collaborated with me in all stages of the survey field work in the Cibao. In addition, Patricia Pessar, Max Castro, Alejandro Portes, Joshua Reichert, Emmanuel Castillo, and Rafael Yunén contributed in essential ways to the collection of the data. The interviews could not have been completed without the careful work of the following interviewers: in the Dominican Republic, Osvaldo Ureña, David Alba, José Acosta, José Vargas, Georgina Zacarias, Margarita Ramírez, Paul Almonte, Victor Martínez, Claudio Jerez, Rosa Ureña, Elena García, Neuli Cordero, Ziamara García, and Hugo Rodríguez. I am also thankful to Christine Rubertone for coding supervision and to Eric Cohen for computer assistance.

3. A snowball sample typically refers to a nonprobability sampling procedure such that cases are initially deliberately selected on the basis of certain variables (in this case undocumented status) and expanded by means of referrals or contacts established by the early interviews. Thus, for example, ten interviews are given with subjects of interest, who then each recommend two or three others, and so on. This kind of procedure is often employed when the population of interest is not likely to appear in adequate numbers by means of representative sampling. The snowball sample, being unrepresentative, involves the risk of unrecognized biases in regard to other variables. It is possible, however, to evaluate the overall representativeness of a snowball sample by comparing it on key variables with other representative samples of the subject population.

4. These figures were arrived at in the following manner:
$a = 16.7\%$ = the percent of sampled households containing at least one migrant
$b = 43,449$ = the N of the total sampled population of households
$c = 1.37$ = the median number of outside migrants per household in the sample

$d = 91{,}250$ = the total economically active population of Santiago
$$(a \times b \times c)/d = 10.9\%$$
5. Return migrants as a percentage of the economically active was calculated as follows:
$a = 11.0\%$ = the percent of sampled households containing at least one return migrant
$b = 43{,}449$ = the N of the total sampled population of households
$c = 1.39$ = the median number of return migrants per household of all return migrant households
$d = 91{,}250$ = the total economically active population of Santiago
$$(a \times b \times c)/d = 7.3\%$$
The values a, b, and c are based on my survey, whereas d is the figure given by the National Statistics Office.

6. This calculation is admittedly a rough estimate. It is based on the following assumptions: (1) that 18.3 percent of 43,449 households received a mean of D.R. $149.56 a month, 12 months a year = D.R. $14,270,118.00; and (2) that 12.0 percent of 43,449 households receive a mean of $66.44 a month but on an irregular basis, which I translate to mean on the average of six times a year = D.R. $2,078,774.00. Therefore, the regular and irregular recipients receive D.R. $16,348,892.00 annually.

REFERENCES

Alba, Francisco. 1978. "Mexico's International Migration as a Manifestation of Its Development Pattern." *International Migration Review* 12:4 (Winter), 502-513.

Baucic, Ivo. 1972. *The Effects of Emigration from Yugoslavia and the Problems of Returning Emigrant Workers*. The Hague: Martinus Nijhoff.

Bray, David. 1983. "Agricultura de exportación, formación de clase, y fuerza de trabajo excedente: El caso de la fuerza de trabajo migratoria en la República Dominicana." Paper presented to the Conference on Dominican Migration to the United States. New York.

Cabrel, Manuel José. 1975. "Inflación, distribución del ingreso y empleo." *Ciencia y Sociedad* I (June), 1-4.

Cardoso, Fernando Henrique, and Enzo Faletto. 1979. *Dependency and Development in Latin America*. Berkeley: University of California Press.

Castells, Manuel. 1975. "Immigrant Workers and Class Struggles in Advanced Capitalism: The Western European Experience." *Politics and Society* 5 (Spring), 33-66.

Catrain, Pedro. 1980. "Estado, hegemonía y clases dominantes en la República Dominicana, 1966-1978." Paper presented to the Second National Sociological Congress of the Association of Dominican Sociologists, Santo Domingo (November).

Cornelius, Wayne. 1976. "Mexican Migration to the United States: View from Rural Sending Communities." Mimeo.

———. 1978. "Mexican Migration to the United States: Causes, Consequences, and U.S. Responses." Mimeo. Massachusetts Institute of Technology Migration and Study Group, Center for International Studies.

———. 1982. "Interviewing Undocumented Immigrants: Methodological Reflections Based on Fieldwork in Mexico and the U.S." *International Migration Review* 6:2 (Summer), 378-411.

de Janvry, Alain. 1982. *The Agrarian Question and Reformism in Latin America*. Baltimore: Johns Hopkins University Press.

Dinerman, Ina R. 1977. "Patterns of Adaptation Among Households of U.S.-Based Migrants from Michoacan, Mexico." Paper presented to the Joint Meeting of the Latin American Studies Association and the African Studies Association, Houston, Texas.

Fernández-Kelly, María Patricia. 1981. "Feminization, Mexican Border Industrialization, and Migration." Ph. D. dissertation, Rutgers University.

Frobel, Folker, Jurgen Heinrichs and Otto Kreye. 1979. *The New International Division of Labour*. New York: Cambridge University Press.

Garrison, Vivian, and Carol I. Weiss. 1979. "Dominican Family Networks and U.S. Immigration Policy: A Case Study." *International Migration Review* 12:2 (Summer), 264-283.

González, Nancie. 1970. "Peasants' Progress: Dominicans in New York." *Caribbean Studies* 10, 154-171.

Grasmuck, Sherri. 1981. "The Impact of Emigration on National Development: Three Sending Communities in the Dominican Republic." Center for Latin American and Caribbean Studies. Occasional Paper no. 33. New York University.

——. 1982. "Migration Within the Periphery: Haitian Labor in the Dominican Sugar and Coffee Industries." *International Migration Review* 16:2 (Summer), pp. 365-377.

——. 1983. "International Stair-Step Migration: Dominican Labor in the United States and Haitian Labor in the Dominican Republic." In *Peripheral Workers*, ed. R. Simpson and I. H. Simpson. Greenwhich, Conn.: JAI Press.

Gurak, Douglas. 1981. "Dominicans and Colombians in New York City." Presentation to the New York Forum on Migration, New York.

Hendricks, Glen. 1974. *The Dominican Diaspora: From the Dominican Republic to New York City. Villagers in Transition*. New York: Teachers College Press.

International Labour Organization. 1975. *Time for Transition*. Geneva: ILO.

Jalee, Pierre. 1973. *Imperialism in the Seventies*. New York: Third Press.

Kayal, Philip M. 1978. "The Dominicans in New York: Part II." *Migration Today* 6, 10-15.

Kritz, Mary. 1981. "International Migration Patterns in the Caribbean Basin: An Overview." In *Global Trends in Migration*. ed. Mary Kritz, Charles Keeley and Silvano Tomasi. Staten Island, N.Y.: Center for Migration Studies.

Krute, Eugenia. 1983. "Las causas de la emigración en una comunidad agrícola del Cibao." Paper presented to the Conference on Dominican Migration to the United States. Museo del Hombre Dominicano, (Abril).

Marshall, Adriana. 1973. *The Import of Labor: The Case of the Netherlands*. Rotterdam: Rotterdam University Press.

Oficina Nacional de Planifiación. 1981. "La situación del empleo en Santo Domingo y Santiago en noviembre de 1970." Santo Domingo: ONAPLAN.

Pérez, Glauco. 1981. "Dominican Illegals in New York: Selected Preliminary Findings." Paper presented to the Center for Inter-American Affairs, New York University (May).

Pessar, Patricia. 1982. "The Role of Households in International Migration: The

Case of U.S.-Bound Migrants from the Dominican Republic." *International Migration Review* 16:2 (Summer), 342-364.

Poinard, Michel, and Michel Roux. 1977. "L'émigration contre le dévéloppement: Les cas portugais et yougoslave." *Revue tiers-monde* 18 (January-March), 21-53.

Portes, Alejandro. 1978. "Migration and Underdevelopment." *Politics and Society* 8:1, 1-48.

———. 1979. "Illegal Immigrants and the International System, Lessons from Recent Illegal Mexican Immigrants to the U.S." *Social Problems* 26:4 (April), 425-438.

Portes, Alejandro, and John Walton. 1981. *Labor, Class and the International System.* New York: Academic Press.

Ramírez, Nelson, Paolo Tactuk and Minerva Breton. 1977. *La migración interna en la República Dominicana.* Santo Domingo: Alfa y Omega.

Reichert, Joshua. 1981. "The Migrant Syndrome: Seasonal U.S. Wage Labor and Rural Development in Central Mexico." *Human Organization* 40:1 (Spring), 56-66.

Roberts, Kenneth. 1981. "Agrarian Structure and Labor Migration in Rural Mexico." Working Papers in U.S.-Mexican Studies, no. 30. La Jolla: University of California at San Diego.

Safa, Helen I. 1981. "Runaway Shops and Female Employment: The Search for Cheap Labor." *Signs* 7:2 (Winter), 418-423.

Sassen-Koob, Saskia. 1978. "The International Circulation of Resources and Development: The Case of Migrant Labour." *Development and Change* 9, 509-546.

Stoddard, Ellwyn. 1976. "A Conceptual Analysis of the 'Alien Invasion': Institutionalized Support of Illegal Mexican Aliens in the U.S." *International Migration Review* 10 (Summer), 157-189.

Ugalde, Antonio, Frank Bean and Gilbert Cárdenas. 1979. "International Migration from the Dominican Republic: Findings from a National Survey." *International Migration Review* 13:2 (Summer), 235-254.

Urrea, Fernando. 1982. "Life Strategies and the Labor Market: Colombians in New York in the 1970s." Paper presented to the conference on "Colombians and Dominicans in New York" Life Strategies in the Household and at Work," Center for Latin American and Caribbean Studies, New York University, occasional paper no. 34.

Veras, Rafael A. 1976. "Santiago y su proceso de desarrollo urbano." *Santiago ante el futuro*. Santo Domingo: Fondo Para el Avance de la Ciencias Sociales, 27-42.

Vuskovic, Pedro. 1982. "Economic Internationalization, Neoliberalism, and Unemployment in Latin America."*Contemporary Marxism* no. 5, 81-87.

Weist, Raymond E. 1970. "Implications of International Labor Migration for Mexican Rural Development." In *Migration Across Frontiers and the United States*, ed. F. Camara and R. V. Kemper. Contributions of the Latin American Anthropology Group, vol. 3. Albany: Institute for Mesoamerican Studies, SUNY Albany, pp. 85-97.

World Bank. 1978. *Dominican Republic: Its Main Economic Development Problems.* Washington, D.C.: World Bank.

———. 1981. "República Dominicana: análisis del sector agrícola," Report prepared for the projects department of Latin American & Caribbean Regional Office.

Evolving Patterns of Puerto Rican Migration

Frank Bonilla and Ricardo Campos

For about 90 seconds in Ana María García's moving new film on the sterilization of Puerto Rican women (*La Operación*), the mayor of a small island town, Barceloneta, proudly takes stock of his role in bringing Puerto Rico's population into line with the needs of the new industrial order. After more than 20 years of emigration and persistent promotion of sterilization, he says, the municipality finally registered a decline in population in the 1970 census. Several primary schools have been closed, since there are now so few children. Women, no longer burdened with child rearing, are busy at work in local factories, whose owners, with enlightened self-interest, allow them to receive birth control counseling on factory time. As the camera follows the mayor on his self-congratulatory stroll through the town's streets, he is finally constrained to comment on the dozens of (maleidlers) observing his passage. The men, he says, have already completed their daily duties elsewhere and are partaking of the pleasures of small town sidewalk conviviality. In a flash the reality of how a population may even in a relatively short time be molded to the passing convenience of a particular form of capital is unequivocally brought home.

There is, of course, a considerable distance between the graphic power of such a representation and a well worked out and documented theory of the interactions between population and the economy under capitalism. The very simplicity of this compressed imagery may be deceptive. Having introduced the necessary notion that population itself may be a consequence, and end point as well as a point of departure, in social analysis and political action, how can we avoid imputing unwarranted powers of purposive social intervention to persons like the mayor and his political and intellectual mentors? How can we reassert, against the mechanistic, linear discourse of the mayor's common-sense account and its dominant social science counterparts, a grasp of the ironies implicit in the historical coming into being of a social reality in which mass sterilization and mass migration can appear as integral features of a defensible project of social construction?

The mayor of Barceloneta, with considerable justification, sees Puerto Rico as an outstanding exemplar of planned industrialization and population control. Without a doubt, Puerto Rico stands today among the most industrialized societies. Equal recognition must be conceded to the successes of population control programs. With some 35 percent of women in reproductive ages sterilized, the island leads the field in the number of its women surgically protected against conception. The demographic effects of this and other methods of population control have exceeded the expectations of Puerto Rican planners and their preceptors in the United States. The island's rate of natural increase has taken a decisive drop, from 2.7 during the decade of the 1950s to 1.7 in the decade ending in 1980. Equally impressive is the nearly 40 percent reduction in fertility between 1960 and 1980 (table 1).

TABLE 1
Age Specific Fertility Rates for Mothers in Puerto Rico

Age group	1960	1980	Percent Change
15-19	100.0	75.4	-24.6
20-24	285.5	185.4	-35.0
25-29	244.6	177.3	-27.5
30-34	157.6	92.6	-41.2
35-39	112.3	39.3	-65.0
40-44	52.0	10.5	-79.8
45-49	9.9	1.4	-85.8
Mean births per mother	4.8	2.9	-39.6

Source: Planning Board, Commonwealth of Puerto Rico, Economic and Social Planning Area, Division of Human Resources, Unpublished data.
Note: Rates calculated as live births for each 1,000 women in each age group.

Undeniably, the reproductive behavior of Puerto Ricans is of a piece with that of the peoples of similarly industrialized societies. At the same time, the island has reproduced the typical internal distribution of its people that is associated with modern, urbanized economies. Today better than half the population (52 percent) is concentrated in the 18 municipalities that make up the metropolitan areas of San Juan, Caguas, Mayagüez, and Ponce. As in other core cities of industrialized regions, these urban centers appear to have come upon some limits to growth (Vining, 1982). After several decades of uninterrupted expansion, their growth rate in the 1970s (1.5 percent) fell below that of the 60 other municipalities on the island. San Juan, the central city of the major metropolitan area, lost more than 30,000 inhabitants in the course of the 1970s, according to the *San Juan Star*.

This turnaround in the internal movement of the population takes place against a backdrop of structural changes in migration patterns that have transformed the island into a center of both exportation and importation of workers. The underlying paradox here is that Puerto Rico, despite an accelerated industrialization, urbanization, systematic population control, and mass emigration (2 million Puerto Ricans are now in the United States), is today more troubled than ever by a growing and apparently uncontrollable problem of surplus population. Given the generalized levels of poverty and unemployment, two-thirds of the island's people eke out a subsistence on food stamps dispensed by the federal government, while the local administration calculates that still rising unemployment reached a critical 25.3 percent in 1983, as reported in the *San Juan Star*.

Reflection on these outcomes, so much at odds with the expectations nurtured by the much-vaunted design for industrialization, may prove instructive. But a well-rounded understanding of how Puerto Rico reproduces on an ever more aggravated scale its chronic problems of poverty and overpopulation, while exporting Puerto Ricans and importing more and more foreign workers, requires a brief recapitulation of earlier phases during which the contemporary relation of capital to population began to take form. We have found it useful in the course of several years of research and thinking to look for the beginnings of this process in the very origins of capitalism on the island a little more than a hundred years ago.

PUERTO RICANS IN THE INTERNATIONAL SYSTEM

The Transnational movement of workers is a constitutive feature of capitalist relations and their expansion. Puerto Rico has passed in about a hundred years and under the aegis of two metropolitan powers from the beginnings of agrarian capitalism through its consolidation and decline, through forced draft externally financed industrialization, and on to become a high-technology, service- and finance-oriented "postindustrial" dependency of the United States (Rodriguez, 1979). On a world scale this process occupied two to three centuries and, of course, uprooted and totally reshuffled hundreds of millions of the world's population. It should come as no surprise that in this short span Puerto Ricans have experienced in especially intense and visible ways all the forms of population change and displacement associated with the course of capitalism to the present day (Krippendorf, 1976).

A first period in the history of these migrations (1873-1947) may be broken down into three phases. The first of these, from 1873 to 1898, is marked by two events essential to the acceleration of the transition to agrarian capitalism: the abolition of slavery and servile labor in 1873; and the gradual appropriation of lands by the emergent sugar *centrales*. Under the dominant mode of accumulation controlled by commercial capitals, the operations of agrarian producers gradually gained sway, institutionalizing patterns of underemployment, prolonged seasonal unemployment, and wage payments in kind or in scrip. It is worth noting that, despite the dislodging of rural peoples from the land and the partial "liberation" of the work force, the persistence of precapitalist relations in the countryside stood in the way of the consolidation of a well-supplied market of "free" workers, leading sugar growers to denounce labor shortages and to import workers from the British Caribbean colonies. At the same time, impoverished smallholders and day workers, caught in the pinch between meager yields of their own and unstable employment in cane cultivation, undertook migrations to the Dominican Republic, Cuba, Venezuela, and elsewhere in the Caribbean in a search for connections to more advanced capitals.

The rudimentary state of the market for free labor was the inevitable counterpart of the virtual absence of a market for capitals in the colony. Financing for technological upgrading, the expansion of installations, the assembling of landholdings, and money wages had to be obtained in Europe and the United States, the principal customers for island production. The failing Spanish metropolis became an exasperating intermediary between the island and the rest of the world. *From its very origins, capitalism in Puerto Rico was marked by effective internationalization of both capital and the labor force.*

The consolidation of agrarian capitalism between 1898 and the world crisis in 1929 accomplished a thorough proletarianization of farm workers and artisans in the small towns, with an astonishing reversal of alleged labor shortages to labor gluts. "Surplus" workers were quickly channeled by U.S. corporations and their agents to the new territories recently acquired. For thousand of Puerto Rican rural families emigration meant entering the working class in the Dominican Republic, Cuba, or places as remote as Hawaii or California. With the further development of the sugar economy and the imposition of U.S. citizenship in 1917, contingents of workers began to move northward in growing numbers on their own, withouth the organized, contractual arrangements common up through World War I.

After 1920 New York became the dominant pole of attraction for island workers. The economic crisis at the end of the decade made the chronic imbalance of jobs to people even more acute, and although the trek northward continued, conditions in the U.S. also drove thousands back to the island between 1930 and 1934. Long before there were any convincing signs of recovery in the U.S., the irresistible pressures in Puerto Rico impelled new thousands to try their luck abroad. The imperative need for a major restructuring of the local economy was devastatingly apparent, but it took a second world war with its massive destruction of capitals and labor power to generate the conditions for a new surge of accumulation. With the passage of the Industrial Incentives Act in 1947, Puerto Rico was finally able to bring together at a timely moment the two inducements that were to draw substantial capitals from the U.S. to the island over the next two decades: abundant cheap labor and generous tax exemptions. But to capitalize the labor power that would remain on the island, new thousands would have to be persuaded to follow the quarter million displaced before the war.

There are distinctive moments as well in the patterns of migration in the decades that follow the launching of Operation Bootstrap. Thousands more broke away from rural poverty and stagnation during the surge of U.S. investment in light industry in the late 1940s and 1950s. Between 1950 and 1960 workers employed in agriculture fell from 38 to 24 percent. Migration peaked in 1953, with nearly 75,000 net departures; in the first 15 postwar years net departures averaged over 40,000 annually. The proliferation of government agencies and public enterprises also began to absorb a growing proportion of the work force. Nevertheless, by the mid-1960s falling profits and competition from other low-wage areas signaled the waning promise of development based on light manufacturing. During this phase of vigorous growth, unemployment was never brought more than a small fraction below 12 percent.

The high-technology capitals brought in to fill this breach were to prove even more niggardly consumers of labor. The cycle of their ascent was also short lived as local recession in the early 1970s and major realignments in the world economy made their effects felt in the pace and composition of investment. As employment in agriculture dwindled further to a scant 7 percent in 1970, government continued to expand its economic role. For several years in the early 1970s, return migration was enough to offset continued outward flows. In these circumstances even greater emphasis was placed on family planning and the wholesale sterilization of women. A variety of schemes to help root emigrants more permanently abroad or discourage their return were openly considered. Paradoxically, this occurred just as the presence of non-Puerto Ricans, chiefly Cubans, Dominicans, and stateside Americans began to be felt in the labor force. In 1970 there were already some 278,000 immigrants resident on the island (Vázquez and Morales del Valle, 1979). The economic and social base for a full-scale internationalization of the island's work force was in place.

In the current phase, industrial finance capital is being overshadowed as an actual and prospective source of jobs by the service sector. Prominent among these services is the unproductive consumption of labor in government, which as early as 1978 carried on its payrolls 40 percent of the employed work force in a vain attempt to stem the thrust of rising unemployment, which has climbed imperturbably from 11 percent in 1970 to the 25 percent already noted in 1983. In the meantime, Puerto Ricans, caught up in a restless circulation between the island and increasingly scattered concentrations of their own in the U.S., are joined in this movement by contingents of foreigners, who add distinctive circuits to this complex intermingling of the capitals and peoples of numerous nations. Having apparently exhausted all the historically known changes in modes of capitalist accumulation, Puerto Rico is said to stand at the threshold of a new phase of expansion based on a variety of financial and other services and requiring an even more radical internationalization of economic activity. A hidden card, the large scale exploitation of nonrenewable resources, long under negotiation with powerful multinational corporations, implies a no less complete internationalization, with the added threats of extensive depopulation, continued substitution of population, and the physical destruction of a large part of the island (Taller Arte Cultura, 1982).

THE DIVISION OF LABOR IN THE SERVICE SOCIETY

A reversal in the proportions of productive versus unproductive labor is a key indicator of how far Puerto Rico has gone in assuming the social configuration of the most advanced capitalist formations. The reduction of agricultural production to inconsequential proportions, technological change, and the export of manufacturing jobs are all elements in the ebbing of productive work. Fewer and fewer workers are engaged in the production of commodities, while more and more are in demand in finance, transport, distribution, merchandising, and security. The social repercussions of these changes are far reaching. It not only generates major social and ideological divisions within the working class but enlarges so-called middle sectors and alters expectations of future development as more and more productive tasks are exported. Illusions of mounting flourishing transnational service platforms, centers of finance, research and communication hubs, opulent complexes of technology and culture, much in the style of a Venetian princely commercial state, are as infectious in the Caribbean as in lower Manhattan. Much harder to face is the reality of having to extract ever large quanta of surplus value from fewer and fewer productive workers to maintain an expanding unproductive class and provide minimal subsistence to a bloated reserve of unused labor. The present situation of Puerto Rico may be taken as paradigmatic of the contradictions arising in the transition to a service-based economy (table 2).

Less than half the active work force is in production. This constitutes a major shift since 1940, when the proportion so engaged was 70 percent. The service economy is a reality, with 60 percent of all workers in various compartments of this dominant sector. It is no surprise, then, to find as many proprietors and managers as skilled craftsmen and foremen, or that professionals and white collar workers exceed semiskilled and unskilled workers. The latter have seen their numbers dwindle to 7.6 percent of workers.

TABLE 2

Productive and Unproductive Division of Labor, October 1982
(Thousands of persons 16 years and older)

Productive (376 = 48.3%)	(000)
craftsmen and foremen	90
operatives	135
laborers	27
farm laborers and foremen	31
farmers and farm managers	16
other services[a]	77
Unproductive (403 = 51.7%)	
professionals[b]	125
proprietors, managers, officials	80
clerical	112
sales	52
private household	7
protective services	27
Total	779

Source: *Department of Labor and Human Resources, Commonwealth of Puerto Rico, Statistical Report*, Vol. 4, 1982, p. 27.

[a] Include unknown number of unproductive public employees.
[b] Includes unknown number of productive salaried professionals.

A slightly different perspective on changes in the social division of labor emerges from a look at the relative position of economic sectors (table 3). As we have remarked, the most important employer is the colonial government, with 40 percent of the employed on its rolls. Statistical stratagems are routinely applied to mask these magnitudes by representing government workers as engaged in services, communications, and even agriculture.[1] Salaries for this inflated bureaucracy depend increasingly on federal transfers, with now cover better than a third of the administrative budget. The slender fiscal base further eroded by subsidies and tax exemptions to business make the flow of these federal funds crucial for employment. Federal policy in the Reagan era poses grave dilemmas for island officials as a principal tool for modulating crises is effectively withdrawn and the repercussions on other jobs of severe cutbacks in public employment loom ever larger.

The decline of industrial employment since 1970 (from 20.6 to 17.9 percent) has affected men and women unevenly. A higher proportion of women than males remain in industry. Women are also notably concentrated in government and services, while males prevail in commerce, and more traditionally, in transport and construction

Labor market trends toward specialization and selectivity are evident and troubling. The thousands excluded from work, it may be said, have the option

TABLE 3
Social Division of Labor, 1981

Economic Sector	Percent males	Percent females	Total (000)	Total Percent
Agriculture, fishing, forestry	7.7	—a	42	5.0
Mining	—b	—a	—c	—b
Construction	9.0	—a	49	5.8
Manufacture	15.8	23.5	155	18.6
Commerce	21.4	13.6	155	18.6
Finance, real estate, insurance	2.6	3.6	25	3.0
Transportation, communications	8.6	2.3	53	6.3
Services	15.6	22.2	150	18.0
Government	19.0	33.9	203	24.4
Total			832	

Source: Puerto Rico, 1982a.
a Less than .07 percent.
b Less than .4 percent.
c Less than 2.000.

of migrating. Males perhaps outnumber women among those now poised for departure. Male participation in the labor force dropped from 69 percent in 1964 to just over 57 percent in 1982. Women have also registered a decline since 1970, but their participation in 1982 (26.3 percent) is still above that in 1964 (22.4 percent). Women have continued to enter the work force, while men in large numbers no longer figure among job seekers. The role of government in job generation may help explain what is happening. Women obtained 55 percent of 121,000 jobs created between 1961 and 1971. Between 1971 and 1979 they obtained 58 percent of new jobs. In the 1980 fiscal period, 62 percent of new jobs went to women. At first blush one might imagine that women's right to work is finally materializing in objective opportunities and that women's gradual incorporation into the work force is a step toward sexual equality. A glance at the comparable pay for men and women in various occupational categories will dispel lingering doubts on the matter. The lower salaries received by women at every level reveal how distant these ideals remain. Not only in the higher-salaried positions but even among the most poorly paid, women's salaries trail those of men. Only in manufacturing and technical jobs does pay for women approach the male average. This inequality is crucial to an understanding of the increase in female employment in recent years. The consumption of low-wage labor is especially advantageous to those who gain through the value added by productive workers. A real though different benefit accrues to employers through payroll savings from unproductive workers. Women, in fact, outnumber men in the jobs that we have designated as unproductive, not only in proportion to their presence in the work force (59 as against 26 percent) but in absolute numbers (about 169,000 as against 106,000). The expansion of the service economy has apparently rested materially on the lower price of female labor (table 4).

TABLE 4
Weekly Average Salary by Occupation and Sex, 1980

Occupation	Males No. (000)	Males Salary	Females No. (000)	Females Salary
Professionals	39	$212.78	59	$158.47
Technicians	9	167.04	5	162.01
Managers and officials	34	230.75	10	170.34
Clerical	38	143.26	77	119.88
Salespeople	27	119.94	10	101.03
Craftsmen and foremen	97	125.80	2	122.54
Operatives	70	119.36	65	114.82
Services	53	122.09	48	87.84
Laborers	51	103.74	—	—
Private household	—	—	5	56.61
Farm administrator	—	—	—	—
Farm workers	27	59.82	—	—
Total	445		281	
Overall average		$136.53		$121.70

Source: Puerto Rico, 1982a.

Women in industry, where they constitute nearly half of the work force (48 percent), are in an even more disadvantaged position. They occupy more than their share of the jobs with salaries in the middle range, such as those in electronics and scientific instruments, but only a third of those in chemicals, which has the highest hourly pay scale. A very substantial 40 percent are underemployed in apparel, textile, and wood product factories, where they receive the lowest industrial wages and have the shortest average work week. Women constitute 84 percent of the work force in the oldest and most rapidly declining sectors such as apparel. Whether as newcomers or worker of long standing, women in Puerto Rico are situated in the least rewarding jobs in the lower reaches of the U.S. labor market, of which they are an organic component (table 5).

TABLE 5
Industrial Division of Labor-August, 1982
(Thousands of persons 16 years and older)

Industry	All Workers	Females	Production Workers	Average Hourly Earnings	Average Weekly Hours
Total	139.5	67.3	110.3	4.66	37.6
Food	20.9	5.3	13.7	4.65	36.0
Tobacco	1.4	0.5	1.2	4.48	38.0
Textiles	2.5	1.2	2.2	4.13	35.2
Apparel	29.5	24.7	27.3	3.76	33.6
Paper	5.0	1.0	2.6	4.75	38.0
Chemicals	15.5	5.2	10.2	6.33	42.1
Oil	5.5	1.5	4.0	5.68	39.7
Hides	5.1	5.4	4.8	3.83	37.1
Wood	3.0	0.5	2.5	3.85	34.3
Clay, Stone, Glass	3.9	0.5	2.9	4.86	38.4
Metal	4.2	0.5	3.3	4.86	37.1
Machinery	9.2	3.7	7.0	5.10	38.6
Electrical equipment	17.3	9.9	14.7	4.71	39.8
Professional instruments	13.2	7.8	11.1	4.73	42.6
Miscellaneous	3.4	1.6	3.0	4.65	36.1

Source: Department of Labor and Human Resources, Commonwealth of Puerto Rico, *Statistical Report*, Vol. 4, 1982, pages 29 and 31. The individual figures do not necessarily add to the totals indicated because of rounding.

Economic stagnation and the depletion of jobs in industry have catapulted unemployment to 1930s depression levels. Without taking into account "discouraged" workers, official rates acknowledged to be on the rise have moved past the 25 percent mark in 1983. A year earlier unemployment was already at 25.6 percent for males and at 15.3 percent for women. The incidence of unemployment by age group reveals the overwhelming impact of unemployment on the young, irrespective of sex. As the average age of the employed has risen, the corresponding figure for the unemployed creeps downward (tables 6 and 7).

Not even higher levels of schooling seem to endow job seekers of the island

TABLE 6
Unemployment Rate by Age, 1982

Age	Males	Females
16-19	61.0	52.3
20-24	49.1	40.1
25-54	21.2	10.0
55 and over	12.9	—

Source: Puerto Rico, 1982a.

TABLE 7
Unemployment Rate by Education, 1981

Years of Schooling	Males	Females	Total
0	2.2	—	2.2
1-3	7.3	—	6.0
4-6	16.1	8.9	14.2
7-9	24.8	15.6	22.4
10-11	12.4	11.1	12.6
12	27.7	37.8	30.0
13 and more	8.8	22.2	12.0

Source: Puerto Rico 1981.
Note: Includes persons 16 years and older.

with any competitive advantage. On the contrary, unemployment is highest among those with most schooling, and women appear once again to be on the short end as regards rewards for investment in training. The most obvious option, of course, for those in this situation is to try their luck in the U.S. There has been considerable ado on both ends of the migration circuits about an impeding wave of university-trained Puerto Ricans heading for the U.S. Although well-schooled Puerto Ricans may figure more abundantly among current and prospective newcomers to the U.S., they can only be a modest part of a larger stream that will continue to be peopled mainly by the semiskilled and unskilled, many seeking their first jobs.

Obviously, the magnitude of the reserves of jobless continues to feed an exodus of native-born workers, now intermingled with migrant flows of Puerto Ricans born abroad and foreigners. Estimates of the size and meaning of net balances in these complicated comings and goings become more and more difficult. In fact, government figures on these net balances may actually distort the numbers of workers actually set into motion by ongoing changes in the labor market in Puerto Rico, the United States, and other places. More aware that most of the knotty problems involved, Puerto Rico's Planning Board has announced the following appraisal of recent trends:

> The fact that net migrations has diminished does not mean that emigration has slowed but rather that immigration has increased. According to the 1979 Study of Immigration, 395,000 persons are estimated to have arrived in Puerto Rico during the decade, a number never observed before in immigration flows to this country. For the migration flows to yield a negative balance, emigration must have been in the neighborhood of 500,000 persons, a flow close to that observed during the 1950s. *This indicates that a process of population substitution has been occurring.* (Emphasis added.) (Economic Report to the Governor, 1981, p. 275)

A majority of immigrants are Puerto Ricans, along with Cubans, Dominicans, and stateside Americans. The study carried out by the Planning Board differentiates returning Puerto Ricans by place of birth and separates foreigners from North Americans. The information made available so far is scant and incomplete. Little in fact has been established about this process of "population substitution" and its main trends. A few items, however, provide some idea of the nature of the population of workers entering Puerto Rico. Immigrants are older (median age 32.2) than the nonmigrant population (21.6), although this varies considerably by nationality. Among Puerto Ricans born on the island, the median age was 37.9 years, while that for the U.S. born was only 14.6. Foreign workers were the oldest (median age 39.6) and, moreover, had an average of 12.5 years of schooling as against 9.2 years for migrant Puerto Ricans and 8.4 years for those never having left the island.

Further clues concerning the local labor market may be inferred from the patterns of accommodation of immigrants. While about a third of nonmigrants live in the San Juan metropolitan area, this figure was only 24.5 percent for island-born immigrants and 30.6 for Puerto Ricans born in the U.S. By contrast, 79.2 of the foreign immigrants and 53.1 percent of those from the U.S. were concentrated in the main metropolitan area. This concentration is in line with the high proportion of foreign immigrants, male and female, engaged in commercial ventures (about two in five). Commerce and services together account for the employment of 79.3 percent of foreigners and 79.2 for non-Puerto Rican newcomers form the U.S. It is worth noting that 32.3 percent of the male foreigners were self-employed, as against 18.1 of island stayers. Better than four in five foreign immigrant women worked in the private sector, while for all Puerto Rican women the principal employer was the government.

In sum, Puerto Rico, the "privileged" colony of the most advanced capitalist power, reflects in particularly transparent ways the driving forces of an ongoing crisis of transformation in capitalism at large and its U.S. compo-

TABLE 8
Nonmigrant and Immigrant Population, 1979

Characteristic	Non-Migrants	Total	Puerto Rican	Puerto Rican Descent	Foreign Born	U.S. Born
Period of arrival						
Before 1960		12.0%	11.2	11.6	19.4	16.5
1960-69		27.5	29.0	21.7	32.4	23.2
1970-79		60.3	59.6	66.5	48.1	60.2
Unemployment rate	17.6	21.8	22.6	29.2	—	—
Participation rate	57.7	64.4	65.7	46.3	73.3	—
males	57.7	64.4	65.7	43.8	93.2	—
females	27.5	29.3	29.6	26.1	37.2	—
Weekly salary						
less $80	22.2	21.9	24.5	15.4	—	
$80-149	54.3	51.0	51.8	57.1	42.4	
$150-329	22.2	24.7	21.5	27.4	46.5	
$330 or more	1.1	22.7	2.0	—		
Employment sector						
Agriculture	5.0	4.9	6.0	—	—	
Industry	30.5	33.2	35.3	31.5	19.9	—
Services	64.4	61.8	58.5	68.4	79.3	79.2
White collar	37.9	44.9	39.3	60.8	73.3	58.4
Blue collar	37.0	37.8	41.5	28.5	17.0	—
Services	14.4	12.8	13.7	10.6	8.9	—

Source: Puerto Rico, 1982a.

nent, of which Puerto Rico has become a regional extension. Locally the crisis manifests itself in the magnitudes of unused and underused labor despite and extravagant and unproductive consumption of labor by the state along with an accelerated internationalization of capital and labor that seems destined to relegate the island population to a permanent and increasingly marginal place in the ongoing restructuring of the island economy. Because the crisis is genuine, the possibilities of econimic collapse or social explosion are present. Severe pressures on the work force have opened the way to a reconstitution of forms of exploitation historically linked to primitive accumulation and the very origins of capitalism. As shall be seen, in all these respects, Puerto Rico may be running in tandem with or even in advance of social processes in the metropolis rather than lagging behind in the historical unfolding of the struggle to construct a new course for capitalist accumulation.

THE UNITY OF CAPITALIST PROCESSES

The interest for history and political economy of the social transformations occurring in Puerto Rico in the last several decades is substantially enhanced by their direct connection to parallel processes at the epicenter of the metropolitan and world economy, New York City. The contradictions of advanced capitalism so acutely evident in the compressed social space of a regional dependency are mirrored on a larger scale in the circuits of capitals and peoples that converge at "the institutional heights of worldwide resource allocation" (Ross and Trachte, 1983, p. 392). A recently noted and transcendent reversal in the operation of those circuits is the accelerated displacement of population from industrial "core" regions to "peripheries" (Vining, 1982). After centuries of migration to industrial heartlands, people are decamping toward new growth poles. This sea shift in population is most clear in the U.S. Northeast, where it is said to have been in the making since 1945 (when, ironically, Puerto Ricans began to arrive in large numbers) and to have been unmistakably operative in the 1970s. Trends in the same direction are documented for this period in Canada, Western Europe, and a variety of Eastern European and Asian nations with well-consolidated, original industrial regions. The process is not one of core expansion; populations are leaping over the outer bounds of established industrial areas to new regions. The explanation advanced for both the earliest concentrations of capital and populations as well as their ongoing redeployment is simple: investment, private and public, gravitates to sites where it can benefit from economies of scale. "Population follows industry. Later in development economies of scale are reduced; industry and population begin to flow to the periphery. One reason for the early and large flow from the U.S. core is that the South and West are well suited to industry" (Vining, 1982, p. 47). Just as some core-periphery thinkers began to discover the periphery within the core (Portes and Walton, 1981), other were coming upon emergent cores on the periphery.

New Yorkers of all social conditions did not have to wait for the 1980 census or the labored insights of social scientists to know that a major turnover of capitals, jobs, and peoples was underway all about them during the 1970s. Job flight and white flight quickly became the buzz words denoting the threatening implications of municipal and regional economic shrinkage. In the South Bronx and other neighborhoods where old and new immigrants faced the realities of "disinvestment," unemployment, and the collapse of social infrastructures, life at the commanding heights of world capitalism looked more and more like the remembered existence in its backwaters. The local impact of untrammeled capital movement was projected to intensify as the decade closed and extend well into the 1980s. One forecast talked of a population loss of about a million whites and almost as many jobs with a half-million nonwhites added to the city's population by 1985 (Hughes and Sternlieb, 1978). Some new jobs were being created, of course, as others, chiefly in manufacturing dwindled. Bluestone and Harrison (1980) calculated that between 1969 and 1976 something over a million new jobs were created in New York State, while about a million and a half were destroyed by closings. For the first time in 1982 the number of jobs in finance (488,000) exceeded jobs in manufacturing (483,000).

There was considerable disagreement, however, about whether the new jobs would suit the population in place or that which could be held in or attracted to the city and whether the jobs being created would constitute any significant improvement over those lost. For the U.S. at large, fewer than three in ten of new private sector jobs were said to be "good" jobs; an estimated five new job seekers were available for every two jobs generated (Ginzberg, 1979, p. 141). According to one empirical analysis of labor segmentation, as early as 1960 only about half of the jobs in the country could be counted as "good" in terms of pay, related benefits, and long-term security (Freedman, 1976, p. 120). While debate in the nation and city raged on about where jobs would come from and who would get them (if they were worth having), a steady stream of newcomers, legal and "undocumented," gained a foothold in the New York metropolitan economy, giving structured form to new dimensions of class and national polarization.

As 1980 census results continue to trickle out, a clearer sense of the demographic changes being worked in the city and region can be obtained.[2] New Yorkers were about a tenth fewer in number in 1980 than a decade earlier, a loss said to be the largest in two hundred years. Hispanics in contrast increased about 10 percent, to about 1.4 million. Together with blacks, who also increased by about 7 percent, and a small but fast growing number of Asians, "nonwhites" came to nearly half of the city's people (47 percent). Statistics on Puerto Rican births and deaths in the city suggest that natural increase over the decade was somewhere between 150,000 and 160,000 (NYC Dept. of Health, 1982). This implies a minimum Puerto Rican *net* outmigration of 135,000 or so, without taking into account fresh arrivals from Puerto Rico or elsewhere along with departures followed by returns to the city. *Job flight and white flight in the 1970s meant Puerto Rican flight as well.*

Although migration data on Puerto Ricans are notoriously spotty, a few clues suggested well before the most recent census that Puerto Ricans were leaving New York in substantial numbers for other parts of the U.S. and Puerto Rico, even as equal or larger contingents left the island for various U.S. cities, including New York. The number of persons of Puerto Rican descent enumerated in the United States in 1980 broke the 2 million mark, an increase of 41 percent since 1970. While the large growth in absolute numbers in nearby states, especially New Jersey, but also Connecticut, Pennsylvania, and Massachusetts, suggest a fanning out from the New York concentration, there were also impressive absolute and percentage gains in states as scattered as

Texas, Florida, Illinois, Hawaii, and Virginia (table 9). A pressing research task for the immediate future is to map the operative contours of these widening migration circuits and to establish whether this further dispersal is associated with any meaningful economic or other gains to the group.

TABLE 9
States with 10,000 or More Persons of Puerto Rican Origin in 1980

Rank	State	Percent Rate of increase 1970-1980	Number 1980	Number 1970
1	New York	7.6	986,389	916,608
2	New Jersey	75.3	243,540	138,896
3	Illinois	47.7	129,165	87,477
4	Florida	236.4	94,775	28,166
5	California	82.7	93,038	50,929
6	Pennsylvania	107.4	91,802	44,263
7	Connecticut	135.0	88,361	37,603
8	Massachusetts	227.7	76,450	23,332
9	Ohio	60.0	32,442	20,272
10	Texas	262.2	22,938	6,333
11	Hawaii	108.4	19,351	9,284
12	Indiana	36.8	12,683	9,269
13	Michigan	100.3	12,425	6,202
14	Wisconsin	44.6	10,483	7,248
15	Virginia	149.6	10,227	4,098
	Selected states	38.4	1,924,069	1,389,980
	United States	40.9	2,013,945	1,429,396

Source: Data from U.S. Census Bureau Published in *El Diario*, September 17, 1982, p. 3.

By 1980 those Puerto Ricans who had remained in the city or had been drawn there in the course of the decade looked demographically a little more like other New Yorkers. The average age for both men and women had increased by about three years, principally through a marked decline in the number of children under 15. Women continued to outnumber men (about 53 as against 47 percent) and were on the average about three years older than men (table 10). Nevertheless, Puerto Ricans remained much younger in the aggregate than the city's white or black populations. These differences are accentuated in places like Manhattan, where white children under 15 are relatively few, and the Bronx, where large concentrations of white elderly are present. In neighborhoods shared by blacks and Puerto Ricans (e.g. East Harlem and Mott Haven) they show fairly similar sex and age distributions (table 11).[3]

TABLE 10
Puerto Rican Population, by Age and Sex, New York City, 1970-1980

Population Group	Number		Percent Distribution	
	1970	1980	1970	1980
Total males	385,379	400,801	100.0	100.0
under 15	157,704	139,073	41.0	34.8
15-19	39,697	46,781	10.3	11.7
20-64	179,462	201,422	46.5	50.2
65 and over	8,516	13,535	2.2	3.3
Median age	18.9	21.9		
Total females	426,464	459,751	100.0	100.0
under 15	151,994	134,008	35.8	29.2
15-19	40,924	48,415	9.6	10.5
20-64	220,380	254,752	51.6	55.4
65 and over	13,166	22,576	3.0	4.9
Median age	21.8	25.2		

Source: Based on table 1B, New York, City. Department of Planning, 1982.

While the proportion of Puerto Ricans living in family households is higher than for the city's population at large (90 as against 82 percent), the last decade saw a sharp plunge in the proportion of Puerto Rican families with husband and wife present. Just over half of all Puerto Rican families are headed by married couples. For the city as a whole this figure is 69 percent. While the main trend is toward an increase in single men and women living alone or sharing living space with nonrelatives, this is not the case for Puerto Ricans. Among Puerto Ricans the most dramatic change is the rise since 1970 from 29.1 to 43.5 percent in families headed by women, almost all with children. Women alone head only slightly more than one in four of all families in the city (table 12).

At this writing, census results for 1980 regarding labor force participation, income, and occupation cannot be disaggregated for subgroups within the Spanish origin category. A fair approximation of the situation of most Puerto Ricans can be obtained, however, by a close look at two of the major concentrations of Puerto Ricans in two longstanding Puerto Rican neighborhoods.

TABLE 11
White, Black, and Puerto Rican Population, by Age and Sex

	New York	Manhattan	East Harlem	Central Harlem	Bronx	Mott Haven
Non-Hispanic White males	1,709,829	331,835	11,572	683	180,598	9,250
Percent under 15	14.8	7.4	24.3	8.1	13.4	32.5
Percent 15-64	68.9	79.0	64.4	79.2	64.3	60.4
Percent 65 and over	16.3	13.6	11.3	12.7	22.3	7.1
Non-Hispanic White females	1,959,116	382,019	14,198	775	216,238	10,990
Percent under 15	12.2	6.1	19.6	14.0	10.4	27.2
Percent 15-64	64.6	71.4	62.7	70.9	58.1	62.3
Percent 65 and over	23.2	22.5	17.7	15.1	31.5	10.5
Non-Hispanic Black males	758,004	133,631	17,705	49,112	153,796	12,847
Percent under 15	28.9	20.1	28.5	19.1	30.6	34.0
Percent 15-64	65.6	69.8	65.4	66.5	63.5	61.4
Percent 65 and over	5.5	10.1	6.1	14.4	4.9	4.6
Non-Hispanic Black females	936,123	156,587	23,706	59,226	194,948	16,638
Percent under 15	23.3	17.1	21.3	16.2	23.8	24.8
Percent 15-64	68.7	67.9	66.9	64.1	68.8	66.3
Percent 65 and over	8.0	15.0	11.8	19.7	7.4	8.9
Puerto Rican males	400,801	74,918	24,396	2,225	147,052	22,889
Percent under 15	34.5	27.9	31.2	19.0	35.5	34.0
Percent 15-64	62.4	67.4	62.6	74.0	61.7	62.5
Percent 65 and over	3.1	4.7	6.2	17.0	2.8	3.5
Puerto Rican females	459,751	86,910	28,645	2,538	173,046	26,133
Percent under 15	28.9	24.4	25.6	26.4	29.2	28.8
Percent 15-64	66.5	68.3	65.7	65.8	66.7	63.4
Percent 65 and over	4.6	7.3	8.7	7.8	4.1	5.8
Total population	7,071,639	1,428,285	101,481	99.198	1,168,972	79,118

Sources: City and county data provided by N.Y.C. Dept. of Planning. Community Board data tabulated al CUNY Data Center.

Just over 85 percent of the Spanish origin population in both these areas (East Harlem and Mott Haven) are of Puerto Rican origin or descent. A heavily black neighborhood, Central Harlem, contiguous with East Harlem, has been included as a reference point for contrasting Puerto Ricans and non-Hispanic blacks. In future treatments we propose to deal with these and other neighborhoods in New York and other cities in a more systematic, qualitative way that takes into account spatial factors in the institutionalization of inequality within cities and regions. In the present analysis, they will be used largely as provisional surrogates for a part of the Puerto Rican and black population.

TABLE 12
Puerto Rican Families by Family Type, New York City, 1970-1980

Family Type	Number		Percent Distribution	
	1970	1980	1970	1980
Married couple family	133,772	109,959	66.7	51.3
Male family householder, no wife	8,526	11,236	4.2	5.2
Female family householder, no husband	55,378	93,193	29.1	43.5
All families	200,676	214,388	100.0	100.0

Source: Based on NYC Department of Planning, 1982, table 3, p. 100.

The configuration taken by the Puerto Rican population as an effect of the rates of natural increase, net outmigration, and changes in the pattern of household formation seem to be directly reflected in labor force participation, job holding, and income, especially among Puerto Rican women. In the city as a whole and in the boroughs of the Bronx and Manhattan, the participation in the labor force and unemployment of Spanish-origin men is generally at a level between that of whites and blacks. Unemployment is higher and participation rate substantially lower for all men in the working-class neighborhoods where Puerto Ricans and blacks are concentrated.[4] Differences among New York City women are much sharper and support the view that sex inequality has become in the last decade a larger component of racial inequality and its reproduction (Bianchi, 1981, p. 134). In the city as a whole, black women are in the labor force in considerably higher proportions (51.5 percent) than either white (46.3 percent) or Spanish-origin women (36.2 percent), and notably so in comparison with Puerto Rican women.[5] In East Harlem and Mott Haven, which in these data are most indicative for Puerto Rican women, 26.8 and 15.1 percent of Spanish origin women, respectively, were in the labor force in 1980. In 1970 the citywide figure for Puerto Rican women was 28.1 percent (Powers and Macisco, 1982, table 14). White women, nevertheless, retain a considerable advantage in employment rates among women in the labor force. Among black and Puerto Rican women on this evidence, unemployment rates are very similar and one and a half to twice the white rates (table 13).

Unfortunately, available 1980 data do not permit a more detailed analysis

TABLE 13
Employed Persons 16 Years and Older, by Industry, New York City and Selected Counties and Neighborhoods, 1980

Industry	New York	Manhattan	East Harlem	Central Harlem	Bronx	Mott Haven
Production						
Agriculture, forestry, fishery, mining	0.2	0.2	0.2	0.2	0.2	—
Construction Manufacturing	2.7	1.4	2.2	1.9	3.2	2.5
Nondurable goods	11.4	12.8	11.8	8.0	10.6	15.0
Durable goods	6.0	4.1	6.5	5.0	6.5	10.6
Transportation	6.9	4.2	5.7	8.2	7.1	5.3
Communications and utilities	3.1	2.4	2.3	3.3	3.4	1.8
Commerce and finance						
Wholesale trade	4.8	4.3	3.1	2.9	4.3	4.4
Retail trade	13.2	12.4	13.2	10.6	13.9	11.8
Finance, real, insurance, estate	12.0	10.6	9.8	8.1	10.6	10.1
Services						
Business and repair	6.6	8.9	5.8	7.1	5.7	6.8
Personal, entertainment, recreation	5.2	7.9	6.9	9.8	4.6	5.7
Professional and related	9.1	8.6	13.8	13.8	11.5	9.6
Health	6.8	7.8	6.3	6.2	7.0	6.1
Other	7.2	10.5	7.5	8.4	6.2	6.0
Public administration	4.8	3.9	4.9	6.5	5.1	4.3
Total	100.0	100.0	100.0	100.0	100.0	100.0
Total number employed	2,918,178	698,727	28,155	37,949	402,872	18,153

Sources: City and county data provided by N.Y.C. Dept. of Planning. Community Board data tabulated at CUNY Data Center.

of the interaction of race, ethnicity, and sex in labor market placement and behavior. Recent efforts in this direction have been inconclusive in assessing the factors responsible for black-white differences in women's participation in work outside the home (discrimination, human capital differences, low earnings of husbands, family structures, labor market rigidities) or differences among Spanish-origin women (education, English proficiency, national origin, migration, regional labor market conditions, available welfare options) (see Wallace, 1980; Borjas and Tienda, 1981; Cooney, 1979). Nevertheless it seems clear that the significance of the income earned by women varies considerably for the groups involved. The relationship of female family headship to labor force participation is complex and varies by race and ethnicity, as does the very process of the constitution of such households. In fact, sustained or increasing participation (e.g. among black women) may be associated with outcomes not very different from those linked to growing withdrawal from the work force (as seems to be happening among Puerto Rican women). The capacity of capital to segment and divide classes and peoples manifests itself in the work life of women as among other components of the population.

If the aggregate figures on the distribution of employed workers by occupation and industry in Puerto Rican neighborhoods in New York City can be taken as rough approximations of prevailing conditions and trends (tables 14 and 15), they would seem to jibe generally with other more carefully documented assessments. These numbers together with others on Puerto

TABLE 14

Employed Persons 16 Years and Older by Occupation, New York City and Selected Counties and Neighborhoods, 1980

Occupation	New York	Manhattan	East Harlem	Central Harlem	Bronx	Mott Haven
Productive workers	(38.2)	(28.3)	(51.2)	(50.7)	(44.8)	(60.6)
Precision production, craft, repair	8.3	4.4	7.5	5.9	9.3	8.6
Operators, including transport	11.0	8.4	14.2	11.5	12.7	20.7
Laborers, nonfarm	3.3	2.0	4.7	4.9	4.3	6.8
Farming, forestry, fishing	.3	.2	.5	.6	.3	.3
Service workers*	15.3	13.3	24.3	27.8	18.2	24.2
Unproductive workers	(61.8)	(71.7)	(48.8)	(49.3)	(55.2)	(39.4)
Executive, administrative, managerial	11.4	16.1	5.5	5.9	7.8	3.9
Professional specialty	14.3	25.6	9.7	8.5	9.9	4.8
Technicians	2.4	2.6	1.8	2.1	2.3	1.0
Sales	8.8	9.4	7.7	5.7	8.0	5.9
Administrative support/clerical	24.9	18.0	24.1	27.1	27.2	23.8
Total number employed	2,918,178	698,727	28,155	37,949	402,872	18,153

Sources: City and county data provided by N.Y.C. Dept. of Planning. Community Board data tabulated at CUNY Data Center.

*Includes domestic service workers, which are 1 percent or less except in East Harlem (22) and Central Harlem (40).

TABLE 15
Education, Income, and Poverty Status, by Race and Spanish Origin, 1980

	New York	Manhattan	East Harlem	Central Harlem	Bronx	Mott Haven
Persons 25 years and older with schooling beyond high school:						
White	33.0	51.8	22.3	29.8	20.3	8.5
Black	23.1	23.1	17.9	16.0	21.7	12.1
Spanish origin	15.6	16.8	8.3	14.3	12.2	6.6
Mean family income in 1979 (dollars)						
White	24,664	37,503	13,417	13,132	19,814	10,953
Black	15,161	13,514	11,829	11,738	14,355	10,150
Spanish origin	12,898	12,130	9,956	11,604	11,643	10,252
Persons in poverty status						
White	12.7	13.6	36.0	34.6	17.0	41.8
Black	29.2	33.0	34.5	40.5	31.4	44.9
Spanish origin	35.4	35.8	46.2	47.4	40.8	49.3

Source: City and County data provided by N.Y.C. Dept. of Planning. Community Board data tabulated al CUNY Data Center.

Ricans in the U.S. at large (Campos and Bonilla, 1976) suggest the continuation of a decline in work force participation going back to 1950 or so. This trend is quite steep for women and more moderate for males. The decline in participation was up to 1970 compensated by reductions in unemployment. It was also accompanied by a shift from jobs in production to mainly white collar jobs, which was also steeper for women than for men. By the 1980s both participation and unemployment were moving regressively. Detailed analyses of the 1970 situation (Early, 1980; Powers and Macisco, 1982; Rodríguez, 1979) pointed to the declining availability of low-skill job opportunities in the Northeast as a major factor in the deteriorating position in employment of Puerto Ricans as a group. Other structural aspects of the New York labor market were given some prominence in these studies. Early suggested that Puerto Ricans were pretty much locked into low-paying positions in manufacturing, retail, and personal services and much underrepresented in construction, transport, communication, finances, professions, and public administration. Duration of residence, he found, appeared to have no impact on sector location. He was the first to articulate an arresting perception: "Puerto Rican males are in at least indirect wage competition with women workers to a much greater extent that are other males in the labor force" (Early, 1980, pp. 328-330). In fact, the thin evidence on hand for the 1980s indicates that approximations of the social division of labor among all Puerto Ricans in the city look much like that for Puerto Rican women employed in New York in 1970. It is worth noting, however, that this new configuration puts *all* Puerto Rican workers much closer, at least on this plane, to all working New Yorkers.

Unfortunately, this realignment among occupations and industries has left Puerto Ricans at the bottom of the heap in earnings. This occurs, of course, because census categories for occupations and industries submerge as much as they reveal about social stratification. The Spanish origin population lags well behind all others in mean income. Spanish origin poverty levels are two to three times those among whites. In a borough like Manhattan with many high earners, mean income among whites is $37,503—3.1 times the Spanish-origin mean, $12,120. There are 2.6 times as many Hispanics as whites living in poverty in Manhattan and close the three times as many in the city as a whole. These differences are much moderated in the Harlems and the South Bronx, where the commonality of the black and Puerto Rican condition is brought home by the slender margin of black advantage over Puerto Ricans in income and poverty despite the considerably higher educational accomplishment of blacks (table 16). Convergences in the distribution of groups by occupational and industry categories, often used as indicators of social ascent and equalization, proceed along with growing polarization in earnings and impoverishment.

In New York as in Puerto Rico, explanations of lagging labor participation, growing unemployment, and displacement of Puerto Ricans through migration rest simply on the notion that Puerto Ricans suffer because they are

TABLE 16
Persons 16 Years and Older in Labor Force and Employed, by Sex, Race and Spanish Origin, 1980

	New York	Manhattan	East Harlem	Central Harlem	Bronx	Mott Haven
Men in labor force						
White	70.9	77.0	56.8	57.6	63.7	59.0
Black	64.7	58.3	57.1	51.6	62.8	52.1
Spanish origin	70.3	69.1	55.8	53.0	65.7	57.3
Men employed						
White	93.2	93.6	89.2	97.5	93.1	85.0
Black	86.8	84.2	86.6	83.1	86.2	79.0
Spanish origin	89.5	88.6	87.2	87.2	88.6	85.0
Women in labor force						
White	46.3	58.8	33.4	35.0	38.1	26.0
Black	51.5	41.3	41.2	40.3	50.5	37.5
Spanish origin	36.2	42.3	26.8	34.9	30.1	25.1
Women employed						
White	93.6	94.3	91.1	96.8	93.0	83.0
Black	90.1	89.6	86.4	89.0	89.9	84.0
Spanish origin	88.2	88.7	86.0	89.6	87.0	83.0

Sources: City and county data provided by N.Y.C. Dept. of Planning. Community Board data tabulated at CUNY Data Center.

concentrated in the low-skill jobs now diminishing in number; such arguments must deal with the fact of the continuing importation of equally unskilled and culturally diverse labor into the very markets from which Puerto Ricans are being driven. As has been noted, New York City in 1980 registered a 10 percent loss in population since 1970. However, nearly 8 percent of those counted in the city in 1980 were living abroad (4.8 percent) or in another state in 1975. Although these proportions are modest, they constitute a sizable contingent in absolute numbers, approximately 566,000 persons. In Manhattan, new arrivals from both sources come to 14.2 percent.[6] These figures are considerably lower in the Bronx and the three high-poverty neighborhoods considered in this analysis. New York City was well below the national average in drawing migrants from other states (3.0 as against 9.7 percent) but drew more than twice the national average from abroad (4.8 percent as against 1.9 percent) (table 17). To the above must be added an indeterminate number of undocumented persons only partially captured in the census enumeration, most of them Dominicans, other Caribbean national, Central and South Americans, along with a respectable sprinkling of Asians and Europeans. It is generally acknowledged that almost all of these new arrivals find or create niches in the local economy that elude or are rejected by earlier settlers and their offspring. This is allegedly partially accomplished by the reconstitution of extra capitalist economic relations or the reproduction of capitalist relations proper to "peripheries" or that are throwbacks to industrial modalities common in early capitalism (e.g. sweatshops and homework).

The remarkable parallels between ongoing structural realignments of

TABLE 17
Selected Population Characteristics, New York City and Selected Counties and Neighborhoods, 1980

Characteristic	New York	Manhattan	East Harlem	Central Harlem	Bronx	Mott Haven
Total population	7,071,639	1,428,285	101,481	99,198	1,168,972	79,118
Percent born abroad	23.6	24.4	24.2	8.4	18.4	9.2
Percent living abroad in 1975	4.8	5.9	3.4	1.4	3.9	3.8
Percent living in another state in 1975	3.0	8.3	1.5	2.4	1.4	0.7
Percent living below poverty level	19.7	21.4	37.0	40.5	27.0	46.7
Percent employed in government	16.8	13.2	24.1	29.6	22.3	19.1

Sources: City and county data provided by N.Y.C. Dept. of Planning. Community Board data tabulated at CUNY Data Center.

population and employment in Puerto Rico and New York, not only from the small perspective of a migrant people but in terms of the global rearticulation of capitals and labor now in process, command attention even in the sketchy account presented here. In our view these data reaffirm the essential unity of capitalist relations and bring strongly into question conceptual formulations that postulate inner dualisms or radical discontinuities within capitalism. Social dislocations associated with the transition in advanced capitalist societies from an accumulation process based on the superiority and command of industrial production to one based on control of financial resources, high technology and research, communication and information management, and other services are being increasingly treated as instances of disturbances in the "core" provoked by intrusions of people, relations, and practices from the "periphery." Thus we have with specific reference to New York City, "the peripheralization of labor in the core" (Ross and Trachte, 1983); "peripheralization of the core with recomposition" (Sassen-Koob, 1982); and the appearance in the core of "parallel economies" originally encountered in the periphery (Portes and Walton, 1981).

These formulations have in common a recognition of the internationalization of capital as the principal moving force behind ongoing changes throughout the world economy, but they insist on the duality of core and periphery even as they document the interpenetration of structures and processes allegedly distinctive of one or the other and announce the emergence of structures transcending both. Our point is not to dismiss the importance of many of the distinctions drawn in the analyses mentioned, nor to slight their contribution to theoretical and practical discourse on related issues. We question rather whether they are methodologically consistent with a dialectical understanding of part-whole relations and alterations in the form and content of structured relations and social institutions within capitalism.

In years of work on the Puerto Rican case, we have been able to document partially the essential commonalities between politico-economic processes in post-World War II Puerto Rico and developments on a world scale, in the U.S. economy as a whole, and in U.S. regions with sizable concentrations of Puerto Ricans. We have proceeded on the premise of the unity and universality of the laws of motion of capitalism, believing that this unity is given rather than brought into question by the uneven development of productive forces within and across capitalist social formations. Coming upon small findings such as the fact that in the United States New York State alone outdoes Puerto Rico in the variety of fiscal incentives it offers to seduce investment has helped us to continue to view the two sites as roughly cognate formations struggling against the same forces of redeployment of world capitals, uneven regional development, and social polarization of the work force.

Noting the forms that division of the working class take in Puerto Rico and U.S. communities where Puerto Ricans are numerous has also made us skeptical about theories of labor segmentation, however derived, that also postulate sharp discontinuities in capital-labor relations and need to reach outside the economic nexus to explain the place of sex, race, or national identity in dividing classes. Theoretical discussions of segmentation that focus on economic categories in Marx's labor theory of value, for example, resort to treating sex, race, and ethnicity as "extra-economic" factors falling outside their analysis and requiring separate treatment (Bowles and Gintis, 1977; Edwards, 1979; Reich, 1981). An attempted historical explanation of labor segmentation (Gordon, Edwards and Reich, 1982) focusing on system of control, technical relations of production, and class struggle at the level of the firm also fail to integrate these factors satisfactorily. While aware of the great difficulties involved, we suggest that divisions within the working class may be more fruitfully explored in relation to the segmentation of capital itself in the cycle of its reproduction. Such an analysis would not treat the divisions that concern us as transhistorical givens, biologically or ideologically grounded, but as active elements in the reproduction of capitalist relations, as these both replicate segmented social strata and validate instances of individual mobility and partial emancipation. An important aspect of such an exploration would touch on the role of the state in the segmentation of the working class. The regulation of immigration, the unequal extension of civil rights and social supports, and policies influencing labor force participation and rewards are only a few ways in which the state shares in the structuring and restructuring of divisions within the working class.

Among the more significant outcomes of our continuing concern with this particular case and its ramifications in the U.S. and elsewhere has been the persistent reconfirmation of the underlying structural unity of the social inequality borne by working classes and their national, ethnic, and sexually defined components. The potential for a political expression of that unity is today more apparent than ever despite the multiethnic-multinational fragmentation of the working class observable the world over. In the U.S. setting, growing contingents of workers from Spanish-speaking countries are coming into close relation with similarly situated groups, while maintaining their ties with the working classes in their countries of origin as well as with more advantageously placed strata of workers in the metropolis. The coming struggle for the creation of jobs to fill the looming void of prolonged joblessness may serve as a unifying force for all workers as it exposes the permanent contradiction of capitalism and its inability to recover impetus or survive except at increasing cost in real income to workers everywhere.

Notes

1. The U.S. Dept. of Commerce, for one, has pointed out that less than .2 percent of agricultural wage workers are in the private sector. USDC, 1979.

2. Litigation undertaken by the city and state to obtain adjustments of the 1980 census for undercount remains unresolved. Census results shown here draw on Census Bureau releases and publications, special tabulations from the CUNY Data Center, a special report prepared under the supervision of Evelyn Mann (NYC Dept. of Planning, 1982).

3. Since tract-level data could not be disaggregated for race and Spanish origin, comparisons with whites at that level are inappropriate.

4. In the smaller areas, as has been noted, comparisons between the white and Spanish origin population must be made with caution, given the overlap in these self-designations.

5. In Manhattan there is a sharp reversal of this pattern, with 58.8 percent of white women in the work forces as against about two in five among other women.

6. In Queens, which had the sharpest growth of Hispanics in the decade, this figure was 6.8 percent.

References

Bianchi, Suzanne M. 1981. *Household Composition and Racial Inequality*. New Brunswick, N.J.: Rutgers University Press.

Bluestone, Barry, and Bennett Harrison. 1980. *Capital and Communities: The Causes and Consequences of Private Disinvestment*. Washington, D.C.: Progressive Alliance.

Bowles, Samuel, and Herbert Gintis. 1977. "The Marxian Theory of Value and Heterogeneous Labor: A Critique and Reformulation." *Cambridge Journal of Economics* 1:2 (June), 173-192.

―――. 1982. "The Crisis of Liberal-Democratic Capitalism: The Case of the United States." *Politics and Society* 11:1, 51-94.

Campos, Ricardo, and Frank Bonilla. 1976. "Industrialization and Migration: Some Effects of the Puerto Rican Working Class." *Latin American Perspectives* 3:3 (Summer), 66-108.

―――. 1982a. "Bootstraps and Enterprise Zones: The Underside of Late Capitalism in Puerto Rico and the United States." *Review* 5:4, 556-590.

―――. 1982b. "Imperialist Initiatives and the Puerto Rican Worker: From Foraker to Reagan." *Contemporary Marxism* 5 (Summer), 1-19.

Castles, Stephen, and Godula Kosack. 1973. *Immigrant Workers and Class Structure in Western Europe*. Oxford: Oxford University Press.

Cooney, Rosemary S. 1979. "Demographic components of growth in white, black, and Puerto Rican female-headed families: comparison of the Cutright and Ross/Sawhill methodologies." *Social Science Research* 8:2 (June), 144-158.

Early, Brian. 1980. "Puerto Ricans in the New York City Labor Market, 1970: A Structural Analysis." Master's thesis, Fordham University.

Edwards, Richard C. 1979. *Contested Terrain*. New York: Basic Books.
Fligstein, Neil. 1981. *Going North*. New York: Academic Press.
Freedman, Marcia K. 1976. *Labor Markets: Segments and Shelters*. Montclair, N. J.: Allanheld Osmun.
Friend, Andrew, and Andy Metcalf. 1981. *Slump City*. London: Pluto Press.
Ginzberg, Eli. 1979. *Good Jobs, Bad Jobs, No Jobs*. Cambridge: Harvard University Press.
Gordon, David, Richard Edwards and Michael Reich. 1982. *Segmented Work, Divided Workers*. Cambridge: Cambridge University Press.
Hiestand, Dale L., and Dean W. Morse. 1979. *Comparative Metropolitan Employment Complexes*. Montclair, N.J.: Allanheld Osmun.
Hughes, James N., and George Sternlieb. 1978. *Jobs and People*. New Brunswick, N.J.: Center for Urban Policy Research.
Junta de Planificación de Puerto Rico. 1982. *Perfil Demográfico y Económico de la Población Inmigrante en Puerto Rico*. San Juan: Junta de Planificación.
. 1981. *Economic Report to the Governor*. San Juan: Junta de Planificación.
Krippendorf, Ekkehart. 1976. *Migration in the Evolution of the International System*. Johns Hopkins University: Bologna Center.
Laurentz, Robert. 1980. *Racial/Ethnic Conflict in the New York City Garment Industry*. Doctoral dissertation. State University of New York at Binghamton.
National Commission for Employment Policy. 1982. *Hispanics and Jobs: Barriers to Progress* Washinton D.C.: NCEP.
New York City Department of Planning. 1982. *Puerto Rican New Yorkers*. New York: Department of Planning.
New York City Department of Health. 1982. *Summary of Vital Statistics, 1981*. New York: Department of Health.
Petras, Elizabeth Maclean. 1981. "The Global Labor Market in the Modern World Economy." In *Global Trends in Migration*, ed. Kritz, Mary, Charles Keely and Silvano Tomasi, pp. 44-63. New York: Center for Migration Studies.
Piore, Michael. 1979. *Birds of Passage*. Cambridge: Cambridge University Press.
Portes, Alejandro and John Walton. 1981. *Labor, Class and the International System*. New York: Academic Press.
Powers, Mary G., and John J. Macisco, Jr. 1982. *Los Puertorriqueños en Nueva York. Un Análisis de su Participación Laboral y Experiencia Migratoria*. Río Piedras: Universidad de Puerto Rico.
Reich, Michael. 1981. *Racial Inequality*. Princeton:Princeton University Press.
Rodríguez, Clara, 1979. "Economic Factors Afecting Puerto Ricans in New York" In *Labor Migration under Capitalism: The Puerto Rican Experience*, History Task Force, Centro de Estudios Puertorriqueños, pp. 197-221. New York: Monthly Review Press.
Rohatyn, Felix. 1981. "Reconstructing America," *New York Review of Books* 28:3 (March 5), 16-20.
Ross, Robert, and Kent Trachte. 1983. "Global Cities and Global Classes: The Peripheralization of Labor in New York City." *Review* 6:3, 393-431.
Sassen Koob, Saskia. 1982. "Recomposition and Peripheralization in the Core," *Contemporary Marxism*. 5, 88-100.

Simon, Julian. 1977. *The Economics of Population Growth*. Princeton: Princeton University Press.
Taller Arte Cultura. 1982. *De la deformación a la destrucción*. Puerto Rico: Adjuntas.
Thurow, Lester. 1981. *The Zero Sum Society*. New York: Penguin Books.
Tienda, Marta. 1981. *Hispanic Origin Workers in U.S. Labor Markets: Comparative tive Analyses of Employment and Earnings*. Springfield, Va.: National Technical Information Service.
U.S. Commission on Civil Rights. 1982. *Unemployment and Underemployment among Blacks, Hispanics and Women*. Clearinghouse Publication no. 74. Washington, D.C.: Government Printing Office.
U.S. Department of Commerce. 1979. *Economic Study of Puerto Rico*. Wasghington, D.C..: Government Printing Office.
Vázquez Calzada, José L., and Zoraida Morales del Valle. 1979. *Características sociodemográficas de los norteamericanos, cubanos y dominicanos residentes en Puerto Rico*. San Juan: Universidad de Puerto Rico, Escuela Graduada de Salud Pública.
Vining, Jr., Daniel R. 1982. "Migration between the Core and Periphery." *Scientific American* 247:6 (December), 44-53.
Walker, Richard A. 1978. "Two Sources of Uneven Development under Advanced Capitalism: Spatial Differentiation and Capital Mobility." *Review of Radical Political Economy* 10:3 (Spring), pp. 28-37.
Wallace, Phyllis A., 1980. *Black Women in the Labor Force* Cambridge: MIT Press.

Contemporary Production and the New International Division of Labor

María Patricia Fernández Kelly

Among the singular events that U.S. dailies and broadcasts have considered newsworthy in the last three years is a large number of plant closings in traditional industrial communities, reducing union membership, increasing willingness of organized labor to grant concessions or to accept wage cuts from employers, and the revival of sweatshops, homework, and the so-called underground economy. Even more visible has been the attention given advanced technology as a radical transformer of social life. What links these phenomena, making them distinct features of our times? This essay provides an answer to that question on the basis of recent writings on contemporary production. In that sense, this is an effort at synthesis. The emphasis on contemporary production entails the recognition that we are witnessing a new stage of capitalist development, differentiated from, although organically related to, previous epochs. But the term *contemporary* is limited in its analytical scope. It is used here merely for descriptive purposes and to probe the nature of current trends in investments, as well as their most immediate consequence: the establishment of a new international division of labor (Emmanuel, 1974; Frobel, Heinrichs and Kreye, 1981; Nash and Fernández, 1983; Palloix, 1973; Wallerstein, 1974).

With regard to a temporal framework, the reader should bear in mind that under the rubric of contemporary production I am referring to the period that began roughly in 1962 and continues to the present. That date marks the year when Fairchild, the electronics manufacturer, opened the first "offshore" semiconductor assembly plant in Hong Kong (Siegel, 1982). In 1966 the same corporation began operations in Korea. General Instruments moved microelectronics assembly to Taiwan in 1964. And only a year later, when the Mexican government intervened to provide incentives for the expansion of the Border Industrialization Program, Transistron, Motorola, and other followed similar path (Fernández, 1983a). The following decade saw the incorporation of Singapore, Malasia, and the Philippines into offshore manufacturing.

These events were far from trivial. Electronics manufacturing has been at the forefront of economic and political trends for the last three decades. As a harbinger of advanced technology it showed a tendency toward internationalization from the beginning. By transferring phases of production overseas, it became tightly woven to the emergence of export processing zones (EPZs), world market factories, and maquiladoras.[1] EPZs offer corporations an unprecedented range of alternatives for the profitable deployment of resources. In addition, advancements in communications, transportation, and technology now enable capital to cross borders freely and to benefit from holiday programs designed by host governments to lure foreign investments.[2]

Export processing zones and World Market Factories in developing countries are the echo of declining industrial sites, diminishing union membership, and the resurgence of sweatshops in advanced economies. The two sets of phenomena are part of a strategy for reducing production costs, maximizing productivity, allowing industry to remain competitive and, perhaps most importantly, controlling workers (NACLA, 1975, 1977; Nash and Fernández, 1983). There are almost 200 EPZs operating in less developed countries with a work force which approximates 3 million. However, stark figures provide only a partial view of a complex picture. The rise in importance of export processing in the periphery is but one of the indications of international economic restructuring. Its consequences are felt in all facets of social life. It foreshadows tendencies that exist in light and capital goods industries.[3]

In the same vein, the impact of international restructuring is felt at the core and in the periphery. While advanced economies increasingly become the locus of technological development, financial outflows, specialized services and centralized decisions over global production, developing countries increase their participation in the world market as sources of manufactures goods.[4] In this sense offshore assembly represents both a break with the past and the beginning of a new mode of insertion of central and peripheral areas into the international system of production.[5]

In the following pages seven characteristics of contemporary production will be discussed. These can be classified into two groups, each one of which represents a different level of analysis. First, I will examine those traits which are fundamental activators in the movement of capital on a global scale (internationalization, mobility, and technological development). Afterward I will focus on those that may be regarded as corollaries or related effects (centralization and geographical dispersal of production, fragmentation and deskilling of labor processes, pseudoregression, and feminization). The two sets frequently overlap. To be sure, then, the separation between them is artificial. But they offer, in this case, a convenient alternative for disaggregating and understanding more fully the various parts of a process that has evolved as an undivided and dynamic whole.

Interest in the first six traits mentioned above will not come as a surprise to most readers. They have all become part of the explicit discourse on contemporary production, although their interpretation varies. The same is not true about feminization. Yet it is one of the central contentions of this essay that the new articulation of core and periphery described earlier cannot be adequately understood without an analysis of the role played by gender in the reorganization of the international economy. Thus, toward the end of the chapter I pause to consider this issue. My argument is that feminization may be understood in two distinct but related ways. On the one hand, contemporary production has brought about an impressive growth of female employment in direct manufacturing in less developed countries. Indeed, between 85 and 90 percent of those employed in export processing zones are women, the majority of whom are young and single (UNIDO, 1980).

At the same time, in advanced industrial countries, a growing number of women become part of the new service economy or toil in the semi-invisible ranks of the informal economy.[6] There are powerful connections between these groups. For example, the remarkable array of electronic paraphernalia assembled by women in the export processing zones of the periphery later become the tools handled by clerks, word processor specialists, typists, and secretaries in core nations. The majority of these are also women.

But an analysis on feminization must go beyond notice of women's increasing participation in the labor markets of central and peripheral economies. We must also consider another fact: a growing number of jobs in countries like the United States are acquiring characteristics formerly associated with female employment. More and more workers of both sexes are now holding jobs which call for minimum levels of skill, provide comparatively low wages, and offer limited possibilities for promotion. These jobs are frequently temporary, unstable, and bereft of the benefits attached in the past to male blue collar employment. However we define feminization, it is clear that only by gaining a better understanding of gender will we be able to move toward a profound explanation of contemporary production. Such an objective is not fulfilled in these pages. However, the reader is invited to consider gender as a consequence and a process rather than as a mere attribute of individuals and to judge the relevance of this for the elaboration of a comprehensive analysis of current trends in capitalist development.

INTERNATIONALIZATION AND MOBILITY OF CAPITAL

The New International Division of Labour, by F. Frobel, J. Heinrichs and O. Kreye, represented an important event in recent scholarship. Since its original publication in German in 1977, the title of this book has provided students of contemporary economic development with a convenient catchphrase to distinguish our baffling times from other historical periods. Yet the content of the term has remained vague. It now runs the risk of becoming an empty truism. We must assess its meaning in the light of ongoing research and place it within a broad set of explanations.[7]

Frobel, Heinrichs and Kreye's work is best understood in the context of Marxist and neo-Marxist theory in that it assumes the unique character of capitalism. The authors agree that, since its inception in the sixteenth century, capitalism was characterized by an international bent. When feudalism gave way in Europe to cosmopolitan class of merchants and financiers, the tendency toward internationalization was manifest in a penchant for geographical exploration. Devoid of romantic interpretations, the discovery of new continents, the taste for exotic goods and spices, and the intent to mold recently found peoples to the dictums of Christianity may only be appreciated as part of an international system whose purpose was the unlimited accumulation of abstract wealth, that is, the valorization of capital (Palloix, 1973, p. 2a; Wallerstein, 1974).

Two and a half centuries later, the advent of the industrial revolution with its startling array of machinery depended largely on investments overseas. These were destined to the exploiting of native labor and the extracting of raw materials for manufacture in central countries. Neither of these two objectives could be achieved without accentuating colonial and consolidating large hegemonic states at the core. Bloody wars of independence and the creation of new technologies in the nineteenth and early twentieth centuries facilitated the incorporating of a still larger number of areas into the world's productive system as clients or spheres of influence of advanced industrial countries. Several attempts at import substitution in the periphery and strong nationalist ideologies did not reduce dependency, nor did they diminish the tendency toward internationalization. By the mid twentieth century, developing countries continued to function primarily as exporters of raw materials and importers of manufactures (O'Brien, 1975).

From this broad historical sketch, sustained by tomes of detailed archival research, it follows that internationalization and the emergence of a global system of production have been constant features of capitalism for more than four centuries. What, then, separates the last two decades—that is, the period during which the new international division of labor has been consolidated—from other stages in modern history? To answer this question it is first necessary to make a distinction between the general dynamics of capital accumulation and expansion and the labor process itself. Afterwards it is necessary to call into play other factors such as the rapidity of capital movements across national borders made partly possible by advanced technology.

In so doing it becomes apparent that what makes the last two decades unique is not so much the continuing internationalization of investments but the manner in which the movements of capital, allied to a particular type of technology, have drastically affected productive processes. More concretely, the internationalization of the economy in the age of computers and efficient transportation has meant the transferring of "manufacturing stages" from the center to the periphery. This, in turn, is forging a new type of relationship between advanced industrial and developing countries and providing, at the same time, specificity to the concept of internationalization. For example, in the past capital investments overseas were mostly used to exploit native resources and labor. At present they can also be used to subdivide the manufacture of a product into distinct phases and relocate each one of them to different geographical areas. World market factories and export processing zones depend on this new trend, whereby a country in the periphery becomes the locus for assembly of products sold in the international market. Managers of multinational corporations are among the most articulate speakers when describing the singularity of this trend. Mr. J., who headed the subsidiary of United Technologies in Ciudad Juárez, Chihuahua (México) in 1980, stated, "To many it seems like a miracle. . . . It is like carving out a production department (while at the same time maximizing output), launching it to Mexico, Taiwan or Hong Kong and keeping headquarters in the U.S." (Fernández, 1980).

This significant achievement has economic and political repercussions. From a strictly economic vantage point, investors and analysts see this type of internationalization as a mechanism meant to maximize productivity and diminish production cost through the employment of low-wage labor in developing countries. Thi `osters greater revenues, but, most importantly, it allows companies to operate competitively on a world scale. Ironically, the transferring of manufactures overseas is frequently explained as a survival strategy forced by "foreign competition." However, the meaning of this term remains uncertain in a context where more and more companies are being swallowed by international consortia (Chaikin, 1976).

From the point of view of political practice, internationalization is also having consequences. Christian Palloix and David Barkin notice that internationalization in the last two decades has affected the extension of the proletariat throughout the world, that is, the incorporation of growing numbers of workers into social relationships marked by the impact of wage transactions. Proletarianization has happened at the core and in the periphery, but in each case it has adopted different forms. In advanced industrial countries, the decline of traditional "smokestack" industries has entailed a shift in the capacity for negotiation between capital and labor in which the latter is being rendered more vulnerable by the same forces that have facilitated the transferring of manufacture overseas (Nash and Fernández, 1983).

On the other hand, developing countries which have opened their borders to the establishment of export platforms now find themselves in competition with one another. Host governments have considered investments in exportable goods valuable enough to warrant the development of stimuli: tax exemptions, the provision of infrastructure, low wages, and in several cases, the reinforcement of a repressive apparatus to maintain workers in line. Expressing ambivalent feelings toward these phenomena, a worker in the Bataan Export Processing Zone (Philippines) explained, "you can't fight the companies. If we strike or make trouble, they threaten to go to another country. So mostly we are quiet and take the jobs because we have to feed our families. But sometimes even that is difficult and we have to fight" (Gray, Bohlen and Grossman, 1981).

The internationalization and mobility of capital investments have also spun ideological webs. Upon the economic and political transformations outlined above, new interpretations have been erected. For example, to business representatives, internationalization is merely the effect of economic interdependence between countries with a different balance of resources. Similar in tone and content to "comparative advantage" paradigms, this perspective argues that international "production sharing" allows countries with an abundance of capital but hindered by labor shortages to enter optimal partnerships with countries where the reverse is true, that is, where capital is scarce but labor plentiful (Drucker, 1979). In these agreements benefits accrue to both types of nations. Industries (particularly those facing acute competition, those operating under the pressure of rapidly changing technology, and those whose production is seriously affected by seasonality or fashion) can lower costs by establishing operations in areas of the world where wages are between 6 and 15 times smaller than those paid in advanced capitalist countries. For example, wages earned in most Asian countries average 35 cents an hour, while in Mexico hourly investments in labor and benefits barely surpass $1.00 (Grossman, 1978). But despite large wage differentials, it is assumed that less developed countries can profitably use foreign investments in export platforms to create badly needed jobs, increase state revenues, and implement alternative strategies for national development (Flamm and Grunwald, n.d.).

What this euphemistic explanation of contemporary development fails to consider are the contradictions resulting from and causing the internationalization of capital investments. In particular, this perspective in unable to account for the presumed labor shortages found at the core. When examined closely, the notion of labor shortage itself reveals its political dimension. It is clear that when adherents of "production sharing" refer to shortages they are referring to specific types of workers, that is, to uncomplaining, vulnerable, low-paid, and low-skilled workers, similar to those found in the developing world or, in previous eras, in central countries as well. By resorting to employment of workers overseas, investors have dealt a rude blow to the historical achievements of organized labor in central countries. Yet, until now, the spirit of international solidarity has been slow in reaching the consciousness of workers. Instead, some labor representatives have despairingly advocated protectionism, isolationism, and retaliation against "foreign competition." These may be futile demands in a world where production sharing is becoming the norm rather than the exception.

Advanced Technology

The new international division of labor may not be understood without paying attention to the spectacular rise of information-processing machines based on the widespread use of semiconductors. Unquestionably, silicon chips have provided the infrastructure for contemporary capitalist production. A profuse and fascinating literature now exists on these miniscule particles of sand and metal, on their multiple feats and notable adventures (Siegel, 1982; O'Connor, 1983). Therefore I shall only mention two relevant points.

First, advanced technology has brought to fulfillment a long-held capitalist dream: increased control and better coordination over the process of production. In the past, companies were limited by conventional technology's ability to store and handle information. In addition, the cumbersome size of early mainframe computers, as well as their high cost, made it possible only for the largest and best-endowed business to involve them in direct production. At present the reverse is true. Even small companies can own technological means to monitor their output, plan manufacturing, and exert efficient inventory supervision. From their headquarters in New York, Dallas, or Geneva, corporate managers are now capable of instantaneously retrieving valuable data to halt or accelerate production in consonance with market fluctuations. By using the same sophisticated means, they can also harmonize the manufacturing activities of several subsidiaries located in distant geographical areas. Without high tech, the fragmentation of labor processes into discrete stages and their allocation to different countries would not be possible.

Second, advanced technology has also contributed to reduce capitalist dependence on workers, making many at the core increasingly redundant and others, at the core and in the periphery, more liable to strict forms of control (Katz, 1983). To understand this it is useful to consider the two levels at which technology is operating: as an ideological construct and as an actual process meant to reduce production cost by eliminating workers.

The extreme example of future labor redundancy is adeptly presented by the students of robotics. Although the substitution of human workers by robots is still in its early development, corporate planners foresee its extension in the future. Again, we must return to the political dimension of these phenomena. The availability of robots controlled by highly sophisticated computers can be subtly used to make workers aware of their superfluousness and of their imminent substitution if demands for wages and benefits persist. However, both robots and computers are still the end result of minute repetitive manual operations. Thus, many workers may be assembling the machines that will eventually replace them.

On the other hand, the design and programming of information-processing machines requires considerable knowledge and skill. And it is upon the basis of this changing knowledge and skill that a new technocratic elite is rapidly taking force. But the manipulation of information-processing devices often requires no expertise and only limited amounts of learned ability. Pressing keyboards and pushing buttons may yet become one of the most widespread form of labor at the core in the age of technological refinement.

At first glance the reduction of physical effort expended on the job appears as a blessing, and under certain circumstances, it may well be. However, under the guise of simplification and rationalization, advanced technology also offers ample possibilities for controlling workers. For example, research on the conditions of employment for word processor specialists and telephone operators, among others, suggests that, while advanced technology makes output more efficient, it also increases the potential for unprecedented supervision and restraint over workers' activities. With the use of telecommunication checks, it is now possible for many companies to obtain detailed information on their employees' output, time management, and productivity and monitor their behavior to the last minute of their shift (Lowe Benston, 1983).

In sum, advanced technology may simply be seen as the creature of human imagination or as a mechanism deliberately created to displace workers. The first position is ahistorical, the second falls under the rubric of "technological determinism." A third and more fruitful course for interpretation is that which contemplates advanced technology as part of a complex cluster of factors affecting contemporary production, neither a cause nor an isolated consequence but a process and a partial resolution to the conflicts created by the constant confrontation between capital and labor.

CENTRALIZATION AND THE DISPERSAL OF PRODUCTION

The internationalization and mobility of capital have highlighted the presence of large corporations all over the world and promoted the homogenization of social relationships in which workers are submerged. Young women employed in the export processing zones of Asia or as part of the Mexican Maquiladora Program wear strikingly similar clothes, enjoy the same music, and watch the same popular movies dubbed in their mother tongue. Moreover, these workers exchange for additional cash and personal decoration the goods manufactured by Avon and Stanley costume jewelry. Certainly more significant is the fact that these workers seem to hold identical jobs and face the same problems; they are part of the "global assembly line" (Grossman, 1978). But the geographical dispersion of production, the transferring of assembly overseas, goes hand in hand with the centralization of control over production in certain areas. Points like New York, San Francisco, and Los Angeles hold a large proportion of research and development facilities, financial and administrative headquarters out of which vital decisions flow that affect the course of industry throughout the world.

Nevertheless, these processes until now described at the international level are taking place, with small variants, inside core economies leading some observers to speak about the "peripheralization" of advanced industrial countries (Bluestone and Harrison, 1982; Sassen-Koob, 1982). In the United States, as capital moves from North to South and "right to work" states, from East to West or Silicon Valley to southern California, it leaves in its wake a trail of dismissals, defunct plants, and changing communities similar to that which follows, in many cases, the transfer of industrial operations to Asia or to the U.S.-Mexican border. Between 1976 and 1982, 650,000 jobs were lost in the New York metropolitan area as a result of the flight of capital to the South or overseas. In the last three years alone, almost 25,000 electronics assembly jobs in California disappeared for similar reasons.[8]

An example of the manner in which these changes could affect central economies is inferred from recent government attempts to undermine minimum wage legislation for youth workers. The current administration has promoted this initiative in addition to a still unsuccessful "Urban Enterprise Zones" project. It should be duly noted that the logic underlying this scheme is to provide businesses with incentives (mainly low-cost labor) for local investment while at the same time providing the bases for the creation of jobs. The concept of urban enterprise one is, therefore, identical to that of export processing zone. Both consist of incentive packages meant to attract companies to areas of high unemployment, abundant labor supplies, and workers who can be paid very low wages. If "urban enterprise zones" were to become a reality, they would shape a scenario where teenagers (blacks, Chicanos, and other minorities) would perform jobs similar to those held by young women in export processing zones located in Asia and Latin America. These new American workers would earn half of the current minimum wage for temporary, menial jobs.

Traditional industrial workers earned relatively high wages and benefits as a result of almost two centuries of conflict and negotiating with capital. At present their accomplishments are severely threatened by the same forces that have set in motion a new international division of labor. A class of newly vulnerable workers is emerging in central countries. The differences of their status when seen in historical perspective lies not so much in the level of poverty or oppression they must endure but in their newly shared experience with workers of other nationalities. This will become even more apparent if employment forecasts for the United States for the next 20 years materialize. The irreversible trend away from manufacturing and towards the proliferation of low-paying, low-status jobs seems certain. Experts predict the continued decline in blue collar manufacturing even if output rises as a result of automation. By the year 2005, only 5-10 percent of the labor force will be involved in manufacturing, compared with 20 percent today. By contrast, according to government records, the U.S. added 1.6 million tavern jobs between 1973 and 1980. That figure represents more than the current total in the steel (327,000) and auto (666,000) industries. During the 1980s more new secretaries (700,000), nurse's aides and orderlies (508,000), janitors (501,000), and sales clerks (470,000) are expected to be hired than workers in any other job categories (BLS, 1983).

Even in industries like electronics which have been seen as potential mechanisms for the revitalization of the U.S. economies, it is doubtful that benefits will accrue for the majority of those employed in it. Overseas relocation has not strengthened U.S. workers' chances for unionization. In fact, electronics factories have been notoriously resistant to organizing drives. They have also had high rates of turnover, low wages, and few opportunities for occupational advancement. Some authors disagree with this pessimistic portrayal, pointing out that even older industries like auto and steel manufacture experienced early phases during which fierce competition and underdeveloped markets fostered extremely low wages, unstable jobs, and bad working conditions. With the passage of time the same industries were able to change favorably, affording benefits to their employees. Something similar, they claim, could occur in electronics (Drucker, 1979; Flamm and Grunwald, n.d.). They fail to consider internationalization. The current stage in electronics manufacture cannot be equated with earlier periods of industrial growth due to a new order of constraints. These include the mobility of capital investments across international borders, offshore production in developing countries, and the rate of technological change. More specifically, at least three other arguments can be made:

First, labor forecasts like the ones outlined above are relevant to the electronics industry. Less than a third of the jobs created in the next two decades will be in specialized, highly remunerative categories. The majority of jobs will be for service workers and assemblers, who will make only modest gains in wages.

Second, technology and automation have restructured or eliminated many middle-level management and administrative positions, inhibiting occupational mobility.

Finally, the size of industrial establishments will place limits upon organizing workers, keeping them divided. In the past, smallness of productive facilities was characteristic of highly competitive economic sectors and low capital-labor ratios. Largeness indicated membership in advanced sectors, considerable capital investments, and internal labor markets. By contrast, the centralization of decisions affecting production and the development of third-

and fourth-generation computer components go hand in hand with small facilities which are also highly specialized and capital intensive. In other cases smallness of a plant can be an effective tool for separating workers into areas of homogeneous and coordinated operation, thus diffusing their potential for unified action. In other words, the maintenance of small-sized firms and, as we shall see, the expansion of subcontracting and the informal economy may lead to further "Balkanization" of the work force in central countries (Scott, in press).

FRAGMENTATION AND DESKILLING OF THE LABOR PROCESS

It has been almost a decade since the publication of Harry Braverman's memorable writing on *Labor and Monopoly Capital* (1974). Enriched by critical review (Burawoy, 1978), this work has lost neither power nor usefulness. An abbreviated description of Braverman's argument includes an emphasis upon the fragmentation of labor processes as part of the trend toward deskilling of jobs. By subdividing production into increasingly simplified stages involving an ever smaller number of operations, investors were able to achieve four equally important objectives:

First, they effected a net reduction of training periods for workers. This was not achieved abruptly rather as a gradual shift whose ultimate consequences has been the uniformization of most jobs and the interchangeability of most workers.

Second, the reduction in the length of time required to train workers is but a symptom of the debasement of labor itself. As the phases of production become more and more compartmentalized, workers are required to possess less and less learned abilities, although they may be called upon to perform more intense production quotas. A paradox of deskilling is that, while a growing number of workers acquire higher levels of education, they must also, with few exceptions, perform less-skilled jobs than their ancestors. Thus, the terms *unskilled* or *semiskilled* are more appropriate to characterize jobs than workers. This is the same as saying that the definition of the level of skill depends more on the organization of production than on the learned abilities of individual workers (Braverman, 1974).

Third, fragmentation and deskilling have also allowed for greater specialization of the work force and for the increase of productivity. Be it assembly work in an Asian export processing zone or activating a digital keyboard in a telecommunication office, specialization is a trait of contemporary production. As jobs become more and more uniform, groups of people, often differentiated only by their ethnic background or sex, enter the labor market in a highly concentrated manner. This applies to the national and international spheres. As intimated earlier, it is on the basis of fragmentation and deskilling that less developed countries are becoming sources of manufactured exports and central nations the focus of technological expertise.

Finally, it is on the basis of fragmentation and deskilling that the geographical dispersion of contemporary production has been possible. Plants operating in EPZs function as part of an integrated process which has been extended to various parts of the world. They are not companies in an older, more conventional sense. Rather, they are sections subordinated to a headquarters located far away. In part because of this they are not capable of creating "internal labor markets" and promoting the occupational mobility of workers within them (Fernández, 1983b). This raises serious doubts about the extent to which export processing zones can be used to replicate, in peripheral and semiperipheral countries, models of development which took shape in advanced industrial economies.

PSEUDOREGRESSION

One of the most perplexing features of contemporary production is the reemergence of modalities in the organization of production which are strikingly reminiscent of earlier periods in the development of capitalism. When formal production started moving away from traditional manufacturing sites like New York, employment in sweatshop, homework, and subcontracting grew. The new sweatshops hire large numbers of Dominican, Colombian, Central American, Caribbean, Mexican, and Asian workers, many of whom have entered the United States without proper documents (Waldinger, 1983).

This apparent return to the conditions of early capitalism is found not only in highly competitive and customarily exploitative branches like garment and textile manufacturing. Through the subcontracting of operations to small, informal establishments, even the sectors most closely linked to advanced technology have generated their own type of sweatshop. For example, ongoing research in Silicon Valley shows a widespread fluorescence of a new form of cottage industry. Women, at least some of whom have been formally employed in electronics plants, are now assembling components at home in their own kitchens: "Working at a plant doesn't pay. But working as a broker between women in their homes and a client company does. We sell a product: accuracy and efficiency. If I can get past the receptionist, past the supervisors and to the engineers, I know I can get part of their operation" (Katz, 1983).

To underground subcontractors like the one quoted above, homework represents the possibility of combining domestic responsibilities with wage labor. To their employers, it is a timely vehicle to cut cost, increase productivity, maintain a flexible labor force, and evade fiscal responsibilities.

A variation of this is found in San Diego County, California. In a sample of 300 Mexican women working as electronics assemblers in their own homes between 1979 and 1981, almost one-third were found to be former *maquiladora* workers (Solorzano Torres, 1983). After being displaced from or giving up dead-end jobs on the Mexican side of the border, most of these women had migrated illegally to the United States. There they had found informal employment at the margins of the electronics industry.

This instance, in particular, provides a vivid depiction of investment circuits and their relationship to labor mobility. On the one hand, capital's migration across the border, and the subsequent development of the Maquiladora Program since 1965, is giving rise to a new class of female industrial workers in Mexico. On the other hand, the failure of the program in generating long-term employment may be precipitating the north bound migration of experienced workers whose undocumented status in the United States makes them vulnerable and attractive as assemblers as well as likely targets for abuse on the part of subcontractors. Additional research in North County indicates that the expansion of the electronics industry in that area is due partly to capital's movement from Silicon Valley to southern California. This, in turn, is in large measure explained by the interest of employers in hiring Mexican migrants and commuters in formal and informal work.

Cottage industries may also be found in the new clerical sector of advanced industrial economies with the emergence of telecommuting offices, the so-called electronics sweatshops. Some companies are now renting equipment to workers (especially women with domestic responsibilities and housebound or handicapped persons) which then they use at home to process various kinds of information for the same firms. At the turn of the century workers in the New York garment industry leased or bought from their employers the sewing machines behind which they toiled for up to 18 hours a day. The commonalities of the two cases are self-evident. As with other points listed here, the new cottage industries pose delicate political questions. Some observers—Alvin Toffler most notoriously—have seen electronic homework as the part toward a futuristic utopia in which individuals acquire greater personal autonomy.

However, other authors have pointed to the fallacies of that assumption. Electronics homework may become the vehicle by which an increasing number of women, children, and minorities labor intensely and in total isolation trying to fulfill high production assignments for low wages, no benefits, and few possibilities for organization (Katz, 1983). It is not accidental that some of the most conservative organizations in the United States (Moral Majority and supporters of the Family Opportunity Act, for example) favor the passage of legislation meant to facilitate industrial homework in electronics and other manufacturing branches. This is seen as a profamily measure which will allow women to earn "supplementary" income without neglecting their domestic responsibilities, a not very original version of the "double shift" syndrome for wives and mothers.

Export processing enclaves in peripheral countries and pseudoregression in central nations are two prongs of the same economic process. Neither are anomalies or replications of past stages of development. They are not equivalent to textile mills or early auto and steel industries. Unlike the latter, EPZs are not a suitable base for the consolidation of a skilled organized work force, the maintenance of consistent growth rates, and the development of internal consumer and labor markets. More significantly, EPZs are frequently superimposed upon efforts to industrialize on the basis of import substitution. It was upon the latter that the hope to implement viable models of industrial development in the so-called Third World was founded in the 1930s and 1940s (O'Brien, 1975). Cottage industries, electronics sweatshops and the new underground economy in central countries are the logical consequence of capital disinvestment and the erosion of basic productive capacities.

FEMINIZATION

This term poses conceptual and empirical questions that can only be sketched in these pages. Mostly, these have to do with our understanding of gender and the manner in which this historically developed social construction affects current political and economic processes.

We may define feminization as two distinct but interrelated phenomena. To do this we may focus either on the number of women who have entered the wage-labor force (mostly services in central economies and services and manufacturing in less developed ones) during the last two decades. Or we can center our analysis upon the changing nature of jobs now available to most workers.

Consider the first alternative. There has been an impressive growth of female employment in the so-called modern sector of industrializing economies. Not surprisingly, the largest increases in women's employment have taken place in export processing zones. Only in Asia (with the notable exception of the People's Republic of China and Japan) half of the work force is employed in electronics production plants. This amounts to more than 300,000 people, most of whom are women. Equally striking is the Mexican case. In little over a decade almost 200,000 *maquiladora* jobs have been created. The vast majority are held by young women. Women also form more than half of the work force in the new service economies of central countries. Altogether, the number of working women in the United States grew by 173 percent from 1947 to 1980 with the highest increases occurring since the early 1960s. During the same period the employment of men grew only by 43 percent. Thus, "women have been at the vortex of sweeping changes in demographic, social and economic patterns" (U.S.Bureau of the Census, 1983).

It is women who sit behind word processors, key punchers, and computer terminals at corporation headquarters, as part of typing pools or in clerical telecommunication offices. It is women who hold the vast majority of jobs as assemblers and low-level administrators and supervisors in the electronics and other high-tech industries. Finally, it is women who work in large numbers in neosweatshops of various kinds.

If, in addition to women's growing employment, we also consider feminization as a factor affecting the nature of available employment, it is soon apparent that an expanding number of jobs are acquiring characteristics similar to those of traditional female work. Even in the most advanced sectors of the new service economies, fragmentation and deskilling have combined to produce an abundance of low-paying, repetitive, monotonous, temporary jobs. The best example of this trend is found among laid-off workers of the auto and steel industries who have been summarily retrained to fill jobs in high-tech jobs. While in the past these men earned wages averaging $11.00 to $15.00 an hour, at present many of them have had to take unskilled jobs for wages barely above the $3.50 minimum. The failure of training programs and the growth of informal employment suggest that these workers will probably never hold jobs similar to those they had in the past.

How can we account for feminization (in both senses of the word) in the age of advanced technology? To provide a satisfactory answer to this question we must evaluate first the lessons derived from more than a decade of research on gender. Such a task leads to the conclusion that, far from being a mere attribute of individuals, gender is also an ongoing social process, according to which workers are chosen for different types of jobs (Safa, 1983). To confuse sex with gender is an analytical error of the first magnitude. Sex can be defined as an assortment of physiological, anatomical, and secondary morphological traits that differentiate male from female members of the species; it is a refined adaptation to complex forms of biological reproduction. Gender, on the other hand, is the result of socialization processes which allocate to men and women different positions and roles in the social division of labor. It is true that gender frequently builds upon sexual differences, using them to justify social developments on the basis of presumed biological constants. But generally, definitions of gender go largely beyond the strict confines of sex. Thus, while sex remains a link to natural evolution, gender is one of the tenets of political and economic history.

Anthropological research provides ample evidence to illustrate this point. There are no known circumstances under which sex is not recognized as a fundamental guideline for social interaction. However, the construction of societies on the basis of gender varies so dramatically as to negate validity to statements equating the two terms. It is on the basis of sex that some African and New Guinean tribes take passivity, idleness, patience, and extreme vanity to be natural attributes of males. In other cultures (including our own) the same features have been thought to be innately and distinctly feminine. In the same vein, the employment of women as assemblers in export processing zones is frequently explained by their putative natural dexterity, acute eyesight, greater sense of responsibility, patience, and preference for minute, detailed operations. Surrounding these praiseworthy feminine characteristics are low wages, dead-end jobs, and unfavorable working conditions. In this case the ideology of gender is used to justify a rather crude economic reality (Benería, 1983).

Feminists and women's advocates have found in similar contradictions between rationalization and economic reality ample evidence of a particular type of social inequality. Since 1955, when women earned 65 percent of what men earned, the gap has widened. Women now are paid roughly 59 percent what men get (U.S. Bureau of the Census, 1983). The persistence of wage differentials between men and women and the sexual segregation of the labor market are symptoms of women's social subordination and vulnerability. The emphasis upon these undeniable, albeit regrettable facts has led to many stimulating inquiries. However, the same emphasis has also erected tautological traps. An example will suffice to illustrate this.

On the basis of empirical observation we know that when holding variables such as education and age constant, women still tend to earn wages one-third smaller than those earned by men employed in comparable occupations. This is a cause of political and economic vulnerability. But economic and political vulnerability may also be said to be the cause of women's reduced earning capacity and their segregation in the labor market. This circular argument prevents us from identifying the specific mechanisms by which women become socially vulnerable. From the same set of propositions we are not able to distinguish between women's vulnerability and that which characterizes other social groups (say blacks, Chicanos, or undocumented migrants of both sexes). It is not enough to state repeatedly that in an unequal social system all differences, including ethnicity and gender, may be used to divide and exploit workers. This may be accurate, but it still lacks explanatory value.

To move beyond tautologies we need to place gender in a historical perspective and to study it as a consequence of the interplay between households and labor markets. This effort must also contain an inquiry into the way in which the state mediates such a relationship (Mallon, 1983). The massive incorporation of women into wage employment has coincided in the past with moments of economic reorganization, when capitalists must resort to the employment of the most vulnerable workers to retain competitiveness and accumulate additional profits. Such was the case during the early stages of industrialization, and such is the case at present. Gender is, therefore, similar to class and ethnicity in that it conditions the incorporation of workers into particular sectors of the labor market. Little more is necessary to conclude that we cannot advance our understanding of contemporary political economy without a more refined understanding of gender.

Conclusions

The purpose of this essay has been to provide guidelines for a fuller understanding of current economic and political processes on a world scale. It has been argued that "the new international division of labor" designates a new articulation between central and peripheral countries in which the latter are increasingly becoming sources of manufactures for the world marked. Several factors, particularly the internationalization of investments, the accelerated geographical mobility within and across national boundaries, and the rate of technological change, have reorganized production. Most importantly, these transformations have resulted in a shift in the negotiating capacity of workers vis-à-vis employers. How this growing contradiction will be resolved is one of the most important challenges confronted by political economy.

Notes

1. For a detailed historical account of the electronics industry, see O'Connor (1983). The term *maquiladora* designates an assembly plant operating as a direct subsidiary or subcontracted firm for the manufacture of export-oriented goods under the Mexican Border Industrialization Program, started in 1965; since 1972 it has been known as the Maquiladora Program.

2. Export processing zones are special areas reserved for the production of goods for the world market. They operate under government programs, which include tax exemptions, property allowances, provision of infrastructure, and other incentives for investment.

3. Although light industries such as electronics and apparel have become heavily dependent on the transfer of stages of production overseas, heavy industries such as automobile and steel production have also followed suit. The largest producers of steel at present have relocated in Korea under the auspices of multinational corporations. In the same vein, most of the electrical systems for U.S.-made cars (including Chrysler and Ford Motor Company lines) are assembled overseas.

4. See Frobel, Heinrichs and Kreye, 1981. "Some typical aspects of the contemporary world economy [indicate] that the old or 'classical' international division of labour is now open for replacement. The decisive evidence for this hypothesis is the fact that developing countries have increasingly become sites for manufacturing-producing manufactured goods which are competitive on the world market" (p.12). "However, the industrialized countries handle 70 percent of international trade and the developing countries only 20 percent. Seventy percent of exports from developing and industrialized countries are meant for industrialized countries and only 20 percent for the developing countries. The foreign trade of developing countries is mostly with the industrialized countries, and not their fellow developing countries. This translates into economic dependency of the developing countries on the industrialized countries" (p.8).

5. According to Anibal Pinto (1980), this represents an irreversible "opening to the exterior" on the part of developing countries.

6. "Informal economy" denotes a variety of productive arrangements not easily couched in available terminology. "Sweatshop" refers to a licensed enterprise whose owners or managers regularly do not comply with federal or state legislation regarding minimum wages, benefits, health and safety standards, etc. "Cottage manufacture" entails small operations in private homes or makeshift facilities where a broker mediates between a licensed firm and an assortment of workers. "Homework" refers to situations where brokers are absent and managers of firms enter into individual arrangements with workers who perform assembly services in their own homes. For further discussion of the underground industrial economy, see Maram, Long and Berg, 1981, and Piore, 1977.

7. A more precise analysis of contemporary production must take into account the internal dynamics of capitalist accumulation and expansion. In particular, the author wishes to draw attention to the relevance of writings that in the past have considered such issues as the falling rate of profit, the impact of financial capital in economic restructuring, and the role of advanced technology as an instrument to assuage some of the accentuating contradictions of international development.

8. Testimony to congressional subcommittees on employment Opportunities and labor-management relations by the Los Angeles Coalition Against Plant Closings. Some of the plants relocated abroad, while others went bankrupt.

REFERENCES

Benería, Lourdes. 1983. "The Labor Process, Subcontracting and Gender Relations." Paper prepared for the Social Science Research Council Workshop on Social Inequality and Gender Hierarchy.

Bluestone, Barry, and Bennett Harrison. 1982. *The Deindustrialization of America.* New York: Basic Books.

Braverman, Harry. 1974. *Labor and Monopoly Capital.* New York: Monthly Review Press.

Burawoy, Michael. 1978. "Toward a Marxist theory of the Labor Process: Braverman and Beyond." *Politics and Society* 8:3,4, 247-312.

Chaikin, Sol. 1976. *The Needed Repeal of Item 807.00 of the Tariff Schedules of the United States. Report Presented Before the Subcommittee on Trade, Committee on Ways and Means. U.S. House of Representatives.*

Drucker, Peter. 1979. "Production Sharing, Concepts and Definitions." *Journal of the Flagstaff Institute* 1, 32-45.

Emmanuel, Arghiri. 1974. *Unequal Exchange: A Study of the Imperialism of Trade.* New York: Monthly Review Press.

Fernández Kelly, María Patricia. 1980. "Notes From the Field." Mimeo.

———. 1983a. "A Cross Cultural Comparison of Export Processing Zones in Asia and the U.S.-Mexico Border." Monograph prepared for the Walsh-Price Fellowship Program, Maryknoll Fathers and Brothers.

———. 1983b. *For We Are Sold, I and My People: Women and Industry in Mexico's Frontier.* Albany: State University of New York Press.

Flamm, K., and J. Grunwald. N.d. "Offshore Production in the International Semiconductor Industry." Mimeo. Washington, D.C.: Brookings Institution.

Frobel, Folker, Jurgen Heinrichs and Otto Kreye. 1981. *The New International Division of Labour*. Cambridge: Cambridge University Press.

Gordon, David. ed. 1977. *Problems in Political Economy: An Urban Perspective*. Lexington, Mass.: Heath.

Gray, Lorraine, Ann Bohlen and Rachael Grossman. 1981. *Oral Histories*. Washington, D.C.: Educational Film and T.V. Center.

Grossman, Rachel. 1978. "Women's Place in the Integrated Circuit." *Southeast Asia Chronicle* 9:5.6, 2-17.

Katz, N. 1983. "Join the Future Now! Women and Work in the Electronics Industry." In *Women, Men and the International Division of Labor*. ed. June Nash and María Patricia Fernández Kelly, pp. 332-345. Albany: State University of New York Press.

Lowe Benston, M.. 1983. "For Women, the Chips are Down." In *The Technological Woman: Interfacing with Tomorrow*, ed. J. Zimmerman, New York: Praeger.

Mallon, F. 1983. "Gender and Class in the Transition to Capitalism." Paper presented at the Social Science Research Council Workshop on Social Inequality and Gender Hierarchy.

Maram, S., S. Long and D. Berg. 1981. "Hispanic Workers in the Garment and Restaurant Industries in Los Angeles County." Working Papers in U.S.-Mexican Studies, no. 12. La Jolla: University of California at San Diego.

Nash, June, and María Patricia Fernández Kelly. eds. 1983. *Women, Men and the International Division of Labor*. Albany: State University of New York Press.

North American Congress on Latin America. (NACLA). 1975. "U.S. Runaway Shops on the Mexican Border." *Latin America and Empire Report* 9:7, 1-22.

———. 1977. "Capital's Flight: The Apparel Industry Moves South." *Latin America and Empire Report* 11:3, 1-25.

O'Brien, P. 1975. "A Critique of Latin American Theories of Dependency." In *Beyond the Sociology of Development*, ed. Ivar Oxaal et al., pp. 7-27. London: Routledge and Kegan Paul.

O'Connor, D. 1983. "Changing Patterns of International Production in the Semiconductor Industry: The Role of Transnational Corporations." Paper presented at the Conference on Microelectronics in Transition.

Oxaal, Ivar, et al. eds. 1975. *Beyond the Sociology of Development*. London: Routledge and Kegan Paul.

Palloix, Christian. 1973. *Les Firmes multinationales et le procès d'internationalization*. Paris: Maspero.

Pinto, Anibal. 1980. "The Opening up of Latin America to the Exterior." *CEPAL Review* 11 (August), 31-56.

Piore, Michael. 1977. "The Dual Labor Market: Theory and Implications." In *Problems in Political Economy: An Urban Perspective*. ed. David Gordon, pp. 93-97. Lexington, Mass.: Heath.

Safa, Helen I.. 1983. "Women, Production and Reproduction in Industrial Capitalism: A Comparison of Brazilian and U.S. Factory Workers." In *Women, Men and the International Division of Labor*. ed. June Nash and María Patricia Fernández Kelly. Albany: State University of New York Press.

Sassen-Koob, Saskia. 1982. "Recomposition and Peripheralization at the Core." *Contemporary Marxism* 5, 88-100.

Scott, A.. In Press. "Industrial Organization and the Logic of Intra-Metropolitan Location I.: Theoretical Considerations." *Economic Geography.*
Siegel, L. 1982. *Delicate Bonds: The Semiconductor Industry.* Oakland, Calif.: Pacific Studies Center.
Solorzano Torres, R. 1983. "Female Mexican Immigrants in San Diego County: Research in Progress." Mimeo.
United Nations Industrial Development Organization. (UNIDO). 1980. "Export Processing Zones in Developing Countries." Working Paper on Structural Change, no. 19 (August).
U.S. Bureau of Labor Statistics. 1983. "Employment Trends for the Eighties." Washington, D.C.: Bureau of Labor Statistics.
U.S. Bureau of the Census. 1983. *Annual Report.* Washington, D.C.: Bureau of the Census.
Waldinger, R.. 1983. "Immigrant Enterprise and Labor Market Structure." Unpublished manuscript.
Wallerstein, Immanuel. 1974. *The Modern World System: Capitalist Agriculture and the Origins of the European World Economy in the Sixteenth Century.* New York: Academic Press.
Zimmerman, J., ed. 1983. *The Technological Woman: Interfacing with Tomorrow.* New York: Praeger.

Capital Mobility and Labor Migration

Saskia Sassen-Koob

Since the middle of the 1960s, three major new migratory flows have developed. Two of these are intraperiphery migrations, one to the oil-exporting countries and the other to industrial zones, most significantly export processing zones (EPZs) and world market factories. The third flow is the migration from Southeast Asia and the Caribbean basin to major core cities, earlier London and more recently cities such as New York and Los Angeles.

Each of these new migrations is articulated with a specific moment in major new circuits along which capital is mobilized and constituted as capital: (1) the redeployment of manufacturing plants and increasingly office work to periphery areas; (2) large scale industrialization in OPEC members; and (3) the restructuring of economic activity in major core cities fed by the globalization of production and the technological transformation of the work process.

There are locations on the capital and labor circuits where the articulation between both processes assumes concrete forms, rather than being a function of the accumulation process that can only be posited in theoretical terms. The migration of women into the new industrial zones in the periphery is one such example (Safa, 1981; Kumar, 1980; Nash and Fernández Kelly, 1983). This articulation is more highly mediated and hence much more difficult to recognize in the cases of immigration into OPEC countries and into major core cities. Recognition in these cases requires prior theoretical elaboration of the concept of capital mobility (Sassen-Koob, 1982). Accelerated industrialization in OPEC countries can be posited as an instance of capital mobility if oil revenues are viewed as a shift of capital and a redeployment of growth poles from the core to the periphery. In the case of major core cities, their new or expanded role as sites for the management and servicing of the globalized production process is inextricably linked with increased capital mobility. Accelerated industrialization in OPEC countries and economic restructuring in core cities have both generated a large supply of low-wage jobs for which immigrants are a desirable labor supply.

The first section seeks to elaborate the concept of capital mobility theoretically and empirically. This allows me to posit an articulation between the major new labor migrations and major components in the current phase of capital mobility. The focus here is particularly on the effects of capital mobility on major cities at the core. This focus is developed further through an empirical analysis of the reorganization of economic activity in these cities and the new large migrations they have received. This case brings to the fore a number of issues central to the current phase of the international division of labor, notably the coexistence in major core cities of a large job loss due to capital relocation to periphery areas and a large immigrant influx. While the massive immigration into new industrial zones in the periphery can be explained easily in terms of an expansion in manufacturing jobs, this is less so in the case of major core cities, which have lost a large component of their manufacturing jobs. I will use data for New York City and Los Angeles from 1960 to 1980 for the empirical elaboration of the argument and the analysis of the political implications, including the findings of a survey on six immigrant groups in New York City (Cohen and Sassen-Koob, 1982).

THEORETICAL ISSUES

Capital mobility and labor migrations have been studied for the most part as unrelated processes. They appear unrelated because they constitute different circuits within the accumulation process (Sassen-Koob, 1981). As social processes each of these is highly specific, with components sufficiently distinct to have generated two almost separate discourses. The closest to a statement about systemic interdependence is the proposition that these represent options maximizing capital's locational opportunities: either capital is moved or labor moves. The market model renders this in a more general form when it states that workers go where the jobs are, or, if feasible, capital is moved where the labor supply is most adequate. These two kinds of statements indeed capture key aspects of the two processes and elaborate them in terms of factor mobility. But there are other aspects of the articulation between these two processes that are not captured in an analysis of factor mobility. These aspects concern the articulation between labor migrations and capital mobility as a constitutive process in the reorganization of production on a world scale and correspondingly the reorganization of the capital-labor relation.[1]

The Reorganization of Production

Studies on capital mobility have tended to focus on the decentralization of manufacturing and thereby posit the spatial dimension of capital mobility.[2] A theoretical elaboration of the concept capital mobility that takes it beyond a spatial dimension allows for an incorporation of other capabilities besides what Storper and Walker (forthcoming) have termed the locational capability of capital. Such an elaboration must reckon with the reorganization of sources of surplus value made possible by massive shifts of capital from one area of the world to another. Notable among these, but usually not recognized as an instance of capital mobility, is the transfer of money from core countries to OPEC members and to the energy industry via an increase in the international price of oil and the reinjection of oil revenues into the world economy via the large-scale import of inputs for the massive development programs launched after 1973.[3]

Such an elaboration must also reckon with the capability of capital to service and maintain control over the global production process. Taking account of this type of capability brings to the fore important questions about the broader organization and control of the economic apparatus in this new phase of capital mobility, which have remained mostly unasked and unexamined. Besides bringing about changes in the organization of production, increased capital mobility also generates a demand for economic activities aimed at ensuring the management, control, and servicing of this new organization of production. That is to say, it generates a demand for what I will refer to as the production of global control capability. The production of management, control, and service operations is concentrated largely in major urban centers at the core and a few in the semiperiphery. These cities have become the sites for this particular kind of production. It is in this sense that the economic restructuring in major core cities can be conceived of as one component in the current phase of capital mobility.

Although not evident on a spatial level, there is a connection between the decentralization of economic activity and the new or expanded role of major cities as producers of management and control functions. Briefly, the decentralization of various kinds of economic activity is one of the key processes feeding into the need for an increasingly centralized apparatus to manage and control the global production process and the global labor force.[4] Capital mobility is constituted not only in spatial terms but also in technical terms, both through the technologies that render capital mobile and through the capability of maintaining control over a vastly decentralized global production system.

The worldwide redeployment of growth poles raises the issue of the incorporation of such growth poles into surplus generating processes for world capital.[5] Although not necessarily guided by this particular question, various studies have focused on aspects of this incorporation, for example, studies on multinational corporations, on direct foreign investment, on international subcontracting, and on several other issues, which together have generated a voluminous literature on the globalization of economic activity. One aspect that has not received this type of attention is what I refer to as global control capability.

Global control capability is a key factor in the incorporation of decentralized growth poles into surplus generating processes for world capital. In using this term I am seeking to displace the focus from the familiar issues of the concentration of economic control over the economy by large corporations, or from issues concerning the control by large corporations over governments, or even the issues of supracorporate concentration of power via interlocking directorates or organizations such as the Trilateral Commission.

I want to focus on what could be referred to as the practice of global control: the specialized activities involved in producing and reproducing the organization and management of the global production system and the global labor force. The focus is on production: the production of those inputs that constitute global control capability. This focus on production brings to the fore the role of major core cities in the new international division of labor. And it brings to the fore the reorganization of the capital-labor relation contained in the production of global control functions and ancillary activities. The reorganization of the capital-labor relation, in turn, brings to the fore the role of the new immigration in such major cities.

The Reorganization of the Capital-Labor Relation

In reorganizing production, increased capital mobility also brings about a reorganization of the capital-labor relation. Again, this is a subject that has received considerable attention in some of its aspects, both in locations losing capital, such as the increased unemployment among well-paid workers and the weakening of their position vis-à-vis employers, and in locations receiving capital, such as the employment of young women from backgrounds that promote discipline and obedience.

But there are elements in the capital-labor relation that have not been recognized as linked to economic restructuring. Notable among these are certain aspects of the new immigration to the U.S., specifically its magnitude, timing, and primary destinations. These aspects need to be examined against the development of several key cities into the centers for the management, control, and servicing of the global economy. For a number of reasons to be discussed below, these new sites of production generate, directly or through agglomeration effects, a large supply of low-wage jobs that are a function of this restructuring and hence not marginal or a distortion of the normal pattern. In this context, the politicization of native low-wage workers since the 1960s is particularly threatening. This is not class struggle as usual. It is struggle in a moment of economic restructuring and in locations that are sites of key control and management operations in the new global economy. It is against this background that we need to examine the large new migrations to major cities, particularly their continuation at ever higher levels throughout the 1970s amid growing unemployment in the U.S. These cities can be seen as one location in the broader process of the reorganization of the capital-labor relation.

Increased capital mobility has brought about a homogenization of economic space, which conceivably could also have homogenized labor. On the one hand, there has been a worldwide standardization of consumer demands and decreasing differentiation among places in terms of cost, quality, and the availability of most inputs (Storper and Walker, in press). On the other, the large size of firms has made it more profitable to internalize transaction and circulation costs, thereby reducing the barriers to capital circulation and raising capital's ability to equalize the profit rate. "The centralization of capital may, therefore, improve rather than diminish the capacity to equalize profits" (Harvey, 1982, p. 145).[6]

Although it is debatable, I will argue that in several fundamental ways this homogenization of labor has not occurred. The decentralization of economic activity has contributed to the reproduction of a structurally differentiated labor supply in this otherwise homogenized economic space. The spatial and social reorganization of production involved in decentralization permits access to peripheralized labor markets, whether abroad or at home, *without undermining* that peripheral condition, even when the jobs are in leading industries at the core. Crucial here is not the fact of access but the fact that this access does not undermine the peripheral status of the workers even when employed at the core and/or in major growth industries. The historical tendency has been for workers employed by advanced sectors of capital such as the steel and auto industry to acquire considerable economic power, that is, to become a labor aristocracy. Under the organization of production prevalent today, labor needs can be met through a highly differentiated labor supply even in a key industry such as electronics. Furthermore, this high level of differentiation is not eroded by the incorporation of workers into an advanced sector of capital. Certain forms of the capital-labor relation can be maintained even in the most advanced and technologically developed sectors of capital.

The decentralization of economic activity can then be seen as a tendency that ensures the reproduction of structurally differentiated labor supplies in a context of global-size firms, which, by internalizing the functions of the market homogenize their space of operation. In this sense decentralization becomes a mechanism to prevent the generalized increase in the capital intensity of the firm or the tendency toward full-scale sociopolitical incorporation of an increasing proportion of workers employed by advanced sectors of capital.

The incorporation of labor migrations in a discussion of capital mobility offers further elaboration on the differentiation of labor as compared with other factors in the production process.[7] This greater spatial differentiation of labor could generate rigidities for capital. Whether highly trained personnel or low-wage unskilled workers, labor can become one of the key locational criteria, for example, the large-scale location of research and design components by high-technology firms in the Austin and San Diego areas in the U.S., or the location of certain production components in Israel by major U.S. electronics firms in order to profit from the abundant supply of highly trained engineers, or yet the location of low-wage assembly plants in periphery countries. But there are a number of economic activities which do not lend themselves to such moves. Notable among these are the large array of service jobs that need to be performed *in situ*: hospitals, restaurants, and office buildings cannot be moved. For these, a pronounced spatial differentiation of labor could generate problems if the local labor supply is inadequate. In the case of the production of control and management operations in highly specialized services concentrated in global cities, there is a locational contingency that gives added meaning to the flexibility introduced by labor migrations. In this case, labor migrations can be conceived of as a component rather than an alternative to capital mobility, insofar as this type of production is central to the globalization of economic activity.

In the remainder of the chapter I will focus on how this restructuring of economic activity creates conditions that induce a high demand for immigrant labor in major core cities.

The Reorganization of the Capital-Labor Relation

It is the expansion in the supply of low-wage jobs as a function of growth sectors that is one of the key factors in the continuation at ever higher levels of the current immigration. Typically immigrants are viewed as providing cheap labor for *declining* sectors of the economy, therewith facilitating the survival of marginal firms. The expansion of low-wage jobs as a function of *growth* trends entails a reorganization of the capital-labor relation. Two sets of analytical distinctions come to the fore: the distinction between the characteristics of jobs and the sectoral location of jobs, that is, low-wage dead-end jobs can be part of highly dynamic, technologically advanced growth sectors; and the distinction between sectoral characteristics and growth patterns, that is, backward sectors such as the downgraded manufacturing sector can be part of major growth trends in a highly industrialized economy. There is a strong tendency to assume backward jobs to be part of backward sectors and backward sectors to be part of decline trends. Although there may have been a historical phase when this was prevalent, it is becoming increasingly less the case over the last decade.[8]

The expansion of low-wage jobs is being fed generally by the shift from a manufacturing to a service economy. This shift has been rather well documented. More complex and indirect is the generation of low-wage jobs associated with the emergence of global and regional centers for the production of management and control functions and highly specialized services. For a number of reasons, some inherited from the past and others new, these major centers also tend to contain rapidly expanding downgraded manufacturing sectors and a vast array of small service operations.

What is of interest here is that these major centers contain both the most dynamic sectors of the economy and the largest share of immigrants. The fact that about half of all immigrants live in the ten largest cities in the U.S., in contrast to only 11 percent of the total U.S. population, can partly be explained by the large concentration of low-wage jobs in major cities. The magnitude, timing, and destination of the current migration to the U.S. becomes more understandable when juxtaposed with these developments. Although changes in U.S. immigration legislation in 1965 and the existence of prior immigrant communities are important factors explaining immigration over the last decade and a half, they are not sufficient to explain the continuation of this flow at the highest levels even in the late 1970s, a time of growing unemployment in the U.S. and rather high employment growth in countries of origin (see table 1).[9] Nor are they sufficient to explain the disproportionate concentration

TABLE 1
Immigrants Admitted by Major Sending Area 1955-1979

	West Indies	Central America	South America	Asia	Total
1955-1959	78,557	26,825	42,278	98,856	246,516
1960-1964	120,337	43,658	100,131	117,140	381,266
1965-1969	351,806	51,344	119,219	258,229	780,698
1970-1974	318,680	44,159	104,676	574,222	1,041,737
1975-1979	413,715	73,794	155,745	879,178	1,522,432
Total	1,283.095	239,780	522,049	1,927,625	3,972,549

Source: INS, Tabulation of Immigrants Admitted by Country of Birth, 1954-1979, (1981, Unpublished).

of immigrants in major cities. Thus, New York and Los Angeles have the largest Hispanic populations of all U.S. cities, 2 million and 1.5 million, respectively, a size significantly larger than that of the next pair, Chicago and Miami, each with about 580,000 Hispanics (see table 2). New York City and Los Angeles also contain, together with San Francisco, the largest concentrations of Asians. Finally, New York City is the major recipient of West Indians.

The expansion in the supply of low-wage jobs, particularly pronounced in major cities, can then be seen as creating objective employment opportunities for immigrants, even as middle-income blue and white collar native workers are experiencing high unemployment because their jobs are being either downgraded, upgraded, or expelled from the production process. Furthermore, a large immigrant population, especially if organized into fairly com-

TABLE 2
Selected Characteristics of Population of Spanish/Hispanic Origin or Descent in SMSA of 1,000,000 or More Population and 25,000 or More Hispanics, 1980

SMSA	Hispanic Median Family Income		Hispanics Below the Poverty Level		Hispanic, 25 yrs. and Over with a High School Degree (%)		Persons Who Speak Spanish in the Home as a % of Hispanics Five yrs. and Over		Hispanics 18 yrs. and Over Who Speak Spanish at Home & Speak English Well or Very Well (%)		Size		Total Hispanics
	Rank	Value	Rank	Value	Rank	Value	Rank	Value	Rank	Value	Rank	Value	
Los Angeles, Long Beach, CA	7	15,447	6	21.2	10	39.1	11	82.4	11	60.1	1		2,066,103
New York, NY-NJ	12	10,347	2	39.3	13	35.4	2	96.4	8	64.0	2		1,492,559
Chicago, IL	4	16,551	8	19.5	11	36.1	6	91.7	10	61.0	3		580,467
Miami, FL	5	16,133	10	15.9	5	53.3	1	101.4	12	57.8	4		580,427
San Antonio, TX	11	13,284	5	26.9	9	40.5	7	90.8	2	83.0	5		481,378
Houston, TX	3	17,185	9	18.1	8	44.9	3	93.1	7	73.5	6		424,957
Dallas, TX	6	15,754	7	20.1	12	35.8	5	91.8	6	74.4	7		247,937
Newark, NJ	8	14,596	4	30.1	7	45.2	8	90.1	9	62.0	8		131,655
Philadelphia, PA-NJ	10	13,287	3	33.4	4	56.8	9	88.9	4	80.1	9		116,869
Washington, D.C., MD-VA	1	22,834	13	10.6	1	74.5	1	101.4	3	82.9	10		93,686
Boston, MA	13	9,586	1	42.0	3	57.3	3	93.1	10	61.0	11		65,696
Fort Lauderdale, Hollywood, FL	2	19,174	12	12.2	2	62.5	4	92.7	5	78.2	12		40,345
Cleveland, OH	9	14,502	11	15.3	6	49.3	10	87.2	1	84.3	13		25,475

Source: Population Research and Analysis Human Resources Division, New York City Department of City Planning.

plex immigrant communities, generates its own demand for immigrant workers from professionals to unskilled laborers (Wilson and Portes, 1980; Marshall, 1983).

THE EXPANSION OF LOW-WAGE JOBS IN GLOBAL CITIES

To evaluate the impact on the job supply resulting from the restructuring in the economic base of major cities, we can use data on the occupational and earnings distribution of industries in conjunction with the locational patterns of such industries.[10] In view of the major shift to services, it is important to note that individual service industries vary greatly in terms of their occupational and earnings distribution.

First, the evidence shows that major growth industries are characterized by a much higher incidence of jobs at the high- and low-paying ends than was the case in what were once the major growth industries, notably manufacturing. Second, earnings vary not only according to occupation but also according to industry for a given occupation (U.S. Bureau of the Census, 1976). Third, the overall result of a different occupational mix and different earnings for occupations in different industries provides an earnings profile for each industry. Some industries, such as consumer and retailing, are low-paying industries: they have low average pay across occupations and a high incidence of low-earning occupations. Distributive services and public administration, on the other hand, have few poorly paid jobs. Among producer and nonprofit services there is a polarization, with concentrations in both well and poorly paid jobs and occupations.

Stanback and Noyelle (1982) ranked the average annual earnings for each industry and occupational subgroup and found distributive services, manufacturing, and public administration to have the highest average rank. Producer services ranked somewhere in the middle, while consumer services and retailing were the worst. The data on earnings classes shows a very high incidence of the next to lowest earning class in all services, except distributive services and public administration. Almost half of all workers in the producer services were in this earnings class, compared with 17 percent of manufacturing and 18.8 percent of construction workers. The other half of workers in producer services are in the two highest earnings classes. On the other hand, half of all construction and manufacturing workers are in the middle earnings class, compared with 2.8 percent of workers in the producer services. The highest single concentration in the top earnings class are in wholesale and in corporate services.

A detailed empirical examination of the major service industries shows a significant subcategory of low-wage jobs: jobs with few if any skill and language requirements and no history of unionization, in brief, jobs that can conceivably be held by immigrant workers. Using the data from the New York State Department of Labor (1979, 1980) occupational survey of major service industries, I identified the full array of this subtype of low-wage jobs in the major service industries in New York City. These data have many limitations. Nonetheless, the results are suggestive (see table 3). First, there were over 16

TABLE 3
Distribution of Total U.S. Labor Force Among Earning Classes, 1970 and 1980

Earnings Classes	Distribution of total U.S. Labor Force (%)	
	1970	1980
1.60 and above	11.3	12.9
	} 32.2	} 37.0
1.59 to 1.30	20.9	24.2
1.29 to 1.00	18.9	12.8
	} 35.8	} 24.5
.99 to .70	16.9	11.7
.69 to .40	22.8	25.2
	} 32.0	} 38.5
.39 and below	9.2	13.3
Total:	100.0	100.0

Source: Based on U.S. Bureau of the Census, 1982. *Money Income of Households, Families and Persons in the United States: 1980.* (Current Population Reports: Series P-60, No. 132); and U.S. Bureau of the Census, 1972, *Money Income of Households, Families and Persons in the United States: 1970.*
Note: Civilian workers 14 years old and over by total money earning.

percent of low-wage unskilled or semiskilled service jobs, lacking language proficiency requirements and mostly offering few if any advancement possibilities. Such jobs accounted for 10.8 percent of jobs in finance, insurance, and real estate; 23.9 percent in business services, and 18 percent in the remaining service industries. Second, the highest incidence of such jobs is found in the fastest growing employment sector in the city (and in the nation as a whole), that is, business services.

The different occupational and earnings distributions of industries in conjunction with the changes in the industrial mix of the economy express themselves in a growing income polarization among workers over the last decade. Using 1970 and 1980 census data, I found a significant reduction in the middle income stratum (see table 4).

TABLE 4
Employment Growth Rates in Mostly Producer Service Industries, New York City, Los Angeles and Detroit, 1977-1981

ISIC Industry	New York City	Los Angeles	Detroit
60 Banking	20.9	44.6	4.1
61 Credit Agencies	29.1	16.0	13.3
62 Commodity Brokers	34.1	14.5	-1.4
63 Insurance Carriers	8.4	5.7	-7.3
64 Insurance Agents	21.8	24.7	13.7
65 Real Estate	1.1	43.9	-3.6
66 Combined R.E. & Insurance	98.2	-30.0	-0.2
67 Holding, Investment Office	7.1	33.8	—
73 Business Services	24.7	33.2	-1.1
731 Advertising	17.3	12.6	-17.8
737 Computer & Data Processing	65.4	41.2	88.2
81 Legal Services	28.3	48.7	31.3
86 Membership Organizations	-0.1	13.8	4.7
89 Miscellaneous Business Ser.	38.0	64.7	20.2
891 Engineering Services	65.0	75.5	—
892 Research Organizations	13.2	29.8	—
893 Accounting, Auditing	17.8	51.3	—
Average Growth Rates	20.1	30.4	11.8

Sources: Based on U.S. Bureau of the Census, *County Business Patterns, New York, 1977; (CBP-77-34); County Business Pattern, New York, 1980* (CBP-80-34); *County Business Patterns, New York, 1981* (CBP-81-34); *County Business Patterns California, 1977* (CBP-77-6); *County Business Patterns, California, 1980* (CBP-80-6); *County Business Patterns, California, 1981* (CBP-81-6); *County Business Patterns, Michigan, 1977* (CBP-77-24); *County Business Patterns, Michigan, 1980* (CBP-80-24); *County Business Patterns, Michigan, 1981* (CBP-81-24).

The different earnings profiles of major industries need to be considered in combination with the different locational patterns of industries, notably the relation between a locality's size and industrial mix. The evidence (Stanback and Noyelle, 1982; Conservation of Human Resources, 1977) earlier shows the largest Standard Metropolitan Statistical Areas (SMSA) to have a disproportionate concentration of producer and distributive services, above average concentration of consumer and nonprofit services, and a below average concentration of manufacturing and government. Thus, the largest SMSAs experience an expansion of industries, with concentrations of highly and poorly paid jobs and a shrinking in the share of industry, with a heavy incidence of high- and medium-income jobs (see tables 5 and 6).

Polarization in major global cities is further fed by several trends that contribute to an additional expansion in the supply of low-wage jobs. First, the existence of a critical mass of very high-income workers has led to high-income residential and commercial gentrification of large areas of these cites. Such

TABLE 5
Employment Share of Producer Services in All Industries, New York City, Los Angeles and Detroit, 1977, 1981

	New York City	Los Angeles	Detroit
1977			
Employment Share	28.1%	22.7%	11.3%
Employment in All Industries (N. in thousands)	(3,188)	(1,367)	(490)
1981			
Employment Share	30.7%	24.9%	12.6%
Employment in All Industries (N. in thousands)	(3,340)	(1,398)	(395)

Sources: Based on U.S. Bureau of the Census, *County Business Patterns* (Various Issues); *Advance Estimates of Social, Economic and Housing Characteristics, California* (1983); *Advance Estimates of Social, Economic and Housing Characteristics, New York* (1983); *Advance Estimates of Social, Economic and Housing Characteristics, Michigan* (1983); City of Detroit, Planning Department, *Annual Overall Economic Development Program Report and Program Projection* (1983).

Note: Producer Services include SIC 60-67, 73, 81, 86 and 89.

TABLE 6
Economic Characteristics by Race and Spanish Origin, 1980

	White	Black	Asian and Pacific Islander	Spanish Origin
Total Labor Force	90,507,346	10,838,021	1,788,369	6,075,414
Employed	84,134,204	9,300,661	1,665,706	5,421,433
Unemployed	5,205,468	1,272,784	85,788	552,723
Female Labor Force	37,558,407	5,243,841	804,083	2,374,838
Employed	35,297,665	4,625,693	758,397	2,127,752
Unemployed	2,161,216	584,947	43,395	239,197
Median Income ($)	20,840	12,618	22,075	14,711
Mean Income ($)	24,279	15,721	25,681	17,360
Persons, Poverty Status Determined	184,431,365	25,661,955	3,610,970	14,343,741
Income in 1979 Below Poverty Level	17,301,567 (9.3%)	7,752,010 (30.2%)	503,089 (13.9%)	3,409,754 (23.8%)

Source: U.S. Bureau of the Census, *1980 Census of Population and Housing: Provisional Estimates of Social, Economic, and Housing Characteristics* (March) 1982.

gentrification requires an army of low-wage workers: residential building attendants, dog walkers, housekeepers for the two-career family, workers in the gourmet restaurants and food shops, French hand laundries, and so on. Part of the goods and services produced in the so-called informal sector that is emerging in major core cities circulate through the modern sector of the economy that caters to these high-income life styles.[11] It would explain why such an informal sector is most developed in major urban centers experiencing very dynamic growth and not in cities like Detroit.

Second, there has been an expansion of low-wage jobs in the manufacturing sector as a result of the social reorganization of the work process, notably the expansion of sweatshops and industrial homework, the technological transformation of the work process that has induced a downgrading of a variety of jobs, and the rapid growth of high-technology industries, which are characterized by a large share of low-wage jobs in production. These three trends have resulted in what I call a *downgraded* manufacturing sector (Sassen-Koob, 1983).[12] The downgrading of the manufacturing sector entails a disenfranchisement of the working class via the restructuring of the job supply and the restructuring of the labor force. It is worth noting that the drop in levels of unionization over the last decade was sharpest in areas with rapid growth in high-tech industries such as the Los Angeles region, particularly Orange County. Furthermore, the expansion of sweatshops and industrial homework has been greatest in major core cities, particularly Los Angeles and New York City not only in garments (Waldinger, 1983; Abeles et al., 1983) but also in footwear, furs, furniture, and electronics as well (N.Y. Department of Labor, 1982a, 1982b; Sassen-Koob, 1983). Indicative of this recomposition is the drop in the average hourly wage in production in these two cites alongside the boom in their financial and specialized services sector.

This recomposition of the manufacturing sector would explain why two such diverse cities as New York City and Los Angeles have experienced an expansion in the share of low-wage jobs in manufacturing and rapid growth of sweatshops and industrial homework. Between 1970 and 1980, when New York City lost a third of a million manufacturing jobs, the Los Angeles region added 225,000, representing a fourth of all new manufacturing jobs from 1970 to 1980. Furthermore, the particular content of the major growth sectors in manufacturing in Los Angeles—high technology industries—could hardly contrast more with New York City's manufacturing base, the garment industry. The aerospace and electronics industries, the high-tech core in the Los Angeles region, represent the largest such concentration in the country and perhaps in the world (Soja, Morales and Wolff, in press). In the decade of the 1970s this cluster grew by 50 percent. The growth in employment in high-tech industries has been larger than the total growth in manufacturing employment in Houston over the same decade. Total employment in electronics in the Los Angeles region is higher than in the other major high-tech center in the country, the so-called Silicon Valley in Santa Clara County. The Los Angeles region has increased its share of total U.S. employment in all these industries, except for aircrafts and parts, where it declined from 22 to 19 percent.

When we disaggregate some of the economic data for these two cities, we find major growth sectors amid New York City's massive decline trends and major declines amid Los Angeles' massive growth trends. Less well known than the scale of New York City's declines and losses is the scale of the growth trends. Although overall employment and population in the city declined in absolute terms, there was a 17 percent increase in employment in the nine major service industries from 1977 to 1980 (U.S. Bureau of Labor Statistics, 1980, 1981). Similarly, although overall figures in manufacturing generally, and garments particularly, declined, there has in fact been a major expansion in manufacturing jobs, but mostly in forms of organization of work that do not get easily recorded in official figures, notably sweatshops and industrial homework, including homework in electronics (N.Y. Department of Labor, 1982a, 1982b).

On the other hand, Los Angeles has experienced a massive decline in its older, established industries, notably automobile, once second only to Detroit, rubber tires, and a cluster of industries associated with the automobile industry (Soja, Morales and Wolf, in press). But it also has had declines in aircrafts and parts. There has been an associated rapid decline in the share of unionized workers, which had fallen to 19 percent by 1980. Interestingly, the sharpest decline, down to 13 percent, happened in Orange County, which also had the sharpest increase in high-tech industries. An examination of the job-supplying high-tech industries shows a massive expansion in low-wage assembly line jobs, mostly not unionized and held by immigrant or native minority women. Finally, well over a third of the net addition of jobs from 1970 to 1980 was in garments. Both in garments and electronics, sweatshops and industrial homework have expanded rapidly.

Behind the remarkably different industrial profiles of these two cities, we find a parallel restructuring of the job supply. Notwithstanding the distinct industrial mix characterizing each of these cities, both have had a major expansion in the supply of low-wage jobs. This expansion is a function of several developments that increasingly present themselves as integral to advanced industrial economies. Technology has made possible the downgrading of a vast array of jobs, transferring the skills from the worker to the machine. Thus, high-tech industries require a large number of workers for routine assembly line operations, many of which have in fact been redeployed to less developed countries. Furthermore, the transformation of the industrial mix has entailed a decline of older, established manufacturing industries with higher rates of unionization and higher shares of well-paid, skilled jobs. Finally, the transformation of the organization of the labor process associated with these two developments has facilitated the expansion of forms of production, such as sweatshops and industrial homework, that rely on cheap, powerless workers.

In sum, we can identify at least three sources for the expansion of low-wage jobs in global cities. First, the general shift to a service economy brings about a great incidence of low-wage jobs. This may be particularly the case in major cities, where the large concentration of people—be they workers, residents, tourists, or shoppers—will induce a disproportionate concentration of service activities. The growth in the supply of low-wage workers will itself further induce a growth of low-cost service operations, from cheap restaurants to cheap retail stores. Second, the combination of rapid growth, locational patterns, and income polarization in the highly specialized services sector contributes to the creation of low-wage jobs both directly and indirectly. The direct creation of low-wage jobs becomes evident once we take account of the infrastructure of menial jobs that underlies even the most technically advanced of these industries. A significant growth in the numbers of financial experts, technical consultants, and international lawyers, will tend to induce an expansion in other aspects of a city's economy, from offices to paper and software, which in turn will induce an expanded need for cleaners, stockclerks, and errand runners. There is an indirect creation of low-wage jobs associated with the expansion of highly specialized services sector because the expansion in the high-income stratum employed in these industries generates a demand for cheap labor to service the life styles of the former. The concentration of these growth industries in major cities, together with their rapid growth, makes the expansion in high income personnel a significant factor in generating a demand for cheap labor: individual high incomes evolve into a new social pattern epitomized by a new consumption structure. Third, the expansion of the downgraded manufacturing sector generates low-wage jobs, both through the downgrading of existing jobs and the development of new industries, notably in high-technology production and assembly plants.

HISPANICS IN NEW YORK CITY: A CASE STUDY

It is against this background that we need to place the evidence on the massive immigrant influx into these two cities, the leading recipients of the new immigration. The 180 census data show blacks and persons of Spanish origin to have the lowest median income and the highest incidence of persons below the poverty level. These two groups clearly provide a significant share of low-wage workers. Asians, on the other hand, show a relatively high median income and a much lower share of persons below the poverty level. The aggregate data suggest that their incidence of low-wage jobs is not as high as among Hispanics and blacks. Yet we know from specialized studies that a growing number of Asians are in low-wage jobs, many of which probably go uncounted. Similarly, the figures for Hispanics, while showing low levels of income, are likely to underestimate the share of low-wage workers in that population.

The more detailed information on Hispanics in New York City and Los Angeles, with the two largest single concentrations of Hispanics in the country, confirm the picture suggested by the aggregate data. It is interesting to note that, although the composition of the two Hispanic populations in New York City and in Los Angeles is very different, they both have some of the worst rankings on various economic characteristics (table 2). The 1980 census puts Hispanics' median income at $15,447 in Los Angeles and $10,300 in New York City and the share of Hispanics below the poverty level at 21 percent in Los Angeles and 39 percent in New York City. The share of Hispanics aged 25 years and older with high school degrees is slightly higher in Los Angeles than in New York City, 39 percent compared with 35.5 percent yet both cities rank poorly among the 13 SMSAs. The 1980 survey of the Equal Employment Opportunity Commission on job patterns for minorities and women in private industry shows that Hispanics in these two cities had by far the highest incidence of low-wage semi- or unskilled jobs: 50 percent of Hispanics in New York City and 56.8 percent in Los Angeles were laborers, service workers, or operatives. The figures for whites were 14.1 percent in New York City and 20 percent in Los Angeles.

This pattern is similar to that found by Cohen and Sassen-Koob (1982) in a 1980 survey of six immigrant groups in New York City. It found Hispanics disproportionately concentrated in service and manufacturing jobs compared with older immigrant groups (see tables 7 and 8). Only 11 percent of Jews and about 30 percent of the major European immigrant groups as well as Puerto Ricans had such jobs, compared with over half of the new Hispanics. Within the Hispanic population of our sample some additional differences emerge.

TABLE 7
Occupational Distribution by Ethnicity, Queens, New York City, 1980
(percentages)

	Blacks	Jews	Italians	Irish	Other European Ethnics	Puerto Ricans	Other Colombians	Hispanics	Asians	Other
Management	8.9	13.4	8.6	11.4	14.7	11.7	11.5	.1.3	2.8	7.9
Professional & Technical	24.6	31.0	18.0	31.4	21.5	13.3	3.8	13.6	41.7	22.8
Sales	6.0	8.8	7.0	1.0	5.1	11.7	3.8	3.4	8.3	7.9
Clerical	14.1	27.2	18.0	24.8	24.9	21.7	15.4	15.9	22.2	18.5
Crafts	7.7	4.2	6.2	5.7	9.0	3.3	15.4	12.5	0.0	13.6
Operatives & Laborers	14.5	3.1	18.0	5.7	7.9	16.6	19.2	20.5	8.3	9.3
Transport	4.8	2.3	6.3	2.9	1.7	1.7	0.0	1.1	0.0	2.9
Services	19.4	10.0	17.9	17.1	15.2	20.0	30.9	21.7	16.7	17.1
Total	100.0	100.0	100.0	100.0	100.0	100.0	100.0	100.0	100.0	100.0
Total N = (1269)	(248)	(261)	(128)	(105)	(177)	(60)	(26)	(88)	(36)	(140)

Source: Cohen and Sassen-Koob (1982).

TABLE 8
Occupational Distribution by National Origin and Sex, Queens (NYC), 1980
(percentages)

	Colombian	Puerto Ricans	Other Hispanic	All Hispanics
White Collar, Total	100.0	100.0	100.0	100.0
Male	44.4	28.6	41.7	37.0
Female	55.6	71.4	58.3	63.0
Blue Collar, Total	100.0	100.0	100.0	100.0
Male	62.5	66.7	55.2	59.2
Female	37.5	33.4	44.8	40.8
Services, Total	100.0	100.0	100.0	100.0
Male	44.4	25.0	43.5	36.5
Female	55.6	75.0	56.5	63.5

Source: Cohen and Sassen-Koob (1982).

Although about 11 percent of Puerto Ricans, Colombians, and other Hispanics had managerial jobs, a significant difference emerges for professional jobs—only 3.8 percent of Colombians compared with over 13 percent each of Puerto Ricans and other Hispanics. The other major new immigrant group, the Asians, had almost 42 percent of its members in this occupational stratum. Colombians, on the other hand, had the highest share in crafts jobs, about 15.5 percent, compared with 3.3 percent of Puerto Ricans, 7.7 percent of blacks, and between 6 and 9 percent for the major European groups. This seems to confirm Immigration and Naturalization Service (INS) data showing a high share of highly skilled workers among the Colombian and other South American immigrants. The highest concentration of new Hispanics is in both operative and service jobs: half of all Colombians and 42 percent of other Hispanics.

Furthermore, two-worker households are more prevalent among the new Hispanics, about 30 percent compared with 10-15 percent among the other ethnic groups in our sample (table 9). Both Urrea Giraldo (1982) and Castro (1982) found a very high incidence of multiple-earner households among Colombians. This characteristic helps explain why the average family income of the new Hispanics is not much different from that of other ethnic groups in our sample, even though their occupational distribution is much more disadvantaged.

These various patterns strongly suggest that the new Hispanic immigration is a labor supply directed toward service jobs and a downgraded manufacturing sector. Furthermore, they are also a labor supply for clerical and low-level managerial jobs, especially in small firms (Urrea Giraldo, 1982). The fact

TABLE 9
Selected Household Characteristics by Ethnicity, Queens, 1980
(percentages)

	Blacks	Jews	Italians	Greeks	Other European Ethnics	Puerto Ricans	Dominicans	Colombians	Other Hispanics	Asians	Others
Average years of education	12.4	14.1	12.4	11.9	12.6	11.7	11.1	11.3	12.3	14.6	12.4
Average family income (in $1000s)	21.0	25.3	21.8	22.6	22.7	23.5	22.8	19.7	20.4	22.7	20.9
Two-job family	13	21	17	18	14	21	32	29	32	33	20
Retired	9	12	17	3	20	1	0	0	0	5	7
Total N = (1639)	(370)	(345)	(170)	(40)	(426)	(76)	(38)	(35)	(104)	(45)	(47)
Percentage of total	22	20	10	2	25	5	2	6	2	3	3

Source: Cohen and Sassen-Koob (1982).

that the occupational distribution of the new Hispanics in New York City diverges considerably from that in their country of origin at the time of departure also points to the extent to which the job supply in the receiving society determines their occupation. The evidence in this regard is probably most clear with respect to women. Castro (1982) found that although over 50 percent of the Colombian women in the Queens sample had jobs in manufacturing, only 12 percent of them had had such jobs in Colombia. A good share of the Colombian men holding low-level managerial positions in New York City have actually experienced downward mobility (Urrea Giraldo, 1982); they represent considerable human capital for a low price to employers. In my earlier fieldwork study of Colombians and Dominicans in Queens (Sassen-Koob, 1979), I found a highly stratified situation. The upper income segments had experienced downward mobility, while the lower-income segments had experienced what according to standard occupational measures would be considered upward mobility, from farm or operative to service work.

Comparing the occupational distribution of the new Hispanics in our sample with that of other major Hispanic groups nationally (U.S. Department of Labor, 1981) we note three major patterns (see table 10). First, all Hispanics, including those in our sample, hold a higher share of blue collar and service jobs compared with workers generally. Second, the new Hispanics in our sample had the highest share of service jobs (24.6 percent), and Puerto Ricans, another major New York City-based group, the next largest share. Third, the new Hispanics in our sample have, together with Cubans, one of the highest shares in white collar jobs. Fourth, the new Hispanics in our sample had a considerably lower share in manufacturing jobs than was typical for all other ma-

TABLE 10

Occupational Distribution of Major Hispanic Groups, United States and Queens, 1980

	United States, 1980						Queens (NYC) 1980
	All Workers	Whites	All Hispanics	Mexicans	Puerto Ricans	Cubans	New Hispanics
White Collar	52.2	53.9	34.2	29.2	38.8	44.7	42.1
Blue Collar	28.1	27.7	41.6	44.7	39.0	39.5	33.3
Services*	16.9	15.4	20.3	20.3	21.6	15.9	24.6
Farm	2.8	2.9	3.8	5.7	0.6	0.0	0.0

Source: U.S. Department of Labor, 1981, *Geographic Profiles of Employment and Unemployment, 1980;* Cohen and Sassen-Koob (1982).
* Transport included in Services.

jor Hispanic groups, although it was higher than that for workers generally. Again, note that the figure for manufacturing excludes what is probably a considerable share of jobs in sweatshops and industrial homework.

In sum, the restructuring of labor demand in major cities contains two major trends. First, there has been a pronounced expansion in the supply of high-income professional and technical jobs associated with the growth of the advanced services and headquarters complex, high-tech industries, and the technological transformation of the work process, which has upgraded a vast array of what used to be middle-income jobs. Second, there has been a pronounced expansion of low-wage jobs associated with a general shift to a service economy and, more particularly, with the recomposition of industry, an outcome of (1) the technological transformation of the work process, which has not only upgraded but also downgraded a vast array of jobs through the transfer of skills into machines, (2) changes in the industrial mix, notably the decline of older established manufacturing industries in Los Angeles and the rise of low-wage assembly plants in high-tech industries, and (3) the transformation of the organization of the labor process, notably the shift of certain jobs from unionized shops to sweatshops or industrial homework. The new migrations to major core cities need to be understood in this context of economic restructuring and polarization in the job supply.

CONCLUSION

In this chapter I sought to link the new immigration to the U.S. with the broader process of economic restructuring in both its urban and global scale. The most common view in the mass media as well as among scholars is that immigrants provide cheap labor that ensures the survival of declining firms in backward sectors. While immigration does indeed play this role, I see it as a minor one compared with its role in growth sectors. A key distinction in my analysis is that between the characteristics of jobs and those of sectors. Today's growth sectors, including highly advanced industries, are generating large numbers of low-wage menial jobs. There is a strong trend toward concentration of growth sectors in major cities. Thus, these cities contain a large share of the low-wage jobs being generated by growth during the current phase. The existence of a large concentration of low-wage workers itself induces an additional expansion of low-wage workers to staff a wide array of low-cost consumer services. Here we find, then, conditions for the absorption of the continuing immigrant influx into cities like New York and Los Angeles, two leading producers of highly specialized services and two leading recipients of the new immigration.

A second central contention in this chapter is that some of these new growth trends in major cities are rooted in the same set of conditions that have brought about the decline of traditional manufacturing, both in those same cities and in manufacturing centers like Detroit. This set of conditions has been variously referred to as the increased mobility of capital, the new international division of labor, the new locational capability of capital, the deindustrialization of advanced capitalist economies, and so on. Each of these terms captures central, often overlapping, aspects of the current phase of the world economy, characterized by the large-scale decentralization and relocation of plants and offices. What is generally overlooked is that this decentralization contributes to the need for an expanded centralized management and control apparatus and the highly specialized services that are its key inputs. These are located in major cities. Management, control, and specialized service activities have come to constitute one of the major and most dynamic growth sectors, a sort of new basic industry alongside the high-technology industries which produce the necessary tools for the former.

When we incorporate the need for an expanded centralized control and servicing operation into the concept of a new international division of labor or a new phase in the mobility of capital, then we have the conditions for understanding immigration as a component of, rather than an alternative to, capital mobility. Major cities are nodal points in the new organization of the economy because they are the sites for the production of global control capability; and since this type of production generates a vast array of low-wage jobs, access to a politically suitable supply of low-wage workers becomes particularly important. The importance of the labor question in these new growth sectors is of a different order from that of declining sectors in need of cheap labor for survival. As major cities are strategic locations in the worldwide restructuring of economic activity, the labor question is going to be strategic as well, be that the labor represented by highly trained financial experts or by unskilled errand runners. In the context of a highly politicized native low-wage labor supply and acquired expectations of upward mobility, the expansion of low-wage jobs in growth sectors emerges as problematic. Access to politically vulnerable immigrants is a rather convenient option. Besides contributing to the survival of firms in decline, the availability of an immigrant labor supply contributes to the operations of growth—given the characteristics of that growth and the circumstances through which it takes place.

Notes

1. Although there are some studies in the migration literature that begin to incorporate this articulation from the migration side (Nash and Fernández Kelly, 1983; Grasmuck, 1982; Morales, 1983; Portes and Walton, 1981; Sassen-Koob, 1981, 1983; Bonilla and Campos, 1982), I could find no such studies in the literature on capital mobility.

2. This emphasis on the spatial dimension occurs both in studies of capital mobility as a locational process and in those positing a new international division of labor. Considerations of technology are put in terms of spatial issues as well, e.g., transportation and communication technologies.

3. Very briefly, my argument is as follows (see Sassen-Koob, 1982). The magnitude of the cumulative money flow from core oil-importing countries to OPEC countries in the post-1973 period makes it qualitatively different from the pre-1973 period. This flow makes possible the launching of vast industrialization programs on a scale and at a pace that render it significant for the world economy. The value of imported goods and services necessary for the realization of these programs eventually reached and surpassed the value of oil revenues in all OPEC countries except the Gulf states. From 1973 to 1978, oil revenues were $700 billion, compared with $80 billion in the decade preceding 1973. Imports increased by an average of 60 percent in the first few years after 1973. From 1973 to 1978, the cumulative value of imports was $530 billion, representing about 76 percent of oil revenues. In sum, accelerated industrialization in OPEC countries can be seen as a mechanism for the reinjection of oil revenues back into the world accumulation process. Luxury consumption in OPEC countries could not have generated this level of reinjection of oil revenues. Given a historically developed need for imported oil, the international price of oil operates as a mechanism generating forced savings and concentrating these diffuse expenditures in one massive flow of money directed to OPEC countries and to the international oil companies. I can think of few systems that would have been so effective in extracting additional surplus and concentrating it into a few highly select targets.

4. Harvey (1982, p. 140) observes that Marx seems to suggest that there is some equilibrium organization of production which is consistent with capital accumulation and the law of value; he further seems to suggest that this point would be struck in theory, at least, by the working out of tendencies toward centralization and decentralization. In *Capital 1* and in the *Grundrisse*, Marx does discuss inducements for capital toward decentralization, notably subcontracting and the move into branches of production that are typically labor-intensive and small-scale.

5. This has also introduced new elements in the relation between capital and the state in core countries, particularly in the case of transnational capital. In the earlier phase of monopoly capital, major growth poles were largely concentrated in core countries. What was good for GM was indeed good for the country, meaning the state. Today this is much less the case. High growth in transnational sectors of capital does not necessarily translate into benefits for the state as was the case up to the immediate post-World War II period. This is one of the elements of the current restructuring at the core that I have sought to capture in the notion of peripheralization at the core (1982).

6. In contrast, there has been a general tendency since World War II for the share of the largest plants to decline. The conjunction of a growing number of plants and growing size and concentration among firms has resulted in an increasing divergence between firm concentration and plant concentration. For example, the 1963 Census of Manufactures data show that the share of the value of all shipments from the eight largest companies in computing machines is twice the share held by the eight largest plants; an extreme example of this divergence was found in gypsum products, where the eight largest companies account for 97 percent of the value of shipments, while the eight largest plants account for 22 percent. Blair (1972, pp. 105-106) notes that in concentrated industries—those where the four largest firms account for 50 percent or more of the output—more than four-fifths of the output comes from fields in which the share of the eight largest companies exceeds that of the eight largest plants by at least 20 percentage points. "For all but a minor segment of the industrial economy the explanation for concentration is clearly to be found in multiplant operations, not in the requirements of

technology to achieve economies of scale." (Blair, 1972, p. 107). Herman (1981, pp. 190-191) found that ten of the largest firms in manufacturing each had from 63 to 328 plants. This multiplant structure includes separate lines of activity and multiple domestic and foreign locations. The data also show that in the mid-1970s 90 of the 100 largest manufacturing firms were active in four industries or more and 33 in more than ten industries, while among medium-sized firms none was active in ten or more industries (Scherer, 1980, p. 75). The evidence suggests that large size in manufacturing is a function of multiple plant operations.

7. Storper and Walker (1982) note that neoclassical economics and location theorists have treated labor in the same terms as "true" commodity inputs and outputs and therewith have underestimated its importance in location decisions.

8. The general direction of technological change has been mostly toward large scales of operations. This has given rise to a whole series of propositions linking profitability and productivity with large size. The current phase of economic development brings to the fore a new set of relationships. What is being produced and how it is being produced have created conditions that make small scales of operations highly profitable and productive. Important here is the fact that this is also happening in leading industries. At the same time, it is worth noting that decentralizing technologies emerged in certain key industries, notably plastics, already in the 1930s. "Up to the 1930s, observers of the industrial scene could be forgiven for having failed to foresee that what had been true of the past would not be true of the future" (Blair, 1972, p. 95). What is different today is that the leading and technologically most developed sectors contain a new relationship to size from what was the case in leading sectors in an earlier phase.

9. Entry levels over the last decade and a half are among the largest in U.S. immigration history. Legal entries numbered 265,000 in 1960, but they reached half a million by the end of that decade, 700,000 during the second half of the 1970s (INS, 1978, p. 1981). Annual entry levels throughout the 1970s were higher than annual entries in the previous four decades. According to the 1980 census, the Asian population had the highest rate of increase, 100 percent between 1970 and 1980, a level surpassed by some nationalities, e.g., the 412 percent increase of South Koreans; the Hispanic population increased by 62 percent (U.S. Bureau of the Census, 1981).

10. The evidence, although inadequate, is quite useful in documenting some of the issues of concern here. The evidence points to the growth and locational concentration of economic activities that generate key inputs for firms, particularly large corporations (U.S. Bureau of the Census, various years; Singlemann, 1978; Stanback and Noyelle, 1982). The evidence also shows the pronounced growth in the export of such inputs and how these exports are associated with the growth of an offshore manufacturing sector (U.S. Department of Commerce, 1980; Economic Consulting Services, 1981; DiLullo, 1981). There is also evidence showing that a few core cities produce such inputs for export to other domestic areas (Conservation of Human Resources Project, 1977; Drennan, 1983; Cohen, 1981; Stanback et al., 1981).

11. The fine, high-price specialty item shop emerges as a key element in this new structure of consumption. It carries consequences for workers. This type of firm operates under different constraints than large department stores, which emerged as the central mechanism for the delivery of goods in the 1950s and 1960s. Lowering the cost of labor becomes very important, there is a considerable input on the part of owners and an emphasis on distinct products addressed to a particular clientele rather than the mass

middle class market of department stores. There are strong inducements for subcontracting certain phases of production and servicing—from garments through decorative items to the preparation of food. Industrial homework and sweatshop production becomes a possible way of organizing production in a way that would have been cumbersome for the large department stores with huge orders of a given item and many different outlets all over a region and even the country. Furthermore, the possibility of lowering the costs of labor would reflect significantly in the rate of profits. The rise of the boutique and the decline of the department store represents much more than a change in shopping patterns: they also stand for different forms of organizing production.

12. Here it is important to emphasize that employers do not simply seek low-wage labor but labor that can be consumed under certain conditions of the organization of the work process. A focus on the different requirements in terms of control over labor associated with various types of organization of the labor process helps to explain differences between immigrant and minority workers, or other low-wage native workers and the varying weight of such differences (Sassen-Koob, 1981).

REFERENCES

Abeles, Scwartz, Hackel, and Silverblatt, Inc. 1983. *The Chinatown Garment Industry Study*. New York: Local 23-25 of the ILGWU and the New York Skirt and Sportswear Association.

Blair, John. 1972. *Economic Concentration*. New York: Holt, Rinehart and Winston.

Bonilla, Frank, and Ricardo Campos. 1982. "Imperialist Initiatives and the Puerto Rican Worker: From Foraker to Reagan." *Contemporary Marxism* 5 (Summer), 1-19.

Borjas, George, and Marta Tienda. eds. 1984. *Hispanics in the U.S. Economy*. New York: Academic Press.

Castro, Mary Garcia. 1982. "Mary and Eve's Social Reproduction in the Big Apple: Colombian Voices." Center for Latin American and Caribbean Studies. Occasional Papers, no. 35. New York University.

Cohen, Robert B. 1981. "The New International Division of Labor, Multinational Corporations, and Urban Hierarchy." In *Urbanization and Urban Planning in Capitalist Society*, ed. M. Dear and A. Scott. London: Methuen.

Cohen, Steven M., and Saskia Sassen-Koob. 1982. *Survey of Six Immigrant Groups in Queens, New York City*. New York: Queens College.

Conservation of Human Resources Project. 1977. *The Corporate Headquarters Complex in New York City*. New York: Columbia University Conservation of Human Resources Project.

Dear, M., and A. Scott, eds. 1981. *Urbanization and Urban Planning in Capitalist Society*. London: Methuen.

DiLullo, Anthony J. 1981. "Service Transactions in the U.S. International Accounts, 1970-1980." *Survey of Current Business* (November), 29-46.

Drennan, Matthew. 1983. "Local Economy and Local Revenues." In *Setting Municipal Priorities, 1984*. ed. Raymond D. Hornton and Charles Brecher. New York: New York University Press.

Economic Consulting Services. 1981. The International Operations of U.S. Service Industries: Current Data Collection and Analysis. Washington, D.C.: Economic Consulting Services.

Friedmann, John, and Goetz Wolf, eds. 1983. "World City Formation." Special issue of *Development and Change.*

Grasmuck, Sherri. 1981. "The Impact of Emigration on Development: Three Sending Communities in the Dominican Republic." Center for Latin American and Caribbean Studies. Occasional Papers, no. 33. New York University.

Harvey, David. 1982. *The Limits to Capital.* Oxford: Basil Blackwell.

Herman, Edward. 1981 *Corporate Control, Corporate Power.* Cambridge: Cambridge University Press.

Hornton, Raymond D., and Charles Brecher, eds. 1983. *Setting Municipal Priorities, 1984.* New York: New York University Press.

Kumar, Krishna, ed. 1980. *Transnational Enterprises: Their Impact on Third World Societies and Cultures.* Boulder, Co.: Westview Press.

Marshall, Adriana. 1983. "Immigration in a Surplus-worker Labor Market: The Case of New York." Center for Latin American and Caribbean Studies. Occasional Papers, no. 39. New York University.

Morales, Rebecca. 1983. "Undocumented Workers in a Changing Automobile Industry: Case Studies in Wheels, Headers and Batteries." In *Proceedings of the Conference on Contemporary Production, Capital Mobility and Labor Migration,* Center for U.S.-Mexican Studies. La Jolla: University of California at San Diego.

Nash, June, and María Patricia Fernández Kelly, eds. 1983. *Women, Men and the International Division of Labor.* Albany: State University of New York Press.

New York Department of Labor. 1979. *Occupational Employment Statistics: Finance, Insurance and Real Estate, New York State, May-June 1978.* Albany: New York DOL.

———. 1980. *Occupational Employment Statistics: Services, New York State, April-June 1978.* Albany: New York DOL.

———. 1982a. *Report to the Governor and the Legislature on the Garment Manufacturing Industry and Industrial Homework.* Albany: New York DOL.

———. 1982b. *Study of State-Federal Employment Standards for Industrial Homeworkers in New York City.* Albany: New York DOL.

Pessar, Patricia. 1982. "Kinship Relations of Production in the Migration Process: The Case of Dominican Emigration to the United States." Center for Latin American and Caribbean Studies. Occasional Papers, no. 32. New York University.

Portes, Alejandro, and John Walton. 1981. *Labor, Class and the International System.* New York: Academic Press.

Safa, Helen I. 1981. "Runaway Shops and Female Employment: The Search for Cheap Labor." *Signs* 7:2 (Winter), 418-433.

Sassen-Koob, Saskia. 1981a. "Towards a Conceptualization of Immigrant Labor." *Social Problems* 29 (October), 65-85.

———. 1981b. "Exporting Captal and Importing Labor: New York City." Center for Latin American and Caribbean Studies. Occasional Papers, no. 28. New York University.

———. 1982. "Recomposition and Peripheralization at the Core." *Contemporary Marxism*. 5 (Summer), 88-100.

———. 1983. "The Structuring of a New Investment Zone for the World Market: Southern California." Center for U.S.-Mexican Studies. Research Report. La Jolla: University of California at San Diego.

———. Forthcoming. "The Foreign Investment Connection: Rethinking Immigration." Unpublished research in progress.

Scherer, F. M. 1980. *Industrial Market Structure and Economic Performance*. 2nd ed. Chicago: Rand McNally.

Singlemann, Joachim. 1978. *From Agriculture to Services: The Transformation of Industrial Employment*. Beverly Hills, Calif.: Sage.

Soja, Edward, Rebecca Morales and Goetz Wolff. In press. "Urban Restructuring: An Analysis of Social and Spatial Change in Los Angeles." *Economic Geography*.

Stanback, Thomas M., Jr., and Thierry J. Noyelle. 1982. *Cities in Transition: Changing Job Structures in Atlanta, Denver, Buffalo, Phoenix, Columbus. Ohio), Nashville, Charlotte*. Montclair, N.J.: Allanheld, Osmun.

Stanback, Thomas M., Jr., et al. 1981. *Services: The New Economy*. Montclair, N.J.: Allanheld, Osmun.

Storper, Michael and David Walker. In press. "The Labor Theory of Location." *International Journal of Urban and Regional Research*.

Urrea Giraldo, Fernando. 1982. "Life Strategies and the Labor Market: Colombians in New York in the 1970s." Center for Latin American and Caribbean Studies. Occasional Papers, no. 34. New York University.

U.S. Bureau of the Census. 1976. *Survey of Income and Education, 1975*. Washington, D.C.: Bureau of the Census.

———. 1981. Public Law File.

U.S. Bureau of Labor Statistics. 1980. *News*. New York: BLS, Mid-Atlantic Region.

———. 1981. *News*. New York: BLS, Mid-Atlantic Region.

U.S. Department of Commerce. 1980. *Current Developments in U.S. International Services Industries*. Washington, D.C.: International Trade Administration.

U.S. Department of Labor. 1981. *Geographic Profiles of Employment and Unemployment, 1980*. Washington, D.C.: Government Printing Office.

U.S. Immigration and Naturalization Service. 1978. *Annual Report*. Washington, D.C.: Government Printing Office.

———. 1981. "Tabulation of Immigrantes Admitted by Country of Birth, 1954-1979." Unpublished.

U.S. Senate. Committee on Banking, Housing and Urban Affairs. 1982. *Foreign Barriers to U.S. Trade: Service Exports. Hearing before the Subcommittee on International Finance and Monetary Policy*. 97th Cong. Washington, D.C.: Government Printing Office.

Vernon, Raymond. 1977. *Storm over the Multinationals*. Cambridge: Harvard University Press.

Waldinger, Roger. Forthcoming. "The Garment Industry in New York City." In *Hispanics in the U.S. Economy*, ed. George Borjas and Marta Tienda. New York: Academic Press.

Whichard, Obie G. 1982. "U.S. Direct Investment Abroad in 1980." *Survey of Current Business* (August), 20-39.

Wilson, Kenneth L., and Alejandro Portes. 1980. "The Immigrant Enclave." *American Journal of Sociology* 86:2 (September), 295-319.

Segmentation of the Work Process in the International Division of Labor

June Nash

With the growing trend toward capital mobility in the international economy and the concomitant deindustrialization of old industrial centers in the United States, patterns of labor segmentation are in flux. The control that managers in core industrial nations exercised throughout the twentieth century in defining the job and determining who will enter it was a corollary of corporate capitalist organization of labor. With the movement overseas of many of the production processes, corporate managerial control over the labor process has been strengthened at the same time that the labor movement and the bargaining position of workers have been weakened.

In this review of the changing work process in a New England community I shall try to show the effect of the global integration of production on the work force. The changes experienced by these workers in an old industrial community of the northeast encompass three major transitions defined by social historians and economists. (1) the shift from craft to routinized jobs that Braverman (1974) analyzed in terms of the debasement of labor; (2) the shift from a "homogenized" to a segmented labor force that Gordon, Reich and Edwards (1973, 1982) have developed from premises of a dual labor market (Doeringer and Piore, 1971); and (3) the shift from assembly and even skilled machinist and toolmaker trades to automated or computerized work processes (Gorz, 1978). The latest tactic of control is to shift—or to threaten to shift—production sites to U.S. areas with the "right to work" legislation or to overseas export processing zones.[1]

These transitions affect a work force segregated by both achieved (training and education) and ascribed (sex, age, and race) criteria differently. In the

---

[1] Research was funded by a grant from the National Endowment for the Humanities and from the National Science Foundation. I am indebted to them for the opportunity to carry out this investigation in the period from June 1982 to January 1983 with the assistance of Max Kirsch.

early stages of the movement of capital overseas, women's jobs in garment, electronics, and textiles were primarily affected (Fernández Kelly, 1980; Safa, 1981). With the location of steel mills and auto production overseas, this movement has begun to affect the male unionized labor force. The differential impact of capital investment policies on sectors of the labor force requires an analysis that takes into account the interplay between status and role defined in the community and in the family with the division of labor in the work place. Patriarchal and racist policies, far from being relegated to marginal enterprises in the contemporary labor market, continue to define the entry into most production jobs in monopoly capitalist enterprises. But because segregation in the work place is not always coterminous with familial and community patterns of interaction, the consciousness developed on the job may be negated in the settings outside of the work place.

For these reasons, neoclassical and Marxist theories of the labor market that restrict themselves to the analysis of the relations of production may fail to see the dynamic process in the formation of class consciousness. Assumptions underlying both neoclassical and neo-Marxist theories of the labor market deny the complex interaction between job roles and socioeconomic strata defined in the family and community. I shall deal with these in turn.

Neoclassical theory relating differential rewards on the job to "human capital investment" provides an ideology but not an explanation for occupational stratification. Bibb and Form (1977) show the failure of an investment in education by women and blacks to net them equal status and pay in the occupational hierarchy. Assumptions about universalistic, rational criteria determining opportunities and rewards are laid to rest when we realize that college-educated women have incomes equivalent to those of male high school dropouts, or that black men with college degrees average earnings of white high school graduates. The education and training required for entry into many jobs masks the racial and ethnic segregation that persist in society.

In common with neoclassical theorists, neo-Marxist analyses of the labor market often assume that the outlook and behavior of workers can be equated with the slot they occupy in industry. This simplistic equation is further distorted when the nuclear family is taken to be "the molecular unit of the class system," as Middleton (1974, p. 184) points out. This error is contained in Gordon, Edwards and Reich's (1982, p. 273) conclusions about the relationship between consciousness and segmentalized labor categories. Identifying the worker with a household as though all members were a unit responding to a single wage earner, they state that "the independent primary workers *and their household*" are likely to focus on political issues concerning quality of life and individual autonomy; that "the subordinate primary workers *and their household*" emphasized the importance of the economic growth and U.S. international dominance to ensure full employment, while "secondary workers *and their household*" are likely to place particular emphasis on access to government services [emphasis added.] But what if, as I have seen most commonly, the primary worker comes home to find his secondary work force wife, who has rushed from her part-time job to cook his supper? And then what if his son drops in to advise them that he has to move back home with them because he just lost his job at MacDonalds? Whose consciousness is going to prevail? With a theory of segmentation that assumes a unique tie to the labor market, the social scientists would have to leave a script that would sum up that consciousness to a TV sitcom writer.

Criticizing the assumptions of labor market theory, Bibb and Form (1977, p. 976) stress that we are dealing not with a competitive labor market but rather with "socially structured mechanisms which link economic and social organization through a wider range of social processes." In their structural model of the relationship between work and its rewards, they consider the kind of technology, the stratification of occupational groups, and the stratal location of the labor force in the community (1977, pp. 977-978). Wages are not a reflection of human capital investment but, rather, the "intersection of differently structured arenas in the enterprise, occupational groups, and the society."

The government sector plays a mediating role, channeling the frustrations of workers blocked by a segregated labor market. As Sokoloff (1980) shows, the technical and professional employees excluded or pushed out of the monopoly sector were formerly absorbed in the competitive enterprises and the state sector. The task of this sector, both in generating employment and in compensating for inequities, is now threatened by national and state budgetary cutbacks just when it is most needed to overcome the stagnation in the economy and the widening gap in wealth distribution.

Segmentation of jobs and of the labor force channeled into them is not a new phenomenon. Differentiation between a core of preferentially treated workers and a temporary, lower-paid group usually assumed to be less skilled has been characteristic of industrialization since its origins. In the 1830s when women were the majority of operatives, the few men employed in textile factories aspired to be foremen by virtue of "good conduct and obedience to the will of their employers" (Montgomery, 1980). Gray (1974, p. 19) writing about "The Labor Aristocracy in the Victorian Class Structure," found, "The inhibiting effect on working class consciousness of structural differentiation is, as social historians are well aware, a phenomenon visible throughout the history of industrial capitalism." While in nineteenth-century textile and shoe mills segmentation was based on differential skills, job seniority, and supervisory functions, by the twentieth century it was additionally influenced by the level of integration of the firm in the global production system. Large corporations with multiple branches within the nation and overseas attracted a preferred work force with higher wages and benefits won by unionized shops. Competitive firms in industry and services draw upon women and ethnically discriminated workers. What differentiates the segmentation of labor in the nineteenth century from that in the twentieth is that it was not yet bureaucratically regulated in the negotiations of union and management.

Currently, deindustrialization is destroying the privileged position of the "primary" work force at the same time that it is eliminating the production processes organized by unions. As these formerly privileged workers fall into the ranks of the "secondary" work force or of the unemployed, the relationships among members sharing the same household are changed. I shall describe some of the strategies of workers and management that are bringing about a restructuring of industrial relations in a New England city dominated by the electrical machinery industry.

THE RISE AND DECLINE OF INDUSTRY IN WESTERN MASSACHUSETTS

I shall draw upon data collected in the study of a city of 50,000 people, which I shall call Pontoosuc, to talk about the emerging labor process in the present industrial restructuring. Industry developed in the western part of Massachusetts at an earlier date than on the East Coast because of lack of transportation and access to markets trading with Britain. During the War of 1812, Eastern mercantile capitalists dependent on trade with Britain did not support the war. In the western part of the state, however, where small manufacturers had developed independently, an early historian of the area stated, "The love of country and the hope of gain thus operated reciprocally upon each other, and harmoniously together, in the encouragement of manufactures" (Smith, 1876, p. 197). The fulling and dyeing mills that had assisted housewives with domestic production of wool since the turn of the century expanded their production to include woolen blankets and uniforms for the U.S. Army. The textile industry developed a competitive position even after the tariffs of 1824 attracted eastern mercantile interests to enter into production in Lowell, Massachusetts, and Manchester, New Hampshire. Segmentation of the labor force was a constant feature of these early mills. Listing the names of long-term employees, Smith (1876, p. 479) commented, "A peculiarity in the management of the Pomeroy mills, which they share with that of other old [Pontoosuc companies], is the long retention of faithful employees." Among those mentioned were Solomon Wilson, superintendent for 50 years, Joel Monthrop, a spinner for 40 years, and Wesley Hansen, a fuller for 35 years. Like the others listed, all were male, and apparently of English or Irish patronyms. Clearly the job was not in itself the determining factor in the preferential retention of this work force, since fullers and spinners were found among the roving work force sporadically employed in response to levels of sales. Personal traits of sobriety, industriousness, and ability to get along with foremen and co-workers were the important characteristics.

Capital generated in the textile mills provided a base for electrical machine manufacturing. William Stanley, who invented the first alternating current generator, was able to raise $27,000 from Pontoosuc's banks and start his first plant in 1887. The rapid growth of the Stanley Co. plant, which employed over a thousand workers by 1903 and which had increased its capital investment tenfold, attracted the attention of Global Enterprises. Incorporated in the late nineteenth century, the corporation had two main plants in the Northeast. From the very beginning of corporate control, local business and labor leaders feared that the company would be closed since it was believed "that the main object of the Global Enterprises [pseudonym inserted] in acquiring control of the property was to remove what might have eventually developed into a formidable competitor" (*Berkshire Eagle*, February 12, 1903). This did not come to pass. The new owners invested $1 million and trained the young men in the plant on larger work.

Throughout the history of the corporation, the plant has had a segmentalized work force. In the 1916 strike, it was the preferred work force of machinists that led the protest for higher wages and shorter hours. It was their union, the International Association of Machinists, that took the lead in organizing the walkout. Machinists and toolmakers have always been the prima donnas of the work place, taking priority over winders and other very skilled but industry-specific training. The fact that they had a skill that they could take to many other industrial plants gave them assurance to stand up to management, one very militant toolmaker told me. Many became strong supporters of industrial unions in the 1930s and after World War II. Their history shows that managerial tactics dividing the work force are not directly related to consciousness.

The work force of 7,100 now employed in Global Enterprises is two-thirds of that employed up to the late 1960s. The corporation is now threatening to shut down an entire division if productivity does not increase dramatically. The present unemployment rate of 8.6 percent seems low in comparison with national rates of 10.5, but the city has lost over 7,000 young workers who have left in the past decade. In the period 1969 to 1975, Massachusetts lost 430,000 jobs, many of them in primary manufacturing (Bluestone and Harrison, 1982). Many of the products formerly manufactured by Global Enterprises are now produced in their overseas branches: radios, electrical bulbs, plastic housings and switches for electrical appliances, and so forth. The latest victim was a entire division producing gynal, which was developed by the corporation and recently sold to a Japanese firm. The most active unit is the ordnance division, where government contracts have increased the demand for workers bumped from other divisions. Paper manufacturing, plastic mold injection firms that grew out of divisions closed down by Global Enterprises, and garment and textile plants that survived the flight to the South in the earlier decades of the twentieth century provide employment along with growing demands for service sector jobs in the tourist industry. Members of the same family are often distributed in different occupational levels within the Global Enterprises and in smaller unorganized shops and service occupations. The differentiations within these firms and among workers employed in firms that are differentially integrated in the world market will be explored in terms of the "emic" categories—those use by the workers and managers themselves to describe their status—and the "etic" categories defined by social scientists. The relations in production are conditioned by the way in which the firm is integrated in the world capitalist system and modified by the way in which it is related to the occupational stratification in the community and family. Both emic and etic categories may mask those relations because they refer to a job and not the labor process. That way of conceptualizing the problem does not capture the workers' consciousness of their condition as it is qualified by their familial relations with members of the household employed in a variety of different jobs. Nor does it take into consideration the levels of expectation that are activated in the socialization in the family and community.

The Work Force in Corporate Capitalist Enterprise

The reference points for managerial classifications of the work force in Global Enterprises are (1) exempt, (2) ineligible for union membership, and (3) eligible production workers. Exempt workers are those whose skill and control of information put them beyond the application of government rulings regarding affirmative action or union rules related to seniority or "bumping" rules. Ineligible is a category that includes routine clerical and keypunch operators along with secretarial and other information processing workers who deal with "confidential" material. Eligible includes the bulk of production workers except for foremen, who, like all supervisors and managers, are ineligible.

Exempt Employees. Most of the jobs in this category are filled by men. It is a professional status requiring training and education that is subdivided into "individual contributors" and others who manage other people. When women broke into these higher positions after the implementation of the Equal Employment and Opportunity Act, they were channeled into the former category to avoid gender confrontation in the management of men by women. Jane, an "individual contributor" with whom I spoke, said: "The exempt category are strictly the professional people. When it comes to laying off in Global Enterprises, they very rarely lay off people in the exempt category. The individual contributors may manage a contract or a project, but they don't manage people."

Job security is the principal benefit for this group but in addition there is an apparently trivial but in fact very potent distinction between exempt and other categories of workers: they do not have to punch in on the time clock. This symbolizes the fact that they are more in control of the management of their time in the plant. Competition exists among even these highly specialized workers. Managers will give the task of solving the same problem to two or more engineers, who will often be pitted against each other in coming up with a solution.

When opportunities for women opened up in the exempt category in the early 1970s, some of the older personnel managers found it difficult to adjust to the new outlook. The young woman quoted above recounted her experience in being interviewed by the personnel manager accustomed to dealing with male applicants:

> I interviewed for one job at G.E. where even though you're not supposed to ask people certain questions regarding their intentions of having families or things like that, I was asked.... Well, it used to be when I wasn't married, "Do you have a boyfriend? A pretty girl like you, you don't have a boyfriend?" I mean roundabout kind of fashion. The way they do it now is they come out and say, "Are you career oriented or family oriented?" It's the same damn question. I had one man come out and say to me, he mumbled something in the middle of an interview, something about a family, and I said, "I beg your pardon? I didn't quite get what you asked me." And he mumbled again and I said, "I'm sorry, I really don't know what you're trying to ask me." And he finally looked at me and he said, "Well, what about a family?" I said, "Do you mean, Do I want to have children and stay home for twenty years and take care of them? Is that what you're trying to ask me?" He said, "I know I'm not supposed to, but that's what I'm asking you." I really was flabbergasted, and I said, "Well, you're right, you're really not supposed to ask me."

When the Equal Employment and Opportunity Act first opened up this category for women and racially discriminated employees, the company was out fishing for candidates. That wave crested in the late 1970s, and management no longer urges individuals to upgrade themselves as they once did. However, the training courses are open to minorities and they have greater access to information about openings than formerly.

Ineligible Employees. The company controls the designation of jobs as ineligible for union membership. Any supervisory employee is automatically designated as ineligible even when he or she is in charge of a small group. Because the corporation controls the definition of the job, management can write into the description that it involves the processing of confidential information, and they are the ones who decide what that means. As the white collar union business agent stated:

> We are excluded from doing "confidential work." So the company says it is confidential work and they can tell you every job in the Global Enterprises is confidential work. If a clerk keypunches the boss's check, or a proprietary budget, that's confidential work. Well, everything in the Global Enterprises is confidential, and they have brought in the use of that word and we've lost our jobs throughout. Our bargaining unit went from 1,296 people eligible twelve years ago to 371 today, and the employment in the ineligible rank went the opposite.

The fact that 86 percent of this unit is female gives one a new perspective on the problem of why women don't join unions. Their clerical functions, routine as they may be, are easily categorized as managerial, from secretaries all through the information-processing chain. Some women have been reclassified as ineligible while working at the same job, but this is tantamount to grievance provocation. Most of the time, the reclassification comes with the introduction of new processing machinery which integrates them with other information processing units that are somewhere along the chain classified as confidential. Because so much of the basis for negotiations rest on knowledge of comparable wage scales in other plants, one can understand why management wants to control this information. The computer may become the instrument whereby workers can gain access to that information.

Elegible Employees. The shrinking number of employees eligible for union membership is a clue to managerial strategies in the manipulation of job descriptions to categorize increasing numbers of the work force as ineligibles. The old distinctions between "skilled" and "unskilled" are rarely if ever used. Nor is the contrasting pair "mental" and "manual" used in the discussions of the job hierarchy by corporation employees in any category. What one hears is the distinction between "production" workers who are "on the floor" and clerical workers in the offices. These older terms seem to be superseded by a changing managerial ideology that has moved away from Taylorism and the debasement of the job to Drucker's approach to motivational management.

Elegible jobs are divided into a complex range of differentially compensated job ratings. In contract negotiations carried out after World War II, job ratings were worked out in production as well as clerical and exempt categories. In the clerical ranks, the lowest is a mail carrier, whose wage in 1982 was $325 a week, followed by general clerks, file clerks, keypunchers, typists, stenotypists, and payroll. Up to the 1970s, women were never hired in ranks above this. The overt reason was that higher ranks should be able to read blueprints. The union fought for and won training courses in blueprint reading. Women now occupy up to grade 12 ratings, where they figure out traffic routes for shipping the large utilities made by the company. The highest pay in this range is $500 a week.

The company has complete control over adding duties or taking away some tasks, lowering the rating on jobs or claiming that work doesn't exist. They are resorting more frequently to Kelly Girls, women employed by a private agency which sends in "temporary" workers. These workers are not unionized and work for about half the wage of regularly employed workers. One whom I met in the course of our random interviews, the spouse of a regularly employed worker, was actually earning one-quarter of the top-ranking white collar workers in Global Enterprises.

The lack of information about future plans for technological change inhibits the union's ability to plan ahead and advise their workers. As the white collar union's business agent said. "I'd like to see a good retraining program we can plan in advance. Say we're getting 19 computers two years from now, we could say, "How many of you people would like to do this at night, take some courses?" Or "We'll pay your tuition at B.C.C. to learn about this." In the new contract the union has negotiated a retraining contingency for coping with technological innovation. This is a possible entry into information of the sort envisioned by the business agent, if handled adroitly.

Production workers have up to 25 ratings supposedly based on skill, difficulty or hazard in the job, and special training. Women never rose above an R14 rating, which was chiefly testing, until the 1970s. Following the passage of the EEOA, jobs were posted and several women applied and gained jobs as truckdrivers, cleaners, and big assembly. The only woman to sign up for the heavy assembly job was a woman in her thirties who had lost $45 in weekly pay when she and all the other workers were taken off piecework. She commented:

> To upgrade yourself after we lost piecework you had to take on a man's job. Foremen tried to discourage you there. It was tough to take on a man's job. "This is heavy, that is heavy; you've got to climb way up there." It was tough to take on harder jobs just to make up the money that you had lost. If you're working for yourself and your family, this is what you had to do.

Joan worked inside the tank loaded with PCB-impregnated oil. There were hundreds of men, and she was the only woman on the night shift, which she took to get 10 percent extra in pay. She moved to an R19 rating, and with the "adder" which was compensation for the lost piece rate, she was making more than her husband, who did the same job. Her marriage went on the rocks after 15 years and 5 kids, but she denied that it had any connection with her new earning status. On the job she wore dungarees and shirts, covered with oil. But after work she changed to street clothes, the trim polyester pant suits with California-style blouses that she wears in her duties as shop steward. From this job she went to woodwork shop, which had also been a male domain. Here she worked with a swing saw. When she started work here, Joan said,

> The boss didn't want the other gal who came in with me because she was too small. As though size made a difference! Because there were little men in there. But we always had to prove ourselves, whereas a man just gets hired. There can be 20 guys in a shop and 1 woman on the job and the supervisor asks, "Is she doing it right? Why is she standing still? Give her a broom to sweep." But you stand out.

The new system of posting jobs and advising the shop of possibilities led to several women applying for jobs formerly held by men only. Women are driving trucks, cleaning tanks, and running forklifts. But not all women wanted these changes. When layoffs came about, the company could fire them if they refused more than two of the jobs offered in bumping workers with less seniority.

Nelly belonged to the generation older than Joan that went to work just before World War II during the Depression. She resisted being put on "men's" work during the war:

> I remember one time they came up with this job. It was something to do with a small bomber. It used to come off the presses in half, and then they'd put them together. And you used to have to buff it, you know, with these wheels. And two or three girls had tried it and they couldn't do it, so he asked me to do it. You know, if those wheels went so fast, they could snap that right out of your hand. And I was short and I didn't reach that big wheel. You couldn't even hold it. A woman couldn't hold it. I told him I couldn't even hold the dishes they're so big. "It's dangerous. I'm not going to do it." So he said, "Well, you go home." So I said, "Well, I'm going home." He says, "You go home and come back when I call you." That was before the union. So I went home. Then he called me back on another job. They had hired men to do that work.

Production workers like Nelly could earn more than the foremen on some jobs:

> The minute they figured out what jobs paid well, they sent in a timer. The boss would always be watching and he could never make it out. So, anyway, he used to say, "You make more money than I do." I said, "Well, I work for it." And he'd say, "Well, I'll catch you yet. I'll find out which job is which." But he never did.

Because Nelly did several jobs she was able to mix the tally cards so that the boss was never sure where the money was. Nelly, who was Italian, was on good terms with her boss, even though she "never brought in any tomato sauce to give to him" like some others did. He "took a liking to me," she said, adding "not a liking like you could bribe him."

In these years, even before the union, Global Enterprises had enough advantages over the textile and paper firms in the area that they could be selective about their employees. Girls who started to work before the age of 16 had to be released one day a week to go to continuation school. This was the case of Vickie, an Italian Swiss who started work in 1923 in the North Adams cotton mills. When she turned 16 she went to work in Global Enterprises in the porcelain plant that was replaced with plastics. Then she went to work on radio bases with 800 women in one department. That went to Concord, New Hampshire, and she went into fan motors. That was moved overseas. Then she was a winder in small transformers, but that went to Shreveport. Her career is a record of capital flight. Although she never went beyond an R10 rating, she was able to make good money on pieces rates. When day rates were instituted, she lost $14 a week. She felt that day work meant a big loss of motivation.

In her early years of work, she was subject to many layoffs. The first came when she got married in 1926. "It was the time that Global Enterprises laid all the married women off. It made no difference whether your husband was working or not, but mine happened not to be, but as far as Global Enterprises was concerned, that was the rule. If you were married, you got laid off."

When she was penalized for her marriage, she went to work at Sprague's in North Adams and worked until the birth of her child, when she took three months off. She lived in a two-family house with her mother and so had no problem with baby-sitting. She always made more money than her husband, who was in construction. As the demand for workers rose during World War II, she returned to ask for a job at Global Enterprises. The manager said she would have to go to "Victory" school along with all the other "girls" to learn the machines. She had worked all of them before so she asked for a chance to demonstrate that she could run them and he hired her. The hardest thing for her was getting used to the swing shift, and they kept alternating these each month. With a family to take care of, doing the cooking and cleaning, she found it hard to get to sleep. When the boys returned from war, she lost her job: "They put the boys back on the machines and there were no women running them. They transferred them elsewhere. I went over on winding. I liked the screw machine because I happened to like machinery."

In the 49 years of active work, Vickie ended up with 28 years and seven months of service because her intermittent employment was subtracted from her cumulative credits. If she could have stayed three months more beyond her sixty-fifth birthday, when retirement was compulsory, she would have had a higher pension.

Competitive Capitalist Firms

Vickie was luckier than some women who dropped out of the primary work force entirely when they married. Mitzie was born in 1922, just a year before Vickie came to America. Her father was a silk weaver who kept moving the family as he went from Canada to the New England mills that closed successively. "You know how the mills are," she said, "they closed and moved South. We kept moving. Rocky Hill was one, Willamatic was one, then Norwich. I was quite young and the mills didn't stay around all that long. Finally he came to work on the Adams wool mill."

Her older brothers were weavers working in wool, silk, and cotton. Her sisters started out as weavers in the mills, but they got married quite young. Her first job when she got out of high school was in Global Enterprises.

> When I got out of high school in 1939, jobs were hard to get. I had applied for an office job in Global, but there was nothing. I got a call from Global personnel who said, "There's an opening in the factory which I could take until there was an office opening." I took the job waiting for the office job, but when it came, I didn't want to take it because the pay was so low—$16 and I was making $70.

She got married in 1943 but did not have to leave as women did before the war. In 1944 she had a still-born child, and she went back to work until 1947. She was making $60-$70 a week and knew she would be leaving soon for her second child. She left work in 1947 when the baby was born and stayed out until 1969, when the youngest of her six children went to college.

With her return to work, she dropped into the secondary work force working in the school cafeteria. She unpacked and heated food sent from the high school. She started at $1.75 and never got more than the minimum wage. Proposition 2½ meant a cutback on jobs held by many women, and she and the others who remained on the job had to work harder. Parents had a hard time paying for the increase in prices for the lunches, which went up to 60 cents and were then cut back to 50 cents because of the drop in sales. CETA workers are hired at wages above what these women are now getting, about $85-$90 a week, even though they supervise the work of these young people. She is head of her union, which they organized four years ago. "We get very few raises, but it is easier to get when we have the union to back us up. Before they were just talking to a bunch of women—take it or leave it. But with the union backing us, people will come in from Boston to fight for us."

Mary started in the work force as a clerk in her sister's store when she was 14. She gave all her wages—$5 a week—to her father, who gave her 50 cents. When she was married at the age of 20 she quit work to have three children in four years. When her husband proved irregular in his support of the family, she went to work as a spare hand spinning and doffing at the woolen mill earning $14 a week in 1932. She quit her job to follow her husband to Connecticut, but there he abandoned her and she was forced to go on welfare. The Connecticut welfare service escorted her and the children back to Massachusetts, and there she went back to work in the factory.

In these competitive capitalist workshops, the work was hard and poorly paid, and there were few benefits. Women were constantly subjected to sexual harassment by foremen but felt they couldn't complain for fear of losing their jobs. Mary was never offered a job at the Global Enterprises like some of her companions, but even some of those who were offered a job stayed on at the textile mill, thinking that there might be more security in a small shop. However, the mill folded before they reached retirement, and they had little more than social security after a lifetime of work.

Sue started work in a garment factory in 1971. She stayed with the same factory despite the low wage because her boss let her take time off for her pregnancies, which she considered a favor. She was also able to come in at 7:30, one-half hour later than her shift because of baby-sitting problems, and her boss was good about letting her stay home when the children were sick. She never had a paid vacation and was just given Thanksgiving, Christmas, and New Year's as paid holidays. She had no health insurance and no retirement plan. She was divorced and almost the only support for her children.

What broke her commitment to the job was when the boss called in a time-rate man when he got a big order from the army to make parkas. The first week he set the rates, the women got much higher than usual wages. Then the boss, who had always set the rates arbitrarily, cut them in half. She earned only $65 and complained along with several workers. When he refused to respond, she and others called in the ILGWU. When the boss heard of it, he threatened them with closing the shop. So they decided to come out in the open and organize. The organizer entered the shop with cards, and when one of the women said hello to him, the boss came raging out and fired her. Sixty-one workers walked out with her, three-quarters of the entire shop.

The workers walked the picket line from May to September, when a court date with the National Labor Relations Board was set in November. In the time of the picket lines, the owner tried to run down the pickets with his car, called them names, and threatened them. He continued to work with a reduced force and subcontracted some of the work to New Jersey.

Sue's answer to one of the question raised in a forum as to why she picketed and exposed her children to the violence was as follows:

> Because I feel very strongly about it as a worker, as a woman and as a mother. I feel I should be able to make a decent week's pay for my children to live. I felt very guilty the entire summer that I was not able to do a single thing with my children except to bring them to the picket line with me. As I said before, I cannot afford to send the children to babysitter. My family is not sympathetic to this. My family has not made an offer in any way to me, whether it is to watch the children for a day, or buy me groceries, or anything like that. My mother incidentally, she works at Global Enterprises, but she will not belong to the union. She doesn't believe in unions. While I know that I don't like my children exposed to the language he is using—I don't use this kind of language—I know that this kind of language is used. They don't repeat it; they understand what it is and where it's coming from. I just want them to know the kind of struggle that's involved.

During the discussion that followed, someone of Sue's mother's generation brought up Ronald Reagan's declaration that September 5, 1982, be declared working mother's day in appreciation of the 18 million American women who work and raise a family. One woman commented, "That's a cheap shot! Where are the appropriations to back it up!" She was Sue's grandmother's age.

Just the summer before, the nurses at the medical center went out on strike and got more support than the garment workers. One nurse spoke at the same forum:

> I'm sure most of you have read the paper and realized the background of the nurses' strike. Nursing is professionally, traditionally, and historically mostly women, and the conditions are disgusting. That is the only way to describe them. Here in Pontoosuc we start at $6.64 an hour and the top of the scale is 7.52 an hour. They give us a title and call us registered nurses, but they don't give us the rights or the benefits of any of the male professional groups. Our working conditions are—well, we're continually short staffed, we have no input into making decisions, we have to work under staffing problems continually. When we meet with the staff, they throw down a wonderful little shopping list to go through. They constantly refer to us as girls, "You girls got to be realistic." The main thrust of them sitting there calling us

girls is that they don't think that we were serious; they didn't think that we would have the strength to get together and pull off a successful strike....

We have very few scabs crossing our lines. We have only 18 out of 400 of our own nurses crossing the picket line, and then there are a sort of rent-a-scabs that the hospital hires from other areas.... We had a negotiating session last week, and they are long and hard. I couldn't really understand what was the matter. It was my worst session. I went home and I thought about it and then I understood why I felt so bad. And finally for the first time I realized that I was absolutely being refused something that I deserved for no other reason than that I was a woman. It hit home that day, and I was angry and frustrated and hurt.

It is in these moments of truth, when workers confront the contradiction in their lives, that militant class consciousness is born. It may happen because the awareness of ascribed status contradicts the ideal of achievement, as in the case of the nurse and the Global Enterprise "individual contributor." Or it may rise directly out of the sense of class exploitation on the job, as in the case of the cafeteria worker becoming aware of the extremely low wage rates when CETA volunteers were hired at a beginning rate higher than the women were earning. However it occurs, the lack of logic in the system becomes visible, and management loses its credibility.

The women who expressed and acted upon a class-conscious basis were those who worked in the marginal factories and in service occupations. The fact that Sue was a divorced head of household supporting two children on a wage that was only a few cents above the minimal wage catapulted her into trade union activity when her boss arbitrarily cut piece rates. Mitzie's husband had always been the chief wage earner in the household when he worked for the G.E., but when kids whom the had to supervise were getting higher hourly rates than she and the other women in the school cafeteria when they came in on a CETA program, she became an organizer of the union. The nurse who triggered union organization in the hospital experienced the full impact of managerial injustice when she recognized the fact that she was a woman made the difference in their willingness to negotiate.

In the declining industrial city of Pontoosuc this awareness of contradictions is occurring among workers in the marginal firms and service jobs more than in the work force employed in the transnational corporation. In Global Enterprises the relatively higher wage rate—$10-$12 an hour compared with $3.75-$7.00 plus the better benefits won in the half century of labor organization—shielded them from some of the harsher economics of the labor market. But as the attrition in the labor force pushes them into the ranks of the unemployed, they are forced to reassess their position. Thus far, the plant has not laid off many workers with seniority of more than a decade. Defense contracts in the ordnance division enabled that part of the plant to absorb workers laid off in other divisions, except in the case of draftsmen, who have been the main victims of computerized processes.

Women's work has always served as the shock absorber in a system subject to economic cycles of expansion and decline. The system has drawn on this labor force almost to the upper limit of its ability to compensate for fluctuations. Married women who worked part time are now almost fully employed. Their paycheck goes not just for extras but for the essentials needed by the family. Divorced women are the principal support for their children, and their imperative to work is the greatest. These are the women who are most conscious of their class position and who have taken the most militant role in recent labor disputes. The women in the garment factory where Sue worked had the longest strike in Pontoosuc's history in 1982. They walked the picket line despite aggravated assault by the owner of the firm, who at one time drove his Cadillac into the line, injuring a picket, who had to be hospitalized. The National Labor Relations Board settlement in July 1983 called upon the owner to reinstate employees fired for organizing with back pay.

The Social Relations of Production and the Reproduction of Family and Community

These women experience in a multiplicity of ways a changing labor process, but their experience is not a passive response. They are reinforcing or transforming the categories in which they experience the impact. Nellie refused to do what she considered to be a man's job during the war, while Joan scorned the supervisor's assumption that she could not do a man's work. Many, like Mary and Sue, chose jobs in marginal factories because they thought that the more personalistic ties with an owner-operated shop would permit greater latitude to accommodate their work with their family responsibilities. Other women chose work in hospitals or school cafeterias because the hours were more flexible and they could choose a shift that matched their children's home coming.

I have selected cases from female respondents because they are the ones who are balancing the conflicting demands of production and reproduction. In their movement in and out of the labor market, and from primary to secondary jobs, it is clear that any attempt to equate consciousness and status in the work force at any one point in time and without consideration of employment of other family members is clearly inadequate. Heightening of consciousness came with an abrupt transition either in the job experience or in their home life. When women entered the jobs that had been sex segregated, they became aware of the stereotypes about them as women. Joan experienced this with foremen on the shop floor somewhat differently than Jane did in management headquarters, but both of them gained a greater sense of their potential in challenging the stereotypes they encountered. Nellie liked the sense of being protected and treated as a woman even though she worked in the factory all her life. When she first went to work at the age of 16 her father saw to it that she was quickly transferred from the night shift, where all these "rough Polish girls worked," to the day shift, and after she got married she deferred to her husband's concern that she shouldn't work on a dirty job. Vickie, who loved working on the machines during the war, was disappointed when she had to go back to assembly work, but she never fought management's prerogative in assigning the job.

Rising unemployment rates exacerbate the pressure both to work full time in order to supplement family income as men are laid off and to accept jobs that may not be compatible with family roles because of the diminishing choices. The only area of growth in the region is tourism, an "industry" that many feel is not only in direct competition with heavy industry for basic resources but in opposition to it. Wages are lower for many of the jobs that have taken up the slack caused by attrition in the major corporation. Young people and women are the major group affected. Although layoffs in the Global Enterprises are governed strictly by seniority, women are less likely to have the same accumulated seniority as a job protection. Affirmative action rulings have imposed a peculiar handicap: because all jobs are presumably open to women, they are expected to accept all jobs when they are bumped from any position. However many women, particularly those of Nelly's generation, do not want to take very heavy jobs, and if they refuse more than two jobs offered, they are out on the street.

As yet, the city has not experienced a closing of their major company, but smaller shops have closed, and all companies, including paper mills, have had some attrition in the numbers of production workers employed. Bluestone and Harrison (1982) show that no one is immune to job loss in the current deindustrialization of America. However they indicate that more blacks and women are likely to be laid off and to find it harder to get reemployed. We are not able to state this precisely for Pontoosuc since we are in the middle of the research. However, as men move into the service jobs that formerly hired youths and women, the latter have fewer jobs to find. In the major corporation, the segmentation by sex is once again crystalizing as the pressure for equal employment is relieved. The very principle of seniority that is institutionalized in union negotiations makes it harder for women and other minorities to retain the jobs they were hired to fill in affirmative action.

To return to the original argument about the impact of a segregated labor market on organization of workers, I have chosen data from interviews with women in monopoly and competitive capitalist enterprises to challenge the argument that workers have never developed a serious political party because it is divided along economic, political, and cultural dimensions and further that this segmentation is a managerial technique of control and represents the last resolution of the capitalist crisis (Gordon, Edwards and Reich, 1982, p. 2). In contrast, I found that segmentation was a continuous technique throughout the industrialization of Pontoosuc in the textile mills of the nineteenth century as well as in corporate capitalist concerns and competitive industries in the twentieth century. However it was often the privileged segments of the work force who led the organization of unions in the early decades of unionization, and the organizations they formed united the masses of workers in industrial unions in the 1930s. The implication of a theory of segmentation determining worker consciousness and organization is that unity and collective action can be achieved only when the work force is completely homogenized. That has never been true for one industry and far less even for the many levels of production we find even in a small industrial city such as Pontoosuc. Workers have been able to achieve hegemonic alliances with a wide variety of differential paid and stratified workers. What broke the unity of the work force in the post World War II period was the campaign of anti-Communism and redbaiting. The resultant split in the union was only partially overcome in the strike waves of the late 1960s as the old division between the unions was overcome in the negotiations.

The divisive factor in the work force is not only that of a primary and secondary work force based on any intrinsic features in the job governing attitudes or behavior. The real divisions in the work place are the management-created categories of ineligibles and exempt personnel that impede unionization. This direct manipulation of the work force determining who may join the unions is quite different from the creation of a preferentially treated hierarchy affecting class consciousness. Historically, workers have been able to overcome cooptation resulting from the job differentiation in times of crisis. Some unions, including the Oil and Chemical Workers Union, have begun to challenge the ineligible classification on a job-by-job basis, but for the most part the consensual accord that characterizes worker-management relations in industry (Burawoy 1979) accepts the managerial prerogative of control over information and definition of the job.

Anthropological monographs on the production process testify to the importance of the family and community in mediating consciousness of class relations in production. This is not just a "primitive" or "precapitalist" conditioning of consciousness. Cultural historians give equally persuasive evidence that working class movements do not begin and end in the shop but rather are sustained by the mobilization of the community.[3] Pontoosuc's own history indicates the importance of community support in the moments of class struggle that issue from the work place but do not necessarily begin and end there. The present struggles and the level of militant class action in Pontoosuc today would be completely unpredictable in terms of segmentation theory: nurses, women—particularly those with full responsibility for maintaining themselves and their children—working in competitive capitalist enterprises are the ones who have "hit the streets" in their demands for a living wage and the right to unionize. Women who live in households with a second wage earner are not as likely to recognize the exploitation they experience in work places where the wage in less than the subsistence needs of the family as are women who are the only support of the family. When Mitzie's husband retired and received less than one-quarter of his former pay as a pension, her income became more important. When she realized how low it was in comparison with CETA employees who were recent graduates of high school, she started to unionize. Sue's moment of truth came when the New Jersey piece-rate timer revealed the comparatively low pay the women in this unorganized shop received in the rates he put on their work, and when the boss reacted by arbitrarily cutting the rate in half. Their accommodation to subordinate jobs and wages came about not because a change in their relations in production but as they began to see their jobs and wages in a larger context. The unionized work force in Global Enterprises has so far accepted the attrition of jobs and a speedup designed to make them more competitive, but a recent four-hour walkout to show their objections to a "checker" system instituted to measure their productivity indicates a deep and growing resentment to corporate practices.

The context for these differentiated responses by workers to the present restructuring of the work force is the world capitalist system and how it impinges on the production process. Marginally surviving enterprises such as the garment shop in which Sue Works are in direct competition with offshore sweatshops, and management is demanding that workers make their labor competitive with that of low-paid operatives throughout the world. Except for one plant that was unionized, the small plastics factories are not organized, and the highest-paid workers get less than a janitor in the Global Enterprises plant. By subcontracting and eliminating entire processes that are relocated overseas, the corporation is cutting its operations down to the only division it considers to be sufficiently profitable—armaments.

A theory of working-class consciousness and how it is tied to relations in production must take into account the mediation of family and community as well as the level of integration of the firm in the world market. It cannot ignore the active intervention of workers in shaping the categories that appear to govern their behavior: the privileges of the "primary" work force were in great part won by the workers themselves. They were not just favors given by management in the interest of coopting a segment of the work force. The task ahead is to weld those hegemonic alliances among differentiated strata of the work force at a time when the very survival of industry is threatened by the flight of capital.

Notes

1. Among those who have studied the offshore plants are Linda Lim (1978), M. Patricia Fernández Kelly (1980), and Helen Safa (1981). Their work, along with that of researchers of electronics assembly plants in Salinas Valley (Katz and Kemnitzer 1983, Keller 1983) show the preponderance of young female assembly line workers who are

assumed to have the biological predispositions to do small, painstaking assembly work without rebelling.

2. See Alverson, 1978; Epstein, 1958; Mitchell, 1956; Nash, 1979; Walker, 1950; Warner, 1941; and many others who have emphasized the significance of community in relation to the work place.

3. In particular, Cumbler, 1979; and Gutman, 1976.

REFERENCES

Alverson, Hoyt. 1978. *Mind in the Heart of Darkness: Value and Self-Identity among the Tswana of Southern Africa.* New Haven: Yale University Press.

Bibb, Robert, and William H. Form. 1977. "The Effects of Industrial, Occupational, and Sex Stratification on Wages in Blue-Collar Markets." *Social Forces* 55:4 (June), 974-996.

Bluestone, Barry, and Bennett Harrison. 1982. *The Deindustrialization of America.* New York: Basic Books.

Braverman, Harry. 1974 *Labor and Monopoly Capital.* New York: Monthly Review Press.

Burawoy, Michael. 1979. *Manufacturing Consent.* Chicago: University of Chicago Press.

Cumbler, J.T. 1979. *Working Class Community in Industrial America: Work, Leisure and Struggle in Two Industrial Cities, 1881-1930.* Westport, Conn.: Greenwood Press.

Doeringer, P.B., and M.J. Piore. 1971. *Internal Labor Market and Manpower Analysis.* Lexington, Mass.: Heath.

Epstein, A.L. 1958. *Politics in an Urban African Community.* Manchester: Manchester University Press.

Fernández Kelly, M. Patricia. 1980. "Chavalas de Maquiladora: A Study of the Female Labor of Ciudad Juarez Offshore Production Plants." Ph.D. dissertation, Rutgers University.

Gordon, David M., Michael Reich and R. C. Edwards. 1973. "A Theory of Labor Market Segmentation." *American Economic Review* 63 (May), 359-365.

―――. 1982. *Segmented Work, Divided Labor.* New York: Cambridge University Press.

Gorz, Andre. 1978. *Farewell to the Working Class.* Boston: South End Press.

Gray, Robert Q. 1974. "The Labour Aristocracy in the Victorian Class Structure." In *The Social Analysis of Class Structure.* ed. F. Parkin, pp. 19-38. London: Tavistock.

Gutman, Herbert. 1976. *Work, Culture and Society in Industrializing America: Essays in American Working Class and Social History.* New York: Knopf.

Hartman, Heidie. 1976. "Capitalism, Patriarchy and Job Segregation by Sex." *Signs* 1 (Spring), 137-169.

Katz, N., and J. Kemnitzer. 1983. "Join the Future Now! Women in the Electronics Industry: Sexism, Structure and Profit." In *Women, Men and the International*

Division of Labor. ed. June Nash and María Patricia Fernández Kelly, pp. 332-345. Albany: State University of New York Press.

Keller, J. 1983. "The Division of Labor in Electronics." In *Women, Men and the International Division of Labor.* ed. June Nash and María Patricia Fernández Kelly, pp. 346-373. Albany: State University of New York Press.

Kreckle, Reinhard. 1982. "Unequal Opportunity Structure and Labor Market Segmentation." *Sociology* 14 (November), 525-550.

Lim, Linda. 1978. "Women Workers in Multinational Corporations: The Case of the Electronics Industry in Malaysia and Singapore." Occasional Papers. Ann Arbor: University of Michigan.

Middleton, Chris. 1974. "Sexual Inequality and Stratification Theory." In *The Social Analysis of Class Structure.* ed. F. Parkin, pp. 169-203. London: Tavistock.

Mitchell, J. Clyde. 1956. "The Kalela Dance". Rhodes-Livingstone Papers, no. 27.

Montgomery, David. 1980. "To Study the People: The American Working Class." *Labor History* 21 (Fall), 485-512.

Nash, June. 1983. "Class Conflict and Community Integration in a New England Industrial Town." Paper presented to the Seventh Political Economy of the World System Conference on Labor and Labor Movements in the World Capitalist System.

Nash, June, and María Patricia Fernández Kelly. eds. 1983. *Women, Men and the International Division of Labor.* Albany: State University of New York Press.

Parkin, F., ed. 1974. *The Social Analysis of Class Structure.* London: Tavistock.

Safa, Helen. 1981. "Runaway Shops and Female Employment: The Search for Cheap Labor." *Signs* 7:2 (Winter), 418-423.

Smith, E. A. 1876. *The History of Pittsfield, Berkshire County, Massachusetts from the Year 1800 to the Year 1876.* Springfield, Mass.: C. W. Bryan.

Sokoloff, Natalie J. 1980. *Between Money and Love: The Dialectics of Women's Home and Market Work.* New York: Praeger.

Walker, C. R. 1950. *Steeltown.* New York: Harper.

Warner, W. L., and P. S. Lunt. 1941. *The Social Life of a Modern Community.* New Haven: Yale University Press.

Selected Bibliography

Agarwala, A. N., and S. P. Singh. eds. 1973. *The Economics of Underdevelopment.* New York: Oxford University Press.

Alba, Francisco. 1978. "Mexico's International Migration as a Manifestation of Its Development Pattern." *International Migration Review* 12:4 (Winter), 502-513.

Amin, Samir. 1975. *Accumulation on a World Scale.* New York: Monthly Review Press.

Arrighi, Giovanni. 1982. "A Crisis of Hegemony." In *Dynamics of Global Crisis*, ed. Samir Amin. New York: Monthly Review Press.

Arroyo, Gonzalo, ed. 1982. *El desarrollo agroindustrial y la economía latinoamericana.* vol. I. Documentos de trabajo para el Desarrollo Agroindustrial, no. 5. Mexico: SARH-CODAI.

Assael, Hector. 1979. "The Internationalization of the Latin American Economies: Some Reservations." *CEPAL Review* 7 (April), 41-55.

Austin, James E. 1974. *Agribusiness in Latin America.* New York: Praeger.

Axline, W. Andrew. 1977. "Underdevelopment, Dependence, and Integration: The Politics of Regionalism in the Third World." *International Organization* 31:1 (Winter), 83-105.

Bach, Robert L. 1978. "Mexican Immigration and the American State." *International Migration Review* 12:4 (Winter), 536-558.

———. 1978. "Mexican Immigration and U.S. Immigration Reforms in the 1960s." *Kapitalistate* 7, 63-80.

———. 1979. "On the Holism of the World-Systems Perspective." In *The Process of the World Economy*, ed. Terence K. Hopkins and Immanuel Wallerstein, pp. 289-310. Beverly Hills, Calif.: Sage.

———. 1980. *Past and Present Legislative Reform: The Immigration and Nationality Efficiency Act of 1979.* Hearings before the Senate Judiciary Committee on S. 1763. 96th Cong., 1st sess. Washington, D.C.: Government Printing Office.

———. Forthcoming. "The Entry of Refugee Populations in the Labor Force." In *The Labor Market Impacts of Immigration.* New York: Rockefeller Foundation.

———, and Lisa A. Schraml. 1982. "Migration, Crisis and Theoretical Conflict." *International Migration Review* 16:2 (Summer), 320-341.

Barkin, David. 1982. "The Impact of Agribusiness on Rural Development." In *Current Perspectives in Social Theory*. ed. Scott McNall, pp. 1-25. Greenwich, Conn.: JAI Press.
———, and Carlos Rozo. 1981. "L'Agriculture et l'internationalization du capital." *Revue tiers-monde* 88 (October-December), 723-745.
———. 1983. "La producción de alimentos y la internacionalización del capital." *El trimestre Económico* 50:3 (Fall), 1603-1626.
———, and Blanca Suárez. 1982. *El fin de autosuficiencia alimentaria*. Mexico: Nueva Imagen
Barnet, Richard, and Ronald Mueller. 1974. *Global Reach: The Power of the Multinational Corporation*. New York: Simon and Schuster.
Baucic, Ivo. 1972. *The Effects of Emigration from Yugoslavia and the Problems of Returning Emigrant Workers*. The Hague: Martinus Nijhoff.
Benería, Lourdes. 1983. "The Labor Process, Subcontracting and Gender Relations." Paper prepared for the Social Science Research Council Workshop on Social Inequality and Gender Hierarchy.
Bergsten, C. Fred. 1975. *The Dilemmas of the Dollar*. New York: New York University Press.
———. 1976. "Interdependence and the Reform of International Institutions." *International Organization* 30:2 (Spring), 361-372.
Bhagwati, Jagdish. ed. 1977. *The New International Economic Order: The North-South Debate*. Cambridge: MIT Press.
Bianchi, Suzanne M. 1981. *Household Composition and Racial Inequality*. New Brunswick, N.J.: Rutgers University Press.
Bibb, Robert, and William H. Form. 1977. "The Effects of Industrial, Occupational, and Sex Stratification on Wages in Blue-Collar Markets." *Social Forces* 55:4 (June), 974-996.
Blair, John. 1972. *Economic Concentration*. New York: Holt, Reinhart.
Bluestone, Barry, and Bennet Harrison. 1980. *Capital and Communities: The Causes and Consequences of Private Disinvestment*. Washington, D.C.: Progressive Alliance.
———. 1982. *The Deindustrialization of America*. New York: Basic Books.
Bonilla, Frank, and Ricardo Campos. 1981. "A Wealth of Poor: Puerto Ricans in the New Economic Order." *Daedalus* (Spring), 133-176.
Bowles, Samuel, and Herbet Gintis. 1977. "The Marxian Theory of Value and Heterogeneous Labor: A Critique and Reformulation." *Cambridge Journal of Economics* 1:2, 173-192.
———. 1982. "The Crisis of Liberal-DemocraticCapitalism: The Case of the United States." *Politics and Society* 11:1, 51-94.
———, David M. Gordon and Thomas E. Weiskopf. 1983. *Beyond the Wasteland: A Democratic Alternative to Economic Decline*. New York: Anchor.

Braverman, Harry. 1974. *Labor and Monopoly Capital*. New York: Monthly Review Press.
Bray, David. 1983. "Agricultura de exportación, formación de clase, y fuerza de trabajo excedente: El caso de la fuerza de trabajo migratoria en la República Dominicana." Paper presented to the Conference on Dominican Migration to the United States. New York.
Bucher, Carl. 1968. *Industrial Evolution*. New York: Augustus M. Kelley.
Bukharin, N. 1973. *Imperialism and World Economy*. New York: Monthly Review Press.
Burawoy, Michael. 1978. "Toward a Marxist Theory of the Labor Process: Braverman and Beyond." *Politics and Society* 8:3,4, 247-312.
———. 1979. *Manufacturing Consent*. Chicago: University of Chicago Press.
Burbach, Roger, and Patricia Flynn. 1980. *Agribusiness in the Americas*. New York: Monthly Review Press.
Business International. 1981. *Trading in Latin America: The Impact of Changing Policies*. New York: Business International.
Cabrel, Manuel José. 1975. "Inflación, distribución del ingreso y empleo." *Ciencia y Sociedad* I (June), 1-4.
Campos, Ricardo, and Frank Bonilla. 1976. "Industrialization and Migration: Some Effects on the Puerto Rican Working Class." *Latin American Perspectives* 3:3 (Summer), 66-108.
———. 1982. "Bootstraps and Enterprise Zones: The Underside of Late Capitalism in Puerto Rico and the United States." *Review* 5:4, 556-590.
———. 1982. "Imperialist Initiatives and the Puerto Rican Worker: From Foraker to Reagan." *Contemporary Marxism* 5 (Summer), 1-19.
Caporaso, James A. 1978. "Dependence, Dependency and Power in the Global System: A Structural and Behavioral Analysis." *International Organization* 32:1 (Winter), 13-44.
———. 1981. "Industrialization in the Periphery: The Evolving Global Division of Labor," *International Studies Quarterly* 25:3 (September), 347-384.
Cardoso, Fernando Henrique, and Enzo Faletto. 1979. *Dependency and Development in Latin America*. Berkeley: University of California Press.
Castells, Manuel. 1975. "Immigrant Workers and Class Struggles in Advanced Capitalism: The Western European Experience." *Politics and Society* 5 (Spring), 33-66.
Castles, Stephen, and Godula Kosack. 1973. *Immigrant Workers and Class Structure in Western Europe*. Oxford: Oxford University Press.
Castro, Mary García. 1982. "Mary and Eve's Social Reproduction in the Big Apple: Colombian Voices." Center for Latin American and Caribbean Studies, Occasional Papers, no. 35. New York University.
Catrain, Pedro. 1980. "Estado, hegemonía y clases dominantes en la República Dominicana, 1966-1978." Paper presented to the Second National

Sociological Congress of the Association of Dominican Sociologists, Santo Domingo (November).
Centro de Estudios Puertorriqueños. 1979. *Labor Migration Under Capitalism: The Puerto Rican Experience.* New York: Monthly Review Press.
Chilcote, Ronald H., and Joel C. Edelstein. 1974. *Latin America: The Struggle with Dependency and Beyond.* Cambridge, Mass.: Shenkman.
Cline, William R., and Sidney Weintraub. eds. 1981. *Economic Stabilization in Developing Countries.* Washington, D.C.: Brookings Institution.
Cohen, Robert B. 1981. "The New International Division of Labor, Multinational Corporations and Urban Hierarchy." In *Urbanization and urban Planning in Capitalist Society,* ed. M. Dear and A. Scott. London: Methuen.
Cooney, Rosemary S. 1979. "Demographic Components of Growth in White, Black, and Puerto Rican Female-Headed Families: Comparison of the Cutright and Ross/Sawhill Methodologies." *Social Science Research* 8:2 (June), 144-158.
Cooper, Richard. 1980. *The Economics of Interdependence.* New York: Columbia University Press.
Cornelius, Wayne. 1976."Mexican Migration to the United States: View From Rural Sending Communities." Mimeo.
———. 1978. "Mexican Migration to the United States: Causes, Consequences, and U.S. Responses." Mimeo. Migration and Study Group, Center for International Studies, MIT.
Cumbler, J. T. 1979. *Working Class Community in Industrial America: Work, Leisure and Struggle in Two Industrial Cities, 1881-1930.* Westport, Conn.: Greenwood Press.
de Janvry, Alain. 1982. *The Agrarian Question and Reformism in Latin America.* Baltimore: Johns Hopkins University Press.
Dinerman, Ina R. 1977. "Patterns of Adaptation Among Households of U.S.-Based Migrants from Michoacan, Mexico." Paper presented to the Joint Meeting of the Latin American Studies Association and the African Studies Association, Houston, Texas.
Doeringer, P. B., and Michael J. Piore. 1971. *Internal Labor Market and Manpower Analysis.* Lexington, Mass.: Heath.
Dougherty, James E., and Robert L. Pfaltzgraff, Jr. 1980. *Contemporary Theories of International Relations.* 2nd ed. Philadelphia: Lippincott.
Drucker, Peter. 1979. "Production Sharing, Concepts and Definitions." *Journal of the Flagstaff Institute* 1.
Edwards, Richard C. 1979. *Contested Terrain.* New York: Basic Books.
———, Michael Reich and David M. Gordon. 1975. *Labor Market Segmentation.* Lexington, Mass.: Heath.
Ellis, H. S., and L. A. Metzler, eds. 1950. *Readings in the Theory of International Trade.* Philadelphia: Blakiston.

Emmanuel, Arghiri. 1974. *Unequal Exchange: A Study of the Imperialism of Trade*. New York: Monthly Review Press.

Epstein, A. L. 1958. *Politics in an Urban African Community*. Manchester: Manchester University Press.

Ernst, Dieter, ed. 1980. *The New International Division of Labor, Technology and Underdevelopment: Consequences for the Third World*. Frankfurt: Campus/Verlag.

———. 1981. Special Issue on "Industrial Redeployment and International Transfer of Technology: Trends and Policy Issues." *Viertel Jahres Berichte* 83 (March).

Evans, Peter. 1979. *Dependent Development: The Alliance of Multinational, State and Local Capital in Brazil*. Princeton: Princeton University Press.

———. 1979. "Shoes, OPIC, and the Unquestioning Persuasion." In *Capitalism and the State in U.S.-Latin American Relations*, ed. Richard R. Fagen, pp. 302-336. Stanford: Stanford University Press.

Fagen, Richard R., ed. 1979. *Capitalism and the State in U.S.-Latin American Relations*. Stanford: Stanford University Press.

Feinberg, Richard. 1983. *The Intemperate Zone: The Third World Challenge to U.S. Foreign Policy*. New York: Norton.

Fernández Kelly, María Patricia. 1980. "Chavalas de Maquiladora: A Study of the Female Labor of Ciudad Juárez Offshore Production Plants." Ph.D. dissertation, Rutgers University.

———. 1983a. *A Cross-Cultural Comparison of Export Processing Zones in Asia and the U.S.-Mexico Border*. Monograph prepared for the Walsh-Price Fellowship Program, Maryknoll Fathers and Brothers.

———. 1983b. *For We Are Sold, I and My People: Women and Industry in Mexico's Frontier*. Albany: State University of New York Press.

Fishlow, Albert. 1978. "Flying Down to Rio." *Foreign Affairs* (Winter), 387-405.

Flamm, K., and J. Grunwald. N.d.. "Offshore Production in the International Semiconductor Industry." Mimeo. Washington, D.C.: Brookings Institution.

Fleisher, Belton M. 1963. "Some Economic Aspects of Puerto Rican Migration to the United States." *Review of Economics and Statistics* 45:3 (August), 245-253.

Fligstein, Neil. 1981. *Going North*. New York: Academic Press.

Fogarty, John. 1982. "Staple Theory and the Development Experiences of Argentina, Australia, and Canada." Paper delivered to the International Congress of Americanists, Manchester, England.

Foxley, Alejandro, and Laurence Whitehead. 1980. "Economic Stabilization in Latin America: Political Dimensions." *World Development* 8:11 (November), 823-832.

Frank, Andre Gunder. 1980. *Crisis in the World Economy*. New York: Holmes and Meier.

Freedman, Marcia K. 1976. *Labor Markets: Segments and Shelters*. Montclair, N.J.: Allanheld Osmun.

Frenkel, Roberto, and Guillermo O'Donnell. 1979. "The 'Stabilization Programs' of the International Monetary Fund and Their Internal Impacts." In *Capitalism and the State in U.S.-Latin American Relations*, ed. Richard R. Fagen, pp. 171-216. Stanford: Stanford University Press.

Friend, Andrew, and Andy Metcalf. 1981. *Slump City*. London: Pluto Press.

Frobel, Folker, Jurgen Heinrichs and Otto Kreye. 1977. "The Tendency Towards a New International Division of Labour." *Review* 1:1 (Summer), 73-88.

———. 1978. "The World Market for Labour and the World Market for Industrial Sites." *Journal of Economic Issues* 12:4 (December), 843-858.

———. 1979. *The New International Division of Labour*. New York: Cambridge University Press.

Furtado, Celso. 1976. *Economic Development of Latin America*. 2nd ed. Cambridge: Cambridge University Press.

Galtung, Johan. 1971. "A Structural Theory of Imperialism." *Journal of Peace Research* 8:2, 81-118.

Gardner, Richard N. 1956. *Sterling-Dollar Diplomacy*. Oxford: Clarendon Press.

Garrison, Vivian, and Carol I. Weiss. 1979. "Dominican Family Networks and U.S. Immigration Policy: A Case Study." *International Migration Review* 12:2 (Summer), 264-283.

George, Susan. 1977. *How the Other Half Dies: The Real Reasons for World Hunger*. Montclair, N.J.: Allanheld, Osmun.

Geschwender, James A., and Rhonda F. Levine. 1983. "Rationalization of Sugar Production in Hawaii, 1946-1960: A Dimension of the Class Struggle." *Social Problems* 30 (February), 352-368.

Giersch, H. ed. 1979. *On the Economics of Intra-Industry Trade*. Tübingen, German Federal Republic: JCB Mohr.

Ginzberg, Eli. 1979. *Good Jobs, Bad Jobs, No Jobs*. Cambridge: Harvard University Press.

Girvan, Norman. 1976. *Corporate Imperialism*. White Plains, N.Y.: M. E. Sharpe.

Goldberg, Ray. 1974. *Agribusiness Management for Developing Countries—Latin America*. Cambridge, Mass.: Ballinger.

Gómes, Gerson, and Antonio Pérez. 1979. "The Process of Modernization in Latin American Agriculture." *CEPAL Review* 8 (August), 55-74.

Gordon, David, ed. 1977. *Problems of Political Economy: An Urban Perspective*. Lexington, Mass.: Heath.

Gordon, David, Richard Edwards and Michael Reich. 1973. "A Theory of Labor Market Segmentation." *American Economic Review* 63 (May), 359-365.

———. 1982. *Segmented Work, Divided Workers*. Cambridge: Cambridge University Press.
Gorz, Andre. 1978. *Farewell to the Working Class*. Boston: South End Press.
Grasmuck, Sherri. 1981a. "Emigration and Development: The Case of the Dominican Republic." Center for Latin American and Caribbean Studies. Occasional Papers, no. 34. New York University.
———. 1981b. "The Impact of Emigration on National Development: Three Sending Communities in the Dominican Republic." Center for Latin American and Caribbean Studies. Occasional Paper no. 33. New York University.
———. 1982. "Migration Within the Periphery: Haitian Labor in the Dominican Sugar and Coffee Industries." *International Migration Review* 16:2 (Summer), pp. 365-377.
———. 1983. "International Stair-Step Migration: Dominican Labor in the United States and Haitian Labor in the Dominican Republic." In *Peripheral Workers*, ed. R. Simpson and I. H. Simpson. Greenwhich, Conn.: JAI Press.
Grossman, R. 1978. "Women's Place in the Integrated Circuit." *Southeast Asia Chronicle* 9:5,6, 2-17.
Grubel, Herbert, and Peter Lloyd. 1975. *Intra-Industry Trade*. London: Macmillan.
Gurak, Douglas. 1981. "Dominicans and Colombians in New York City." Presentation to the New York Forum on Migration, New York.
Gutman, Herbert. 1976. *Work, Culture and Society in Industrializing America: Essays in American Working Class and Social History*. New York: Knopf.
"Hands off the IMF". 1982. *Economist* 284:7253 (September 4), 15-16.
Hartman, Heidie. 1976. "Capitalism, Patriarchy and Job Segregation by Sex." *Signs* 1 (Spring), 137-169.
Harvey, David. 1982. *The Limits to Capital*. Oxford: Basil Blackwell.
Heckscher, Eli. 1919. "The Effects of Foreign Trade on the Distribution of Income." Reprinted in *Readings in the Theory of International Trade*, ed. H. S. Ellis and L. A. Metzler, pp. 272-300. Philadelphia: Blakiston, 1949.
Helleiner, G.K. 1977. "Transnational Enterprises and the New Political Economy of U.S. Trade Policy." *Oxford Economic Papers* 29:1 (March), 102-116.
———. 1979. "Transnational Corporations and Trade Structure: The Role of Intra-firm Trade." In *On the Economics of Intra-Industry Trade*, ed. H. Giersch, pp. 159-181. Tübinen, German Federal Republic: JCB Mohr.
Hernández-Álvarez, J. 1968. "The Movement and Settlement of Puerto Rican Migrants within the United States, 1950-1960." *International Migration Review* 2:2 (Spring), 40-52.
Hiestand, Dale L., and Dean W. Morse. 1979. *Comparative Metropolitan Employment Complexes*. Montclair, N.J.: Allanheld Osmun.

Hopkins, Raymond F., and Donald J. Puchala. 1980. *Global Food Interdependence: Challenge to American Foreign Policy.* New York: Columbia University Press.
———. eds. 1978. *The Global Political Economy of Food.* Madison: University of Wisconsin Press.
Hopkins, Terence and Immanuel Wallerstein. 1977. "Patterns of Development of the Modern World-System." *Review* 1:2.
———. 1979. *The Process of the World Economy.* Beverly Hills, Calif.: Sage.
Hughes, James N., and George Sternlieb. 1978. *Jobs and People.* New Brunswick, N.J.: Center for Urban Policy Research.
Huntington, Samuel P. 1968. "The Bases of Accommodation." *Foreign Affairs* 46:4 (July), 642-656.
Hymer, Stephen. 1972. "The Internationalization of Capital." *Journal of Economic Issues* 6:1 (March), 91-111.
———. 1980. *The Multinational Corporation.* Cambridge: Cambridge University Press.
Inter-American Development Bank. 1982. *Economic and Social Progress in Latin America: The External Sector.* Washington, D.C.: IDB.
International Labour Organization. 1975. *Time for Transition.* Geneva: ILO.
Jalee, Pierre. 1973. *Imperialism in the Seventies.* New York: Third Press.
Jenkins, J. Craig. 1978. "The Demand for Immigrant Workers: Labor Scarcity or Social Control?" *International Migration Review* 12:4 (Winter), 514-535.
Johnson, A. 1928. "How Present Congress is Dealing with Proposals to Change Immigration." *Congressional Digest* 7, 152-154.
Johnson, Harry. 1958. *International Trade and Economic Growth.* London: Allen and Unwin.
Junta de Planificación de Puerto Rico. 1982. *Perfil demográfico y económico de la población inmigrante en Puerto Rico.* San Juan: Junta de Planificación.
Katz, N., and J. Kemnitzer. 1983. "Join the Future Now! Women in the Electronics Industry: Sexism, Structure and Profit." In *Women, Men and the International Division of Labor*, ed. June Nash and María Patricia Fernández Kelly, pp. 332-345. Albany: State University of New York Press.
Katzenstein, Peter J. 1975. "International Interdependence: Some Longterm and Recent Changes." *International Organization* 29:4 (Autumn), 1021-1034.
Keesing, Donald B. 1979. "Trade Policy in Developing Countries." World Bank Staff Working Paper, no. 353. August.
Keller, J. 1983. "The Division of Labor in Electronics." In *Women, Men and the International Division of Labor*, ed. June Nash and María Patricia Fernández Kelly, pp. 346-373. Albany: State University of New York Press.

Keohane, Robert, and Joseph Nye. 1977. *Power and Interdependence: World Politics in Transition*. Boston: Little, Brown.

Kramer, Peter. 1966. *The Offshores: A Study of Foreign Farm Labor in Florida*. St. Petersburg, Fla.: Community Action Fund.

Krasner, Stephen. ed. 1982. "International Regimes." Special issue of *International Organization* 36:2 (Spring).

Kreckle, Reinhard. 1982. "Unequal Opportunity Structure and Labor Market Segmentation." *Sociology* 14. (November), 525-50.

Kredietbank. 1978. "The New International Division of Labor." *Weekly Bulletin* 33:37 (October), 1-6.

Krippendorf, Ekkehart. 1976. *Migration in the Evolution of the International System*. Bologna: Johns Hopkins University, Bologna Center.

Kritz, Mary. 1981. "International Migration Patterns in the Caribbean Basin: An Overview." In *Global Trends in Migration*. ed. Mary Kritz, Charles Keeley and Silvano Tomasi. Staten Island, N.Y.: Center for Migration Studies.

Kritz, Mary, Charles Keeley, and Silvano Tomasi. eds. 1981. *Global Trends in Migration*. Staten Island, N.Y.: Center for Migration Studies.

Krute, Eugenia. 1983. "Las causas de la emigración en una comunidad agrícola del Cibao." Paper presented to the Conference on Dominican Migration to the United States. Museo del Hombre Dominicano, (Abril).

Lawrence, Paul R., and Davis Dyer. 1983. *Renewing American Industry*. New York: Free Press.

Lewis, W. Arthur. 1954. "Economic Development with Unlimited Supplies of Labor." Reprinted in *The Economics of Underdevlopment*, ed. A. N. Agarwala and S. P. Singh, pp. 400-449. New York: Oxford University Press.

Lim, Linda. 1978. "Women Workers in Multinational Corporations: The Case of the Electronics Industry in Malaysia and Singapore." Occasional Papers. Ann Arbor: University of Michigan.

Lipietz, Alain. 1982. "Marx or Rostow?" *New Left Review* 132 (March), 48-58.

Luxemburg, Rosa. 1968. *The Accumulation of Capital*. New York: Monthly Review Press.

Magee, Stephen P. 1977. "Information and Multinational Corporation: An Appropriability Theory of Direct Foreign Investment." In *The New International Economic Order: North-South Debate*, ed. Jagdish Bhagwati, pp. 317-340. Cambridge: MIT Press.

Maldonado, Rita M. 1976. "Why Puerto Ricans Migrated to the United States in 1947-1973." *Monthly Labor Review* 99:9 (September), 7-18.

Mallon, F. 1983. "Gender and Class in the Transition to Capitalism." Unpublished manuscript.

Malloy, James. ed. 1977. *Authoritarianism and Corporatism in Latin America*. Princeton: Princeton University Press.

Manning, Robert D. 1981. "The Interaction of Race, Nationality and Class in the American Labor Market: A Comparative Study of Mexican-American and Afro-American Labor Migration (1842-1981)." Master's thesis, Northern Illinois University.

Maram, S., S. Long and D. Berg. 1981. "Hispanic Workers in the Garment and Restaurant Industries in Los Angeles County." Working Papers in U.S.-Mexican Studies no. 12. La Jolla: University of California at San Diego.

Marshall, Adriana. 1973. *The Import of Labor: The Case of the Netherlands.* Rotterdam: Rotterdam University Press.

———. 1983. "Immigration in a Surplus-worker Labor Market: The Case of New York." Center for Latin American and Caribbean Studies Occasional Papers, no. 39. New York University.

Marshall, F. R. 1975. "Economic Factors Influencing the International Migration of Workers." *Mexican-United States Border*. San Antonio: Weatherhead Foundation.

McCoy, Terry. 1982. "Significance of Comprehensive Immigration Law Reform for the State of Florida: Temporary Workers Provisions." Paper presented to the fourth annual Earl Warren Symposium, University of California at San Diego.

———, and Charles H. Wood. 1982. "Caribbean Workers in the Florida Sugar Industry." Caribbean Migration Program Occasional Paper no. 2. Center for Latin American Studies, University of Florida.

McNall, Scott. ed. 1982. *Current Perspectives in Social Theory*. vol. 3. Greenwich, Conn.: JAI Press.

McNeill, W. H., and R. S. Adams. eds. 1978. *Human Migration: Patterns and Policies*. Bloomington, Ind.: American Academy of Arts and Sciences.

Middleton, Chris. 1974. "Sexual Inequality and Stratification Theory." In *The Social Analyiss of Class Structure*, ed. F. Parkin, pp. 169-203. London: Tavistock.

Mighell, Ronald, and Lawrence Jones. 1963. *Vertical Coordination in Agriculture*. Washington, D.C.: USDA.

Montes de Oca, Rosa Elena, and Gerardo Escudero. 1981. "Las empresas transnacionales en la industria alimentaria mexicana." *Comercio Exterior* 31:9 (September).

Montgomery, David. 1980. "To Study the People: The American Working Class." *Labor History* 21 (Fall), 485-512.

Moore Lappé, Frances, and Joseph Collins. 1977. *Food First: Beyond the Myth of Scarcity*. Boston: Houghton Mifflin.

Moran, Theodore H. 1973), "Foreign Expansion as an 'Institutional Necessity' for U.S. Corporate Capitalism," *World Politics* 25:3 (April), 369-386.

Morrissy, J. David. 1974. *Agricultural Modernization through Production*

Contracting: *The Role of the Fruit and Vegetable Producer in Mexico and Central America.* New York: Praeger.

Mortimer, D. M., and R. Bryce-Laporte, eds. 1981. *Female Immigrants to the United States: Caribbean, Latin American, and African Experiences.* RIIES Occasional Papers no. 2. Washington, D.C.: Smithsonian Institution.

Muller, Geraldo. 1979. "Agroindustria e multinacionais: Acerca da recente expansão da soja no Brasil." Unpublished ms.

Myint, H. 1954, "The Gains from International Trade and the Backward Countries," *Review of Economic Studies* 22:2, 129-142.

———.1958. "The Classical Theory of International Trade and the Underdeveloped Countries." *Economic Journal* 68:270 (June), 317-337.

Nash, June. 1983. "Class Conflict and Community Integration in a New England Industrial Town." Paper presented to the seventh Political Economy of the World System Conference on Labor and Labor Movements in the World Capitalist System, Duke University.

———, and María Patricia Fernández Kelly. eds. 1983. *Women, Men and the International Division of Labor.* Albany: State University of New York Press.

National Commission for Employment Policy. 1982. *Hispanics and Jobs: Barriers to Progress.* Washington, D.C.: National Commission for Employment Policy.

Nau, Henry R. 1978. "The Diplomacy of World Food." In *Global Food Interdependence: Challenge to American Foreign Policy.* ed. Raymond Hopkins and Donald J. Puchala, pp. 201-235. New York: Columbia University Press.

New York City. Department of City Planning. 1982. *Puerto Rican New Yorkers.* New York: Department of City Planning.

New York, Department of Labor. 1982. *Employment Standards: Industrial Homeworkers in New York City.* Albany: DOL.

North American Congress on Latin America (NACLA). 1975. "U.S. Runaway Shops on the Mexican Border." *NACLA Report on the Americas,* 9:7.

———. 1977. "Capital's Flight: The Apparel Industry Moves South." *NACLA Report on the Americas,* 11:3.

O'Brien, Philip. 1975. "A Critique of Latin American Theories of Dependency." In *Beyond the Sociology of Development.* ed. Ivar Oxaal, et al., pp. 7-27. London: Routledge and Kegan Paul.

O'Connor, D. 1983. "Changing Patterns of International Production in the Semiconductor Industry: The Role of the Transnational Corporation." Unpublished manuscript.

O'Connor, James. 1982. *The Fiscal Crisis of the State.* 2nd ed. New York: St. Martin's Press.

Ohlin, B. 1935. *Interregional Trade and International Trade*. Cambridge: Harvard University Press.
Oxaal, Ivar, et al. eds. 1975. *Beyond the Sociology of Development*. London: Routledge and Kegan Paul.
Palloix, Christian. 1977. *Las firmas multinacionales y el proceso de internacionalización*. Mexico: Siglo XXI. In French, *Les Firmes multinationales et le proces d'internationalization*. Paris: Maspero, 1974.
———. 1979. *Proces de production et crise du capitalisme*. Paris: Maspero.
Parkin, F. ed. 1974. *The Social Analysis of Class Structure*. London: Tavistock.
Perelman, Michael. 1977. *Farming for Profit in a Hungry World: Capital and Crisis in Agriculture*. Montclair, N.J.: Allanheld, Osmun.
Pérez, Glauco. 1981. "Dominican Illegals in New York: Selected Preliminary Findings." Paper presented to the Center for Inter-American Affairs, New York University (May).
Pessar, Patricia. 1982. "The Role of Households in International Migration: The Case of U.S.-Bound Migrants from the Dominican Republic." *International Migration Review* 16:2 (Summer), 342-364.
Petras, Elizabeth Maclean. 1981. "The Global Market in the Modern World Economy." In *Global Trends in Migration*, ed. Mary Kritz, Charles Keeley and Silvano Tomasi, pp. 44-63. Staten Island, N.Y.: Center for Migration Studies.
Pinto, Anibal. 1979. "The Periphery and the Internationalization of the World Economy," *CEPAL Review* 9 (December), 45-67.
Piore, Michael. 1975. "Notes for a Theory of Labor Market Stratification." In *Labor Market Segmentation*, ed. Richard Edwards, Michael Reich and David M. Gordon, Lexington, Mass.: Heath.
———. 1977. "The Dual Labor Market: Theory and Implications." In *Problems of Political Economy: An Urban Perspective*, ed. David M. Gordon, pp .93-97. Lexington, Mass.: Heath.
———. 1979. *Birds of Passage*. Cambridge: Cambridge University Press.
Poinard, Michel, and Michel Roux. 1977. "L'émigration contre le développement: Les cas portugais et yougoslave." *Revue tiers-monde* 18 (January-March), 21-53.
Portes, Alejandro. 1977. "Labor Functions of Illegal Aliens." *Society* 14 (September-October), 31-37.
———. 1978. "Migration and Underdevelopment." *Politics and Society* 8:1, 1-48.
———. 1979. "Illegal Immigrants and the International System, Lessons from Recent Illegal Mexican Immigrants to the U.S." *Social Problems* 26:4 (April), 425-438.
———. 1982. "Of Borders and States: A Skeptical Note on the Legislative Control of Immigration." Paper presented to the fourth annual Earl Warren Symposium, University of California at San Diego.

Portes, Alejandro, and Robert L. Bach. Forthcoming. *Latin Journey: Mexican and Cuban Immigrants in the United States*. Berkeley: University of California Press.

Portes, Alejandro, and John Walton. 1981. *Labor, Class and the International System*. New York: Academic Press.

Powers, Mary G., and John J. Macisco, Jr. 1982. *Los puertorriqueños en Nueva York: Un análisis de su participación laboral y experiencia migratoria*. Río Piedras: Universidad de Puerto Rico.

Purcell, Susan K. ed. 1981. *Mexico-United States Relations*. New York: American Academy of Political Science.

Rama, Ruth. 1980. *Transnacionales, estado y acumulación agrícola: La caña de azucar en México*. Mexico: UNAM.

―――, and Fernando Rello. 1980. *Estrategias de las agroindustrias transnacionales y política alimentaria en México*. Mexico: Nueva Imagen.

―――, and Raúl Vigorito. 1979. *Transnacionales en América Latina: El complejo de frutas y legumbres en México*. Mexico: Nueva Imagen.

Ramesh, J., and Charles Weiss. 1979. *Mobilizing Technology for World Development*. New York: Praeger and Overseas Development Corporation.

Ramírez, Nelson, Paolo Tactuk and Minerva Breton. 1977. *La migración interna en la República Dominicana*. Santo Domingo: Alfa y Omega.

Redclift, Michael. 1981. "Development Policymaking in Mexico: The Sistema Alimentario Mexicano." Working Papers in U.S.-Mexican Studies, no. 24. La Jolla: University of California at San Diego.

Reich, Robert. 1982. *The Next American Frontier*. New York: New York Times Books.

Reichert, Joshua. 1981. "The Migrant Syndrome: Seasonal U.S. Wage Labor and Rural Development in Central Mexico." *Human Organization* 40:1, (Spring), 56-66.

Reisler, Mark. 1976. *By the Sweat of Their Brow: Mexican Immigrant Labor in the United States, 1900-1940*. Westport, Conn.: Greenwood Press.

Reubins, Edwin P. 1978. "Policy Dimensions of the H-2 Program (Temporary Importation of Foreign Workers." Paper prepared for the National Commission for Manpower Policy, U.S. Department of Labor.

Reynolds, Clark W. 1981. "The Structure of the Economic Relationship." In *Mexico-United States Relations*. ed. Susan K. Purcell, pp. 125-135. New York: American Academy of Political Science.

Roberts, Kenneth. 1981. "Agrarian Structure and Labor Migration in Rural Mexico." Working Papers in U.S.-Mexican Studies, no. 30. La Jolla: University of California at San Diego.

Rodríguez, Clara. 1979. "Economic Factors Affecting Puerto Ricans in New York." In *Labor Migration Under Capitalism: The Puerto Rican Experience*, Centro de Estudios Puertorriqueños, pp. 197-221. New York: Monthly Review Press.

Rohatyn, Felix. 1981. "Reconstructing America." *New York Review of Books* 28:3 (March 5), 16-20.

Rosecrance, Richard, et al. 1977. "Whither Interdependence?" *International Organization* 31:1 (Winter), 83-105.

Ross, Robert, and Kent Trachte. 1983. "Global Cities and Global Classes: The Peripheralization of Labor in New York City." *Review* 6:3, 393-431.

Rothstein, Robert L. 1977. *The Weak in the World of the Strong*. New York: Columbia University Press.

———. 1979. *Global Bargaining: UNCTAD and the Quest for a New International Economic Order*. Princeton: Princeton University Press.

Safa, Helen I. 1981. "Runaway Shops and Female Employment: The Search for Cheap Labor." *Signs* 7:2 (Winter), 418-423.

———. 1983. "Women, Production and Reproduction in Industrial Capitalism: A Comparison of Brazilian and U.S. Factory Workers." In *Women, Men and the International Division of Labor*. ed. June Nash and María Patricia Fernández Kelly. Albany: State University of New York Press.

Sanderson, Steven E. 1981. "Florida Tomatoes, U.S.-Mexican Relations and the International Division of Labor." *Inter-American Economic Affairs* 31:3 (Winter), 23-52.

———. 1983. "Presidential Succession and Political Rationality in Mexico, *World Politics* 35:3 (April), 315-334.

Sassen-Koob, Saskia. 1980. "The Internationalization of the Labor Force." *Studies in Comparative International Development* 15 (Winter), 3-23.

———. 1981a. "Exporting Capital and Importing Labor: The Role of Women." In *Female Immigrants to the United States: Caribbean, Latin American, and African Experiences*. ed. D. M. Mortimer and R. Bryce-Laporte. Washington, D.C.: Smithsonian Institution.

———. 1981b. "Towards a Conceptualization of Immigrant Labor." *Social Problems* 29 (October), 65-85.

———. 1982. "Recomposition and Peripheralization at the Core." *Contemporary Marxism* 5, 88-100.

———. 1983. "The Structuring of a New Investment Zone for the World Market: Southern California." Research Report. Center for U.S.-Mexican Studies, University of California at San Diego.

Schmitz, Andrew, Robert S. Firch and Jimmye S. Hillman. 1981. "Agricultural Export Dumping: The Case of Mexican Winter Vegetables in the U.S. Market." *American Journal of Agricultural Economics* 63:4 (November), 645-654.

Servan-Schreiber, Jean-Jacques. 1968. *The American Challenge*. New York: Atheneum.

Siegel, L. 1982. "Delicate Bonds: The Semiconductor Industry." Oakland: Pacific Studies Center.

Simpson, R. M. and I. H. Simpson. eds. 1983. *Peripheral Workers*. Greenwich, Conn.: JAI Press.

Singlemann, Joachim. 1978. *From Agriculture to Services: The Transformation of Industrial Employment*. Beverly Hills, Calif.: Sage.

Skidmore, Thomas. 1977. "The Politics of Economic Stabilization in Postwar Latin America." In *Authoritarianism and Corporatism in Latin America*. ed. James L. Malloy, pp. 149-190. Princeton: Princeton University Press.

Slutzky, Daniel. 1982. "La agroindustria de la carne en Honduras." In *El desarrollo agroindustrial y la economía latinoamericana*, ed. Gonzalo Arroyo. Mexico: SARH-CODAI.

Sokoloff, Natalie J. 1980. *Between Money and Love: The Dialectics of Women's Home and Market Work*. New York: Praeger.

Sorenson, Vernon. 1975. *International Trade Policy: Agriculture and Development*. East Lansing: Michigan State University International Business and Economic Studies.

Spero, Joan Edelman. 1981. *The Politics of International Economic Relations*. 2nd ed. New York: St. Martin's Press.

Stanback, Thomas M., Jr., and Thierry J. Noyelle. 1982. *Cities in Transition: Changing Job Structures in Atlanta, Denver, Buffalo, Phoenix, Columbus (Ohio), Nashville, Charlotte*. Montclair, N.J.: Allanheld, Osmun.

Stoddard, Ellwyn. 1976. "A Conceptual Analysis of the 'Alien Invasion': Institutionalized Support of Illegal Mexican Aliens in the U.S." *International Migration Review* 10 (Summer), 157-189.

Storper, Michael and David Walker. 1983. "The Labor Theory of Location." *International Journal of Urban and Regional Research*.

Sunkel, Osvaldo. 1971. "Capitalismo transnacional y desintegración nacional en América Latina." *Estudios Internacionales* 4:16 (January-March), 3-61.

Thompson, Holly J. 1979. "An Economic Analysis of the Role of the Sugar Industry in the South Florida Economy." Master's thesis, University of Florida.

Thurow, Lester. 1981. *The Zero Sum Society*. New York: Penguin Books.

Tienda, Marta. 1981. *Hispanic Origin Workers in U.S. Labor Markets: Comparative Analysis of Employment and Earnings*. Springfield, Va.: National Technical Information Service.

Tucker, Robert W. 1977. *The Inequality of Nations*. New York: Basic Books.

United Nations Center on Transnational Corporations. 1981. *Transnational Corporations in Food and Beverage Processing*. New York: United Nations.

United Nations. Industrial Development Organization. 1980. *Export Processing Zones in Developing Countries*. UNIDO Working Paper on Structural Change, no. 19. Vienna, Austria: UNIDO.

────. 1981. *Restructuring World Industry in a Period of Crisis-The Role of Innovation: An Analysis of Recent Development in the Semiconductor Industry*. Vienna, Austria: UNIDO.

U.S. Commission on Civil Rights. 1982. *Unemployment and Underemployment among Blacks, Hispanics and Women*. Clearinghouse Publication no. 74. Washington, D.C.: Government Printing Office.

U.S. Department of Commerce. 1979. *Economic Study of Puerto Rico*. Washington, D.C.: Government Printing Office.

Vázquez Calzada, José L., and Zoraida Morales del Valle. 1979. *Características sociodemográficas de los norteamericanos, cubanos y dominicanos residentes en Puerto Rico*. San Juan: University of Puerto Rico, Escuela Graduada de Salud Pública.

Vernon, Raymond. 1966. "International Investment and International Trade in the Product Cycle." *Quarterly Journal of Economics* 80:2 (May), 190-207.

———. 1970. *The Technology Factor in International Trade*. New York: Columbia University Press for the National Bureau of Economic Research.

———. 1977. *Storm over the Multinationals*. Cambridge: Harvard University Press.

Vining, Jr., Daniel R. 1982. "Migration Between the Core and the Periphery." *Scientific American* (December), 247:6, 44-53.

Waldinger, Roger. 1983. "Immigrant Enterprise and Labor Market Structure." Unpublished manuscript.

Walker, Richard A. 1978. "Two Sources of Uneven Development under Advanced Capitalism: Spatial Differentiation and Capital Mobility." *Review of Radical Political Economics* 10:3 (Spring), 28-37.

Watkins, Melville H. 1963. "A Staple Theory of Economic Growth." *Canadian Journal of Economics and Political Science* 29:2 (May), 141-158.

Weber, William T. 1978. "The Complexities of Agripower." *Agricultural History* 52:4 (October), 526-537.

Whitehead, Laurence. 1980. "Mexico from Bust to Boom: A Political Evaluation of the 1976-1979 Stabilization Programme." *World Development* 8:11 (November), 843-846.

Wilson, Kenneth L., and Alejandro Portes. 1980. "The Immigrant Enclave." *American Journal of Sociology* 86:2 (September), 295-319.

Winrock International. 1981. *The World Livestock Product, Feedstuff, and Food Grain System*. Morrilton, Ark.: Winrock International.

Wolf, Eric. 1982. *Europe and the People Without History*. Berkeley: University of California Press.

Zolberg, Aristide. 1978. "International Migration Policies in a Changing World System." In *Human Migration: Patterns and Policies*. ed. W. H. McNeill and R. S. Adams, pp. 241-286. Bloomington, Ind.: American Academy of Arts and Sciences.

About the Contributors

Steven E. Sanderson is Associate Professor of Political Science at the University of Florida. His most recent book is *The Transformation of Mexican Agriculture: International Structure and the Politics of Rural Change*. He is currently conducting research on U.S. trade policy and the development of Latin America.

Robert L. Bach is Assistant Professor of Sociology at the State University of New York at Binghamton. He is coauthor, with Alejandro Portes, of *Latin Journey: Mexicans and Cubans in the United States*, as well as author of numerous articles on migration and refugee flows, state policies, and labor markets.

David Barkin is Professor of Economics at the Universidad Autónoma Metropolitana, Xochimilco, Mexico, and Senior Research Associate at the Centro de Ecodesarrollo, Mexico City. He is the author of numerous books and articles on rural development, agricultural production, international capital, and economic development. His book with Gustavo Esteva, *Inflación y Democracia*, won the National Economics Prize in Mexico.

Frank Bonilla is Director of the Centro de Estudios Puertorriqueños at Hunter College of the City University of New York and Professor of Sociology and Political Science, CUNY doctoral programs.

Ricardo Campos is a political scientist and research director of the History and Migration Task Force of the Centro de Estudios Puertorriqueños at Hunter College of the City University of New York. Together with Frank Bonilla he is coauthor of numerous publications on migration, including *Labor Migration under Capitalism: The Puerto Rican Experience*, and articles in *Daedalus, Review,* and *Contemporary Marxism*.

María Patricia Fernández Kelly is a Fellow at the Center for U.S.-Mexican Studies at the University of California, San Diego. She has written *For We Are Sold, I and My People: Women and Industry in Mexico's Frontier*, as well as articles on border industrialization, women and development, and migration.

Sherri Grasmuck is Assistant Professor of Sociology at Temple University. She has conducted research in Scotland on ethnic separatism and uneven development and in the Dominican Republic on the impact of international labor migration on sending societies.

Terry McCoy is Associate Director of the Center for Latin American Studies at the University of Florida. He was trained as a political scientist, and his special interests are politics and public policies in Latin America and the Caribbean. His publications cover agrarian reform and population policies in these two regions. With Charles Wood, he is currently finishing a study of international seasonal labor migration from the Caribbean to the Florida sugar industry.

June Nash is Professor of Anthropology at the City College of the City University of New York. She is currently studying the impact of industry on a New England industrial community. She recently edited a book with María Patricia Fernández Kelly, entitled *Women, Men and the International Division of Labor*, published by SUNY Press, Albany, in a series, called Anthropology of Work, of which she is general editor.

Ruth Rama is an Uruguayan economist who has conducted research at the Institute of Transnational Studies and acted as consultant to the United Nations Centre on Transnational Corporations and the Sistema Alimentario Mexicano. She is currently Coordinator of the Section of Agriculture and Agroindustries of the Postgraduate Division of Economics, National University of Mexico. She has written various books and articles dealing with transnational corporations in Latin American agriculture.

Helen I. Safa is Professor of Anthropology and Director of the Center for Latin American Studies at the University of Florida and the current president of the Latin American Studies Association. She is author of *The Urban Poor of Puerto Rico* and the editor of several other books. Her articles on migration, housing, race, and women and national development have appeared in a variety of scholarly journals.

Saskia Sassen-Koob is Associate Professor of Sociology at Queens College and the Graduate School, City University of New York. She has published numerous articles on immigration, focusing particularly on development issues in migrant-sending countries and on the labor market in receiving countries.

Charles Wood is Associate Professor of Sociology at the University of Florida. He is coauthor with José Alberto de Carvalho of *The Demography of Inequality in Brazil*. He has written numerous articles on migration, Amazon development, infant mortality, and income distribution in Latin America.

Index

AFDC, 121
Agribusiness, viii, 6, 13-14, 47, 50, 52-54
Agriculture, *see also* Mexico, agriculture, viii, ix, x, 5, 13, 20, 37-38, 48-94, 181
   crisis, 71-73, 77, 89
   exports, 6, 50-52, 54-56
   fruits and vegetables, 73, 82
   imports, xi, 36, 50-52, 62
   labor, 181,
   specialization, 73
   technology, 6
   trade, 36
Agroindustry, *see also* Industry, food processing, 6, 9, 21, 49-50, 52-54, 56-65, 69-94
Alverson, Hoyt, 271n
Amazon, 3
Amin, Samir, 51
Anderson Clayton, 80
Argentina, 5, 9, 19, 49ff, 146
   exports, 48
Asia, 219
   east, 35
   southeast, 103, 116, 118, 226
Atari, 11
Austin, James E. and Gustavo Esteva, 42n
Aviculture, *see* Poultry
Bach, Robert L., xi, 7, 16, 19, 20
Banana, 49
Barbados, vii, 127
Barkin, David, ix, 7, 11, 16, 19, 20, 210
Barley, 53
Barnet, Richard and Ronald Mueller, 42n
Beatrice Foods, 13
Beef cattle, 48, 54, 55ff, 73, 84
Beer, 56
Bibb, Robert and William H. Form, 255
Blair, John, 247n
Bluestone, Barry and Bennet Harrison, 191, 268
Bonilla, Frank and Ricardo Campos, x, 16, 21

Border Industrial Program (Mexico), 99, 109, 206, 222n
Bowles, Samuel, David Gordon and Thomas Weisskopf, 42n
Bracero Program (P.L. 78), 109, 111-112, 122n, 130, 131
Brain drain, 146
Braverman, Harry, 42n, 253
Brazil, 6, 9, 17, 19, 21, 46, 49ff
   exports, 48, 83
   imports, 9
Bretton Woods system, 8
Bukharin, N., 107, 122n
BWICLO, 127, 131
Cacao, 84
California, 84, 180, 217,
Cambodia, 120
Campos, Ricardo *see* Bonilla, Frank and
Canada, 116
Cane cutters, *see* Sugar
Capital, 4
   centralization, 230
   decentralization, 227
   foreign, viii
   international expansion, 29, 33
   -labor relation, 229-234
   locational capability, 228
   mobility, 213, 226-252
   segmentation of, 202
   valorization, 209
   world-scale, 96
Caribbean, 3, 5, 96, 117, 125-144, 180, 200, 226
   Basin Initiative (CBI), 121, 172
   cane cutters, 125-144
   Offshore Industries, 3
Carter, President James, 120
Caterpillar, 11
Castells, Manuel, 140
Castro, Fidel, 131
Castro, Mary García, 244
Central America, 121, 200
Chicago, 107, 232
Chicanos, 106-107

Index

Chile, 9, 15, 16, 19, 20, 21, 48, 63, 65n
  exports, 48
Citrus, 54
Civil Rights Act (US), 112
Class struggle, 28, 229
Coffee, 48, 52, 65n
Cohen, Robert B. and S. Sassen-Koob, 241
Colombia, 49ff
  exports, 48
  workers, 5, 242-244
Comparative advantage, 211
CONASUPO (Mexico), 81-82
Connecticut, 107
Consumption patterns, 38-41, 83-86, 90-91
Cornelius, Wayne, 151
Costa Rica, 103
Cottage industry, 218, 219, 223n
Cotton, 49
Crisis, 27, 28, 42n, 60, 70
Cuba, 103, 114-121, 131-133, 180
  Refugee Program, 115-116
  Relations with US, 114-115
  Revolution, 114, 126
Cumbler, J. T., 271n
de Janvry, Alain, 51
Debt, 16, 17, 18, 19, 22, 30-31, 34, 41
Decentralization, 227, 230, 245
Deindustrialization, 20, 246, 256, 268
Dematurity, 21
Denationalization, 53
Dependence, 8
Dependency school, 4
Deskilling, see Labor
Detroit, 238, 239, 245
Differentiation, see Standardization
Dominican Republic, see also Migration, Dominican, vii, x, 114, 145-176
  National Statistics Office, 150-174
  Santiago, 145-176
  Santo Domingo, 159,
  workers, 5, 200, 244
Egypt, 146
Employment, 183
Epstein, A. L., 271n
Equal Opportunity Commission, 241

Export, see also Agriculture, viii, xi, 6, 9, 11, 14, 16, 17, 19, 21, 30
  dependence, 16, 46
  manufactured, 9, 63
  platform, 9, 17,
  processing zone (EPZ), 207, 208, 210, 211, 213, 217, 219, 220, 226
  promotion, 20, 21
  substitution, 3, 63
Fairchild, 206
Fajnzylber, Fernando, 43n
Feminization, see Women
Fernández Kelly, María Patricia, vii, ix, x, 17, 270n
Feudalism, 209
Fiscal crisis, viii, 65
Fishmeal, 49
Florida, 26, 58, 115-118, 125-144, 192
  Fruit and Vegetable Association (FFVA), 127
  sugar industry, 125
Flowers, 56
Foreign policy, 22
Frozen Orange Juice Concentrate (FOJC), 57-58, 65n
Food, see also Agriculture, 31, 37
  crisis, 70
  policy, 88
  power, 64
  security, 3, 16, 64
  self-sufficiency, xi, 30, 37-38, 72, 83, 88
  shortage, xi, 31, 35
  systems, see also SAM, 13, 50, 61, 70, 90
Forakker Act, 106
Frank, Andre Gunder, 42n
Free-trade
  policy, 21
  zones, 3, 99, 172
Frobel, Folker, Jurgen Heinrichs and Otto Kreye, 95-96, 98, 99, 122n, 208-209
Gains from trade, 8, 9, 16
García, Ana María, 177
GATT, 63
General Instruments Company, 206

Global, *see also* Internationalization,
  production, 231
  cities, 236, 234-240
  control capability, 228-229
  integration, 253
  proletarianization, 10-12, 15, 19, 22, 26-45
  sourcing, 3, 36, 41
  system, 10, 26
Gordon, David, Michael Reich and Richard Edwards, 253, 254
Grasmuck, Sherri, x, 7, 16
Great Britain, 5, 47
Great Depression, 129, 140
Great Society, 111
Greece, 147
Growth poles, 46, 228
Guatemala, 5
Gutman, Herbert, 271*n*
H-2 immigration program, 20, 125, 129, 136, 137, 139, 140, 142
Haiti
  migrants, 5
  refugees, 121, 133
  workers, 148
Harvey, David, 247*n*
Havana, 116-117
Hawaii, 140, 180, 192
Heckscher, Eli, 43*n*
Herman, Edward, 248*n*
Homework, 97, 200, 206, 218, 223*n*, 238*ff*, 245
Homogenization, *see* Standardization
Hong Kong, 171, 206, 210
Houston, 238
Human capital, 21, 169, 244, 254
Huntington, Samuel P., 116
Illinois, 107, 192
ILWU, 141
ILGWU, 265
Immigrants, 188, 231, 232, 239
Immigration, 2, 104-114, 133-141, 226-7, 229, 231, 240, 242, 245
  Act of 1917 (US), 105, 129, 130
  and Naturalization Act of 1965 (US), 112-113, 125
  policy, 17, 97, 103, 104, 113, 114-121, 128-144, 232
Import, *see also* Industrialization, import substitution, 19, 21, 35
  dependence, 16, 30, 62
Impulsora Agrícola, 63
Income
  concentration of, 240
  distribution of, 17, 148, 234-235
Industrial
  Incentives Act (Puerto Rico), 181
  organization, 12, 13
  restructuring 229
Industrialization, 179, 247*n*
  accelerated, 226
  export-based, ix
  import substitution, vii, 6, 35, 46, 51, 52, 60-63, 149
Industries
  aerospace, 238
  animal feed, 49, 80, 83
  distribution, 234
  electronics, 207, 230, 238
  food processing, 39, 49, 56-60
  garment, 217, 238
  high-technology, 238, 246
  manufacturing, 234
  meat packing, 49
  service, 234, 239
  textile, 217, 256-267
Inequality, 4
Informal
  economy, 208, 222*n*
  sector, 238
Interdependence, 4, 8
International Labour Office, 43*n*
International Monetary Fund, 8
International Multifoods, 113
International
  production sharing, 211
  restructuring, 207
  specialization, 15-16, 98
  technology, 207
  trade, 91, 37
  trade policy, 19, 36, 64, 99
  trade theory, 35
Internationalization, 3*ff*, 22, 98-99, 180, 207, 210, 215

294   *Index*

of agriculture, vii, viii, ix, 21, 46-94
of capital, 10, 12, 17, 26-45, 47, 180, 201, 211, 213
of food, 39, 41
of industry, vii, viii, ix
of labor, vii, x, 5, 17, 38, 125-144, 180, 181
of production, 10, 17, 98, 209, 226
Israel, 230
Italy, 116
Japan, 219
Jenkins, J. Craig, 138
Job
   low-wage, 234-240
   security, 258
Johnson, President Lyndon B., 112, 115, 120
Jones Act, 106
Kampuchea, 117, 122n
Kelly Girls, 260
Kennedy, Robert, 112
Kramer, Peter, 131
Labor, *see also* Employment, Internationalization, 29
   deskilling, 32, 207, 216-217
   differentiation, 230
   division of, 182-189
   female, *see* Women
   global, 228
   homogenized, 230, 253
   Mexican, 96, 104-105, 109-111, 217
   mobility, 7, 15
   participation, 198
   process, viii, ix, 3, 8, 10-20, 29, 207, 226, 239, 245, 249n, 253-272
   proletarianization, 26-41, 61, 210
   Puerto Rican, 96, 106-108
   restructuring, 244
   rural, 11
   scarcity, 145, 211
   segregation, 254
   segmentation, 197, 202, 253, 255
   skilled, 146
   surplus, 146, 147, 158-168, 180
   undocumented, 5, 162, 217
Labor process vs. industrial organization, 12

Laos, 117, 120
Lewis, W. Arthur, 141-142
Lim, Linda, 270n
London, 226
López Mateos, President Adolfo, 112
Los Angeles, 214, 226, 232, 238ff
Luxemburg, Rosa, 42n
MacDonalds, 255
Maize, 48, 77
Malaysia, 207
Maquiladora, ix, 207, 219, 222n
Marglin, Steven, 42n
Marshall Plan, 18
Marx, Karl, 247n
McCoy, Terry, *see* Wood, Charles and
Meat, 83-87
Mexico, vii, ix, 3, 9, 13, 17, 21, 49ff, 69-94, 114, 117, 147, 149, 210, 211, 218, 219
   agriculture, 17, 47, 99
   exports, 6, 73-76
   imports, 9
Mexican Food System, *see* SAM.
Miami, 232
Middleton, Chris, 254
Migration, vii, x, xi, 10, 16, 65, 95-124, 145-205, 226-252
   Caribbean, 147, 180, 217
   Dominican, x, 145-176, 180, 217
   Hispanic, x, 232
   Mexican 5, 104-105, 147, 164
   Puerto Rican, 106-111, 177-205
   return, 163-168
   remittances, 154-155
   rural-urban, 148-150
   urban, 147, 152-157
Mitchell, J. Clyde, 271n
Motorola, 206
Multinational corporation, *see* Transnational corporation
Mutual structural adjustment, 20-22
Nash, June, vii, x, 21, 271n
National Labor Relations Board (U.S.), 265, 265-267
National Rural Credit Bank (Mexico), 81-82
New Deal, 103, 110-111

New Jersey, 98, 191
New York, 98, 151*ff*, 177-205, 214, 226, 232-246
   City, 107
   City, immigrants in, 226-252
   Hispanic population, 191, 240-245
   migration to, 151-174
   labor market, 198
   Puerto Ricans in, 191*ff*
   Queens, 244
Newly industrialized countries (NICs), 6, 36, 37, 43*n*
North-south relations, 37, 63
Occupation, 234
OECD, 6, 8, 9, 10, 14, 20, 42*n*
Offshore industries, 3
Ohlin, B., 43*n*
Oil, 228
Oilseeds, 76-83
OPEC, 226-227, 247*n*
Operation Bootstrap, x, 105, 181
Operation Wetback, 105, 109
Orange County, 238*ff*
Palloix, Christian, 9, 210
Parallel exchange rate, 169,
Peasant, vii*ff*, 11, 30, 31, 40, 41, 51, 53, 61, 64-65, 90-91
Pennsylvania, 191
People's Republic of China, 219
Periphery, 201, 207, 214, 226, 230
Peru, 9, 46, 49
   exports, 48
Pessar, Patricia, 173*n*
Philippines, 207, 211
Pineapple, 55, 56
Pinto, Anibal, 222*n*
P.L. 480, 72, 88
Population
   Asians, 242, 248*n*
   Chinese, 122*n*
   control, 178*ff*
   Hispanic, 232, 240-245, 248*n*
Pork, 59-60
Portugal, 147
Poultry, 52, 57, 58-60, 74, 79
Product life cycle, 9
Production

contracting, 14, 53, 55
decentralization, 227, 228, 230, 247*n*
global, 228, 232
integration, vii
process, 212-213
Protectionism, *see* International, trade policy,
Pseudoregression, 207-208, 217-219
Puerto Rico, x-xi, 149, , 117, 149, 177-205
   agriculture, xi
   Junta de Planificación, 188
   population, 241-244
Ralston Purina, 80
Rama, Ruth, 6, 11, 16, 17, 21
Ramesh, J. and Charles Weiss, 43*n*
Redeployment, 27, 29, 226, 228
Refugee, 97, 104, 112, 114-121
Reich, Michael, 42*n*
Reig, Nicolas, 85
Reindustrialization, 3, 21
Rodríguez G., Gonzalo, 92*n*
Rostow, Walt, 113-114
Rozo, Carlos, 42*n*
Safa, Helen I., 270*n*
Safflower oil, 56
Saigon, 117
SAM (Sistema Alimentario Mexicano), 42*n*, 58, 66*n*, 69, 88,
San Diego, 217
San Francisco, 214, 232
Sanderson, Steven E., vii, 6, 11, 16
Sassen-Koob, Saskia, x, 11, 17, 140, 146
Schwartz, Abba, 113
Self-sufficiency, *see* Food, self-sufficiency
Service economy, 40, 182-189, 231
Silicon Valley, 214, 217, 218, 239
Singapore, 171, 207
Smith, Adam, 100
Smokestack industries, 20
Sokoloff, Natalie J., 255
Sony, 11
Sorghum, 80-81
South Korea, 146, 171, 206, 222*n*, 248*n*
Soybeans, 48
SSI, 121

Stanback, Thomas M. Jr., and Thierry J. Noyelle, 234
Standard Brands, 56
Standardization/differentiation, 11, 27, 29, 33
State power, 18-20,22, 96
Sterling Bloc, 18
Sterilization, 177
Storper, Michael and David Walker, 228, 248n
Strawberry, 52, 73,
Sugar, 48, 49, 55, 56, 85, 125-144
  cane industry, south Florida, vii
  cane cutters, 5, 125-144
Sweatshop, 200, 206, 223n, 245
Switzerland, 116
Taiwan, 206, 210
Technology, 17, 26-33, 40, 52, 53, 70, 92n, 149, 212-213, 219, 226, 230, 238, 239
Texas, 84, 99, 104, 192
Textile industry, 256
Tobacco, 84-85, 150
Tomatoes, vii, 20
Transistron, 206
Transnational corporation (TNC), 7, 8, 10, 12, 29ff, 40, 49ff, 69-71, 79, 82, 84, 95, 210, 228, 247n
Trilateral Commission, 229
Tucker, Robert W., 4,
Undocumented workers, 138
Unemployment, 31, 35, 108, 145, 186-187, 232
Unequal exchange, viii
Uneven development, 170
Unions, 206, 239, 245, 258
United Fruit, 56
United Nations
  Economic Commission for Latin America (ECLA), 9
  Food and Agricultural Organization (FAO), 9
United States, 3-21, 47, 48, 49, 63, 86-87, 101-103, 128, 147
  Border Patrol, 105
  Department of Agriculture, 130
  Department of Commerce, 203n
  Department of Labor, 127, 132, 141
  Emergency Farm Program 1947, 130
  Employment Service, 105
  export-bill, 8
  Immigration and Naturalization Service (INS), 127, 138, 242
  Office of Management and Budget, 103
  State Department, 113
  Sugar Corporation, 125, 127
  working class, 102
United Technologies, 210
Urban Enterprise Zone, 214
Vegetable, 5
  pickers
  winter exports, 55
Venezuela, 5, 48, 49, 180
Vernon, Raymond, 43n
Vertical integration and coordination, 13-15, 17, 22, 50, 53
Vietnam, 116-122
Virginia, 192
Walker, C. R., 271n
Walter-McCarran Act, 112
Warner, W.L., 271n
West Indies,
  migration, vii, x
  workers, 133-144, 232
Women, vii, viii, ix, x, 29, 171, 177, 185-186, 195-197, 207, 208, 217, 219-221, 226, 238, 253-272
Wood, Charles H. and Terry McCoy, vii, x, 7, 20
Work, *see also* Labor
  process, 253-272
  segmentation, 253-272
Working-class consciousness, 270
World Bank, 148
World
  car, 11
  labor, 95
  markets, 3, 95, 101
  market factories, 207, 210, 226
Worldwide sourcing, *see* Global sourcing
Yugoslavia, 146